The Fast

Z Grills

WOOD PELLET GRILL

AND SMOKER COOKBOOK

500 EASY AND QUICK TO GRILL AND SMOKE

RECIPES FOR BEGINNERS

DARLENE VERA

CONTENTS

VEGETABLES RECIPES 109

POULTRY RECIPES 137

COCKTAILS RECIPES....207

RECIPE INDEX....220

INTRODUCTION

How Your Z Grills Wood Pellet Grill Works

The name itself refers to the method of heating. Pellet grills use a different fuel to traditional grills (which rely upon sources like charcoal or gas)–they use up and burn wooden pellets. These wooden pellets look like little tablets or tiny rolled cigars; they're actually just compressed sawdust.

These wooden pellets are rotated into the fire pot, where they are exposed to intense heat, combust and emit heat and smoke of their own. This process is stoked by an internal fan, which then sends and distributes the heat throughout the grill. As you can see, this is a different method of heating–almost a combination of traditional ovens and flame cooking.

The method of cooking is called convection heating, which is the same method used by traditional smoke boxes.

The advantage of this is that the food is separated from the fire by a metal plate–which means there are no flare-ups and no grease falls into the fire pit (which can, in turn, burn up and produce an unwelcome flavor, along with being a pain to clean).

Seeing the Benefits of Your Z Grills Wood Pellet Grill

1. Easy To Manage Temperature

One of biggest obstacles people have when it comes to grilling and smoking meats is getting the fire started and controlling the temperatures.

If folks want to use a charcoal grill then they deal with getting the charcoal lit, adjusting the vents, waiting for temperatures to stabilize, adding more fuel during a cook, etc. If they are using a gas grill then getting it lit is easy but dialing in a temperature is difficult. Gas grills are designed for Low, Medium and High. What exactly those settings means is going to depend upon your grill, the ambient weather, etc.

Dealing with temperature control is the problem that dives so many people to using electric smokers where they can just dial in a temperature, sit back and relax.

When it comes to temperature control, using a pellet smoker is just as easy as using an electric smoker! You dial in a temperature, wait 15-20 minutes for the grill to stabilize and then start grilling!

2. Flavor Is An Upgrade Over Electric And Propane

Without question, meat cooked on a pellet grill tastes better than meat cooked with an electric smoker or on a gas grill.

When you use an electric smoker the smoke flavor comes from smoldering wood chips that have to be replenished throughout the cook. When you are cooking on a pellet grill the smoke comes from the continually burning wood. The smoke from burning wood smells and tastes better than that from smoldering wood and gives a better smoke ring to boot. Same goes for meat cooked on a gas grill or smoker.

3. Minimal Flare Ups

The basic design of almost all pellet grills places shields between the flames in the fire pot and the dripping grease. This design has the intrinsic benefit of reducing flare ups to just about zero.

If you have been grilling on a cheap gas grill or directly over lit charcoal then you know that if you are not paying attention then a sudden flare up can happen and scorch whatever you are cooking.

4. Relatively Large Capacity

It doesn't cost much more money for a manufacturer to produce a large pellet grill vs a small one. The core expenses of the stand, electronics, auger, fan, smoke stack, pellet hopper, etc are constant. The only difference is making the cook chamber a little longer and the grates a little bigger.

Better to Use Your Wood Pellet Grill

1. Use Your Pellet Grill Like You Use Your Oven

One of the simplest and best tricks I have learned is to use your pellet grill like you use your oven.

Not every food is great with smoke added, but most things are! So experiment.

Any recipe that calls for roasting or baking in your kitchen oven can be transferred to your pellet smoker, simply by cooking for the same length of time and at the same temperature.

2. Use a Thermometer, Not Your Clock

Following on from the above oven tip, using a thermometer to gauge the internal temperatures of your meat will ensure a better cook rather than using time alone.

After all, it might have been cooking for the suggested time, but if it doesn't reach the right temperature inside, you could severely overcook your food. Or worse, undercook it and make yourself and your guests very ill.

Using a thermometer will also save you from opening the cooking chamber, just to keep checking on the progress of your meat.

The saying goes 'if you're looking, you ain't cooking!'. This is because as you open the door, you let all the heat escape, preventing all that hot smokey goodness from progressing the cook.

So, if your pellet smoker doesn't come with an integrated thermometer, we recommend investing in a good quality, 3rd party digital one. This way, you can monitor the cook via your thermometer and let the grill do its thing!

3. Use Those Upper Racks

Not only do upper racks give you extra space inside your grill, but they also mean the meat you've placed on them is further from the heat source.

This means the meat is being cooked more by convection, rather than radiant heat, which offers a more even cook.

Utilize every space and rack you have, and you'll also get more bang for your buck with the wood pellets you burn, as well as have a lot more food to go around!

4. Get Your Reverse Searing On

To sear or reverse sear? That is the question! But know that pellet grills are brilliant at reverse searing your meat, and not enough grillers do it!

To get that medium-rare finish edge to edge, with a perfectly seared smokey edge, we recommend you learn how to reverse sear.

Think of this process, almost like sous vide cooking. You create the perfect finish throughout the entire steak that you are looking for, cooking with a very low and gentle heat, to ensure none of it, not even the surface, is overcooked.

Only after reaching the perfect doneness throughout, do you then sear to create the Maillard crust and caramelized edge that creates a succulent sensory experience on top of that tender meat.

Depending on the model of your pellet grill and what you're cooking, set your grill temperature to 225f and place your meat in.

Once the internal temperature of your meat reaches 125f, which typically takes 45 minutes to an hour for a 2" thick steak (for medium-rare), take your meat out.

Crank up the grill to 500f, allowing it to heat through thoroughly, and then move the meat back into the grill, on a lower rack, and sear it for a couple of minutes with the lid closed, turning it once, until you have a great crust.

The result will be perfectly medium-rare meat throughout, with a great crust. And not a hint of that grey, overcooked outer edge you often get with the traditional sear.

5. Creating a Smokier Flavor

This tip is for those larger cuts of meat that you want to pull more smoke into, such as beef brisket or a chuck roast.

Smoke loves cold meats, 'condensing' onto the surface more readily than it does to warm surfaces. So the colder it is, the more chance you'll give the smoke to adhere to it.

So, instead of allowing your meat to come up to room temperature – as many recipes request you to do – whip it straight out of the fridge with the dry rub you placed on it the night before and put it straight into the pellet smoker.

As usual, set it to a low smoking temperature and allow it that extra time with the smoke, to get a more pronounced smoke flavor.

Cleaning Tricks for Your Z Grills Wood Pellet Grill

1.Burning Off the Grill after Grilling

Depends on how much gunk/food residue is left, I like to give the grill a good brush down, then fire up to max temperature for 5 minutes. Then a follow up brushing and turning off/cooling down sequence.

2. Grill Cleaning a Few Options

You can just go for a wire brush (check that you pellet grill grill can handle an abrasive brush, some can, some can't) or get a specific tool that is a bit more thorough, design specific.

TIP: If you don't have either of these tools, you can use a scrunched up bit of tin foil to clean in between the grates.

If your not into cleaning the pellet grill after each cook, a minimum of cleaning after each 40 lb of pellets should be done.

3.Ash Removal After Each Cook

Once off and cool I take the ash out, do a quick check inside to see if there is any grease build up.

Even though there won't be much, I like to always empty the ash after a cook.

Getting rid of the ash is always a good idea after each cook, and some pellet grills like the Campchef's have simple pull out knobs for ash removal.

4. Clean Probe In Pellet Grill

The internal temperature probe, once cooled, should have a wipe.

A small amount of vinegar and water, with a scourer or scrubber, is an easy technique to keep the probe clean.

BAKING RECIPES

Baked Green Chile Mac & Cheese By Doug Scheiding

Servings: 8
Cooking Time: 120 Minutes

Ingredients:

- 24 Ounce shredded cheddar cheese, divided
- 8 Ounce mozzarella cheese, shredded
- 6 Tablespoon unsalted butter
- 16 Ounce large dry elbow macaroni noodles
- 2 1/2 Cup half-and-half
- 2 Cup heavy whipping cream
- 8 Ounce cream cheese
- 16 Ounce 505 Southwestern Hatch Valley Flame Roasted Green Chile
- 2 Tablespoon Prime Rib Rub

Directions:

1. Supply your smoker with wood pellets and follow the start-up procedure. Preheat the grill, with the lid closed, to 165° F.
2. Place 16 ounces of the shredded cheddar and the 8 ounces of shredded mozzarella cheese into a shallow pan or cookie sheet and place the pan directly on the grill grate. Smoke for 30 to 40 minutes. Remove from grill and set aside. Grill: 165 °F
3. Increase the grill temperature to 300°F and place a large disposable aluminum half pan in the Traeger with the butter. Remove the pan from the grill after the butter has fully melted. Grill: 300 °F
4. Add the noodles to the pan, along with half-and-half, heavy whipping cream, 16 ounces of the cold smoked cheddar, all of the smoked mozzarella cheese and cream cheese broken into small pieces. Add the green chiles to taste (12 ounces for mild and 16 ounces for spicy) and stir to combine.
5. Place the pan in the grill and bake for 2 hours, stirring every 20 minutes. If macaroni and cheese looks like it is getting dry, add a little more half-and-half and stir to combine. Grill: 300 °F
6. During the last 20 minutes of cooking, sprinkle the remaining (unsmoked) cheddar cheese on top and add a light dusting of Traeger Prime Rib Rub. Serve hot. Enjoy!

Basil Margherita Pizza

Servings: 6
Cooking Time: 25 Minutes

Ingredients:

- Basil, Chopped
- 2 Cups Flour, All-Purpose
- Mozzarella Cheese, Sliced Rounds
- 1 Cup Pizza Sauce
- 1 Teaspoon Salt
- 1 Teaspoon Sugar
- 1 Tomato, Sliced
- 1 Cup Water, Warm
- 1 Teaspoon Yeast, Instant

Directions:

1. Combine the water, yeast, and sugar in a small bowl and let sit for about 5 minutes.
2. In a large bowl, stir together the flour and salt. Pour in the yeast mixture and mix until a soft dough forms. Knead for about 2 minutes. Place in an oiled bowl and cover with a cloth. Let the dough sit and rise for about 45 minutes or until the dough has doubled in size.
3. Roll out on a flat, floured surface (or on a pizza stone) until you''ve reached your desired shape and thickness.
4. Supply your smoker with wood pellets and follow the start-up procedure. Preheat the grill, with the lid closed, to 350° F.
5. On the rolled out dough, pour on the pizza sauce, cheese, and then tomatoes and basil. Place in your Grill and bake for about 25 minutes, or until the cheese is melted and slightly golden brown.

Chocolate Lava Cake With Smoked Whipped Cream

Servings: 4
Cooking Time: 45 Minutes

Ingredients:

- 1 Pint heavy whipping cream
- 9 Tablespoon Butter
- 220 G Semisweet Chocolate
- 1 1/4 Cup powdered sugar
- 2 Large eggs
- 2 egg yolk
- 6 Tablespoon flour
- 1 Tablespoon Bourbon Vanilla
- Powdered Sugar
- cocoa powder

Directions:

1. Supply your smoker with wood pellets and follow the start-up procedure. Preheat the grill, with the lid closed, to 180° F.
2. For the Smoked Whipped Cream: Add cream to a shallow, aluminum baking pan. Place the pan on the grill and smoke for 30 minutes.
3. Pour the smoked cream into a large mixing bowl and refrigerate for later use. Grill: 180 ˚F
4. Increase the grill temperature to 375°F and preheat. Grill: 375 ˚F
5. Brush 4 small soufflé cups with 1 tablespoon melted butter.
6. Melt the chocolate and remaining butter in a heatproof bowl over simmering water, stir until smooth.
7. Stir in powdered sugar. Add eggs and egg yolks, stirring continuously. Whisk in flour until blended completely.
8. Pour batter into the prepared soufflé cups. Place them on the Traeger and bake for 13-14 minutes, or until the sides are set. Grill: 375 ˚F
9. For the Whipped Cream: Remove the chilled smoked cream from the refrigerator, add the bourbon vanilla and whip until airy.
10. Add confectioners sugar and continue whipping until whipped cream forms stiff peaks.
11. Dust lava cakes with confectioners sugar and cocoa, top with a dollop of smoke-infused whipped cream. Enjoy!

Easy Smoked Cornbread

Servings: 4
Cooking Time: 75 Minutes

Ingredients:

- 2 cups self rising flour
- 1 1/2 cups white corn meal
- 2 cups sharp cheddar cheese
- 1/2 cup sour cream
- 1/2 cup sugar
- 1 Tbsp baking powder
- 1 teaspoon sea salt
- 1 12 oz can of evaporated milk
- 1/2 cup vegetable oil
- 2 large eggs beaten

Directions:

1. Mix all ingredients together well and fold into a greased baking pan (such as a round cake Pan).
2. Supply your smoker with wood pellets and follow the start-up procedure. Preheat the grill, with the lid closed, to 375° F. Smoke on 375 ˚F for 1 hour and 15 minutes or until toothpick comes clean and edges look brown.
3. Rub some butter on top and sprinkle a little Fred's Butt Rub on top before serving.
4. Enjoy!

Onion Cheese Nachos

Servings: 6
Cooking Time: 10 Minutes

Ingredients:

- 1 Pound Beef, Ground
- 3 Cups Cheddar Cheese, Shredded
- 1 Green Bell Pepper, Diced
- 1/2 Cup Green Onion
- 1/2 Cup Red Onion, Diced
- 1 Large Bag Tortilla Chip

Directions:

1. Supply your smoker with wood pellets and follow the start-up procedure. Preheat the grill, with the lid closed, to 350° F.
2. While you're waiting, empty a large bag of nacho chips evenly onto a cast iron pan. Start loading up with toppings - cooked ground beef, red onion, red pepper, cheese, green onions. These are just the toppings we had on hand, so feel free to add anything you like! Make sure you do a couple layers of chips so everyone gets a good serving of nachos. And don't be skimpy with the cheese - lay it on heavy!
3. Place your loaded nachos on the grill and let the hot smoke melt your toppings into one cheesy creation. Heat at 350°F for 10 minutes or until the cheese has fully melted. Remove and serve with sour-cream and salsa.

Skillet Buttermilk Cornbread

Servings: 6
Cooking Time: 25 Minutes

Ingredients:

- 1 Cup Cornmeal
- 1 Cup all-purpose flour
- 1/3 Cup granulated sugar
- 1 Teaspoon salt
- 1 Teaspoon baking powder
- 1 1/2 Cup buttermilk
- 2 Whole eggs
- 8 Tablespoon butter, melted

Directions:

1. Grease a cast iron skillet or 9-inch square baking pan with bacon fat. Put a 10-inch well-seasoned cast iron skillet on the grill grate. If using a regular baking pan, do not preheat.
2. Supply your smoker with wood pellets and follow the start-up procedure. Preheat the grill, with the lid closed, to 400° F.
3. In a large mixing bowl, combine the cornmeal, flour, sugar, salt, and baking powder and whisk to mix thoroughly. Make a well in the center of the dry ingredients.
4. In a separate mixing bowl, whisk together the buttermilk and eggs until well-combined. Add the melted butter. Pour into the dry ingredients and mix until the batter is fairly smooth. Do not overmix.
5. Carefully pour the batter into the preheated skillet. Bake for 20 to 25 minutes, or until the top is firm and a tester inserted in the center of the cornbread comes out clean. Be careful when removing the skillet from the grill as it will be very hot. Let the cornbread cool slightly on a trivet or cooling rack before slicing into wedges or squares.

Spiced Lemon Cherry Pie

Servings: 6-8
Cooking Time: 60 Minutes

Ingredients:

- 1/2 Teaspoon Cinnamon, Ground
- 1/2 Teaspoon Cloves, Ground
- 1/2 Cup Cornstarch
- 1 Pound Frozen Sweet Dark Cherries, Thawed
- 1 Teaspoon Water (Beaten With Egg) 1 Egg
- 1 Lemon, Juice
- 1 Lemon, Zest
- 2 Prepared Store Bought Or Homemade Pie Crust
- 1 Teaspoon Hickory Honey Sea Salt Seasoning
- 1 Cup Sugar, Granulated
- 1 Teaspoon Vanilla Extract

Directions:

1. In a large bowl, mix together the thawed cherries and their juices, sugar, cornstarch, lemon zest, lemon juice, cinnamon, clove, vanilla extract and Hickory Honey Sea Salt. Allow to sit for 30 minutes.
2. Flour a work surface and roll out one of the prepared pie crusts so that it fits a 9 inch pie tin. Fill with the cherry pie filling and refrigerate. When the pie is chilled, roll out the second pie crust, brush the edge of the first pie crust with the egg mixture, top with the second pie crust, crimp the edge with a fork, and chill. Alternatively, cut the second pie crust into strips and form a lattice pattern, attaching the strips with the egg mixture. Chill the pie for 15-30 minutes, or until the dough is very cold and firm. Brush the top of the pie with the remaining egg mixture.

3. Supply your smoker with wood pellets and follow the start-up procedure. Preheat the grill, with the lid closed, to 350° F and grill for 45 minutes to 1 hour, or until the pie crust is golden and firm and the filling is bubbly. Remove from the grill and allow to cool at room temperature for at least 4 hours to set the filling, then serve and enjoy!

Cinnamon Pull-aparts

Servings: 6
Cooking Time: 20 Minutes

Ingredients:

- 16.3 Ounce Biscuits, Homestyle, Canned
- 1 Cup packed brown sugar
- 1/2 Cup butter
- 1/4 Cup water
- 1 Teaspoon ground cinnamon
- 1/2 Cup Nuts (optional)

Directions:

1. Cut each biscuit into 4 pieces and peel each piece in half; set aside.
2. Combine brown sugar, butter and water in a large saucepan and bring to a boil; reduce heat and simmer for 1 minute. Stir in cinnamon and nuts; add biscuit quarters and mix to coat. Pour into greased 13 by 9 inch casserole dish and spread evenly in the dish.
3. Supply your smoker with wood pellets and follow the start-up procedure. Preheat the grill, with the lid closed, to 350° F.
4. Place the casserole dish on the grill; close lid and cook for 20 to 25 minutes or until the biscuits are done. Grill: 350 °F
5. Remove from the grill and transfer to a serving platter making sure to get all the gooey syrup onto the biscuits. Serve warm. Enjoy!

Donut Bread Pudding

Servings: 8
Cooking Time: 40 Minutes

Ingredients:

- 16 Cake Donuts
- 1/2 Cup Raisins, seedless
- 5 eggs
- 3/4 Cup sugar
- 2 Cup heavy cream
- 2 Teaspoon vanilla extract
- 1 Teaspoon ground cinnamon
- 3/4 Cup Butter, melted, cooled slightly
- Ice Cream

Directions:

1. Lightly butter a 9- by 13-inch baking pan. Layer the donuts in an even thickness in the pan. Distribute the raisins over the top, if using. Drizzle evenly with the butter.
2. Make the custard: In a medium bowl, whisk together the sugar, eggs, cream, vanilla, and cinnamon. Whisk in the butter. Pour over the donuts. Let sit for 10 to 15 minutes, periodically pushing the donuts down into the custard. Cover with foil.
3. Supply your smoker with wood pellets and follow the start-up procedure. Preheat the grill, with the lid closed, to 350° F.
4. Bake the bread pudding for 30 to 40 minutes, or until the custard is set. Remove the foil and continue to bake for 10 additional minutes to lightly brown the top. Grill: 350 °F
5. Let cool slightly before cutting into squares. Drizzle with melted ice cream, if desired. Enjoy!

Baked Potatoes & Celery Root Au Gratin

Servings: 2
Cooking Time: 60 Minutes

Ingredients:

- 5 Tablespoon butter, softened
- 2 Large leeks, white parts only, cleaned and sliced into half moons
- kosher salt
- freshly ground black pepper
- 5 Small Yukon Gold potatoes, sliced 1/4 inch thick
- 2 Whole celery root, peeled and sliced 1/4 inch thick
- 2 Cup cream
- 1 Tablespoon minced sage
- 1 Cup shredded Gruyere or other hearty Swiss cheese, divided

Directions:

1. Supply your smoker with wood pellets and follow the start-up procedure. Preheat the grill, with the lid closed, to 400° F.
2. Butter a 9x13 baking dish with 1 tablespoon of the softened butter. In a medium frying pan over medium heat, melt the remaining butter. Add the leeks and a generous pinch of salt and pepper and cook, stirring often until softened, about 5 minutes.
3. Remove from the heat and allow to cool. Place the potato and celery root slices into a large mixing bowl. Add the cream, leek mixture, minced sage, 1 teaspoon salt, 1/2 teaspoon pepper and 1 cup cheese. Stir gently to coat.
4. Arrange a layer of potato and celery root slices so they're slightly overlapping in the prepared baking dish. Repeat two more times so there are three layers of potatoes. Pour remaining cream from the bowl over the gratin, then sprinkle the top with the remaining cup of cheese.
5. Cover the dish loosely with foil and bake on the grill for 45 minutes. Remove the foil and continue baking until the top is golden and bubbly and the potatoes are tender when pierced, about 30 to 45 minutes longer. Let stand for 10 minutes before serving. Enjoy!

Marbled Brownies With Amaretto & Ricotta

Servings: 4

Cooking Time: 30 Minutes

Ingredients:

- 1 Cup Ricotta Cheese
- 1 eggs
- 1 Tablespoon Amaretto Liqueur
- 1/4 Cup sugar
- 2 Teaspoon cornstarch
- 1/2 Teaspoon vanilla extract
- 1 Brownie Mix

Directions:

1. Coat a 9- by 13-inch nonstick baking pan with cooking spray or softened butter and set aside. (If you do not have a nonstick pan, line a regular one with buttered foil or parchment paper.)
2. In a medium bowl, combine the ricotta, egg, amaretto, sugar, cornstarch, and vanilla and whisk together thoroughly. Set aside.
3. Prepare the brownie mix according to the package directions. Spread the brownie batter evenly in the prepared pan. Randomly drop dollops of the ricotta mixture over the batter. Run a plastic knife through the ricotta mixture to give the brownies a marbled look. (A plastic knife is less likely to scratch your pan's nonstick surface.)
4. Supply your smoker with wood pellets and follow the start-up procedure. Preheat the grill, with the lid closed, to 350° F.
5. Put the pan with the brownie mixture directly on the grill grate and bake, about 25 to 30 minutes. Insert a bamboo skewer or toothpick in the center of the brownies to determine if they are done: the batter should not be wet. Grill: 350 °F
6. Transfer the brownies to a wire cooling rack to cool completely. Cut into squares.

Focaccia

Servings: 6

Cooking Time: 40 Minutes

Ingredients:

- 1 Cup warm water (110°F to 115°F)
- 1/2 Ounce Yeast, active
- 1 Teaspoon sugar
- 2 1/2 Cup flour
- 1 Teaspoon salt
- 1/4 Cup extra-virgin olive oil
- 1 1/2 Teaspoon Italian herbs, dried
- 1/8 Teaspoon red pepper flakes
- As Needed coarse sea salt

Directions:

1. Measure the water in a glass-measuring cup. Stir in the yeast and sugar. Let rest for in a warm place. After 5 to 10 minutes, the mixture should be foamy, indicating the yeast is "alive." If it does not foam, discard it and start again.

2. Pour the water/yeast mixture in the bowl of a food processor. Add 1 cup of the flour as well as the salt and 1/4 cup of olive oil. Pulse several times to blend. Add the remaining flour, Italian herbs, and hot pepper flakes.
3. Process the dough until it's smooth and elastic and pulls away from the sides of the bowl, adding small amounts of flour or water through the feed tube if the dough is respectively too wet or too dry.
4. Let the dough rise in the covered food processor bowl in a warm place until doubled in bulk, about 1 hour5. Remove the dough from the food processor (it will deflate) and turn onto a lightly floured surface.
5. Oil two 8- to 9-inch round cake pans generously with olive oil. (Just pour a couple of glugs in and tilt the pan to spread the oil.) Divide the dough into two equal pieces, shape into disks, and put one in each prepared cake pan.
6. Oil the top of each disk with olive oil and dimple the dough with your fingertips. Sprinkle lightly with coarse salt, and if desired, additional dried Italian herbs.
7. Cover the focaccia dough with plastic wrap and let the dough rise in a warm place, about 45 minutes to an hour.
8. When ready to cook, start the smoker grill and set the temperature to 400F and preheat, lid closed, for 10 to 15 minutes.
9. Put the pans with the focaccia dough directly on the grill grate. Bake until the focaccia breads are light golden in color and baked through, 35 to 40 minutes, rotating the pans halfway through the baking time.
10. Let cool slightly before removing from the pans. Cut into wedges for serving.

Baked Chocolate Brownie Cookies With Egg Nog

Servings: 6
Cooking Time: 12 Minutes

Ingredients:

- 16 Ounce Bar bittersweet chocolate, finely chopped
- 4 Tablespoon unsalted butter, room temperature
- 4 eggs
- 1 1/3 Cup granulated sugar
- 1 Teaspoon vanilla extract
- 1 1/2 Cup all-purpose flour
- 1/2 Teaspoon baking powder
- 1 Cup semisweet chocolate chips

Directions:

1. Supply your smoker with wood pellets and follow the start-up procedure. Preheat the grill, with the lid closed, to 350° F.
2. Line two baking sheets with parchment paper.
3. Put the finely chopped chocolate and butter in a heatproof bowl and set over a saucepan of barely simmering water; stir occasionally until chocolate is completely melted and smooth. Set aside and allow to cool to room temperature.
4. Whisk together eggs, sugar and vanilla extract in a medium bowl. Set aside.
5. Sift together the flour and baking powder in a small bowl. Add the melted chocolate mixture to the egg mixture and stir with a rubber spatula until completely combined.
6. Add the flour mixture in three batches, folding gently into the batter with a spatula. Once all of the flour has been incorporated, stir in the chocolate chips.
7. Scoop 1-1/2 tablespoons of dough onto prepared baking sheets. Bake for 10 to 12 minutes or until they are firm on the outside. Do not over bake. Grill:350° F
8. Leave to cool completely on the baking sheets. Enjoy!

Smoker Wheat Bread

Servings: 6
Cooking Time: 60 Minutes

Ingredients:

- As Needed extra-virgin olive oil
- 2 Cup all-purpose flour
- 1 Cup whole wheat flour
- 1 1/4 Ounce Packet, Active Dry Yeast
- 1 1/4 Teaspoon salt
- 1 1/2 Cup water
- As Needed Cornmeal

Directions:

1. Oil a large mixing bowl and set aside. In a second mixing bowl, combine the flours, yeast, and salt.
2. Push your sleeve up to your elbow and form your fingers into a claw. Mix the dry ingredients until well-combined.
3. Add the water and mix until blended. The dough will be wet, shaggy, and somewhat stringy.
4. Tip the dough into the oiled mixing bowl and cover with plastic wrap.
5. Allow the dough to rise at room temperature--about 70 degrees-- for 2 hours, or until the surface is bubbled.
6. Turn the dough out onto a lightly floured work surface and lightly flour the top. With floured hands, fold the dough over on itself twice. Cover loosely with plastic wrap and allow the dough to rest for 15 minutes.
7. Dust a clean lint-free cotton towel with cornmeal, wheat bran, or flour. With floured hands, gently form the dough into a ball and place it, seam side down, on the towel.
8. Dust the top of the ball with cornmeal, wheat bran, or flour, and cover the dough with a second towel. Let the dough rise until doubled in size; the dough will not spring back when poked with a finger.
9. In the meantime, start the smoker grill and set temperature to 450 F. Preheat, lid closed, for 10-15 minutes.
10. Put a lidded 6- to 8-quart cast iron Dutch oven - preferably one coated with enamel, on the grill grate.
11. When the dough has risen, remove the top towel, slide your hand under the bottom towel to support the dough, then carefully tip the dough, seam side up, into the preheated pot.
12. Remove the towel. Shake the pot a couple of times if the dough looks lopsided: It will straighten out as it bakes.
13. Cover the pot with the lid and bake the bread for 30 minutes. Remove the lid and continue to bake the bread for 15 to 30 minutes more, or until it is nicely browned and sounds hollow when rapped with your knuckles.
14. Turn onto a wire rack to cool. Slice with a serrated knife. Enjoy!

Vanilla Chocolate Chip Cookies

Servings: 12

Cooking Time: 20 Minutes

Ingredients:

- 3/4 cup brown sugar
- 3/4 cup white sugar
- 1 stick butter, room temp
- 2 eggs
- 1 tsp vanilla
- 2 1/2 cups flour
- 1/2 tsp salt
- 1 tsp baking soda
- 1 cup Chocolate Chips

Directions:

1. Cream your butter and sugar together in a mixing bowl using a hand mixer or stand mixer on medium speed for about 4-5 minutes.
2. Once the butter is creamed, add the eggs and vanilla. Continue mixing for an additional minute.
3. Put flour, salt, and baking soda in a sifter. Sift it into your creamed butter mixture.
4. Scrape the sides of your mixing bowl with a rubber spatula, and then turn your mixer on to low speed.
5. Let it mix a little, and then scrape the sides again. Stop mixing when there are one or two streaks of flour left in the cookie dough.
6. Scrape the sides of your bowl and pour in a cup of chocolate chips, and turn the mixer to low again to mix the chocolate. It should take just a few turns for the chocolate pieces to be well incorporated.
7. Line a large baking sheet with parchment paper. Using a medium cookie scoop (about 1.5 tbsp), drop evenly spaced dollops of cookie dough onto the cookie sheet.
8. Supply your smoker with wood pellets and follow the start-up procedure. Preheat the grill, with the lid closed, to 350° F. Place the cookie sheet in your smoker, and let them cook for about 12 minutes.
9. Let them sit on a cooling rack while you continue to cook the additional cookies.
10. Cool for a few minutes to let cookies set.
11. Enjoy!

Sourdough Pizza

Servings: 4

Cooking Time: 12 Minutes

Ingredients:

- 1 1/2 Cup Fresh Sourdough Starter
- 1 Tablespoon olive oil
- 1 Teaspoon Jacobsen Salt Co. Pure Kosher Sea Salt
- 1 1/4 Cup all-purpose flour

Directions:

1. Supply your smoker with wood pellets and follow the start-up procedure. Preheat the grill, with the lid closed, to 450° F.
2. Mix together the fresh sourdough starter, one tablespoon of oil, Jacobsen salt and 1-1/4 cups of flour. Add more flour, a little at a time, as needed to form a pizza dough consistency.
3. Allow the dough to rest for 30 minutes, to allow for easier rolling. Roll the dough out into a circle, using a small amount of flour to prevent sticking.
4. Place on a pizza stone. Bake the crust for approximately 7 minutes Grill: 450 °F
5. Remove the crust from the grill; brush on remaining oil to prevent toppings from soaking into the crust. Add the desired toppings and return pizza to grill; bake until the crust browns and the cheese melts.

Eyeball Cookies

Servings: 20

Cooking Time: 35 Minutes

Ingredients:

- 2 Packages Candy Eyeballs
- Green, Blue And Purple Food Coloring
- 1 Box Of Yellow Gluten Free Cake Mix
- 1/2 Cup (Optional) Granulated Sugar
- 2 Large Eggs
- 1/3 Cup Powdered Sugar
- 1 Teaspoon Pure Vanilla Extract
- 6 Tablespoon Melted Vegan Butter (Unsalted)

Directions:

1. Supply your smoker with wood pellets and follow the start-up procedure. Preheat the grill, with the lid closed, to 350° F.
2. Line two large baking sheets with parchment paper. In a large bowl, combine cake mix, melted butter, eggs (or egg substitute), powdered sugar, sugar (optional), and vanilla and stir until combined. (substitute 2 flax eggs for Vegan – 1 tbsp flax seed meal and 5 tbsp water per egg).
3. Divide dough between 3 bowls and dye each bowl a different color.(We used green, blue and purple).
4. Roll dough into tablespoon-sized balls.
5. Place about 2" apart on the baking sheet and grill until tops have cracked and the tops look set, 8 to 10 minutes. – Turn half way through baking, after 4-5 minutes.
6. Immediately, while the cookies are still warm, stick candy eyeballs all over the cookies.
7. Let cool completely before serving.

Savory Beaver Tails

Servings: 8

Cooking Time: 2 Minutes

Ingredients:

- 2 Tbsp Butter, Melted
- 1 Tbsp Cinnamon, Ground
- 1 Egg
- 2 1/2 Cups Flour, All-Purpose
- 1/2 Cup Milk, Warm
- 1/2 Tsp Salt
- 1 Tsp Sugar
- 1/2 Tsp Vanilla
- 1 L Vegetable Oil
- 1/4 Cup Water, Warm
- 2 1/2 Tsp Active Yeast, Instant

Directions:

1. In a small bowl, combine water, milk, yeast, and sugar. Let it sit for about 10 minutes or until frothy.
2. In another bowl, pour in the flour and make a well in the middle. Pour in butter, sugar, salt, vanilla and egg. Mix everything together until the dough is smooth. Knead for about 5 minutes and set the dough in a

greased bowl. Cover with a towel and set aside for about an hour, or until the dough has doubled in size.

3. After one hour, supply your smoker with wood pellets and follow the start-up procedure. Preheat the grill, with the lid open, to 450° F.Pour 1L of vegetable oil into a cast iron pan and place on the grates of your Grill. Keep your flame broiler closed so as to prevent grease flareups. Preheat the oil so that it is 350 degrees F.
4. While you"re waiting for the oil to heat up, punch down the dough and separate into 8 small balls. Shape each piece of dough into a flat circle. Fry the dough in the preheated oil for about 1 minute per side, or until the dough is golden brown.
5. Sprinkle with cinnamon sugar immediately, or top with your desired toppings. Enjoy!

Rosemary Cranberry Apple Sage Stuffing

Servings: 7
Cooking Time: 45 Minutes

Ingredients:

- 10 Cups Day Old Diced Bread, Sliced Loaf
- 2 1/2 Cups Broth, Chicken
- 1 Cup Butter, Unsalted
- 1 Cup Diced Celery, Cut
- 1 1/2 Cups Fresh Cranberries
- 1 Beaten Egg
- 1 Medium Granny Smith Apple, Peel, Core And Dice
- 2 Tbsp Minced Parsley, Fresh
- 1 Tbsp Minced Rosemary, Fresh
- 2 Tbsp Roughly Chopped Sage
- Salt And Pepper
- 1 Tbsp Minced Thyme
- 2 Cups Diced Yellow Onion, Sliced

Directions:

1. Supply your smoker with wood pellets and follow the start-up procedure. Preheat the grill, with the lid closed, to 350° F.
2. Melt butter over medium heat. Add onions then celery and cook until onions start to become translucent.
3. In a large bowl, mix together bread, apples, cranberries, cooked onion and celery mixture, and fresh herbs.
4. Add half of the chicken broth to the mixture and stir.
5. Beat together eggs and the rest of the chicken broth in a small bowl. Pour into the bread mixture and stir until completely combined.
6. Add salt and pepper to taste.
7. Pour stuffing into a cast iron pan or baking dish. Cover with foil and bake on the grill for 30 minutes. Remove the foil and cook for an additional 15 minutes.
8. Serve immediately and enjoy!

Bacon Chocolate Chip Cookies

Servings: 2
Cooking Time: 10-12 Minutes

Ingredients:

- 2¾ cups all-purpose flour
- 1½ teaspoons baking soda
- ½ teaspoon salt
- 12 tablespoons (1½ sticks) unsalted butter, softened
- 1 cup light brown sugar
- 1 cup granulated sugar
- 2 eggs, at room temperature
- 2½ teaspoons apple cider vinegar
- 1 teaspoon vanilla extract
- 2 cups semisweet chocolate chips
- 8 slices bacon, cooked and crumbled

Directions:

1. In a large bowl, combine the flour, baking soda, and salt, and mix well.
2. In a separate large bowl, using an electric mixer on medium speed, cream the butter and sugars. Reduce the speed to low and mix in the eggs, vinegar, and vanilla.
3. With the mixer speed still on low, slowly incorporate the dry ingredients, chocolate chips, and bacon pieces.
4. Supply your smoker with wood pellets and follow the start-up procedure. Preheat, with the lid closed, to 375°F.
5. Line a large baking sheet with parchment paper.
6. Drop rounded teaspoonfuls of cookie batter onto the prepared baking sheet and place on the grill grate. Close the lid and smoke for 10 to 12 minutes, or until the cookies are browned around the edges.

Pineapple Cake

Servings: 4

Cooking Time: 30 Minutes

Ingredients:

- 2/3 cup of vegetable oil (olive oil works great, not virgin)
- 3 eggs
- 1/3 cup brown sugar (not too sweet)
- 3/4 cup self raising plain flour
- 1/4 cup wholemeal self raising flour
- 1/3 cup saltanas
- 1/3 cup diced canned pineapple (drained)
- 1/3 cup diced raw walnuts
- 2 large carrots grated
- Icing Ingredients
- 250 grams cream cheese
- 35 grams icing sugar (not too sweet)
- Whole lemon or orange zest

Directions:

1. Mix all ingredients in a large bowl.
2. Place into 6″ greased baking tray or un-greased silicone tray.
3. Supply your smoker with wood pellets and follow the start-up procedure. Preheat the grill, with the lid closed, to 190 °F. Cook for 25-30min until golden brown and no dough when probed.
4. Let cool on rack (not directly on plate or board) then apply icing.
5. Whip icing ingredients and place in fridge until ready to coat the cake.

Blueberry Pancakes

Servings: 4

Cooking Time: 10 Minutes

Ingredients:

- 2 Cups Blueberries, Fresh
- 1 Cup Pancake Mix
- 1/2 Cup Sugar
- 3/4 Cup Water, Warm

Directions:

1. Supply your smoker with wood pellets and follow the start-up procedure. Preheat the grill, with the lid closed, to 350° F.
2. Place the cast iron griddle on the grates of your grill.
3. In a large bowl, pour water, pancake mix and 1/2 cup of the blueberries and mix until combined.
4. Pour the batter onto the griddle in 4 equal parts. Cook with the lid closed for about 6 minutes, or until the edges of the pancakes are slightly cooked. Flip each pancake and continue cooking for another 4 minutes.
5. Pour the hot blueberry sauce over your freshly cooked pancakes and enjoy!

Sweet And Spicy Baked Pork Beans

Servings: 20

Cooking Time: 120 Minutes

Ingredients:

- 1 - 21 Oz Apple Pie Filling, Can
- 1 Gallon Baked Beans
- 1 Tbs Chilli, Powder
- 1 Green Bell Pepper, Diced
- 1 10 Oz Drained Jalapeno, Can Diced
- 1 Cup Maple Syrup
- 1 Onion, Diced
- 1 Lb Pork, Pulled

Directions:

1. Supply your smoker with wood pellets and follow the start-up procedure. Preheat the grill, with the lid closed, to 350° F.
2. Place all ingredients in mixing bowl and mix well.
3. Pour bean mixture into foil pans.
4. Bake in grill till bubbling throughout – about 2 hours.
5. Rest at least 15 minutes before serving.

Italian Herb & Parmesan Scones

Servings: 8

Cooking Time: 20 Minutes

Ingredients:

- 2 1/2 Cup all-purpose flour
- 2 Teaspoon baking powder
- 1 Teaspoon baking soda

- 1/2 Teaspoon garlic salt
- 1 Tablespoon Italian Seasoning
- 1 Cup Parmesan cheese, grated
- 2 Large eggs
- 1 1/2 Cup buttermilk
- 1/4 Cup olive oil

Directions:

1. In a large mixing bowl, combine flour, baking powder, baking powder, soda, garlic salt, Italian seasoning, and 1/2 cup of the cheese. Make a well in the center.
2. In a smaller bowl, whisk together eggs, buttermilk, and olive oil.
3. Pour into the well in the dry ingredients, and stir batter just until it's combined. It will appear lumpy.
4. Oil 12 muffin cups, spray with cooking spray, or line with disposable paper liners.
5. Divide the batter evenly between the cups. Sprinkle the tops of the muffins with the remaining Parmesan cheese.
6. Supply your smoker with wood pellets and follow the start-up procedure. Preheat the grill, with the lid closed, to 400° F.
7. Arrange the muffin tin directly on the grill grate and bake the muffins for 20 to 25 minutes, or until a toothpick inserted in the center of the muffin comes out clean.
8. Cool for several minutes before removing from the muffin tin. Serve warm with butter or olive oil. Enjoy!

The Dan Patrick Show Pull-apart Pesto Bread

Servings: 8

Cooking Time: 25 Minutes

Ingredients:

- 1 Sourdough Bread, loaf
- 1/2 Cup butter, melted
- 1 Cup Pesto Sauce
- 1 1/2 Cup Italian Cheese Blend

Directions:

1. Supply your smoker with wood pellets and follow the start-up procedure. Preheat the grill, with the lid closed, to 350° F.
2. Using a serrated knife, make 1" diagonal cuts through the bread leaving the bottom crust intact. Turn the bread and make diagonal cuts in the opposite direction, creating diamonds.
3. Place the bread on a sheet of foil large enough to wrap around the entire loaf. Pour the melted butter into the cracks in the bread. Using a spoon spread the pesto into the cracks then follow with the cheese stuffing it down into each crack.
4. Fold up the edges of the foil to wrap up the loaf and transfer to a baking sheet. Place the baking sheet directly on the grill grate.
5. Bake for 15 minutes then unwrap the foil and cook for an additional 10 minutes. Remove from the grill and serve. Enjoy! Grill: 350 ˚F
6. Follow along as we give you a recipe each day this week from The Dan Patrick Show Game Day Recipes eBook.

S'mores Dip Skillet

Servings: 4-6

Cooking Time: 8 Minutes

Ingredients:

- 2 tablespoons salted butter, melted
- ¼ cup milk
- 12 ounces semisweet chocolate chips
- 16 ounces Jet-Puffed marshmallows
- Graham crackers and apple wedges, for serving

Directions:

1. Supply your smoker with wood pellets and follow the start-up procedure. Preheat, with the lid closed, to 450˚F.
2. Place a cast iron skillet on the preheated grill grate and pour in the melted butter and milk, stirring for about 1 minute.
3. Once the mixture starts to heat, top with the chocolate chips in an even layer and arrange the marshmallows standing up to cover all of the chocolate.

4. Close the lid and smoke for 5 to 7 minutes, or until the marshmallows are lightly toasted.
5. Remove from the heat and serve immediately with graham crackers and apple wedges for dipping.

Baked Cheesy Parmesan Grits

Servings: 4
Cooking Time: 60 Minutes

Ingredients:

- 4 Cup chicken stock
- 3 Tablespoon butter
- 3/4 Teaspoon salt
- 1 Cup quick grits
- 1 Cup shredded cheddar cheese
- pepper
- 1/2 Cup Monterey Jack cheese, shredded
- 1/2 Cup whole milk
- 2 Large eggs

Directions:

1. Supply your smoker with wood pellets and follow the start-up procedure. Preheat the grill, with the lid closed, to 350° F.
2. Butter an 8" baking dish or a 10" cast iron pan.
3. Bring the chicken stock, butter, and salt to boil in medium saucepan. Gradually whisk in grits.
4. Reduce heat to medium and cook until mixture thickens slightly, stirring often about 8 minutes. Remove from heat.
5. Add cheeses and stir until melted. Season with pepper and salt to taste.
6. Whisk together milk and eggs in small bowl. Gradually whisk mixture into grits.
7. Pour the cheese grits into the buttered cast iron pan. Bake until grits feel firm to touch, about 1 hour. Grill: 350 °F
8. Remove from grill and let stand 10 minutes before serving. Enjoy!

Tarte Tatin

Servings: 6
Cooking Time: 55 Minutes

Ingredients:

- 2 Cup all-purpose flour
- 1 Teaspoon salt
- 1 Cup butter
- 5 Tablespoon cold water
- 1/4 Cup unsalted butter
- 3/4 Cup granulated sugar
- 10 Granny Smith Apples, Cut Into Wedges

Directions:

1. Supply your smoker with wood pellets and follow the start-up procedure. Preheat the grill, with the lid closed, to 350° F.
2. For the crust: Place flour and salt in a food processer and pulse to mix. Add butter a little at a time while pulsing. Once it starts to looks like cornmeal, add the water until dough start to come together. Form a round with the dough, wrap in plastic and let it cool in the refrigerator.
3. While dough cools, place a pie dish or a 10-inch round cake pan on the grill; add butter and sugar to pie dish. Let it caramelize.
4. When the sugar caramelizes and has come to a dark amber color, take off grill. Arrange apple wedges in a fan formation covering the caramel.
5. Roll the pie crust into a circle big enough to cover the pan. Prick the pie dough with a fork and cover the pan with the pie dough. Trim the crust leaving room for shrinkage.
6. Place on the grill and bake for 55 minutes until apples are soft. Let sit for 3 minutes. While pan is still hot, place a plate over pie and flip over. Grill: 350 °F
7. Serve warm, topped with ice cream or whipped cream. Enjoy!

Crescent Rolls

Servings: 8
Cooking Time: 12 Minutes

Ingredients:

- 1 Crescent Dough, Can

Directions:

1. Supply your smoker with wood pellets and follow the start-up procedure. Preheat the grill, with the lid closed, to 375° F.

2. Unroll the dough and separate into triangles. Roll up the triangles and place on an ungreased nonstick cookie sheet. Bake for 10 -12 minutes on your Grill. You will know that they are finished when the rolls are golden brown.

Pretzel Rolls

Servings: 6
Cooking Time: 20 Minutes

Ingredients:

- 2 3/4 Cup Bread Flour
- 1 Quick-Rising Yeast, envelope
- 1 Teaspoon salt
- 1 Teaspoon sugar
- 1/2 Teaspoon celery seed
- 1/2 Teaspoon Caraway Seeds
- 1 Cup hot water
- As Needed Cornmeal
- 8 Cup water
- 1/4 Cup baking soda
- 2 Tablespoon sugar
- 1 Whole Egg White
- Coarse salt

Directions:

1. Combine bread flour, 1 envelope yeast, salt, 1 teaspoon sugar, caraway seeds and celery seeds in food processor or standing mixer with dough hook and blend.
2. With machine running, gradually pour hot water, adding enough water to form smooth elastic dough. Process 1 minute to knead. (You could also knead it by hand for a few minutes.)
3. Grease medium bowl. Add dough to bowl, turning to coat. Cover bowl with plastic wrap, then towel; let dough rise in warm draft-free area until doubled in volume, about 35 minutes.
4. Flour a large baking sheet. Punch dough down and knead on lightly floured surface until smooth. Divide into 8 pieces. Form each dough piece into a ball.
5. Place dough balls on prepared sheet, flattening each slightly. Using serrated knife, cut X in top center of each dough ball. Cover with towel and let dough balls rise until almost doubled in volume, about 20 minutes.
6. When ready to cook, start the smoker on Smoke with the lid open until a fire is established (4-5 minutes). Turn temperature to 375 F (190 C) and preheat, lid closed, for 10 to 15 minutes.
7. Grease another baking sheet and sprinkle with cornmeal. Bring water to boil in large saucepan. Add baking soda and sugar (water will foam up). Add 3 rolls (or however many will fit comfortably in the pot) and cook 30 seconds per side.
8. Using slotted spoon, transfer rolls to prepared sheet, arranging X side up. Repeat with remaining rolls. Brush rolls with egg white glaze. Sprinkle rolls generously with coarse salt.
9. Bake rolls until brown, about 20 to 25 minutes. Transfer to racks and cool 10 minutes. Serve rolls warm or at room temperature. Enjoy!

Lemon Chicken, Broccoli, String Beans Foil Packs

Servings: 4
Cooking Time: 20 Minutes

Ingredients:

- 2 Cups Broccoli
- 3 Tbsp Butter, Melted
- 4 Chicken, Boneless/Skinless
- 1 Garlic, Minced
- 1 1/2 Tsp Italian Seasoning, Dried
- 1 Lemon, Sliced
- Pepper
- Salt
- 1 Cup String Beans

Directions:

1. Supply your smoker with wood pellets and follow the start-up procedure. Preheat the grill, with the lid closed, to 450° F.
2. Lay four 12 x 12 inch pieces of foil out on a flat surface, then place one chicken breast in the middle of each foil.
3. Divide the broccoli and string beans between the four foil packs. Thinly slice the lemon, split them between each foil pack, and place the slices on, in and around the chicken and vegetables.

4. Mix the butter, garlic, juice of the remaining lemon, and Italian seasoning together, and then brush over the chicken and vegetables. Sprinkle with salt and pepper to taste.
5. Fold the foil over the chicken and vegetables to close the pack, and pinch the ends together so the pack will remain closed.
6. Grill for 7-9 minutes on each side. Turn off grill, remove the foil packets, and serve immediately.

Pull-apart Dinner Rolls

Servings: 8
Cooking Time: 10 Minutes

Ingredients:

- 1/4 Cup warm water (110°F to 115°F)
- 1/3 Cup vegetable oil
- 2 Tablespoon active dry yeast
- 1/4 Cup sugar
- 1/2 Teaspoon salt
- 1 egg
- 3 1/2 Cup all-purpose flour
- cooking spray

Directions:

1. Supply your smoker with wood pellets and follow the start-up procedure. Preheat the grill, with the lid closed, to 400° F.
2. In the bowl of a stand mixer, combine warm water, oil, yeast and sugar. Let mixture rest for 5 to 10 minutes, or until frothy and bubbly.
3. With a dough hook, mix in salt, egg and 2 cups of flour until combined. Add remaining flour 1/2 cup at a time (dough will be sticky).
4. Prepare a cast iron pan with cooking spray and set aside.
5. Spray your hands with cooking spray and shape the dough into 12 balls.
6. After shaped, place in the prepared cast iron pan and let rest for 10 minutes. Bake in Traeger for about 10 to 12 minutes, or until tops are lightly golden. Enjoy! Grill: 400 °F

Green Bean Casserole Circa 1955

Servings: 6
Cooking Time: 30 Minutes

Ingredients:

- 1 1/2 Pound Green Beans, fresh
- 1 Can cream of mushroom soup
- 1/2 Cup milk
- 2 Teaspoon soy sauce
- 1/2 Teaspoon Worcestershire sauce
- 1/2 Teaspoon black pepper
- 1.334 Cup French's Original Crispy Fried Onions
- 1/4 Cup red bell pepper, diced

Directions:

1. In a mixing bowl, combine the beans (trimmed and cooked until tender, or may use 2 16 oz. cans), soup, milk, soy sauce, Worcestershire sauce, black pepper, 2/3 cup of the onion rings, and red pepper, if using. Transfer to a 1-1/2 quart casserole dish.
2. Supply your smoker with wood pellets and follow the start-up procedure. Preheat the grill, with the lid closed, to 375° F.
3. Cook the casserole until the filling is hot and bubbling, 25 to 30 minutes. Top with the remaining onions and cook for 5 to 10 minutes more, or until the onions are crisp and beginning to brown. Grill: 375 °F

Delicious Baked Protein Bars

Servings: 6
Cooking Time: 25 Minutes

Ingredients:

- 2 Cup Frozen Sweet Cherries
- 1 Cup Apricots, Frozen
- 1 Scoop Vanilla Protein Powder
- 2 Tablespoon honey
- 1 Teaspoon vanilla extract
- 1 Cup rolled oats

Directions:

1. Supply your smoker with wood pellets and follow the start-up procedure. Preheat the grill, with the lid closed, to 350° F.

2. In the bowl of a food processor, add cherries, apricots (revived in hot water for 5 minutes and drained), vanilla protein powder, honey, and vanilla. Pulse about 10 to 15 times, to break the fruit into smaller pieces and to mix all ingredients.
3. In a separate bowl, fold together oats and fruit mixture. Transfer mixture to a loaf pan or silicone mold and place in grill.
4. Bake for approximately 20 to 25 minutes. Grill: 350 °F
5. Let cool completely and cut into 8 pieces. Enjoy!

Vanilla Cheesecake Skillet Brownie

Servings: 2
Cooking Time: 30 Minutes

Ingredients:

- 1 Box Brownie Mix
- 1 Package Cream Cheese
- 2 Egg
- 1/2 Cup Oil
- 1 Can Pie Filling, Blueberry
- 1/2 Cup Sugar
- 1 Tsp Vanilla
- 1/4 Cup Water, Warm

Directions:

1. Combine all brownie ingredients and mix. In a separate bowl, combine cream cheese, sugar, egg and vanilla and mix until smooth. Grease skillets and pour in brownie batter. Top with cheesecake and cherry pie filling, using a knife to blend to give it that marbled look.
2. Supply your smoker with wood pellets and follow the start-up procedure. Preheat the grill, with the lid closed, to 350°F and bake for about 30 minutes.
3. Let cool for about 10 minutes and enjoy!

Mexican Black Bean Cornbread Casserole

Servings: 6
Cooking Time: 30 Minutes

Ingredients:

- 1 Lb Beef, Ground
- 1 15Oz Drained Black Beans, Can
- 1 Box Corn Muffin Mix
- 1 15Oz Enchilada Sauce, Can
- 1 Onion, Chopped
- 1 15Oz Drained Pinto Beans, Can

Directions:

1. Supply your smoker with wood pellets and follow the start-up procedure. Preheat the grill, with the lid closed, to 300° F.
2. Mix corn muffin mix according to directions.
3. Place cast iron skillet over flame broiler and heat for a few minutes, leaving Grill lid open.
4. Add onion and ground beef/sausage to skillet and break up
5. Cook until meat is done about 5 to 10 minutes.
6. Add both cans of beans, and enchilada sauce, stir to combine.
7. Bring mixture to a simmer.
8. Carefully close flame broiler and turn Grill up to 400 degrees.
9. Spread prepared corn muffin mix over top of meat and bean mixture and bake for 15 minutes until cornbread mixture is lightly browned.
10. Let sit 15 minutes before serving.

Double Chocolate Chip Brownie Pie

Servings: 8-12
Cooking Time: 45 Minutes

Ingredients:

- 1/2 Cup Semisweet Chocolate Chips
- 1 Cup butter
- 1 Cup brown sugar
- 1 Cup sugar
- 4 Whole eggs
- 2 Teaspoon vanilla extract
- 2 Cup all-purpose flour
- 333/500 Cup Cocoa Powder, Unsweetened
- 1 Teaspoon baking soda
- 1 Teaspoon salt
- 1 Cup Semisweet Chocolate Chips
- 3/4 Cup White Chocolate Chips
- 3/4 Cup Nuts (optional)
- 1 Whole Hot Fudge Sauce, 8oz
- 2 Tablespoon Guinness Beer

Directions:

1. Coat the inside of a 10-inch (25 cm) pie plate with non-stick cooking spray.
2. When ready to cook, set the grill temperature to 350°F (180 C)and preheat, lid closed for 15 minutes.
3. Melt 1/2 cup (100 g) of the semi sweet chocolate chips in the microwave. Cream together butter, brown sugar and granulated sugar. Beat in the eggs, adding one at a time and mixing after each egg, and the vanilla. Add in the melted chocolate chips.
4. On a large piece of wax paper, sift together the cocoa powder, flour, baking soda and salt. Lift up the corners of the paper and pour slowly into the butter mixture.
5. Beat until the dry ingredients are just incorporated. Stir in the remaining semi sweet chocolate chips, white chocolate chips, and the nuts. Press the dough into the prepared pie pan.
6. Place the brownie pie on the grill and bake for 45-50 minutes or until the pie is set in the middle. Rotate the pan halfway through cooking. If the top or edges begin to brown, cover the top with a piece of aluminum foil.
7. In a microwave-safe measuring cup, heat the fudge sauce in the microwave. Stir in the Guinness.
8. Once the brownie pie is done, allow to sit for 20 minutes. Slice into wedges and top with the fudge sauce. Enjoy.

Garlic Cheese Pull Apart Bread

Servings: 2

Cooking Time: 20 Minutes

Ingredients:

- 1 Loaf Bread, Sourdough Round
- 2 1/2 Tbsp Butter, Salted
- 8 Oz Fontina Cheese
- 1 Grated Garlic, Roasted
- 1/4 Cup Parsley, Minced Fresh
- 1 Tsp Red Flakes Pepper
- 1 Pinch Salt

Directions:

1. Start your Grill on "smoke" with the lid open until a fire is established in the burn pot (3-7 minutes). Supply your smoker with wood pellets and follow the start-up procedure. Preheat the grill, with the lid closed, to 300° F.
2. In a small bowl, add the soft butter, grated garlic, red pepper flakes, sea salt, and ¼ cup of the chopped parsley, and whisk together. With a bread serrated knife, cut 1-inch slices into the bread, not cutting all the way through the bottom of the load. With a butter knife, spread a thin layer of the butter mixture on each slice of the bread. Take the serrated knife again, and cut across the loaf to form 1 inch squares. Next, slice the cheese into small thin slices, then stuff one slice into each bread opening. Place the bread on a baking sheet, and cover tightly with aluminum foil. Place on the grill for about 10 minutes, remove the foil, and grill for a few more minutes until the top is nicely golden and the cheese is oozing. Remove from the grill, sprinkle with fresh parsley leaves, then serve.

Delicious Smoked Candied Pecan Pie

Servings: 4

Cooking Time: 55 Minutes

Ingredients:

- 1 cup brown sugar
- 1/4 cup granulated sugar
- 1 1/2 teaspoon vanilla
- 1/2 teaspoon corn starch
- 1/2 teaspoon orange zest
- 1/2 teaspoon salt
- 3/4 cup light corn syrup
- 1/2 cup butter (aka- 1 stick), melted
- 3 eggs, beaten
- 1 1/2 cups smoked candied pecans
- 1 pie crust

Directions:

1. Supply your smoker with wood pellets and follow the start-up procedure. Preheat the grill, with the lid closed, to 350° F.
2. Put brown sugar, granulated sugar, vanilla, corn starch, orange zest, salt, light corn syrup, melted butter, and three eggs in a medium mixing bowl. Stir ingredients together.

3. Lightly grease a pie pan and put your rolled out pie crust in. Make sure pie crust conforms to the pie tin. Sprinkle half of your pecans onto pie crust in pie pan. Pour ingredients from mixing bowl into pie pan, then evenly top with the remaining pecans.
4. Cover pie in foil and put on the grill. After 30 minutes, remove foil and cook for another 25 minutes.
5. Remove the pecan pie from grill and let it cool to room temperature before serving.

Mint Butter Chocolate Chip Cookies

Servings: 24
Cooking Time: 12 Minutes

Ingredients:

- 1/2 Cup Butter, Melted
- 1 Package Chocolate Chip Cookie Mix
- 8-10 Drop Food Coloring
- 1/2 Tsp Mint, Extract

Directions:

1. Supply your smoker with wood pellets and follow the start-up procedure. Preheat the grill, with the lid closed, to 350° F.
2. Follow the directions on the back of the Chocolate Chip Cookie mix and also add the mint extract and green food coloring. Mix until combined.
3. On a baking sheet lined with parchment paper, drop balls of dough about 2 tbsp in size onto the pan.
4. Place in your Grill and bake for 10-12 minutes. Let cool for a couple minutes before removing from the pan. Enjoy!

Baked Bourbon Monkey Bread

Servings: 6
Cooking Time: 40 Minutes

Ingredients:

- 3 Can Pillsbury Grands Buttermilk Biscuits
- 1 Cup sugar
- 3 Teaspoon ground cinnamon
- 1 Cup Butter, unsalted
- 1 Cup dark brown sugar
- Tablespoon bourbon

Directions:

1. Supply your smoker with wood pellets and follow the start-up procedure. Preheat the grill, with the lid closed, to 350° F.
2. Cut each biscuit into quarters. In a Ziploc bag, combine sugar and cinnamon and add quartered biscuits. Toss to coat in cinnamon sugar.
3. Dump coated biscuit dough into a bundt pan coated with non-stick spray.
4. In a small saucepan, combine the brown sugar, butter, and bourbon. Cook over medium heat until the sugar has dissolved.
5. Pour the butter mixture over the biscuits in the bundt pan.
6. Place in the center of the grill and cook for 40 minutes or until dark golden brown.
7. Let cool on the counter for 5-10 minutes, then flip out onto a serving plate. Enjoy!

Butternut Squash Macaroni And Cheese

Servings: 2
Cooking Time: 50 Minutes

Ingredients:

- 1 Medium butternut squash
- 2 Cup macaroni, uncooked
- 1 Small yellow onion
- 1/2 Cup chicken broth
- 1 Cup milk
- salt
- pepper
- 1 Cup cheese, grated

Directions:

1. Supply your smoker with wood pellets and follow the start-up procedure. Preheat the grill, with the lid closed, to 225° F.
2. Puncture butternut squash with a fork several times and place on grill grate. Cook until tender, about 40 minutes to an hour. When cooked, scoop out meat and discard seeds. Grill: 225 °F
3. Cook elbow macaroni according to package instructions. Drain and set aside.
4. In a medium skillet, sauté chopped onion until fragrant and golden. Add broth, milk, salt, onions and

butternut squash to a food processor. Puree until smooth and creamy. Add salt and pepper to taste.

5. Pour pureed sauce over cooked noodles and add the shredded cheese. Stir to melt the cheese and add milk to reach desired consistency. Serve warm. Enjoy!

Bananas Rum Foster

Servings: 4

Cooking Time: 10 Minutes

Ingredients:

- 1/3 Cup Banana Nectar
- 4 Bananas, Quartered
- 3/4 Cup Brown Sugar
- 1/4 Cup Butter
- 1/2 Tsp Cinnamon, Ground
- 1/3 Cup Dark Rum
- Vanilla Ice Cream

Directions:

1. Supply your smoker with wood pellets and follow the start-up procedure. Preheat the grill, with the lid closed, to medium heat. If using a gas or charcoal grill, preheat a cast iron skillet.
2. Place a large skillet on the griddle, then melt butter in the skillet. Whisk in brown sugar and cinnamon, stirring until sugar dissolves.
3. Add the banana nectar and bananas. Stir to coat
4. Once the bananas begin to soften and turn brown, add the rum. Stir, then ignite the sauce with a stick lighter. After the flames subside, simmer the sauce for 2 minutes.
5. Divide the bananas among 4 scoops/bowls of vanilla ice cream, then spoon the warm sauce over the top of the ice cream. Serve immediately.

Smoky Apple Crepes

Servings: 6

Cooking Time: 60 Minutes

Ingredients:

- 1/2 Cup Apple Juice
- 2 Lbs Apples
- 2 Tbsp Brown Sugar
- 5 Tbsp Butter
- 3 Tbsp Butter, Melted
- Tt Caramel
- 3/4 Tsp Cinnamon, Ground
- Tt Cinnamon-Sugar
- 3/4 Tsp Cornstarch
- 2 Eggs
- 1 Cup Flour
- 2 Tsp Lemon Juice
- Tennessee Apple Butter Seasoning
- 1/2 Cup Water
- 3/4 Cup Milk

Directions:

1. Supply your smoker with wood pellets and follow the start-up procedure. Preheat the grill, with the lid closed, to 225° F. If using a gas or charcoal grill, set it up for low, indirect heat.
2. Peel, halve, and core apples.
3. Season apples with Tennessee Apple Butter then place directly on the grill grate, and smoke for 1 hour.
4. Meanwhile, prepare crêpe batter: combine eggs, milk, water, flour, and 3 tbsp of melted butter in a blender, and blend until smooth.
5. Refrigerate for 30 minutes.
6. Remove apples from grill, cool slightly, then slice thin.
7. Place a cast iron skillet on the grill and melt 3 tbsp butter with brown sugar, cinnamon, cornstarch, apple and lemon juices. Cook for 5 minutes until thick.
8. Add apples and cook for another 3 to 5 minutes, stirring to coat apples in sauce.
9. Remove from grill and set aside.
10. Preheat griddle to medium-low. If using a standard grill, preheat a cast iron skillet on medium-low heat.
11. Melt 1 teaspoon of butter on the griddle.
12. Then add ½ cup of batter, and spread with the bottom of a metal spatula, working quickly, as the batter cooks fast.
13. Cook one minute per side, until edges begin to brown. Remove from griddle, set aside, and repeat with remaining batter.
14. Spoon ¼ cup of apple filling into the center of each crêpe, then quarter-fold into a triangle.

15. Serve warm with additional apple filling, drizzle of warm caramel, and a dusting of cinnamon-sugar.

Baked Wood-fired Pizza

Servings: 6

Cooking Time: 12 Minutes

Ingredients:

- 2/3 Cup warm water (110°F to 115°F)
- 2 1/2 Teaspoon active dry yeast
- 1/2 Teaspoon granulated sugar
- 1 Teaspoon kosher salt
- 1 Tablespoon oil
- 2 Cup all-purpose flour
- 1/4 Cup fine cornmeal
- 1 Large grilled portobello mushroom, sliced
- 1 Jar pickled artichoke hearts, drained and chopped
- 1 Cup shredded fontina cheese
- 1/2 Cup shaved Parmigiano-Reggiano cheese, divided
- To Taste Roasted Garlic, minced
- 1/4 Cup extra-virgin olive oil
- To Taste banana peppers

Directions:

1. In a glass bowl, stir together the warm water, yeast and sugar. Let stand until the mixture starts to foam, about 10 minutes. In a mixer, combine 1-3/4 cup flour, sugar and salt. Stir oil into the yeast mixture. Slowly add the liquid to the dry ingredients while slowly increasing the mixers speed until fully combined. The dough should be smooth and not sticky.
2. Knead the dough on a floured surface, gradually adding the remaining flour as needed to prevent the dough from sticking, until smooth, about 5 to 10 minutes.
3. Form the dough into a ball. Apply a thin layer of olive oil to a large bowl. Place the dough into the bowl and coat the dough ball with a small amount of olive oil. Cover and let rise in a warm place for about 1 hour or until doubled in size.
4. When ready to cook, set smoker temperature to 450°F and preheat, lid closed for 15 minutes.
5. Place a pizza stone in the grill while it preheats.
6. Punch the dough down and roll it out into a 12-inch circle on a floured surface.
7. Spread the cornmeal evenly on the pizza peel. Place the dough on the pizza peel and assemble the toppings evenly in the following order: olive oil, roasted garlic, fontina, portobello, artichoke hearts, Parmigiano-Reggiano and banana peppers.
8. Carefully slide the assembled pizza from the pizza peel to the preheated pizza stone and bake until the crust is golden brown, about 10 to 12 minutes. Enjoy!

Cornbread Chicken Stuffing

Servings: 6 - 8

Cooking Time: 95 Minutes

Ingredients:

- 2 Tbsp Butter
- 1 Cup Chicken Stock
- 6 Cups Cornbread, Cubed
- ½ Cup Dried Cranberries
- 1 Egg
- ½ Cup Heavy Whipping Cream
- 1 Lb. Italian Sausage
- 1 Diced Onion
- 1 ½ Tsp Pulled Pork Rub
- 2 Tbsp Sage, Fresh
- ½ Tsp Fresh Thyme

Directions:

1. Supply your smoker with wood pellets and follow the start-up procedure. Preheat the grill, with the lid closed, to 250° F. If using a gas or charcoal grill, set the temp to low heat.
2. Portion sausage into quarter-size pieces and place on mesh grate. Place grate on the grill and cook for 1 hour. Sausage pieces will have a smoky deep brown color. Move the mesh tray of sausage to the side of the grill with indirect heat.
3. Open the Flame Broiler Plate and increase the temperature to 350°F. Place a large cast iron skillet on the grill, over direct flame. Add butter and onions and cook until the onions caramelize lightly, stirring often. Add the sage and thyme and stir to combine.

4. Gently fold in the dried cranberries and cubed cornbread, then add sausage directly from mesh grate.
5. In a small mixing bowl, whisk together the heavy cream, chicken stock, egg, and Pulled Pork Rub. Pour mixture over the cornbread stuffing mix.
6. Cover grill and cook 30 minutes or until heated through and crispy on top.

Carrot Cake

Servings: 4-6
Cooking Time: 60 Minutes

Ingredients:

- 8 carrots, peeled and grated
- 4 eggs, at room temperature
- 1 cup vegetable oil
- ½ cup milk
- 1 teaspoon vanilla extract
- 2 cups sugar
- 2 cups self-rising or cake flour
- 2 teaspoons baking soda
- 1 teaspoon salt
- 1 cup finely chopped pecans
- Nonstick cooking spray or butter, for greasing
- 8 ounces cream cheese
- 1 cup confectioners' sugar
- 8 tablespoons (1 stick) unsalted butter, at room temperature
- 1 teaspoon vanilla extract
- ½ teaspoon salt
- 2 tablespoons to ¼ cup milk

Directions:

1. For the cake:
2. Supply your smoker with wood pellets and follow the start-up procedure. Preheat, with the lid closed, to 350°F.
3. In a food processor or blender, combine the grated carrots, eggs, oil, milk, and vanilla, and process until the carrots are finely minced.
4. In a large mixing bowl, combine the sugar, flour, baking soda, and salt.
5. Add the carrot mixture to the flour mixture and stir until well incorporated. Fold in the chopped pecans.
6. Coat a 9-by-13-inch baking pan with cooking spray.
7. Pour the batter into prepared pan and place on the grill grate. Close the lid and smoke for about 1 hour, or until a toothpick inserted in the center comes out clean.
8. Remove the cake from the grill and let cool completely.
9. For the frosting:
10. Using an electric mixer on low speed, beat the cream cheese, confectioners' sugar, butter, vanilla, and salt, adding 2 tablespoons to ¼ cup of milk to thin the frosting as needed.
11. Frost the cooled cake and slice to serve.

Blueberry Bread Pudding

Servings: 4
Cooking Time: 60 Minutes

Ingredients:

- 5 eggs
- 3 Cup sugar
- 2 1/2 Cup milk
- 1 1/2 Teaspoon vanilla
- 1 Teaspoon cinnamon
- 1 Pinch salt
- 5 Cup Bread
- 3 Cup blueberries

Directions:

1. Beat the eggs in a large mixing bowl. Whisk in the sugar, milk, vanilla, cinnamon, and salt.
2. In another large bowl, combine the bread and 2 cups (200 g) of the blueberries.
3. Pour the egg mixture over the bread-blueberry mixture and let sit for 30 minutes. Meanwhile, place muffin liners in a muffin tin.
4. Supply your smoker with wood pellets and follow the start-up procedure. Preheat the grill, with the lid open.
5. Spoon the bread-blueberry mixture into the prepared cups; evenly top each with the remaining cup of blueberries, pressing them gently into the pudding with the back of a spoon.
6. Dust the top with sugar.

7. Arrange the pan directly on the grill grate and smoke for 30 minutes. Grill:180°F
8. Increase the temperature to 350F (180 C), and bake until the pudding is set and golden brown on top, about 25 minutes. Grill:350°F
9. Let cool slightly, then sift powdered sugar on top. Serve warm with sweetened whipped cream or vanilla ice cream, if desired.

Grilled Beer Cheese Dip

Servings: 6
Cooking Time: 20 Minutes

Ingredients:

- 6 Oz Beer, Can
- 8 Oz Cream Cheese
- 1 Tsp Onion Powder
- ½ Tsp Pepper
- ½ Tsp Salt
- 2 Cups Shredded Cheese

Directions:

1. Supply your smoker with wood pellets and follow the start-up procedure. Preheat the grill, with the lid closed, to 350° F. If you're using a gas or charcoal grill, set it up for medium high heat. Preheat with lid closed for 10-15 minutes.
2. In the cast iron pan add cream cheese, shredded cheese, beer, onion powder, salt and pepper. Once grill is at 350°F place cast iron skillet onto the grill and cook for about 10 minutes, stir and cook for another 5-10 minutes.
3. Top with more shredded cheese and fresh parsley. Serve with fresh baked pretzels as well.

Baked Buttermilk Biscuits

Servings: 4
Cooking Time: 15 Minutes

Ingredients:

- 2 Cup all-purpose flour
- 1/4 Cup butter
- 3/4 Cup buttermilk

Directions:

1. Supply your smoker with wood pellets and follow the start-up procedure. Preheat the grill, with the lid closed, to High heat. Spoon the flour into a measuring cup and level with a knife.
2. Put the flour into a mixing bowl. Using a pastry blender, cut the butter into the flour until the mixture resembles coarse crumbs.
3. With a fork, gently stir in just enough of the buttermilk so the dough leaves the sides of the bowl. (You may not need all the buttermilk.) For the most tender biscuits, do not overmix.
4. Lightly flour a work surface as well as your hands. Tip the dough onto the floured surface and gently bring together using your fingertips. (Re-flour your hands or the board if the dough is too sticky.) Knead two or three times, just to bring the dough together.
5. With a floured rolling pin, lightly and quickly roll the dough out to a thickness of about 1/2". Using a 1-1/2" floured cutter, cut out as many biscuits as you can. (Do not twist the cutter; push it straight down.) You can reroll the scraps if desired, but the "second string" biscuits will be tougher.
6. Transfer the biscuits to an ungreased baking sheet. Using a pastry brush, brush the tops with melted butter. Bake until golden brown, 10 to 15 minutes. Enjoy! Grill: 500 °F

Cherry Ice Cream Cobbler

Servings: 8
Cooking Time: 45 Minutes

Ingredients:

- 1 Tsp Baking Powder
- 3 Tbsp Butter, Melted
- 1 Cup Flour
- Ice Cream, Prepared
- 1/4 Tsp Salt
- 3/4 Cup Sugar
- 1/2 Cup Milk

Directions:

1. Supply your smoker with wood pellets and follow the start-up procedure. Preheat the grill, with the lid closed, to 350° F.

2. In a bowl, combine flour, sugar, baking powder, salt and mix to incorporate. Stir in butter and milk and mix until combined. In a cast iron pan, dump in cherry pie filling and pile on the prepared topping to cover.
3. Place in your Grill and bake for about 45 minutes, or until the topping is golden brown.
4. Let cool for a couple minutes and serve with ice cream.

Baked Molten Chocolate Cake

Servings: 4
Cooking Time: 20 Minutes

Ingredients:

- all-purpose flour
- butter
- 4 Ounce butter
- 6 Ounce Chocolate, Bittersweet
- 2 eggs
- 2 egg yolk
- 1/2 Cup sugar
- 1 Pinch salt

Directions:

1. Supply your smoker with wood pellets and follow the start-up procedure. Preheat the grill, with the lid closed, to 450° F.
2. Butter and flour four (6oz) ramekins. Tap out excess flour. Place ramekins on a baking sheet and reserve.
3. Melt butter and chocolate in a double boiler over simmering water. In a medium bowl, beat eggs and yolks with sugar and salt on high until thick and pale.
4. Whisk in chocolate until smooth and quickly fold into the egg mixture along with flour.
5. Spoon the batter into prepared ramekins and bake for 20 minutes or until sides are firm but centers are soft. Grill: 450 °F
6. Let cool for 1 minute, then cover each with an inverted dessert plate. Carefully turn each over, let stand 10 seconds, then unmold.
7. Serve immediately with Maple Ice Cream with Candied Bacon. Enjoy!

Quick Baked Dinner Rolls

Servings: 8
Cooking Time: 30 Minutes

Ingredients:

- 2 Tablespoon quick-rise yeast
- 1 Teaspoon salt
- 1/4 Cup sugar
- 3 1/3 Cup flour
- 1/4 Cup unsalted butter, softened
- 1 egg
- cooking spray
- 1 egg, for egg wash

Directions:

1. Combine yeast and warm water in a small bowl to activate the yeast. Let sit until foamy, about 5-10 minutes.
2. Combine salt, sugar, and flour in the bowl of a stand mixer fitted with the dough hook. Pour water and yeast into the dry ingredients with the machine running on low.
3. Add butter and egg and mix for 10 minutes gradually increasing the speed from low to high.
4. Form the dough into a ball and place in a buttered bowl. Cover with a cloth and let the dough rise for approximately 40 minutes.
5. Transfer the risen dough to a lightly floured surface and divide into 8 pieces forming a ball with each.
6. Lightly spray a cast iron pan with cooking spray and arrange balls in the pan. Cover with a cloth and let rise 20 minutes.
7. Supply your smoker with wood pellets and follow the start-up procedure. Preheat the grill, with the lid closed, to 375° F.
8. Brush rolls with egg wash and then bake for 30 minutes until lightly browned. Serve hot. Enjoy! Grill: 375 °F

Baked Bourbon Maple Pumpkin Pie

Servings: 6-8

Cooking Time: 60 Minutes

Ingredients:

- 1/4 Cup Cocoa Powder, Unsweetened
- 1 Tablespoon Cocoa Powder, Unsweetened
- 3 1/2 Tablespoon sugar
- 1 Teaspoon salt
- 1 1/4 Cup all-purpose flour
- 1 Tablespoon all-purpose flour
- 6 Tablespoon butter
- 2 Tablespoon vegetable oil
- 1 Large Egg Yolk
- 1/2 Teaspoon apple cider vinegar
- 1/4 Cup ice water
- 1 Large egg, beaten
- 15 Ounce Pumpkin, canned
- 1/4 Cup sour cream
- 2 Tablespoon bourbon
- 1 Teaspoon ground cinnamon
- 1/2 Teaspoon salt
- 1/4 Teaspoon ground ginger
- 1/4 Teaspoon ground nutmeg
- 1/8 Teaspoon Allspice, ground
- 1/8 Teaspoon Mace, ground
- 3 Large eggs
- 3/4 Cup maple syrup
- 2 Tablespoon sugar
- 1/2 Vanilla Bean, halved
- 1 Cup heavy cream

Directions:

1. For the Chocolate Pie Dough: Pulse cocoa powder, granulated sugar, salt, and 1-1/4 cups plus 1 Tbsp flour in a food processor to combine. Add butter and shortening and pulse until mixture resembles coarse meal with a few pea-sized pieces of butter remaining. Transfer to a large bowl.
2. Whisk together the egg yolk, vinegar, and 1/4 cup ice water in a small bowl. Drizzle half of the egg mixture over flour mixture and, using a fork, mix gently just until combined. Add remaining egg mixture and mix until the dough just comes together (you will have some unincorporated pieces).
3. Turn out dough onto a lightly floured surface, flatten slightly, and cut into quarters. Stack pieces on top of one another. Placing unincorporated dry pieces of dough between layers, and press down to combine. Repeat process twice more (all pieces of dough should be incorporated at this point). Form dough into a 1" thick disk. Wrap in plastic; chill at least 1 hour.
4. Roll out a disk of dough on a lightly floured surface into a 14" round. Transfer to a 9" pie dish. Lift up the edge and allow the dough to slump down into the dish. Trim. Leaving about 1" overhang. Fold overhang under and crimp edge. Chill in freezer 15 minutes.
5. When ready to cook, set the smoker to 350°F and preheat, lid closed for 15 minutes.
6. Line pie with parchment paper or heavy-duty foil, leaving a 1-1/2" overhang. Fill with pie weights or dried beans. Bake until crust is dry around the edge, about 20 minutes.
7. Remove paper and weights and bake until surface of the crust looks dry, 5-10 minutes.
8. Brush bottom and sides of crust with 1 beaten egg. Return to grill and bake until dry and set, about 3 minutes longer.
9. For the Pumpkin Maple Filling: Whisk together pumpkin puree, sour cream, bourbon, cinnamon, salt, ginger, nutmeg, allspice, mace (optional) and remaining 3 eggs in a large bowl; set aside.
10. Pour maple syrup and 2 tbsp sugar in a small saucepan. Scrape in the seeds from vanilla bean (reserve pod for another use) or add vanilla extract and bring syrup to a boil. Reduce heat to medium-high and simmer, stirring occasionally, until mixture is thickened and small puffs of steam start to release about 3 minutes.
11. Remove from heat and add cream in 3 additions, stirring with a wooden spoon after each addition until smooth. Gradually whisk hot maple cream into pumpkin mixture.
12. Place pie dish on a rimmed baking sheet and pour in pumpkin filling. Bake pie, rotating halfway through, until set around edge but center barely jiggles 50-60 minutes.
13. Transfer pie dish to a wire rack and let the pie cool. Slice and serve. Enjoy!

Smoked Sweet Beer Bread

Servings: 6
Cooking Time: 60 Minutes

Ingredients:

- 3 cups all-purpose flour, sifted
- 2 tbsp. sugar
- 1 tbsp. baking powder
- 1 tsp. salt
- 1 (12 oz) can or bottle beer (not too dark or bitter)
- 2 tbsp. honey or agave, warmed
- 6 tbsp. butter, melted

Directions:

1. Supply your smoker with wood pellets and follow the start-up procedure. Preheat the grill, with the lid closed, to 350° F.
2. Lightly grease a 9 ×5 inch loaf pan.
3. In a large mixing bowl, put in the flour, sugar, baking powder, and salt. Whisk to combine and aerate, using a wire whisk. Add the beer and honey and stir with a wooden spoon until the batter is properly mixed (Do not over-mix).
4. Pour half of the melted butter into the prepared loaf pan and pour in the batter. Pour the remaining butter over the top of the loaf.
5. Place the loaf pan on the grill grate and bake for 50 to 60 minutes or until the bread is golden brown.
6. Allow the loaf to cool slightly in the pan before removing it from the pan. Leftovers make great toast.

Dark Chocolate Brownies With Bacon-salted Caramel

Servings: 8
Cooking Time: 40 Minutes

Ingredients:

- 8 Strips bacon
- 1/2 Cup kosher salt
- 1 Whole Brownie Mix
- 1 Jar caramel sauce

Directions:

1. For the bacon salt: Cook a few strips of bacon (6 to 8) until very crisp: 350 degrees for about 25 minutes should do it. Let cool, then pulse in a food processor until finely chopped. Mix with 1/2 cup kosher salt. Store in the refrigerator until ready to use.
2. Supply your smoker with wood pellets and follow the start-up procedure. Preheat the grill, with the lid closed, to 350° F.
3. Mix the brownies according to package directions and pour into a greased pan. Drizzle approximately 2 tablespoons of the caramel sauce over the brownie batter. Sprinkle with approximately 1 teaspoon of the bacon salt. Place directly on the grill grate of your preheated Traeger.
4. Bake the brownies for 20-25 minutes, until the batter has started to set up. Remove from the grill and drizzle with 2 more tablespoons of caramel sauce and sprinkle with more bacon salt. Return to the grill for 20-25 more minutes, or until a toothpick inserted in the middle of the brownies comes out clean.
5. If you like extra caramel, drizzle another layer of caramel on the hot brownies and sprinkle with a final bit of bacon salt. Allow the brownies to cool completely before cutting them into squares. Clean your knife in between each slice to prevent the brownies from sticking to the knife. Enjoy!

Pumpkin Bread

Servings: 6
Cooking Time: 60 Minutes

Ingredients:

- 1 Cup Pumpkin, canned
- 2 eggs
- 2/3 Cup vegetable oil
- 1/2 Cup sour cream
- 1 Teaspoon vanilla extract
- 2 1/2 Cup flour
- 1 1/2 Teaspoon baking soda
- 1 Teaspoon salt
- 1/2 Teaspoon ground cinnamon
- 1/4 Teaspoon ground nutmeg
- 1/4 Teaspoon ground cloves
- 1/4 Teaspoon ground ginger
- As Needed butter

Directions:

1. In a large mixing bowl, combine the pumpkin, eggs, vegetable oil, sour cream, and vanilla and whisk to blend.
2. In a separate bowl, combine the flour, baking soda, salt, cinnamon, nutmeg, cloves, and ginger. Add the dry ingredients to the wet ingredients and stir to combine. Do not overmix.
3. If desired, stir in one or more of the optional ingredients (walnuts, dried cranberries, raisins, or chocolate chips). Butter the interiors of two loaf pans.
4. Sprinkle with flour to coat the buttered surfaces, and tap out any excess. Divide the batter evenly between the two pans.
5. When ready to cook, set the smoker to 350°F and preheat, lid closed for 15 minutes.
6. Arrange the loaf pans directly on the grill grate. Bake for 45 to 50 minutes, or until a skewer or toothpick inserted in the center comes out clean. Also, the top of the loaf should spring back when pressed gently with a finger.
7. Transfer the loaf pans to a cooling rack and let cool for 10 minutes before carefully turning out the pumpkin bread. Let the loaves cool thoroughly before slicing. Wrap in aluminum foil or plastic wrap if not eating right away. Serve and enjoy!

Cake With Smoked Berry Sauce

Servings: 12

Cooking Time: 90 Minutes

Ingredients:

- 12 Oz Blackberries
- 18 Oz Blueberries, Fresh
- 1/4 Cup Brown Sugar
- 2 Tsp Cinnamon, Ground
- 4 Eggs
- 2 Tbsp Flour
- 1 3/4 Cup Granulated Sugar
- 1 Lemon, Juice & Zest
- 1/2 Cup Unsalted Butter
- 3.4 Ounce Box Vanilla Instant Pudding Mix
- 3/4 Cup Vegetable Oil
- 3/4 Cup Water
- 1 Cup White Wine
- 1 Box Yellow Cake Mix

Directions:

1. Fire up your Grill and set to Smoke mode. If using a gas or charcoal grill, set it up for low, indirect heat. Supply your smoker with wood pellets and follow the start-up procedure. Preheat the grill, with the lid closed, to 450° F.
2. Place blueberries and blackberries on a sheet tray, then transfer to upper shelf of smoking cabinet. Make sure that the sear slide and side dampers are open, then preheat the grill, with the lid closed, to 375° F, to ensure the cabinet maintains temperature between 225° F and 250° F. Smoke for 30 to 45 minutes.
3. Place cast iron skillet on grill grate. Add sugar, lemon juice and zest, and wine to skillet. Stir with a wooden spoon until sugar dissolves, then add berries from smoking cabinet.
4. Simmer berries for 15 minutes, then remove sauce from grill to cool.
5. While berries are smoking, prepare cake pans and batter. Grease and flour 2 - 9-inch round cake pans. Set aside.
6. In a large mixing bowl, combine cake mix, brown sugar, granulated sugar, pudding mix, cinnamon, eggs, water, oil, and white wine. Using a hand mixer, mix on low speed for 1 minute, then slowly increase mixing speed to high, and beat an additional 2 to 3 minutes, or until batter is smooth.
7. Evenly distribute batter among cake pans, then place pans on grill shelf and bake at 350° F, for 25 to 30 minutes, or until a toothpick inserted comes out clean. Remove from grill and set aside to cool slightly.
8. While cake is cooling, prepare glaze. Melt butter with sugar in a sauce pot on the grill. Stir for 3 minutes, then add wine. Remove from grill and set aside.
9. Turn out cake onto a sheet tray lined with parchment. Use a toothpick to poke holes in the cake, then slowly pour hot glaze over cake.
10. Spread half of smoked berry sauce on top of one layer, then place second cake layer on top. Pour additional sauce on top of cake and dust with powdered sugar, if desired. Serve warm, or room temperature.

Caramelized Bourbon Baked Pears

Servings: 4
Cooking Time: 30 Minutes

Ingredients:

- 3 Whole Pears, fresh
- 1/4 Cup brown sugar
- 1/4 Cup bourbon
- 2 Tablespoon butter, melted
- 1 Teaspoon vanilla extract
- 1/2 Teaspoon salt

Directions:

1. Supply your smoker with wood pellets and follow the start-up procedure. Preheat the grill, with the lid closed, to 325° F.
2. Peel and core the pears. Arrange them in a buttered baking dish.
3. In a small bowl, combine the brown sugar, bourbon, butter, vanilla, cinnamon and salt. Pour the bourbon mixture over the pears.
4. Place the baking dish on the grill grate, close the lid and bake for 30-35 minutes or until the pears are fork tender. Grill: 325 °F
5. Transfer to a serving plate and spoon the caramelized bourbon mixture over the pears.
6. Serve warm over vanilla ice cream. Enjoy!

Baked Pumpkin Pie

Servings: 6
Cooking Time: 50 Minutes

Ingredients:

- 4 Ounce cream cheese
- 15 Ounce pumpkin puree
- 1/3 Cup Cream, whipping
- 1/2 Cup brown sugar
- 1 Teaspoon pumpkin pie spice
- 3 Large eggs
- 1 frozen pie crust, thawed

Directions:

1. Supply your smoker with wood pellets and follow the start-up procedure. Preheat the grill, with the lid closed, to 325° F.
2. Mix cream cheese, puree, milk, sugar, and spice. One at a time, incorporate an egg to the mixture. Pour mixture into pie shell.
3. Bake for 50 minutes, edges should be golden and pie should be firm around edges with slight movement in middle. Let cool before whip cream is applied. Serve and enjoy! Grill: 325 °F

Ultimate Baked Garlic Bread

Servings: 4
Cooking Time: 20 Minutes

Ingredients:

- 1 baguette
- 1/2 Cup softened butter
- 1/2 Cup mayonnaise
- 4 Tablespoon chopped Italian parsley
- 6 Clove garlic, minced
- salt
- chile flakes
- 1 Cup mozzarella cheese
- 1/2 Cup Parmesan cheese

Directions:

1. Supply your smoker with wood pellets and follow the start-up procedure. Preheat the grill, with the lid closed, to 375° F.
2. Lay baguette on a cutting board and cut it in half lengthwise.
3. In a bowl, add butter, mayonnaise, parsley, garlic, salt and chile flakes. Mix well.
4. Spread butter mixture on baguette halves and top with mozzarella and Parmesan cheese.
5. Place baguette on the grill (if you like the bread crisp, do not use foil and if you like it soft, wrap with foil). Grill for approximately 15 to 25 minutes. Serve warm. Enjoy! Grill: 375 °F

Vanilla Chocolate Bacon Cupcakes

Servings: 12
Cooking Time: 120 Minutes

Ingredients:

- 1 Lb Bacon
- 1 1/2 Tsp Baking Powder

- 1 1/2 Tsp Baking Soda
- 1 Cup Cocoa, Powder
- 2 Egg
- 1 3/4 Cups Flour
- 1 Cup Milk, Whole
- 1/2 Cup Oil
- 1 Tsp Salt
- 2 Cups Sugar
- 2 Tsp Vanilla

Directions:

1. Supply your smoker with wood pellets and follow the start-up procedure. Preheat the grill, with the lid closed, to 250° F.
2. Once your grill is preheated, place bacon strips on the grates. Smoke for 1hr-1 ½ hours or until desired crispiness is achieved.
3. Remove the bacon from the grill and set aside.
4. Increase set the temperature to 350°F and preheat.
5. Mix the rest of the ingredients in a bowl with an electric mixer until it is nice and smooth.
6. Pour the mixture into a cupcake tin.
7. Transfer the tin to your grill and bake for about 20 - 25 minutes.
8. Allow the cupcakes to cool on a wire rack. Once cooled, top with your favorite premade icing and a half of strip of the bacon. Serve and enjoy!

Baked Parker House Rolls

Servings: 8

Cooking Time: 15 Minutes

Ingredients:

- 1/2 Ounce (2 packets) active dry yeast
- 6 Tablespoon plus 1 teaspoon cane sugar
- 1 Cup warm water (110°F to 115°F)
- 5 Cup all-purpose flour, plus more as needed
- 2 Teaspoon salt
- 1 Cup warm milk (110°-115°F)
- 1 Large eggs
- oil
- 4 Tablespoon melted butter, divided
- 1 Tablespoon Maldon Sea Salt Flakes
- 2 Tablespoon poppy seeds
- 2 Tablespoon white sesame seeds
- 1 Tablespoon garlic flakes

Directions:

1. Place the yeast, 1 teaspoon of cane sugar and warm water in a mixing bowl or the base of a stand mixer. Stir to combine. Allow the yeast to proof for 5 minutes- it should start to bubble a bit, showing that the yeast is alive.
2. Sprinkle the flour, salt and remaining 6 tablespoons of sugar over the yeast mixture. Using a dough hook or a wooden spoon, stir for 30 seconds. Pour in the warm milk and egg.
3. Knead again on the medium-low setting, or on a floured work surface by hand until the dough is very soft, adding up to one more cup of flour so the dough is soft and smooth and has lost its sticky quality.
4. Coat the bowl with a small film of oil and place the dough in the bowl, turning to coat dough evenly with the oil. Cover the bowl with a clean cloth, place in a warm spot in the kitchen and allow to proof about 45 minutes. The dough will almost double in size.
5. Punch down the dough and place on a floured work surface. Divide the dough in half, then divide each half into 12 equal pieces.
6. Using your hands, tuck in the seams of each piece of dough then place the dough on a lightly floured surface.
7. Place your fingers around the piece of dough, and roll it in a circular motion to create a smooth, even ball. Alternately, roll the dough between your two hands to create a round ball shape. Repeat with the remaining 23 pieces.
8. Butter a 9x13 inch baking pan with a tablespoon of the melted butter. Place the dough balls evenly in the pan, creating rows of 4 pieces of dough across and 6 down. Cover again with a clean towel and allow the dough to rise in a warm spot, about 30 minutes longer.
9. While the dough is proofing, supply your smoker with wood pellets and follow the start-up procedure. Preheat the grill, with the lid closed, to 325° F. Brush the remaining 3 tablespoons of butter on the bread and sprinkle with the flake salt, seeds and garlic flakes.
10. Place the pan on the grill, cover and bake about 15 to 20 minutes, or until rolls are lightly browned on top and cooked through. When done, you should be able to pull apart two pieces and see that the dough is cooked and the bottoms are lightly browned. Grill: 325 °F

Chili Cheese Fries

Servings: 6
Cooking Time: 10 Minutes

Ingredients:

- 1 Cup Cheddar Cheese, Shredded
- 1 Cup Chili Con Carne, Prepared
- 1 Bag French Fries
- 1 Tablespoon Olive Oil
- 1 Tablespoon Sweet Heat Rub

Directions:

1. Supply your smoker with wood pellets and follow the start-up procedure. Preheat the grill, with the lid closed, to 350° F. If you're using charcoal or gas, set it up for medium high heat.
2. Bake the fries according to manufacturer's instructions. Once the fries are done, place them in a large bowl and add the olive oil and Sweet Heat Rub. Toss the fries to coat. Once everything is well coated with the oil and seasoning, spread the fries on a baking sheet.
3. Top the fries with the chili and the shredded cheddar cheese. Place the baking sheet on the grill and grill for 7-10 minutes, or until the cheese is melted and bubbly, and the chili is warm all the way through.
4. Remove the baking sheet from the grill and serve the fries immediately.

Smoked Cheesy Alfredo Sauce

Servings: 2
Cooking Time: 40 Minutes

Ingredients:

- 1 Cup heavy cream
- 1 Stick butter
- 1 block Parmesan cheese
- 1 Sprig fresh sage
- 2 Pinch Nutmeg

Directions:

1. Supply your smoker with wood pellets and follow the start-up procedure. Preheat the grill, with the lid closed, to 180° F.
2. Pour the cream into a saucepan along with the butter and place on the Traeger grill grate to smoke along with the parmesan cheese.
3. Smoke for 30 minutes to 1 hour, depending on how much smoke flavor you want. Turn the heat on the Traeger up to 300℉. Grill: 180 ˚F
4. Shred the parmesan cheese and add it and the sage sprig into the pan with the cream and butter.
5. Whisk until the cheese has all melted and season to taste with the salt and pepper and a pinch or two of the ground nutmeg.
6. While warm, pour this sauce on anything. Enjoy!

Chicken Pizza On The Grill

Servings: 4
Cooking Time: 10 Minutes

Ingredients:

- 3 Boneless, Skinless Chicken Breast
- 5 Cups Flour, Strong
- 3 Cups Georgia Style Bbq Sauce
- 3 Cups Mozzarella Cheese, Shredded
- 1 Tsp Olive Oil
- 3 Cups Georgia Style BBQ_Sauce
- 1 1/2 Cups Red Bell Peppers, Diced
- 1 1/2 Cups Red Onion, Diced
- 1 Tsp Sugar
- 1/2 Cup Water, Hot
- 1 1/4 Cup Water, Warm
- 2 Tsb Active Yeast, Instant

Directions:

1. Roll your pizza dough so it forms a base about a 1/2 inch thick. To impress your friends and family, you'll want to aim for a nice, pizza like shape. HINT: use a sprinkle of cornmeal on the countertop to aid in moving the dough.
2. Now for the toppings! Start by spreading 1 cup of Georgia Style BBQ_sauce onto each base. Make sure to leave a small portion for the crust! Next, load up with sliced, cooked chicken breasts, diced red onions and red bell peppers before finishing off with a two cups of shredded mozzarella cheese.

3. Supply your smoker with wood pellets and follow the start-up procedure. Preheat the grill, with the lid closed, to 500° F. Place the pizza stone in your grill. Pick up your pizza using a flat surface like a chopping board and slide the pizza carefully onto the hot stone. Close the lid and let your homemade wood-fired pizza bake for 10 - 12 minutes. Remove once your pizza has a golden crust and the cheese is bubbling. Cut and serve for pizza you'll hardly want to share.

Smoked Lemon Tea

Servings: 6 - 8

Cooking Time: 60 Minutes

Ingredients:

- 8 Black Tea Bags
- 4 Cups Boiling Water
- 2 Cups Ice
- 8 Lemons
- 2 Cups Sugar
- 2 Cups Water

Directions:

1. Place the tea bags in a heat-safe pitcher. Bring 4 Cups of water to a boil and pour over tea bags. Let steep for 5-10 minutes. Remove tea bags and set pitcher aside to cool.
2. Turn on your grill and set to smoke mode. Combine 2 cups of sugar and 2 cups water in a small aluminum pan. Smoke for about 45 minutes, stirring occasionally, or until the mixture reduces to a thick, simple syrup. Remove from the grill and let it cool.
3. Supply your smoker with wood pellets and follow the start-up procedure. Preheat the grill, with the lid closed, to 450° F. If using a charcoal or gas grill, set heat to high.
4. Cut the lemons in half and sear over the flame broiler until charred, about 7 minutes. Remove from grill and set aside to cool.
5. Juice the lemons into a medium bowl. Pour lemon juice through a metal strainer into the tea pitcher to remove seeds and pulp.
6. Pour the cooled simple syrup into pitcher and stir until fully incorporated with tea and lemons. Add 2 cups of ice and refrigerate until serving.

Smoked Blackberry Pie

Servings: 4-6

Cooking Time: 25 Minutes

Ingredients:

- Nonstick cooking spray or butter, for greasing
- 1 box (2 sheets) refrigerated piecrusts
- 8 tablespoons (1 stick) unsalted butter, melted, plus 8 tablespoons (1 stick) cut into pieces
- ½ cup all-purpose flour
- 2 cups sugar, divided
- 2 pints blackberries
- ½ cup milk
- Vanilla ice cream, for serving

Directions:

1. Supply your smoker with wood pellets and follow the start-up procedure. Preheat, with the lid closed, to 375°F.
2. Coat a cast iron skillet with cooking spray.
3. Unroll 1 refrigerated piecrust and place in the bottom and up the side of the skillet. Using a fork, poke holes in the crust in several places.
4. Set the skillet on the grill grate, close the lid, and smoke for 5 minutes, or until lightly browned. Remove from the grill and set aside.
5. In a large bowl, combine the stick of melted butter with the flour and 1½ cups of sugar.
6. Add the blackberries to the flour-sugar mixture and toss until well coated.
7. Spread the berry mixture evenly in the skillet and sprinkle the milk on top. Scatter half of the cut pieces of butter randomly over the mixture.
8. Unroll the remaining piecrust and place it over the top of skillet or slice the dough into even strips and weave it into a lattice. Scatter the remaining pieces of butter along the top of the crust.
9. Sprinkle the remaining ½ cup of sugar on top of the crust and return the skillet to the smoker.

10. Close the lid and smoke for 15 to 20 minutes, or until bubbly and brown on top. It may be necessary to use some aluminum foil around the edges near the end of the cooking time to prevent the crust from burning.
11. Serve the pie hot with vanilla ice cream.

Pound Cake

Servings: 8
Cooking Time: 60 Minutes

Ingredients:

- 1 1/2 Cup butter
- 8 Ounce cream cheese
- 3 Cup sugar
- 6 eggs
- 3 Teaspoon Bourbon Vanilla
- 1 Tablespoon lemon zest
- fresh strawberries
- whipped cream

Directions:

1. In a large bowl, cream the butter, cream cheese, and sugar. Add eggs one at a time, whipping in between. Add vanilla and lemon zest, whip.
2. Pour batter into greased loaf pans, about halfway full to allow cake to rise.
3. Supply your smoker with wood pellets and follow the start-up procedure. Preheat the grill, with the lid closed, to 325° F.
4. Place loaf pans on grill and cook for 1 hour - 1 hour and 15 minutes. Check the cake at 45 minutes, if golden brown, cover loosely with foil and continue to cook until a toothpick inserted comes out clean. Grill: 325 °F
5. Cool loaf in pan for 10 minutes before removing to a wire rack.
6. Cut into 1 inch slices and serve with fresh sliced strawberries, top with smoked whip cream.

Cheese Mac

Servings: 6 - 10
Cooking Time: 60 Minutes

Ingredients:

- 5 Tbsp All-Purpose Flour
- 4 Strips Bacon
- Black Pepper
- 2 Cups Breadcrumbs
- 4 Oz Brie
- 4 Oz Brie Cheese
- ½ Cup Butter, Melted
- 12 Oz Cheddar Cheese, Grated
- 3 Cloves Garlic, Minced
- 2 Tbsp Extra Virgin Olive Oil
- 1 Tsp Fresh Grated Nutmeg
- 1 Tsp Ground Cayenne
- 8 Oz, Grated Gruyere Cheese
- 1 Cup Heavy Cream
- 1, Minced Jalapeno Pepper
- 4 Oz Mozzarella Cheese, Grated
- 2 Tbsp Parsley, Minced Fresh
- 12 Oz Raclette
- To Taste Salt
- 5 Tbsp Unsalted Butter
- 4 Oz Whole Milk, Warm
- 1 Yellow Onion, Diced

Directions:

1. Supply your smoker with wood pellets and follow the start-up procedure. Preheat the grill, with the lid closed, to 350° F. Bring a large saucepan of water to a boil. Add the pasta and cook according to the package instructions for al dente. Drain.
2. Heat the oil in a large saucepan over medium-high heat.
3. Add the onion and cook for about 5 minutes, stirring often, until lightly colored, then add the garlic and the jalapeño and cook for 2 more minutes.
4. Reduce the heat to medium, add the butter, and stir until melted. Add the flour and cook, stirring often, for 5 minutes to form a light roux.
5. Add the cheeses, the milk, and cream, reduce the heat to medium-low, and cook, stirring often, until the cheese is melted, and a smooth sauce comes together, about 7 minutes.
6. Stir in the cayenne and truffle oil, then add the pasta and stir to fully coat it in the sauce. Season with salt and pepper. Transfer the mixture to a 12-inch cast-iron skillet and cover with aluminum foil.

7. Place on the grill and bake for 20 minutes. Remove the foil and cover the mac and cheese with the breadcrumbs.
8. Return to the grill and bake for another 15 to 20 minutes, until the cheese is bubbling and the breadcrumbs are golden brown. Serve family style right out of the skillet.

Chicken Pot Pie

Servings: 6
Cooking Time: 60 Minutes

Ingredients:

- 2 Chicken, Boneless/Skinless
- 1 Cream Of Chicken Soup, Can
- 1 Tsp Curry Powder
- 1/2 Cup Mayo
- 1 1/2 Cups Mixed Frozen Vegetables
- 1 Onion, Sliced
- 2 Frozen Pie Shell, Deep
- 1/2 Cup Sour Cream

Directions:

1. Supply your smoker with wood pellets and follow the start-up procedure. Preheat the grill, with the lid closed, to 425° F.
2. Cut the onion in half and place on the grates of the grill. If you''re using fresh chicken breasts, barbecue the chicken at the same time as the onions. The chicken is fully cooked when the internal temperature reached 170F. While the onion and chicken are cooking, prepare the pie crust by putting one crust in a pie plate. When the chicken and onions are done, shred chicken and chop onion into small pieces and place in the prepared pie plate along with the mixed vegetables.
3. Combine cream of chicken soup, mayo, sour cream, and curry powder in a bowl. Pour into the pie crust with the chicken and mix to combine. Wet the sides of the bottom crust with a small amount of water and top with the second pie crust. Push gently along the sides of the crust to seal the two pie crusts together.
4. Place in the and bake for 40 minutes, or until the crust is golden brown. Serve hot.

Baked Pear Tarte Tatin

Servings: 6
Cooking Time: 45 Minutes

Ingredients:

- 2 1/2 Cup all-purpose flour
- 2 Tablespoon sugar
- butter chilled
- 8 Tablespoon cold water
- 1/4 Cup granulated sugar
- 1/4 Cup butter
- 8 Whole Bartlett Pear

Directions:

1. Supply your smoker with wood pellets and follow the start-up procedure. Preheat the grill, with the lid closed, to 350° F.
2. For the crust: Place flour and sugar in a food processor and pulse to mix. Add butter a little at a time while pulsing. Once it starts to looks like cornmeal, add the water until dough start to come together.
3. Form a round with the dough, wrap in plastic and let it cool in the refrigerator.
4. While dough cools, make the caramel sauce. In a sauce pan, add 1/4 cup granulated sugar and 1/4 cup butter. Cook butter and sugar until it becomes a dark caramel, a couple minutes.
5. Pour caramel in the bottom of 10 inch deep cake pan. While the caramel is still hot, arrange pear wedges in a fan formation covering the caramel.
6. Roll the chilled pie dough into a circle big enough to cover the pan. Prick the pie dough with a fork and cover the pan with the pie dough. Trim the crust leaving room for shrinkage.
7. Place on the grill and bake for 45 minutes or until pears are soft. The pears will be soft and most of the juice will evaporate and thicken.
8. Let sit for 3 minutes. While pan is still hot, place a plate over pie and flip over. Slowly lift the plate.
9. Serve warm, topped with vanilla ice cream or whipped cream. Enjoy!

Smoked Vanilla Apple Pie

Servings: 6

Cooking Time: 45 Minutes

Ingredients:

- 1 1/2 cups of self-raising flour
- 3/4 cup of sugar
- 0.3 lbs of butter melted
- 1 tsp of vanilla extract
- 1 egg
- 0.9-lb tin of pie apples
- sugar & cinnamon for dusting

Directions:

1. Supply your smoker with wood pellets and follow the start-up procedure. Preheat the grill, with the lid closed, to 350° F.
2. Combine the self-raising flour, sugar, melted butter, vanilla, and egg in a large bowl until a golden dough texture is formed.
3. Spread half the mixture in a pie dish and press the bottoms and up the sides of the dish.
4. Pour pie apple tin into the pie and spread out evenly.
5. Sprinkle the remaining mixture over the top of the apple evenly and place in the smoker.
6. Leave for 45 minutes or until the golden crust forms on the top.
7. Dust with cinnamon and a little sugar if desired.
8. Serve warm with custard, ice cream, or both.

Spiced Carrot Cake

Servings: 10

Cooking Time: 35 Minutes

Ingredients:

- 1/2 Cup Apple Sauce, Unsweetened
- 2 Tsp Baking Powder
- 1 Tsp Baking Soda
- 1 1/2 Cups Brown Sugar
- 1/2 Cup Butter, Room Temp
- 3/4 Cup Canola Oil
- 3 Cups Carrot, Grated
- 1 1/2 Tsp Cinnamon, Ground
- 2 (8-Ounce) Packages Cream Cheese, Room Temperature
- 4 Egg
- 2 Cups Flour, All-Purpose
- 1/2 Tsp Ginger, Ground
- 1/4 Tsp Nutmeg, Ground
- 1/2 Tsp Salt
- 1/2 Cup Sugar
- 3 Cups Sugar, Icing

Directions:

1. Supply your smoker with wood pellets and follow the start-up procedure. Preheat the grill, with the lid closed, to 350° F.
2. Line the bottom of 2 9-inch cake pans with parchment paper and spray the sides with cooking spray. Set aside.
3. In a large bowl, combine flour, baking powder and soda, spices and salt.
4. In a smaller bowl, combine oil, eggs, sugars, and applesauce and whisk together. Add carrots and stir until well combined.
5. Pour the wet ingredients into the dry. Stir until combined but take care not to over mix. Pour the batter evenly between the two cake pans. Bake for about 35 minutes in your Grill, rotating the cake pans halfway between the cook. Remove once a toothpick is inserted in the middle of the cake and comes out clean.
6. While the cake is cooling, prepare the frosting. Beat the cream cheese until smooth with a hand mixer. Add the butter and icing sugar and mix until fully combined.
7. On a clean plate or cake stand, place one half of the cake and top with a good layer of cream cheese frosting. Place the second half on top and cover with the remaining frosting. Icing tip: try not to lift your knife while icing. Instead make long, smooth strokes. Lifting the knife often make cause crumbs to get into your icing. Top with pecans if desired.

Chocolate Peanut Cookies

Servings: 4

Cooking Time: 12 Minutes

Ingredients:

- 1/2 Tsp Baking Soda
- 1/2 Cup Brown Sugar

- 1/2 Cup + 1 Tbsp Butter, Unsalted
- 1/3 Cup Cocoa Powder, Dark And Unsweetened
- 2 Eggs, Beaten
- 1 1/2 Cups Flour, All-Purpose
- 1/3 Cup Miniature Chocolate Chips
- 2 Cups Peanut Butter Chips, Divided
- 1/4 Tsp Sea Salt
- 1/2 Cup Sugar, Granulated
- 1 Tsp Vanilla Extract

Directions:

1. Supply your smoker with wood pellets and follow the start-up procedure. Preheat the grill, with the lid closed, to medium-low heat. If using a gas or charcoal grill, preheat a cast iron skillet.
2. In a mixing bowl, whisk together the flour, cocoa powder, baking soda, and salt. Set aside.
3. Set a metal saucepan on the griddle, then add ½ cup of butter to melt. Whisk in the sugars and vanilla extract and cook for 2 minutes. Remove the pan from the griddle, and transfer contents to a large mixing bowl.
4. Slowly pour the beaten eggs into the sugar mixture, whisking constantly to temper the eggs.
5. Add the dry mixture to the wet ingredients until just combined. Fold in 1 cup of peanut butter chips and chocolate chips. Refrigerate mixture for 15 to 30 minutes.
6. Remove the dough from the refrigerator, then add an additional cup of peanut butter chips.
7. Portion dough into 16 to 18 cookie balls.
8. Melt 1 tablespoon of butter on the griddle, then transfer the cookie balls to the griddle. Press down gently on the cookies, then cook for 10 to 12 minutes, flipping halfway.
9. Transfer cookies to a cooling rack for 5 minutes before enjoying.

SEAFOOD RECIPES

Garlic Bacon Wrapped Shrimp

Servings: 4
Cooking Time: 11 Minutes

Ingredients:

- 8 Bacon, Strip
- 1/4 Cup Butter Style Shortening (Melted)
- 1 Clove Garlic, Minced
- 1 Tsp Lemon, Juice
- Pepper
- Salt
- 16 (Peeled And Veined) Shrimp, Jumbo

Directions:

1. Supply your smoker with wood pellets and follow the start-up procedure. Preheat the grill, with the lid closed, to 450° F.
2. Take one slice of bacon, and wrap it around each piece of shrimp, and lock it in place with a wooden toothpick.
3. Place the shortening into a mixing bowl and whisk in the garlic and lemon juice. Brush each shrimp with the sauce on both sides.
4. Place on the grill, and barbecue for 11 minutes.
5. Turn the grill off, remove the shrimp, serve and enjoy!

Wood-fired Halibut

Servings: 4
Cooking Time: 20 Minutes

Ingredients:

- 1 pound halibut fillet
- 1 batch Dill Seafood Rub

Directions:

1. Supply your smoker with wood pellets and follow the start-up procedure. Preheat the grill, with the lid closed, to 325°F.
2. Sprinkle the halibut fillet on all sides with the rub. Using your hands, work the rub into the meat.
3. Place the halibut directly on the grill grate and grill until its internal temperature reaches 145°F. Remove the halibut from the grill and serve immediately.

Grilled Tilapia With Blistered Cherry Tomatoes

Servings: 4
Cooking Time: 15 Minutes

Ingredients:

- 1½lb (680g) tilapia fillets or other mild white fish fillets
- chopped fresh curly or flat-leaf parsley
- for the marinade
- ½ cup extra virgin olive oil
- 1 garlic clove, peeled and smashed with a chef's knife
- 3 tbsp freshly squeezed lemon juice
- 1 tsp smoked paprika
- ½ tsp coarse salt
- ¼ tsp freshly ground black pepper
- for the tomatoes
- 2 tbsp extra virgin olive oil
- 2 pints (1 liter) cherry tomatoes (red, yellow, or heirloom varieties)
- coarse salt
- freshly ground black pepper

Directions:

1. Place a cast iron skillet on the grate. Supply your smoker with wood pellets and follow the start-up procedure. Preheat the grill, with the lid closed, to 400° F.
2. In a jar with a tight-fitting lid, make the marinade by combining the ingredients. Shake the jar vigorously to emulsify the ingredients.
3. Place the fillets in a single layer in a nonreactive baking dish. Pour half the marinade over them and turn the fillets to thoroughly coat. Cover with plastic wrap and refrigerate for 15 minutes. (Refrigerate no more than 30 minutes or the acid in the marinade will begin to cook the fish.)

4. Place the olive oil in the skillet. Add the tomatoes and season with salt and pepper. Stir to coat. Cook the tomatoes until they begin to blister and collapse, about 5 minutes, stirring once or twice. Remove the skillet from the grill and transfer the tomatoes to a bowl.
5. Carefully lift each fish fillet from the marinade and let the excess drip off. Place the fillets on the grate at a slight angle to the bars. Lightly season with salt and pepper. Grill until the fish flakes easily when pressed with a fork, about 4 to 5 minutes per side, turning carefully with a thin-bladed spatula.
6. Transfer the fillets to a warmed platter. Top with some of the tomatoes. (Place the remaining tomatoes in a serving bowl.) Scatter the parsley around the platter. Drizzle some of the remaining marinade over the top. Serve immediately.

Pacific Northwest Salmon

Servings: 4
Cooking Time: 75 Minutes

Ingredients:

- 1 (2-pound) half salmon fillet
- 1 batch Dill Seafood Rub
- 2 tablespoons butter, cut into 3 or 4 slices

Directions:

1. Supply your smoker with wood pellets and follow the start-up procedure. Preheat the grill, with the lid closed, to 180°F.
2. Season the salmon all over with the rub. Using your hands, work the rub into the flesh.
3. Place the salmon directly on the grill grate, skin-side down, and smoke for 1 hour.
4. Place the butter slices on the salmon, equally spaced. Increase the grill's temperature to 300°F and continue to cook until the salmon's internal temperature reaches 145°F. Remove the salmon from the grill and serve immediately.

Smoked Trout

Servings: 6
Cooking Time: 120 Minutes

Ingredients:

- 8 rainbow trout fillets
- 1 Gallon water
- 1/4 Cup salt
- 1/2 Cup brown sugar
- 1 Tablespoon black pepper
- 2 Tablespoon soy sauce

Directions:

1. Clean the fresh fish and butterfly them.
2. For the Brine: Combine one gallon water, brown sugar, soy sauce, salt and pepper and stir until salt and sugar are dissolved. Brine the trout in the refrigerator for 60 minutes.
3. Supply your smoker with wood pellets and follow the start-up procedure. Preheat the grill, with the lid closed, to 225° F.
4. Remove the fish from the brine and pat dry. Place fish directly on grill grate for 1-1/2 to 2 hours, depending on the thickness of the trout. Fish is done when it turns opaque and starts to flake. Serve hot or cold. Enjoy! Grill: 225 °F
5. Fish is done when it turns opaque and starts to flake. Serve hot or cold. Enjoy!

Grilled Lemon Lobster Tails

Servings: 3
Cooking Time: 7 Minutes

Ingredients:

- 6 lobster tails
- 1/4 cup melted butter
- 1/4 cup fresh lemon juice
- 1 tablespoon fresh dill
- 1 teaspoon salt
- 6 lime wedges

Directions:

1. Supply your smoker with wood pellets and follow the start-up procedure. Preheat the grill, with the lid closed, to 375° F.
2. Split the lobster tails in half place then back side down.
3. Cut down through the center to the shell the whole length of each tail.
4. Pull the shell back, exposing the meat.

5. Pat the lobster tails with paper towel to dry.
6. Combine in a small mixing bowl the butter, lemon juice, dill, and salt until the salt has dissolved.
7. Brush the mixture onto the flesh side of each lobster tail.
8. Place the lobster tails onto the grill and cook for 5 to 7 minutes, turning them once during the cooking process. (The shells should turn a bright pink).
9. Remove the heat.
10. Serve with lime wedges!

Mezcal Shrimp With Salsa De Molcajete

Servings: 4
Cooking Time: 14 Minutes

Ingredients:

- 18 to 24 jumbo shrimp, about 1½lb (680g) total, peeled and deveined
- ⅓ cup mezcal
- juice of ½ lime
- 2 tbsp extra virgin olive oil
- 2 tsp coarse salt
- 1 tsp ground cumin
- lime wedges
- for the salsa
- 2 Roma tomatoes
- 2 tomatillos, husked and washed
- 2 garlic cloves, peeled and impaled on a toothpick
- 1 jalapeño or serrano pepper
- 1 small white onion, halved
- ½ tsp coarse salt, plus more
- juice of ½ lime
- ¼ cup loosely packed fresh cilantro leaves

Directions:

1. Supply your smoker with wood pellets and follow the start-up procedure. Preheat the grill, with the lid closed, to 450° F.
2. In a large bowl, combine the shrimp, mezcal, lime juice, olive oil, salt, and ground cumin. Toss with your hands to mix thoroughly. Set aside for 15 minutes and then toss once more.
3. Begin to make the salsa by placing the tomatoes, tomatillos, garlic, jalapeño, and onion on the grate. Grill until they begin to char, about 3 minutes for the garlic and about 6 to 8 minutes for the other vegetables, turning as needed. Transfer the vegetables to a rimmed sheet pan. Remove the skewers from the garlic. Let everything cool. Coarsely chop the vegetables and leave them in separate piles.
4. Place the garlic in the molcajete and add the salt. Mash the garlic to a purée using the temolote. Add the onion and grind it into the garlic paste. Stir in the jalapeño (deseeded for a milder salsa), tomatoes, and tomatillos. Stir in the lime juice and cilantro leaves. Taste, adding salt. (If you don't own a molcajete or temolote, prepare the salsa using a small food processor.)
5. Drain the shrimp and discard the marinade. Thread the shrimp on wood or bamboo skewers. Place the shrimp on the grate and grill until they're white and opaque, about 4 to 6 minutes, tossing with tongs.
6. Transfer the shrimp to a platter. Serve with the salsa and lime wedges.

Grilled Garlic Shrimp With Cajun Dip

Servings: 4
Cooking Time: 15 Minutes

Ingredients:

- 1 Grated Garlic Cloves, Peeled
- 1 Tsp Lemon Juice
- ½ Cup Mayonnaise
- 2 Tbsp Olive Oil
- 1 ½ Tbsp Hickory Bacon Rub
- Scallions
- ½ Lb Shelled And Deveined Shrimp
- 1 Cup Sour Cream

Directions:

1. Supply your smoker with wood pellets and follow the start-up procedure. Preheat the grill, with the lid closed, to 350° F. If you're using a gas or charcoal grill, set it to medium heat.
2. In a glass mixing bowl, add mayonnaise, sour cream, Cajun seasoning, garlic, lemon juice, hot sauce, and Hickory Bacon. Whisk together until well combined.

3. Cajun shrimp: In a small bowl, add shrimp, olive oil, Cajun-style seasoning and Hickory Bacon seasoning and toss to combine. Set aside.
4. Transfer dip mixture into cast iron ramekin or small Dutch oven and cover with foil. Place on preheated grill and cook for 10-15 minutes, or until dip begins to bubble along the edges. At the same time, place cast iron pan on grill and add shrimp. Cook for about 3-5 minutes on each side or until shrimp are opaque.
5. Remove dip from grill and top with Cajun shrimp and scallions. Serve warm alongside garlic toast squares and enjoy!

Smoked Fish Chowder

Servings: 4
Cooking Time: 60 Minutes

Ingredients:

- 12 Ounce (1-1/2 to 2 lb) skin-on salmon fillet, preferably wild-caught
- Fin & Feather Rub
- 2 Corn Husks
- 3 Slices Bacon, sliced
- 4 Can Cream of Potato Soup, Condensed
- 3 Cup whole milk
- 8 Ounce cream cheese
- 3 green onions, thinly sliced
- 2 Teaspoon hot sauce

Directions:

1. Supply your smoker with wood pellets and follow the start-up procedure. Preheat the grill, with the lid closed, to 180° F.
2. Sprinkle Traeger Fin & Feather rub as needed on salmon. Arrange the salmon skin-side down on the grill grate. Smoke for 30 minutes. Grill: 180 °F
3. Increase the grill temperature to 350°F. Grill: 350 °F
4. Cook the salmon for 30 minutes, or until the fish flakes easily with a fork. (The exact time will depend on the thickness of the fillet.) There is no need to turn the fish. Using a large thin spatula, transfer the salmon to a wire rack to cool. Remove the skin. (The salmon can be made a day ahead, wrapped in plastic wrap and refrigerated.) Break into flakes and set aside.
5. Arrange the corn and bacon strips on the grill grate. (The salmon will be roasting while you do this.) Roast the corn and the bacon until the corn is cooked through and browned in spots, turning as needed, and the bacon is crisp, about 15 minutes.
6. In the meantime, bring the cream of potato soup and the milk to a simmer over medium heat in a large saucepan or Dutch oven on the stovetop. Gradually stir in the cream cheese and whisk to blend. Chop the bacon into bits and slice the corn off the cobs using long strokes of a chef's knife.
7. Add to the soup along with the green onions. Stir in the salmon. Heat gently for 5 to 10 minutes. Add the hot sauce to taste. If the chowder is too thick, add more milk. Serve at once. Enjoy!

Bacon Wrapped Scallops

Servings: 8
Cooking Time: 20 Minutes

Ingredients:

- 24 jumbo deep sea diver scallops, dry-packed
- 1/2 Cup butter
- salt
- freshly ground black pepper
- 1 Clove garlic, minced
- 12 Slices thin-cut bacon, cut in half crosswise
- lemon wedges, for serving

Directions:

1. Remove the small, crescent-shaped muscle from the side of each scallop, if still attached. Dry the scallops thoroughly on paper towels, then transfer to a medium bowl.
2. Melt butter in a small saucepan, add garlic and cook for 1 minute. Let cool slightly then pour over the scallops. Season with salt and pepper and gently toss to coat.
3. Wrap a piece of bacon around each scallop and secure with a toothpick.
4. Supply your smoker with wood pellets and follow the start-up procedure. Preheat the grill, with the lid closed, to 400° F.

5. Arrange the scallops directly on the grill grate. Grill for 15 to 20 minutes, or until the scallop is opaque and the bacon has begun to crisp. If desired, you can turn the scallops on their side, bacon-side down, turning occasionally to crisp the bacon. Do not overcook. Grill: 400 °F

6. Transfer the scallops to a platter and serve with lemon wedges.

Grilled Pepper Lobster Tails

Servings: 3

Cooking Time: 10 Minutes

Ingredients:

- Tt Black Pepper
- 3/4 Stick Butter, Room Temp
- 2 Tablespoons Chives, Chopped
- 1 Clove Garlic, Minced
- Lemon, Sliced
- 3 (7-Ounce) Lobster, Tail
- Tt Salt, Kosher

Directions:

1. Start your Grill on "SMOKE" with the lid open until a fire is established in the burn pot (3-7 minutes).
2. Supply your smoker with wood pellets and follow the start-up procedure. Preheat the grill, with the lid closed, to 350° F.
3. Blend butter, chives, minced garlic, and black pepper in a small bowl. Cover with plastic wrap and set aside.
4. Butterfly the tails down the middle of the softer underside of the shell. Don't cut entirely through the center of the meat. Brush the tails with olive oil and season with salt, to your liking.
5. Grill lobsters cut side down about 5 minutes until the shells are bright red in color. Flip the tails over and top with a generous tablespoon of herb butter. Grill for another 4 minutes, or until the lobster meat is an opaque white color.
6. Remove from the grill and serve with more herb butter and lemon wedges.

Sweet Smoked Salmon Jerky

Servings: 6

Cooking Time: 300 Minutes

Ingredients:

- 2 Quart water
- 3/4 Cup kosher salt
- 1 Cup Morton Tender Quick Home Meat Cure, optional
- 4 Cup dark brown sugar
- 2 Cup maple syrup, divided
- 1 (2-3 lb) wild caught salmon fillet, skinned and pin bones removed

Directions:

1. In a large nonreactive bowl, combine 2 quarts water, salt, curing salt (if using), brown sugar and 1 cup of the maple syrup. Stir with a long-handled spoon to dissolve the salts and sugar.
2. With a sharp, serrated knife, slice the salmon into 1/2 inch thick slices with the short side parallel to you on the cutting board. In other words, make your cuts from the head end to the tail end. (This is considerably easier if the fish is frozen.) Cut each strip crosswise into 4 or 5 inch lengths.
3. Immerse the strips in the brine, weighing down with a plate or a bag of ice. Cover with plastic wrap and refrigerate for 12 hours.
4. Supply your smoker with wood pellets and follow the start-up procedure. Preheat the grill, with the lid closed, to 180° F.
5. Drain the salmon strips and discard the brine. Arrange the salmon strips in a single layer directly on the grill grate. Smoke for several hours (5 to 6), or until the jerky is dry but not rock-hard. You want it to yield when you bite into it. Halfway through the smoking time, mix the remaining cup of maple syrup with 1/4 cup of warm water and brush the salmon strips on all sides with the mixture. Grill: 180 °F
6. Transfer to a resealable bag while the jerky is still warm. Let the jerky rest for an hour at room temperature. Squeeze any air from the bag, and refrigerate the jerky. Enjoy!

Cold-smoked Salmon Gravlax

Servings: 6

Cooking Time: 30 Minutes

Ingredients:

- 1 Cup kosher salt
- 1 Cup sugar
- 1 Tablespoon freshly ground black pepper
- 2 Pound Sushi-Grad Salmon Fillet, Skin-on, Pin Bones Removed
- 2 Bunch Dill Weed, fresh
- capers, drained
- red onion, sliced
- cream cheese
- lemons

Directions:

1. In a bowl stir together the salt, sugar and black pepper until thoroughly combined. On a work surface, turn salmon skin side up and sprinkle about half of salt mixture all over and rub in.
2. Arrange half the dill on the bottom of a baking dish large enough to hold the salmon. Set salmon skin side down on bed of dill.
3. Rub remaining salt mixture all over top and sides of salmon, then top with remaining dill. Cover with plastic, then top with a weight on a smaller baking dish or a plate with cans of beans on top, then place in refrigerator and allow to cure for 2 days.
4. Remove salmon from refrigerator, rinse under cold water and pat dry with paper towels. Allow to sit at room temperature on the counter for 1 hour
5. Supply your smoker with wood pellets and follow the start-up procedure. Preheat the grill, with the lid closed, to 180° F. Place salmon onto a baking pan. Fill another baking pan with ice and place baking pan with salmon over ice. Place onto grill and smoke for 30 minutes.
6. Remove from grill and slice thin. Serve with capers, red onion, dill, cream cheese, and lemon. Enjoy!

Grilled Salmon Gravlax

Servings: 4

Cooking Time: 10 Minutes

Ingredients:

- 1 center-cut salmon fillet, about 2lb (1kg), preferably wild caught, skin on
- ½ cup aquavit or vodka
- 4 whole juniper berries
- ¼ cup finely chopped fresh dill, plus more
- lemon wedges
- for the rub
- 3 tbsp granulated light brown sugar or low-carb substitute
- 2 tbsp coarse salt
- 2 tsp freshly ground black pepper
- 1 tsp freshly ground white pepper
- 1 tsp ground coriander

Directions:

1. Run your fingers over the fillet, feeling for bones. Remove them with kitchen tweezers or needle-nosed pliers. Rinse the salmon under cold running water and pat dry with paper towels.
2. Place the salmon skin side down in a nonreactive baking dish and pour the aquavit over it. Crush the berries with the flat of a chef's knife and add them to the dish. Cover and refrigerate for 1 hour.
3. In a small bowl, make the rub by combining the ingredients.
4. Remove the salmon from the aquavit and pat dry with paper towels. Discard the soaking liquid and juniper berries. Rinse out the baking dish and place the salmon in the dish. Lightly but evenly sprinkle the rub on the flesh side of the fillet and gently distribute it with your fingertips. Scatter the dill over the top. Cover the dish and refrigerate for 4 hours.
5. Supply your smoker with wood pellets and follow the start-up procedure. Preheat the grill, with the lid closed, to 400° F.
6. With a sharp knife, slice the fillet into 4 equal portions. Place the fillets on the grate and grill until the fish is somewhat opaque but still translucent in the center and the internal temperature reaches 125°F (52°C), about 3 to 5 minutes per side.
7. Transfer the fillets to a platter. Scatter more dill over the top. Serve with lemon wedges.

Grilled Oysters With Mignonette

Servings: 2
Cooking Time: 15 Minutes

Ingredients:

- 4 Cup rock salt
- 18 Large oysters
- 4 Tablespoon unsalted butter
- 2 Clove garlic, minced
- kosher salt
- 12 Medium lemon wedges, for serving
- 2 Tablespoon minced shallot
- 1/4 Cup red wine vinegar
- 1/2 Teaspoon freshly ground black pepper

Directions:

1. Choose a shallow serving platter that will hold all of the oysters. Pour the rock salt onto the platter to create a 1/2 inch base. This will steady the oysters for serving.
2. To prepare the oysters, check to ensure they are completely closed. Discard oysters that are not. Wash and lightly scrub the oysters to ensure there is no grit on the surface. This will prevent the grit from entering the oyster once shucked.
3. Using a thick glove or kitchen towel, sturdy the oyster in the hand opposite of the one holding the knife. Using an oyster knife or very sturdy paring knife, locate the "hinge" on each oyster. Place the point of the knife in the hinge, and wiggle the tip of the knife into the oyster until it feels sturdy. Firmly turn the knife to apply a torquing pressure to gently open the oyster.
4. Remove the top shell of the oyster. Using the tip of the knife, loosen the oyster from its shell, leaving the juices intact. Place each loosened oyster on its half shell on a baking sheet.
5. Supply your smoker with wood pellets and follow the start-up procedure. Preheat the grill, with the lid closed, to 450° F.
6. In a small saucepan, melt the butter over medium-low heat. Add the garlic and a generous pinch of salt, and cook until fragrant but not burned, about 1 minute. Remove from the heat. Grill: 450 °F
7. For the Mignonette: Combine the minced shallot, red wine vinegar and 1/2 teaspoon freshly ground black pepper. Set aside.
8. Spoon 1 teaspoon of the garlic butter sauce onto each oyster in its half shell. Carefully place each oyster directly on the grill grates, ensuring they don't slip. Close the lid and allow them to cook for 3 to 4 minutes, until the edges of the oysters have pulled away from the shell. Remove carefully with tongs to keep the juices and butter in the shells. Place directly on the rock salt to balance them. Serve immediately with the mignonette and lemon wedges to squeeze onto the oysters. Enjoy!

Barbecued Scallops

Servings: 4
Cooking Time: 10 Minutes

Ingredients:

- 1 pound large scallops
- 2 tablespoons olive oil
- 1 batch Dill Seafood Rub

Directions:

1. Supply your smoker with wood pellets and follow the start-up procedure. Preheat the grill, with the lid closed, to 375°F.
2. Coat the scallops all over with olive oil and season all sides with the rub.
3. Place the scallops directly on the grill grate and grill for 5 minutes per side. Remove the scallops from the grill and serve immediately.

Grilled Lemon Salmon

Servings: 4
Cooking Time: 60 Minutes

Ingredients:

- Dill, Fresh
- 1 Lemon, Sliced
- 1 1/2 - 2 Lbs Salmon, Fresh

Directions:

1. Supply your smoker with wood pellets and follow the start-up procedure. Preheat the grill, with the lid closed, to 225° F.

2. Place the salmon on a cedar plank. Lay the lemon slices along the top of the salmon. Smoke in your Grill for about 60 minutes.
3. Top with fresh dill and serve.

Grilled Salmon Steaks With Dill Sauce

Servings: 4
Cooking Time: 8 Minutes

Ingredients:

- 4 salmon steaks, each about 6 to 8oz (170 to 225g) and 1 inch (2.5cm) thick
- extra virgin olive oil
- coarse salt
- freshly ground rainbow peppercorns or freshly ground black pepper
- lemon wedges
- for the sauce
- 1 cup reduced-fat mayo
- ⅓ cup light sour cream
- ¼ cup chopped fresh dill
- 2 tbsp freshly squeezed lemon juice
- coarse salt
- freshly ground black pepper
- sprigs of fresh dill

Directions:

1. Supply your smoker with wood pellets and follow the start-up procedure. Preheat the grill, with the lid closed, to 450° F.
2. In a small bowl, make the dill sauce by combining the mayo, sour cream, dill, and lemon juice. Mix until smooth. Season with salt and pepper to taste. Transfer to a serving bowl. Scatter the dill sprigs over the top. Cover and refrigerate until ready to serve.
3. Brush the salmon with olive oil and season with salt and pepper. Place the salmon on the grate at an angle to the bars. Grill until grill marks begin to appear, about 4 minutes. Use a thin-bladed spatula to turn the salmon. Grill until the internal temperature reaches 140°F (60°C), about 4 minutes more.
4. Transfer the salmon to a platter. Serve immediately with the lemon wedges and dill sauce.

Planked Trout With Fennel, Bacon & Orange

Servings: 4
Cooking Time: 40minutes

Ingredients:

- 4 whole trout, each about 14 to 16oz (400 to 450g), cleaned and gutted, fins removed
- coarse salt
- freshly ground black pepper
- for the filling
- 1 large navel orange
- 4 slices of thick-cut bacon, diced
- 1 large fennel bulb, trimmed, halved, decored, and diced, green fronds reserved
- 4oz (110g) baby spinach, about 6 cups
- coarse salt
- freshly ground black pepper

Directions:

1. Supply your smoker with wood pellets and follow the start-up procedure. Preheat the grill, with the lid closed, to 450° F. Place 4 cedar planks on the grate and allow them to singe slightly on both sides. Remove them from the grill and place them on a heatproof surface to cool.
2. Lower the temperature to 300°F (149°C).
3. Slice 4 thin rounds from the center of the orange and then slice each in half for 8 pieces total. Zest the remainder of the orange and set aside.
4. In a cold skillet on the stovetop over medium heat, sauté the bacon, until the fat has rendered and the bacon is golden brown, about 6 to 8 minutes, stirring frequently. Use a slotted spoon to transfer the bacon to paper towels to drain. Add the fennel to the fat in the skillet and cook until tender crisp, about 5 minutes. Add the spinach and stir until it wilts, about 1 to 2 minutes. Squeeze the juice of one of the reserved orange ends over the mixture. Add the drained bacon. Season with salt and pepper and then stir. Remove the skillet from the stovetop and set aside.
5. Rinse each trout inside and out under cold running water and pat dry with paper towels. Place three 12-inch (30.5cm) pieces of butcher's twine on each plank and place a trout on top. Season the inside of each fish with

salt and pepper. Place two half-rounds of orange in each belly, rind side facing out. Top with some of the filling. Tie the trout with the butcher's twine and trim any ends. Repeat with the remaining trout.

6. Place the planks on the grate and cook the trout until they're cooked through, about 30 to 40 minutes.

7. Remove the planks from the grill and remove the twine. Top each trout with a few curls of orange zest and some reserved fennel fronds. Serve the trout on the planks.

Bbq Oysters

Servings: 4

Cooking Time: 6 Minutes

Ingredients:

- 1 Pound unsalted butter, softened
- 1 Tablespoon Meat Church Holy Gospel BBQ Rub
- 1 Bunch green onions, chopped
- 2 Clove garlic, minced
- 12 oysters
- 1/4 Cup seasoned breadcrumbs
- 8 Ounce shredded pepper jack cheese
- Sweet & Heat BBQ Sauce
- 1/2 Bunch green onions, minced

Directions:

1. Supply your smoker with wood pellets and follow the start-up procedure. Preheat the grill, with the lid closed, to 375° F.

2. For the compound butter: Combine butter, garlic, onion and Meat Church Rub thoroughly.

3. Lay the butter on parchment paper or plastic wrap. Roll it up to form a log and tie each end with butcher's twine. Place in the freezer for an hour to solidify. You can use this butter on any grilled meat to enhance the flavor. You can also use a high-quality butter to replace the compound butter.

4. Shuck the oysters, keeping all of the juice in the shell. Sprinkle the oysters with breadcrumbs and place directly on the Traeger. Cook them for 5 minutes. You will be looking for the edge of the oyster to start to curl slightly.

5. After 5 minutes, place a spoonful of compound butter in the oysters. After the butter melts, add a pinch of pepper jack cheese.

6. Remove the oysters after 6 minutes on the grill total. Top oysters with a squirt of Traeger Sweet & Heat BBQ Sauce and a few chopped onions. Allow to cool for 5 minutes, then enjoy!

Seared Ahi Tuna Steak With Soy Sauce

Servings: 2

Cooking Time: 60 Minutes

Ingredients:

- 1/2 Cup Gluten Free Soy Sauce
- 1 Large Sushi Grade Ahi Tuna Steak, Patted Dry
- 1/4 Cup Lime Juice
- 2 Tablespoons Rice Wine Vinegar
- 2 Tablespoons Sesame Oil, Divided
- 2 Tablespoons Sriracha Sauce
- 4 Tablespoons Sweet Heat Rub
- 2 Cups Water

Directions:

1. Supply your smoker with wood pellets and follow the start-up procedure. Preheat the grill, with the lid closed, to 400° F. If using gas or charcoal, set it up for high heat over direct heat.

2. In the glass baking dish, pour in the water, soy sauce, lime juice, rice wine vinegar, 1 tablespoon sesame oil, sriracha sauce, and mirin. Whisk the marinade together with the whisk until everything is well combine. Place the ahi steak into the marinade and place the glass baking dish with the ahi steak in the refrigerator for 30 minutes. After 30 minutes, flip the ahi steak over so that the ahi has the chance to fully marinate on all sides, and allow to marinate for 30 more minutes.

3. After the tuna steak has finished marinating, drain off the marinade and pat the steak dry with paper towels on all sides. Pour the Sweet Heat Rub onto the plate and rub the remaining tablespoon of sesame oil generously on all sides of the tuna steak, and then gently place the tuna steak into the seasoning on the plate, turning on all sides to coat evenly.

4. Insert a temperature probe into the thickest part of the ahi steak and place the steak on the hottest part of the grill. Grill the ahi tuna steak for 45 seconds on each side, or just until the outside is opaque and has grill marks. Flip the steak and allow it to grill for another 45 seconds until the outside is just cooked through. The ahi tuna steak's internal temperature should be just at 115°F.
5. Remove the steak from the grill once it reaches 115°F, and immediately slice and serve. The inside of the steak should still be cool and ruby pink.

Lemon Scallops Wrapped In Bacon

Servings: 4
Cooking Time: 20 Minutes

Ingredients:

- 3 Tbsp Lemon, Juice
- Pepper
- 12 Scallop

Directions:

1. Start your grill on smoke with the lid open until a fire is established in the burn pot (3-7 minutes).
2. Supply your smoker with wood pellets and follow the start-up procedure. Preheat the grill, with the lid closed, to 400° F.Cut the bacon rashers in half, wrap each half around a scallop and use a toothpick to keep it in place.
3. Next drizzle the lemon juice over the scallops, and then place them on a baking tray.
4. Place in the grill, and grill for about 15-20 minutes, or until the bacon is crisp, remove from the grill, then serve.

Oysters In The Shell

Servings: 4
Cooking Time: 20 Minutes

Ingredients:

- 8 medium oysters, unopened, in the shell, rinsed and scrubbed
- 1 batch Lemon Butter Mop for Seafood

Directions:

1. Supply your smoker with wood pellets and follow the start-up procedure. Preheat the grill, with the lid closed, to 375°F.
2. Place the unopened oysters directly on the grill grate and grill for about 20 minutes, or until the oysters are done and their shells open.
3. Discard any oysters that do not open. Shuck the remaining oysters, transfer them to a bowl, and add the mop. Serve immediately.

Delicious Jerk Shrimp

Servings: 8
Cooking Time: 10 Minutes

Ingredients:

- 1 Tablespoon brown sugar
- 1 Tablespoon smoked paprika
- 1 Teaspoon garlic powder
- 1/4 Teaspoon Thyme, ground
- 1/4 Teaspoon ground cayenne pepper
- 1 Teaspoon sea salt
- 1 lime zest
- 2 Pound shrimp in shell
- 3 Tablespoon olive oil

Directions:

1. Combine spices, salt, and lime zest in a small bowl and mix. Place shrimp into a large bowl, then drizzle in the olive oil, Add the spice mixture and toss to combine, making sure every shrimp is kissed with deliciousness.
2. Supply your smoker with wood pellets and follow the start-up procedure. Preheat the grill, with the lid closed, to 450° F.
3. Arrange the shrimp on the grill and cook for 2 – 3 minutes per side, until firm, opaque, and cooked through. Grill: 450 °F
4. Serve with lime wedges, fresh cilantro, mint, and Caribbean Hot Pepper Sauce. Enjoy!

Cedar Smoked Garlic Salmon

Servings: 6
Cooking Time: 60 Minutes

Ingredients:

- 1 Tsp Black Pepper

- 3 Cedar Plank, Untreated
- 1 Tsp Garlic, Minced
- 1/3 Cup Olive Oil
- 1 Tsp Onion, Salt
- 1 Tsp Parsley, Minced Fresh
- 1 1/2 Tbsp Rice Vinegar
- 2 Salmon, Fillets (Skin Removed)
- 1 Tsp Sesame Oil
- 1/3 Cup Soy Sauce

Directions:

1. Soak the cedar planks in warm water for an hour or more.
2. In a bowl, mix together the olive oil, rice vinegar, sesame oil, soy sauce, and minced garlic.
3. Add in the salmon and let it marinate for about 30 minutes.
4. Start your grill on smoke with the lid open until a fire is established in the burn pot (3-7 minutes).
5. Supply your smoker with wood pellets and follow the start-up procedure. Preheat the grill, with the lid closed, to 225° F.
6. Place the planks on the grate. Once the boards start to smoke and crackle a little, it's ready for the fish.
7. Remove the fish from the marinade, season it with the onion powder, parsley and black pepper, then discard the marinade.
8. Place the salmon on the planks and grill until it reaches 140°F internal temperature (start checking temp after the salmon has been on the grill for 30 minutes).
9. Remove from the grill, let it rest for 10 minutes, then serve.

Smoked Sugar Halibut

Servings: 8

Cooking Time: 120 Minutes

Ingredients:

- 1/4 cup granulated sugar
- 1/4 cup brown sugar
- 1/2 cup kosher salt
- 1 tsp ground coriander
- 2 lbs fresh halibut

Directions:

1. In a small bowl, mix the sugars, salt,and coriander together. Season the halibut on all sides.
2. Wrap the halibut in plastic wrap, place on a rimmed sheet pan,and brine in the fridge for 3 hours.
3. Remove the plastic wrap and rinse the fish. Pat it dry. Set it on a drying rack over a sheet pan for 1-2 hours in the fridge.
4. Supply your smoker with wood pellets and follow the start-up procedure. Preheat the grill, with the lid closed, to 200° F. Smoke the fish for 2 hours or until its internal temperature reaches 140 °F.
5. Serve your preferred sauce with the fish.

Salmon Cakes With Homemade Tartar Sauce

Servings: 4

Cooking Time: 15 Minutes

Ingredients:

- 1 1/2 Cups Breadcrumb, Dry
- 1/2 Tablespoon Capers, Diced
- 1/4 Cup Dill Pickle Relish
- 2 Eggs
- 1 1/4 Cup Mayonnaise, Divided
- 1 Tablespoon Mustard, Grainy
- 1/2 Tablespoon Olive Oil
- 1/2 Red Pepper, Diced Finely
- 1/2 Tablespoon Sweet Rib Rub
- 1 Cup Cooked Salmon, Flaked

Directions:

1. In a large bowl, mix together the salmon, eggs, ¼ cup mayonnaise, breadcrumbs, red bell pepper, Sweet Rib Rub, and mustard. Allow the mixture to sit for 15 minutes to hydrate the breadcrumbs.
2. Supply your smoker with wood pellets and follow the start-up procedure. Preheat the grill, with the lid closed, to 350° F.
3. In a small bowl, mix together the remaining mayonnaise, dill pickle relish, and diced capers. Set aside.
4. Place the baking sheet on the grill to preheat. Once the baking sheet is hot, drizzle the olive oil over the pan and drop rounded tablespoons of the salmon mixture onto the sheet pan. Press the mixture down into a flat patty with a spatula. Allow to grill for 3 to 5 minutes, then flip and grill for 1 to 2 more minutes. Remove from the grill and serve with the reserved tartar sauce.

Swordfish With Sicilian Olive Oil Sauce

Servings: 4
Cooking Time: 10 Minutes

Ingredients:

- 1/2 Cup extra-virgin olive oil, plus 2 tablespoons for oiling the fish
- 1 Whole lemon, juiced
- 2 Clove garlic, minced
- 3 Tablespoon finely chopped fresh parsley
- 1 Tablespoon finely chopped fresh oregano or 1 teaspoon dried oregano
- 1 Tablespoon brined capers, drained (optional)
- 4 (6 to 8 oz) swordfish, halibut, tuna or salmon steaks, 1 inch thick
- salt and pepper

Directions:

1. Put 1/2 cup of olive oil in a small saucepan and warm over low heat.
2. Whisk in lemon juice and 2 tablespoons hot water. Stir in garlic, parsley, oregano, capers (if using), and salt and pepper to taste (go easy on the salt if you're using capers). Keep warm.
3. Supply your smoker with wood pellets and follow the start-up procedure. Preheat the grill, with the lid closed, to 400° F.
4. Brush the fish steaks with 2 tablespoons of olive oil and season with salt and pepper. Grill: 400 °F
5. Arrange on the grill grate and grill until the fish is opaque and flakes easily when pressed with a fork, about 18 minutes. (If you prefer your tuna or salmon on the rare side, cook them for less time.) Grill: 400 °F
6. Transfer the fish steaks to a platter or plates and drizzle with the warm olive oil sauce.
7. Serve the remaining sauce on the side. Enjoy!

Bbq Roasted Salmon

Servings: 4
Cooking Time: 15 Minutes

Ingredients:

- 1/3 Cup honey
- 3 Tablespoon Mustard, whole-grain
- 1 Cup ketchup
- 1/2 Cup dark brown sugar
- 1 Teaspoon Cider Vinegar
- 1/2 Teaspoon Thyme Leaves, finely chopped
- 1/8 Teaspoon Jacobsen Salt Co. Pure Kosher Sea Salt
- 1/8 Teaspoon freshly ground black pepper
- 4 Whole Salmon Fillets, 6oz each, skin-on

Directions:

1. Combine all sauce ingredients in a large bowl, preferably one day prior to making the salmon.
2. Rub salmon fillets on both sides with sauce. Reserve any extra, unused sauce.
3. Supply your smoker with wood pellets and follow the start-up procedure. Preheat the grill, with the lid closed, to 350° F.
4. Place fillets on grill, skin-side down, and cook for 15 minutes. Grill: 350 °F
5. Let the fish rest for about 3-5 minutes. Serve with extra sauce. Enjoy!

Smoked Honey Salmon

Servings: 2
Cooking Time: 25 Minutes

Ingredients:

- 1 lb. salmon fillets
- 1/2 tsp. pepper
- 1/4 tsp. salt
- 2 tbsp. sriracha
- 2 tsp. honey
- 2 tsp. chili sauce
- 1 tsp. lime juice
- 1/2 tsp. fish sauce

Directions:

1. Supply your smoker with wood pellets and follow the start-up procedure. Preheat the grill, with the lid closed, to 350° F.
2. Sprinkle the salmon with salt and pepper.
3. In a bowl, whisk together the sriracha, honey, chili sauce, lime juice, and fish sauce.
4. Once the grill is hot, place the salmon on the grill and leave for 15 minutes.

5. After 15 minutes, brush the salmon with the sriracha chili sauce and keep cooking for 5-10minutes. The salmon should be firm to the touch and crispy on the edges.
6. Serve hot!

Smoky Crab Dip

Servings: 6
Cooking Time: 20 Minutes

Ingredients:

- 1/3 Cup mayonnaise
- 3 Ounce sour cream
- 1 Teaspoon smoked paprika
- 1/4 Teaspoon cayenne pepper
- 1 1/2 Pound Crab meat, lump
- salt and pepper
- scallions, chopped
- butter crackers

Directions:

1. Supply your smoker with wood pellets and follow the start-up procedure. Preheat the grill, with the lid closed, to 350° F.
2. Meanwhile, in a large bowl gently stir together all of the ingredients except the crackers, garnish scallions and the crab meat until thoroughly combined. Gently fold in the crab meat, being careful not to break it up too much.
3. Season to taste and transfer to an oven-safe serving dish.
4. Bake for 20 to 25 minutes, until bubbly and golden on top. Grill: 350 °F
5. Garnish with the additional chopped scallions and serve warm with butter crackers. Enjoy!

Smoke-roasted Halibut With Mixed Herb Vinaigrette

Servings: 4
Cooking Time: 12 Minutes

Ingredients:

- 4 halibut fillets, each about 6 to 8oz (170 to 225g)
- for the vinaigrette
- 2 tbsp white wine vinegar or sherry vinegar, plus more
- ¼ tsp coarse salt, plus more
- ¼ tsp freshly ground black pepper, plus more
- ½ cup extra virgin olive oil
- 2 tbsp minced fresh herbs, such as dill, flat-leaf parsley, or oregano
- for serving
- 4 cups loosely packed baby arugula, spinach, or other mixed greens
- 1 lemon, cut lengthwise into 4 wedges

Directions:

1. Supply your smoker with wood pellets and follow the start-up procedure. Preheat the grill, with the lid closed, to 400° F.
2. In a small bowl, make the vinaigrette by whisking together the vinegar, and salt and pepper. Whisk until the salt dissolves. Continue to whisk while slowly adding the olive oil. Whisk until the vinaigrette is emulsified. Stir in the herbs. Taste, adding vinegar or salt and pepper to taste. Pour 1⁄3 of the vinaigrette into a separate container. Reserve the remainder.
3. Place the fillets on a rimmed sheet pan. Lightly brush both sides with the smaller portion of vinaigrette. (Dividing the vinaigrette into two containers prevents cross-contamination.) Lightly season with salt and pepper.
4. Place the fillets on the grate at an angle to the bars. Grill until the edges begin to look opaque, about 4 to 6 minutes. Gently turn and grill until the fish is cooked through, about 4 to 6 minutes more. (A fillet will break into clean flakes when pressed with a fork when it's done.)
5. Remove the fish from the grill. Place the greens in a large bowl and toss them with 2 to 3 tablespoons of the reserved vinaigrette (you want the greens lightly coated) and divide between 4 plates. Place a fillet on the greens on each plate. Drizzle a bit more of the vinaigrette over the top. Serve with lemon wedges.

Florentine Shrimp Al Cartoccio

Servings: 4

Cooking Time: 13 Minutes

Ingredients:

- 6 tbsp unsalted butter, melted
- ½ cup heavy whipping cream
- ½ cup grated Parmesan cheese
- 2 garlic cloves, peeled and minced
- 1 cup thinly sliced button mushrooms, cleaned and destemmed
- 1 cup baby spinach leaves
- 2 tbsp chopped sun-dried, oil-packed tomatoes
- ½ tsp dried oregano
- ½ tsp dried basil
- ½ tsp crushed red pepper flakes, plus more
- ½ tsp coarse salt
- ½ tsp freshly ground black pepper
- 20 to 24 jumbo shrimp, about 1lb (450g) total, peeled and deveined
- sprigs of fresh rosemary, basil, thyme, or oregano

Directions:

1. Supply your smoker with wood pellets and follow the start-up procedure. Preheat the grill, with the lid closed, to 400° F.
2. In a large bowl, combine the butter and whipping cream. Stir in the Parmesan, garlic, mushrooms, spinach, tomatoes, oregano, basil, red pepper flakes, and salt and pepper. Add the shrimp and stir gently to coat.
3. Place four 12-inch (30.5cm) sheets of wide heavy-duty aluminum foil on a workspace and pull up the sides. Divide the shrimp mixture evenly between the sheets of foil. Roll and crimp the top and sides of the foil to create sealed packages.
4. Place the packets seam side up on the grate and grill until the shrimp are cooked through, about 10 to 13 minutes. (You can carefully open one package to check on the shrimp.)
5. Transfer the packets to plates. Carefully open the packets to avoid any steam. Scatter fresh herbs over the shrimp before serving.

Thai-style Swordfish Steaks With Peanut Sauce

Servings: 4

Cooking Time: 8 Minutes

Ingredients:

- 4 center-cut swordfish steaks, each about 6oz (170g) and 1 inch (2.5cm) thick
- Peanut Sauce
- lime wedges
- for the marinade
- 1/2 cup light Thai-style unsweetened coconut milk
- 2 garlic cloves, peeled and smashed with a chef's knife
- juice and zest of 1 lime
- 1-inch (2.5cm) piece of fresh ginger, peeled and roughly chopped
- ½ Thai bird's eye chili pepper or serrano pepper, deseeded and thinly sliced, plus more
- 2 tbsp fresh cilantro leaves, coarsely chopped
- 1 tbsp Asian fish sauce
- 1 tbsp light soy sauce or liquid aminos
- 1 tbsp light brown sugar or low-carb substitute
- 1 tsp ground coriander
- ½ tsp ground turmeric

Directions:

1. In a medium bowl, make the marinade by whisking together the ingredients. Whisk until the brown sugar dissolves.
2. Place the swordfish steaks in a single layer in a nonreactive baking dish and pour the marinade over them, turning the steaks to coat thoroughly. Refrigerate for 1 hour.
3. Supply your smoker with wood pellets and follow the start-up procedure. Preheat the grill, with the lid closed, to 450° F.
4. Remove the swordfish from the marinade and scrape off any solids. (Discard the marinade.) Place the steaks on the grate and grill until the fish easily flakes when pressed with a fork, about 3 to 4 minutes per side, turning with a thin-bladed spatula.
5. Transfer the swordfish steaks to a platter. Serve with the peanut sauce and lime wedges.

Delicious Smoked Trout

Servings: 8
Cooking Time: 120 Minutes

Ingredients:

- 6 rainbow trout fillets
- Brine:
- 2 Tablespoons kosher salt
- 2 Tablespoons brown sugar
- 4 cups cool water

Directions:

1. For the brine, dissolve the kosher salt and brown sugar in water.
2. Place the trout fillets in the brine, skin side up, and brine the fillets for 15 minutes.
3. Supply your smoker with wood pellets and follow the start-up procedure. Preheat the grill, with the lid closed, to 180° F.
4. Remove the trout from the brine and transfer it to the grill grates.
5. Smoke the trout for 1.5 to 2 hours with the lid closed, depending on the thickness of your fillets.
6. Smoke until the trout reaches an internal temperature of 145 °F, or until the trout flakes easily.
7. Remove the trout from the smoker and serve warm, or let it cool completely and serve chilled with your favorite accouterments.

Tequila & Lime Shrimp With Smoked Tomato Sauce

Servings: 4
Cooking Time: 6 Minutes

Ingredients:

- 24 to 28 jumbo shrimp, about 2lb (1kg) total, peeled and deveined
- 1 lime, quartered
- Smoked Tomato Sauce
- for the marinade
- ½ cup tequila or mezcal
- juice and zest of 1 lime
- 2 garlic cloves, peeled and roughly chopped
- ½ cup freshly squeezed orange juice
- ¼ cup extra virgin olive oil
- 2 tsp agave, light brown sugar, or low-carb substitute
- 2 tsp Mexican hot sauce, plus more
- 1½ tsp coarse salt
- 1 tsp baking soda
- 1 tsp chili powder
- ½ tsp ground cumin

Directions:

1. In a medium bowl, make the marinade by whisking together the ingredients. Whisk until the salt dissolves. Taste for seasoning, adding more hot sauce if desired.
2. Place the shrimp in a resealable plastic bag and pour the marinade over them, turning the bag several times to coat thoroughly. Refrigerate for 30 minutes.
3. Supply your smoker with wood pellets and follow the start-up procedure. Preheat the grill, with the lid closed, to 450° F.
4. Drain the shrimp and discard the marinade. Pat the shrimp dry with paper towels. Thread the shrimp on 4 bamboo skewers (preferably flat ones). Make sure all the shrimp face the same direction. Finish each skewer with a lime wedge.
5. Place the skewers on the grate and grill until the shrimp are white and opaque, about 2 to 3 minutes per side, turning once. (Don't overcook.)
6. Remove the shrimp from the grill. Serve immediately with the warm tomato sauce.

Prosciutto-wrapped Scallops

Servings: 4
Cooking Time: 10 Minutes

Ingredients:

- 1½lb (680g) jumbo sea or diver scallops (size U-10)
- 8 to 10 thin slices of prosciutto, each halved lengthwise
- coarse salt
- freshly ground black pepper
- for the butter
- 8oz (225g) unsalted butter
- 2 tsp minced fresh curly or flat-leaf parsley
- 1½ tsp finely grated orange zest
- 1 tbsp freshly squeezed orange juice

- 1 tsp finely grated lemon zest
- 1 tsp finely grated lime zest
- ½ tsp coarse salt

Directions:

1. Supply your smoker with wood pellets and follow the start-up procedure. Preheat the grill, with the lid closed, to 450° F.
2. In a small saucepan on the stovetop over medium-low heat, make the citrus butter by melting the butter. Add the remaining ingredients and simmer for 3 to 5 minutes to blend the flavors. Keep warm.
3. Rinse the scallops under cold running water and dry with paper towels. Place each scallop on its side at the end of a piece of prosciutto and wrap the prosciutto around the scallop. Secure with a toothpick. Season the exposed sides of the scallop with salt and pepper.
4. Place the scallops exposed sides down on the grate and grill until the edges of the prosciutto begin to frizzle and the scallop is warm inside, about 3 to 5 minutes per side.
5. Transfer the scallops to a platter. Brush with some of the warm citrus butter before serving. Serve the remaining butter on the side.

Garlic Grilled Shrimp Skewers

Servings: 3

Cooking Time: 6 Minutes

Ingredients:

- 1 pound large shrimp
- 1/4 cup olive oil
- 1/4 cup fresh cilantro, finely chopped
- 1/4 cup fresh parsley, finely chopped
- 4 cloves garlic, minced
- 1 tablespoon lemon juice
- 1/2 teaspoon salt
- 1/4 teaspoon black pepper
- Pinch cayenne pepper, adjust to spice preference

Directions:

1. Add the olive oil, herbs, and spices to a small mixing bowl and whisk together.
2. Place the shrimp in a bowl and pour 3/4 of the marinade on top of the shrimp. Mix together gently to coat the shrimp evenly.
3. Cover the bowl and marinate the shrimp for 30 minutes to an hour.
4. Thread the shrimp on the skewers and make sure to get all the good garlic and herbs from the bowl and spread on to the shrimp.
5. Supply your smoker with wood pellets and follow the start-up procedure. Preheat the grill, with the lid closed, to medium high heat.
6. Once the grill is hot, arrange the shrimp skewers on the grill and cook for 2-3 minutes per side, or until they turn pink and opaque.
7. Remove the shrimp skewers to a plate and spoon the remaining marinade on top before serving.

Cider Hot-smoked Salmon

Servings: 4

Cooking Time: 60 Minutes

Ingredients:

- 1 1/2 Pound Wild Caught Salmon Fillet, skinned, pin bones removed
- 12 Ounce apple juice or cider
- 4 Pieces juniper berries
- 1 Pieces Star Anise, Broken
- 1 Pieces bay leaf, coarsely crumbled
- 1/2 Cup kosher salt
- 1/4 Cup brown sugar
- 2 Teaspoon Blackened Saskatchewan Rub
- 1 Teaspoon coarse ground black pepper, divided

Directions:

1. Rinse the salmon fillet under cold running water and check for pin bones by running a finger over the fleshy part of the fillet. If you feel a bone, remove it with kitchen tweezers or a needle-nose pliers.
2. In a sturdy resealable plastic bag, combine the cider, crushed juniper berries, star anise, and bay leaf. Add the salmon fillet and put the bag in a bowl or pan in the refrigerator. Let sit for at least 8 hours, or overnight.
3. Remove the salmon from the bag and discard the cider mixture. Dry the salmon well on paper towels.

Make the cure: In a small mixing bowl, combine the kosher salt, brown sugar, and Traeger rub.

4. Pour half into a shallow plate, or baking dish. Put the salmon fillet, skin-side down, on top of the cure. Generously sprinkle the top with the remaining cure, cover with plastic wrap, and refrigerate for 1 to 1-1/2 hours. Any longer, and the fish will get too salty.
5. Remove the salmon from the cure and pat dry with paper towels. Sprinkle the black pepper on top of the fillet.
6. Supply your smoker with wood pellets and follow the start-up procedure. Preheat the grill, with the lid closed, to 200° F.
7. Lay the salmon skin-side down on the grill grate. Cook for 1 hour, or until the internal temperature in the thickest part of the fish reaches 150 or the fish flakes easily when pressed with a finger or fork. Grill: 200 ˚F Probe: 150 ˚F
8. Let cool slightly. Turn the fillet over and remove the skin; it should come off in one piece.
9. If not serving immediately, let the salmon cool completely, then wrap in plastic wrap and refrigerate for up to 2 days. Transfer to a platter and serve with some or all of the suggested accompaniments. Enjoy!

Lemon Lobster Rolls

Servings: 4

Cooking Time: 35 Minutes

Ingredients:

- 1/2 Cup Butter
- 4 Hot Dog Bun(S)
- 1 Lemon, Whole
- 4 Lobster, Tail
- 1/4 Cup Mayo
- Pepper

Directions:

1. Supply your smoker with wood pellets and follow the start-up procedure. Preheat the grill, with the lid closed, to 300° F.
2. Using kitchen shears, cut the shell of the tail and crack in half so that the meat is exposed. Pour in butter and season with pepper. Place the tails meat side up on the grill and cook until the shell has turned red and the meat is white, about 35 minutes.
3. Remove from the grill and separate the shell from the meat. Place the meat in a bowl with mayo, lemon juice and rind and season with pepper. Stir to combine and evenly distribute into the hot dog buns.

Grilled Albacore Tuna With Potato-tomato Casserole

Servings: 8

Cooking Time: 20 Minutes

Ingredients:

- 6 Tuna Steaks, 6oz
- 1 Whole lemon zest
- 1 chile de árbol, thinly sliced
- 1 Tablespoon thyme
- 1 Tablespoon fresh parsley

Directions:

1. To make the fish: Season the fish with the lemon zest, chile, thyme, and parsley. Cover and refrigerate at least 4 hours.
2. Remove fish from the refrigerator 30 minutes before cooking to come to room temperature.
3. Season the fish with salt and pepper on both sides. Grill 2-3 minutes per side (next to the cast iron with the casserole) rotating it once or twice. The tuna should be well seared but still rare.

Citrus-smoked Trout

Servings: 6

Cooking Time: 120 Minutes

Ingredients:

- 6 to 8 skin-on rainbow trout, cleaned and scaled
- 1 gallon orange juice
- ½ cup packed light brown sugar
- ¼ cup salt
- 1 tablespoon freshly ground black pepper
- Nonstick spray, oil, or butter, for greasing
- 1 tablespoon chopped fresh parsley
- 1 lemon, sliced

Directions:

1. Fillet the fish and pat dry with paper towels.
2. Pour the orange juice into a large container with a lid and stir in the brown sugar, salt, and pepper.
3. Place the trout in the brine, cover, and refrigerate for 1 hour.
4. Cover the grill grate with heavy-duty aluminum foil. Poke holes in the foil and spray with cooking spray (see Tip).
5. Supply your smoker with wood pellets and follow the start-up procedure. Preheat, with the lid closed, to 225°F.
6. Remove the trout from the brine and pat dry. Arrange the fish on the foil-covered grill grate, close the lid, and smoke for 1 hour 30 minutes to 2 hours, or until flaky.
7. Remove the fish from the heat. Serve garnished with the fresh parsley and lemon slices.

Smoked Salt Cured Lox

Servings: 8

Cooking Time: 30 Minutes

Ingredients:

- 1 Cup kosher salt
- 1 Cup sugar
- 1 Tablespoon cracked black pepper
- 1 Whole lemon zest
- 1 Whole orange zest
- 1 Whole Packaged Dill, roughly chopped including stems
- 2 Pound salmon fillet, skin on

Directions:

1. Mix together salt, sugar, black pepper, lemon zest, orange zest, and dill.
2. Slice salmon in half. Coat all flesh of salmon completely with salt sugar mixture. Sandwich the 2 pieces together, flesh to flesh and completely cover with salt sugar mixture.
3. Wrap tightly with plastic wrap and place into a gallon zip top bag. Squeeze out as much air as possible. Place wrapped salmon into a baking dish and place something heavy on top like a pot filled with water or a brick wrapped in foil. Place into the refrigerator for 10 hours. After 10 hours, flip over and put the weight back on top. Refrigerate for another 10 hours.
4. Remove from refrigerator, unwrap and rinse of remaining salt with cold water. Pat dry and leave on counter for 1 hour.
5. Supply your smoker with wood pellets and follow the start-up procedure. Preheat the grill, with the lid closed, to 180° F.
6. Place salmon onto a baking pan. Fill another baking pan with ice and place baking pan with salmon over ice.
7. Place onto grill and smoke for 30 minutes. Remove from grill and slice thin. Grill: 180 °F
8. Serve with bagels, cream cheese, capers, dill, lemon wedges, sliced tomatoes, and red onion. Enjoy!

Grilled Crab Legs With Herb Butter

Servings: 2

Cooking Time: 15 Minutes

Ingredients:

- 12 Tablespoon butter
- 3 Tablespoon Fresh Herbs (Parsley, Chives, Tarragon), finely chopped
- 4 Pound King Crab Legs or Dungeness Crab Leg Clusters
- 3 Whole Lemons, cut into wedges

Directions:

1. Supply your smoker with wood pellets and follow the start-up procedure. Preheat the grill, with the lid closed, to 375° F.
2. Place the butter, garlic, herbs, and a pinch of salt into a small cast iron sauce pan. Place on grill for 5 minutes to melt. Remove from grill and stir. Grill: 375 °F
3. If using king crab legs, split down the center and pour herb butter over meat reserving a quarter for serving. If using crab clusters, toss clusters with herb butter in a large mixing bowl reserving a quarter for serving.
4. Place crab legs directly on the grill grate, meat side up. Grill for 5 to 10 minutes or until hot and beginning to develop a little char on the shell. Grill: 375 °F
5. Serve crab legs with lemon wedges and reserved herb butter. Enjoy!

Coconut Shrimp Jalapeño Poppers

Servings: 6

Cooking Time: 55 Minutes

Ingredients:

- 8 Whole shrimp, peeled and deveined
- 1/2 Teaspoon Chicken Rub, plus more as needed
- olive oil
- 6 Whole jalapeños
- 8 Ounce cream cheese, softened
- 2 Tablespoon fresh chopped cilantro
- 1/2 Cup unsweetened coconut flakes
- 12 Slices bacon

Directions:

1. Supply your smoker with wood pellets and follow the start-up procedure. Preheat the grill, with the lid closed, to 425° F.
2. Rinse and season the shrimp with the Traeger Chicken Rub.
3. Drizzle the shrimp with olive oil and cook on the Traeger for about 5 minutes per side, or until the shrimp is opaque. Grill: 425 °F
4. Remove the shrimp and let cool.
5. Reduce Traeger temperature to 350°F. Grill: 350 °F
6. Meanwhile, get those poppers going. Cut the jalapeños in half then remove the stems and seeds.
7. Chop the shrimp. Mix together the softened cream cheese, chopped shrimp, 1/2 teaspoon Traeger Chicken Rub and 2 tablespoons chopped cilantro.
8. Load a generous amount of the filling in each pepper half. Top with a sprinkle of coconut.
9. Wrap each stuffed pepper with a slice of bacon and place on a foil-lined baking sheet.
10. Cook the peppers on the Traeger for about 45 minutes, or until the bacon fat has rendered and the cream cheese is golden. Enjoy! Grill: 350 °F

Smoked Mango Shrimp

Servings: 4

Cooking Time: 5 Minutes

Ingredients:

- 2 Tablespoon Olive Oil
- 1 Pound Raw Tail-On, Thawed And Deveined Shrimp, Uncooked

Directions:

1. Supply your smoker with wood pellets and follow the start-up procedure. Preheat the grill, with the lid closed, to 425° F. Rinse shrimp off in sink with cold water. Place in bowl and season generously with Mango Magic seasoning and olive oil. Toss well in bowl.
2. Thread several shrimp onto a skewer, so that they are all just touching each other. Repeat with other skewers and remaining shrimp.
3. Grill shrimp for 2 - 3 minutes on each side, or until pink and opaque all the way through. Remove from grill and serve immediately.

Shrimp Cabbage Tacos With Lime Cream

Servings: 4

Cooking Time: 10 Minutes

Ingredients:

- 1/4 Cabbage, Shredded
- 2 Tsp Cilantro, Chopped
- Corn Tortillas
- 1/2 Lime, Wedges
- 1/4 Cup Mayonnaise
- Blackened Sriracha Rub
- 1/4 Red Bell Pepper, Chopped
- 1 Lb Shrimp, Peeled & Deveined
- 1/4 Cup Sour Cream
- 2 Tsp Vegetable Oil
- 1/2 White Onion, Chopped

Directions:

1. Place shrimp In a medium bowl. Season with Blackened Sriracha Rub, then drizzle with vegetable oil. Toss by hand to coat well then set aside.
2. In a small mixing bowl, stir together mayonnaise, sour cream, and fresh lime juice. Season to taste with Blackened Sriracha. Set aside.
3. In a small mixing bowl, combine jalapeño, onion, red bell pepper, and cilantro. Set aside.
4. Supply your smoker with wood pellets and follow the start-up procedure. Preheat the grill, with the lid

closed, till over medium heat. If using a grill, preheat a cast iron skillet over medium-heat.
5. Place tortillas on the griddle to warm each side, then turn off the burner below.
6. Transfer shrimp to the hot griddle, and cook for 4 to 6 minutes, tossing occasionally, until opaque. For spicier shrimp, season with additional Blackened Sriracha.
7. Assemble tacos: shredded cabbage, shrimp, pepper mixture, then drizzle with sauce. Serve warm with fresh lime wedges.

Lemon Herb Grilled Salmon

Servings: 4
Cooking Time: 25 Minutes

Ingredients:

- 1 1/2 pounds salmon with skin
- 1/2 tablespoon lemon zest
- 1 tablespoon lemon juice
- 1 tablespoon unsalted butter
- 1/2 teaspoon sea salt
- 1/2 teaspoon ground black pepper
- 2 teaspoons freshly chopped dill
- 1 teaspoon freshly chopped parsley
- lemon slices for the garnish

Directions:

1. Supply your smoker with wood pellets and follow the start-up procedure. Preheat the grill, with the lid closed, to 325° F.
2. In a small bowl, combine the lemon zest, lemon juice, softened unsalted butter, dill, parsley, sea salt, and ground black pepper.
3. Generously slather the top of the salmon fillet with the mixture and top with a slice of lemon. You may allow marinating for about 10 minutes or so to absorb the mixture.
4. Place the salmon fillets on the hot grill grate, skin-side facing down.
5. Cook the salmon for 20 to 25 minutes, until it reaches an internal temperature of 145 °F and flakes easily, or until the salmon is cooked to your preferred taste.
6. Serve with lemon slices. Enjoy!

Spicy Lime Shrimp

Servings: 4
Cooking Time: 10 Minutes

Ingredients:

- 2 Tsp Chili Paste
- 1/2 Tsp Cumin
- 2 Cloves Garlic, Minced
- 1 Large Lime, Juiced
- 1/4 Tsp Paprika, Powder
- 1/4 Tsp Red Flakes Pepper
- 1/2 Tsp Salt

Directions:

1. In a bowl, whisk together the lime juice, olive oil, garlic, chili powder, cumin, paprika, salt, pepper, and red pepper flakes.
2. Then pour it into a resealable bag, add the shrimp, toss the coat, let it marinate for 30 minutes.
3. Supply your smoker with wood pellets and follow the start-up procedure. Preheat the grill, with the lid closed, to 400° F.
4. Next place the shrimp on skewers, place on the grill, and grill each side for about two minutes until it's done. One finished, remove the shrimp from the grill and enjoy!

Lemon Shrimp Scampi

Servings: 3
Cooking Time: 10 Minutes

Ingredients:

- 2 Tsp Blackened Sriracha Rub Seasoning
- 1/2 Cup Butter, Cubed, Divided
- 1/2 Tsp Chili Pepper Flakes
- 3 Garlic Cloves, Minced
- To Taste, Lemon Wedges, For Serving
- 1 Lemon, Juice & Zest
- Linguine, Cooked
- 3 Tbsp Parsley, Chopped
- 1 1/2 Lbs Shrimp, Peeled & Deveined
- Toasted Baguette, For Serving

Directions:

1. Supply your smoker with wood pellets and follow the start-up procedure. Preheat the grill, with the lid closed, to medium-high heat. If using a gas or charcoal grill, set it up for medium-high heat.
2. Add half of the butter to the griddle, then sauté the garlic, Blackened Sriracha, and chili flakes for 1 minute, until fragrant.
3. Add the shrimp, turning occasionally for 2 minutes, until opaque.
4. Add the remaining butter, parsley, lemon zest and juice. Toss the shrimp to coat in lemon butter, then remove from the griddle, and transfer to a serving bowl.
5. Serve immediately, with fresh lemon wedges, and toasted baguette. Serve over linguine, spaghetti or zucchini noodles, if desired.

Bacon Wrapped Shrimp

Servings: 6
Cooking Time: 20 Minutes

Ingredients:

- 1 1/2 Pound Jumbo Shrimp, Peeled And Deveined
- 10 Strips Bacon
- Cheesy Grits, For Serving
- 1/4 Cup extra-virgin olive oil
- 2 Tablespoon lemon juice
- 1 Teaspoon Fresh Chopped Parsley
- 1 Tablespoon lemon zest
- 1 Teaspoon garlic, minced
- 1 Teaspoon salt
- 1/2 Teaspoon black pepper

Directions:

1. Rinse the shrimp under cold running water and dry thoroughly on paper towels.
2. Transfer to a re-sealable plastic bag or a bowl.
3. For the marinade: Combine the olive oil, lemon juice, lemon zest, garlic, salt, pepper, and parsley in a small jar with a tight-fitting lid and shake vigorously until combined.
4. Pour over the shrimp and refrigerate for 30 minutes to 1 hour.
5. Supply your smoker with wood pellets and follow the start-up procedure. Preheat the grill, with the lid closed, to 400° F.
6. Lay the bacon strips diagonally on the grill grate and grill for 10 to 12 minutes, or until the bacon is partially cooked but still very pliable.
7. Cut each strip in half width-wise. Leave the grill on.
8. Drain the shrimp, discarding the marinade. Wrap a strip of bacon around the body of each shrimp, securing with a toothpick. Grill for 4 minutes per side, turning once. Enjoy! Grill: 400 °F
9. Wrap a strip of bacon around the body of each shrimp, securing with a toothpick.
10. Grill for 4 minutes per side, turning once. Serve over cheesy grits, if desired. Enjoy!

Grilled Tuna Steaks With Lemon & Caper Butter

Servings: 4
Cooking Time: 8 Minutes

Ingredients:

- 4 tuna steaks, each about 8oz (225g) and 1 inch (2.5cm) thick
- extra virgin olive oil
- coarse salt
- freshly ground black pepper
- for the butter
- 6 tbsp unsalted butter, chilled, divided
- 1 garlic clove, peeled and minced
- 3 tbsp brined capers, drained and coarsely chopped
- 1 tbsp freshly squeezed lemon juice, plus more
- 1 tsp lemon zest
- 1 tbsp minced fresh chives or flat-leaf parsley

Directions:

1. Supply your smoker with wood pellets and follow the start-up procedure. Preheat the grill, with the lid closed, to 450° F.
2. In a small saucepan on the stovetop over medium-low heat, begin making the butter by melting 1 tablespoon of butter. (Cut the remaining butter into ½-inch (1.25cm) cubes and keep them cold.) Add the garlic and capers. Cook until the garlic is softened, about 3

minutes. Stir in the lemon juice and zest. Remove the saucepan from the heat and set aside.

3. Lightly brush the tuna steaks with olive oil. Season with salt and pepper. Place the steaks on the grate and grill until seared, about 3 to 4 minutes per side. (The tuna will be quite rare in the center, almost like sashimi. If you prefer your tuna more well done, add 4 to 6 minutes to the grilling time.)

4. Transfer the steaks to a platter and let rest for 5 minutes.

5. Reheat the butter and caper mixture over low heat. Whisk in the chilled butter one or two cubes at a time until the sauce has emulsified. Stir in the chives. Ladle the sauce over the tuna. Serve immediately.

Garlic Pepper Shrimp Pesto Bruschetta

Servings: 12

Cooking Time: 15 Minutes

Ingredients:

- 12 Slices Bread, Baguette
- 1/2 Tsp Chili Pepper Flakes
- 1/2 Tsp Garlic Powder
- 4 Cloves Garlic, Minced
- 2 Tbsp Olive Oil
- 1/2 Tsp Paprika, Smoked
- 1/4 Tsp Parsley, Leaves
- Pepper
- Pesto
- Salt
- 12 Shrimp, Jumbo

Directions:

1. Supply your smoker with wood pellets and follow the start-up procedure. Preheat the grill, with the lid closed, to 350° F. Place the baguette slices on a baking sheet lined with foil. Stir together the olive oil, and minced garlic, then brush both sides of the baguette slices with the mix. Place the pan inside the grill, and bake for about 10-15 minutes.

2. In a skillet, add a splash of olive oil, shrimp, chili powder, garlic powder, smoked paprika, salt pepper, and grill on medium-high heat for about 5 minutes (until the shrimp is pink). Be sure to stir often. Once pink, remove pan from heat. Once the baguettes are toasted, let them cool for 5 minutes, then spread a layer of pesto onto each one, then top with a shrimp, and serve.

Garlic Blackened Catfish

Servings: 4

Cooking Time: 10 Minutes

Ingredients:

- ½ Cup Cajun Seasoning
- ¼ Tsp Cayenne Pepper
- 1 Tsp Granulated Garlic
- 1 Tsp Ground Thyme
- 1 Tsp Onion Powder
- 1 Tsp Ground Oregano
- 1 Tsp Pepper
- 4 (5-Oz.) Skinless Catfish Fillets
- 1 Tbsp Smoked Paprika
- 1 Stick Unsalted Butter

Directions:

1. In a small bowl, combine the Cajun seasoning, smoked paprika, onion powder, granulated garlic, ground oregano, ground thyme, pepper and cayenne pepper.

2. Sprinkle fish with salt and let rest for 20 minutes.

3. Supply your smoker with wood pellets and follow the start-up procedure. Preheat the grill, with the lid closed, to 450° F. If you're using a gas or charcoal grill, set it up for medium-high heat. Place cast iron skillet on the grill and let it preheat.

4. While grill is preheating, sprinkle catfish fillets with seasoning mixture, pressing gently to adhere. Add half the butter to preheated cast iron skillet and swirl to coat, add more butter if needed. Place fillets in hot skillet and cook 3-5 minutes or until a dark crust has been formed. Flip and cook an additional 3-5 minutes or until the fish flakes apart when pressed gently with your finger.

5. Remove fish from grill and sprinkle evenly with fresh parsley. Serve with lemon wedges and enjoy!

Mango Rice Wine Thai Shrimp

Servings: 4

Cooking Time: 15 Minutes

Ingredients:

- 2 Tablespoons Brown Sugar
- 2 Tablespoons Mango Magic Seasoning
- 1 Pinch (Optional) Red Pepper Flakes
- 1/2 Tablespoons Rice Wine Vinegar
- 1 Pound Raw Tail-On, Thaw And Deveined Shrimp, Uncooked
- 2 Tablespoons Soy Sauce
- 1 Teaspoon Sriracha Hot Sauce
- 1/2 Cup Sweet Chili Sauce

Directions:

1. Supply your smoker with wood pellets and follow the start-up procedure. Preheat the grill, with the lid closed, to 425° F. Rinse shrimp off in sink with cold water. Place in bowl and put in all of the ingredients listed above. Let marinade for 2 - 4 hours.
2. Thread several shrimp onto a skewer, so that they are all just touching each other. Repeat with other skewers and remaining shrimp.
3. Grill shrimp for 2 - 3 minutes on each side, or until pink and opaque all the way through. Remove from grill and serve immediately.

Spicy Shrimp Skewers

Servings: 4

Cooking Time: 6 Minutes

Ingredients:

- 2 Pound shrimp, peeled and deveined
- 6 Thai chiles
- 6 Clove garlic
- 2 Tablespoon Winemaker's Napa Valley Rub
- 1 1/2 Teaspoon sugar
- 1 1/2 Tablespoon white vinegar
- 3 Tablespoon olive oil

Directions:

1. If using bamboo skewers, place them in cold water to soak for 1 hour before grilling.
2. Place shrimp in a bowl and set aside. Combine all remaining ingredients in a blender and blend until a coarse-textured paste is reached. Note: if a milder flavor is preferred, feel free to adjust amount of chiles to taste.
3. Add chile-garlic mixture to the shrimp and place in fridge to marinate for at least 30 minutes.
4. Remove from fridge and thread shrimp onto bamboo or metal skewers.
5. Supply your smoker with wood pellets and follow the start-up procedure. Preheat the grill, with the lid closed, to 450° F.
6. Place shrimp on grill and cook for 2 to 3 minutes per side or until shrimp are pink and firm to touch. Enjoy! Grill: 450 °F

Sweet Mandarin Salmon

Servings: 2

Cooking Time: 10 Minutes

Ingredients:

- 1 Whole lime juice
- 1 Teaspoon sesame oil
- 1 1/2 Cup Mandarin Orange Sauce
- 1 1/2 Tablespoon soy sauce
- 2 Tablespoon cilantro, finely chopped
- Freshly cracked black pepper
- 1 Whole (4 oz) wild salmon fillets

Directions:

1. Supply your smoker with wood pellets and follow the start-up procedure. Preheat the grill, with the lid closed, to 375° F.
2. For the glaze, combine Mandarin orange sauce, lime juice, sesame oil, soy sauce, cilantro and fresh cracked black pepper. Mix together.
3. Cut the salmon into 4 fillets. Brush with glaze and place directly on the grill grate, skin side down.
4. Cook until salmon reaches an internal temperature of 155 degrees F (about 15-20 minutes). Half way through cook time, brush salmon again with the glaze.
5. Remove the salmon from the grill and serve with remaining glaze if desired. Enjoy!

Lime Mahi Mahi Fillets

Servings: 4

Cooking Time: 8 Minutes

Ingredients:

- 3/4 cup extra-virgin olive oil
- 1 clove garlic, minced
- 1/8 teaspoon ground black pepper
- 1/2 teaspoon cayenne pepper
- 2 tablespoons dill weed.
- 1 pinch salt
- 2 tablespoons lime juice
- 1/8 teaspoon grated lime peel
- 2 (4 ounce) mahi mahi fillets

Directions:

1. Supply your smoker with wood pellets and follow the start-up procedure. Preheat the grill, with the lid closed, to 325° F.
2. Lightly oil the grate.
3. Combine in a bowl the extra-virgin olive oil, minced garlic, black pepper, cayenne pepper, salt, lime juice, and grated lime zest.
4. Wisk to prepare the marinade.
5. Place the mahi mahi fillets in the marinade and turn to coat.
6. Allow to marinate at least 15 minutes.
7. Cook on preheated grill until fish flakes easily with a fork and is lightly browned (Typically 3 to 4 minutes per side).
8. Garnish with the twists of lime zest to serve.

Grilled Garlic Lobster Tails

Servings: 2

Cooking Time: 11 Minutes

Ingredients:

- 4 Lobster Tails (8 oz Each)
- 3 Sticks Unsalted Butter
- 4 Cloves Garlic Minced
- ½ Cup Fresh Parsley Chopped
- Juice of 1 Lemon
- 2 Tablespoons Fresh Lemon Zest
- 2 Teaspoons Crushed Red Pepper
- ¼ Cup Olive Oil
- 1 TBS Kosher Salt
- 1 TBS Cracked Black Pepper

Directions:

1. Supply your smoker with wood pellets and follow the start-up procedure. Preheat the grill, with the lid closed, to 375° F.
2. Split lobster tails in half lengthwise and season with salt, pepper, and olive oil.
3. Place butter in an aluminum pan and put the pan on the hot side of the grill to melt the butter.
4. Add garlic, parsley, lemon zest, lemon juice, and red pepper to butter and simmer for 5 minutes.
5. Place lobster tails meat side down on the grill and cook for 6 minutes. Baste the shell side with the butter mixture.
6. Dunk each tail in the butter mixture and then transfer to the grill, shell side down. Baste meat again with butter mixture.
7. Cook for an additional 5 minutes or until the lobster meat turns opaque and shells are bright pink.
8. Serve with remaining butter mixture, fresh parsley, and lemon wedges.

Grilled Artichoke Cheese Salmon

Servings: 12

Cooking Time: 270 Minutes

Ingredients:

- 28 Oz Artichoke Hearts, Whole, Canned
- 1/2 Cup Breadcrumbs
- 1/2 Cup Brown Sugar
- 8 Oz Cream Cheese
- 1 Tbsp Garlic Powder
- 1 Cup Italian Cheese Blend, Shredded
- 1/4 Cup Kosher Salt
- 1 Cup Mayonnaise
- 2 Tsp Olive Oil
- 1 Tbsp Onion Powder
- 1/2 Cup Parmesan Cheese
- 2 Tbsp Parsley, Chopped
- Blackened Sriracha Rub
- 1 1/4 Lbs Salmon, Fillet, Scaled And Deboned
- Sour Cream

- 1/2 Tsp White Pepper, Ground

Directions:

1. In a small mixing bowl, whisk together the brown sugar, salt, garlic powder, onion powder, and white pepper. This will make twice the cure needed, so be sure and place the remaining half in a resealable plastic bag and save for smoking fish at a later date.
2. Lay a sheet of plastic wrap on a sheet tray and sprinkle a thin layer of the cure on it. Place the salmon skin-side down on top of the cure, then sprinkle a couple tablespoons of cure on top. Gently press the cure on top of the salmon flesh, then wrap in plastic wrap.
3. Refrigerate for 8 hours, or overnight.
4. Remove salmon from the refrigerator and wash off the cure in the sink, under cold water.
5. Blot salmon with a paper towel, then set salmon skin side on a wire rack. Dry at room temperature for two hours, or until a yellowish shimmer appears on the salmon.
6. Supply your smoker with wood pellets and follow the start-up procedure. Preheat the grill, with the lid closed, to 250° F. If using a gas, charcoal or other grill, set it to low, indirect heat.
7. Place the salmon in the upper cabinet. Smoke for 2 hours, then increase the grill temperature to 350° F to maintain a cabinet temperature of 225°F and smoke another 1 to 2 hours, until salmon reaches an internal temperature of 145° F.
8. Remove salmon from the cabinet and set aside to rest for 15 minutes, then flake apart. Reserve ½ cup to top dip after grilling.
9. While the salmon is resting, drain the artichokes, then skewer onto metal skewers (if using wooden skewers, make sure to soak in water for 1 hour prior to grilling, or you can use a grill basket as well).
10. Season with Blackened Sriracha, then set on the grill. Grill for 2 to 3 minutes, until lightly browned.
11. Remove from the grill, cool slightly, then roughly chop. Set aside.
12. In a mixing bowl, combine shredded Italian cheese, grated parmesan, breadcrumbs and parsley. Set aside.
13. Place cream cheese, mayonnaise, and sour cream in a cast iron skillet. Stir frequently, with a wooden spoon, for about 5 minutes, until the mixture is smooth.
14. Carefully fold in flaked salmon and grilled artichoke hearts, then spread breadcrumb mixture over dip.
15. Drizzle with olive oil, then close the grill lid and bake for 25 to 30 minutes, until dip begins to bubble around the edges, and cheese begins to caramelize on top.
16. Remove dip from the grill, top with reserved salmon and a pinch of parsley. Serve warm with bagel chips, crackers, or crusty bread.

Grilled Maple Syrup Salmon

Servings: 6

Cooking Time: 30 Minutes

Ingredients:

- 1 large salmon fillet (around 3 pounds)
- 1/2 cup salted butter (melted)
- 2 tablespoons soy sauce
- Salt and pepper
- 1/4 cup maple syrup

Directions:

1. Supply your smoker with wood pellets and follow the start-up procedure. Preheat the grill, with the lid closed, to 400° F.
2. Place the salmon fillet in a baking pan lined with parchment paper.
3. Sprinkle the fish with salt and pepper.
4. Add half of the melted butter to the salmon and place the baking pan on the grill.
5. Grill for 15-20 minutes or until fish is roughly 70% cooked. It will feel still gelatinous in the thickest parts of the salmon.
6. Combine the remaining melted butter, soy sauce, and maple syrup and pour over the salmon.It will run off the sides so use a spoon to pour it back over the fish. It's also perfectly fine that some will be left on the sides of the pan.
7. Cook for 5 to 10 additional minutes or until the fish is cooked through. The fish should be firm to the touch but still moist and soft when pressed on,and the ridges will flake or pull apart if pressed on.

Flavour Fire Spiced Shrimp

Servings: 2
Cooking Time: 8 Minutes

Ingredients:

- 1 pound of extra large raw whole wild shrimp
- 1 tablespoon vegetable oil
- 1 tablespoon chili powder
- 1 teaspoon garlic powder
- 1/2 teaspoon onion powder
- 1/2 teaspoon cayenne pepper
- 1/4 teaspoon paprika
- 1/4 teaspoon dried oregano
- Pinch of Kosher salt

Directions:

1. Supply your smoker with wood pellets and follow the start-up procedure. Preheat the grill, with the lid closed, to High heat.
2. While grill is preheating, remove the shrimp shells, leaving the heads.
3. Butterfly shrimp by using a knife to cut each shrimp down the middle, from the head down to the tail.
4. Remove the vein, rinse off the shrimp and lightly dry off with paper towels.
5. Place the shrimp in a large bowl, sprinkle with all the seasonings and the oil.
6. Mix together, ensuring the mixture evenly covers each shrimp.
7. Using a skewer, impale the whole body of a shrimp, from head to tail. (Wrap them in aluminum foil if using wooden skewers).
8. Place the whole shrimp on the grill and cook for 3-4 minutes on each side (Or until shells turns pink and the shrimp is opaque).
9. Serve with your favorite sauce or condiment.

Smoked Cedar Plank Salmon

Servings: 4
Cooking Time: 20 Minutes

Ingredients:

- 1/4 Cup Brown Sugar
- 1/2 Tablespoon Olive Oil
- Competition Smoked Seasoning
- 4 Salmon Fillets, Skin Off

Directions:

1. Soak the untreated cedar plank in water for 24 hours before grilling. When ready to grill, remove and wipe down.
2. Supply your smoker with wood pellets and follow the start-up procedure. Preheat the grill, with the lid closed, to 350° F.
3. In a small bowl, mix the brown sugar, oil, and Lemon Pepper, Garlic, and Herb seasoning. Rub generously over the salmon fillets.
4. Place the plank over indirect heat, then lay the salmon on the plank and grill for 15-20 minutes, or until the salmon is cooked through and flakes easily with a fork. Remove from the heat and serve immediately.

Charleston Crab Cakes With Remoulade

Servings: 4
Cooking Time: 45 Minutes

Ingredients:

- 1¼ cups mayonnaise
- ¼ cup yellow mustard
- 2 tablespoons sweet pickle relish, with its juices
- 1 tablespoon smoked paprika
- 2 teaspoons Cajun seasoning
- 2 teaspoons prepared horseradish
- 1 teaspoon hot sauce
- 1 garlic clove, finely minced
- 2 pounds fresh lump crabmeat, picked clean
- 20 butter crackers (such as Ritz brand), crushed
- 2 tablespoons Dijon mustard
- 1 cup mayonnaise
- 2 tablespoons freshly squeezed lemon juice
- 1 tablespoon salted butter, melted
- 1 tablespoon Worcestershire sauce
- 1 tablespoon Old Bay seasoning
- 2 teaspoons chopped fresh parsley
- 1 teaspoon ground mustard
- 2 eggs, beaten
- ¼ cup extra-virgin olive oil, divided

Directions:

1. For the remoulade:

2. In a small bowl, combine the mayonnaise, mustard, pickle relish, paprika, Cajun seasoning, horseradish, hot sauce, and garlic.
3. Refrigerate until ready to serve.
4. For the crab cakes:
5. Supply your smoker with wood pellets and follow the start-up procedure. Preheat, with the lid closed, to 375°F.
6. Spread the crabmeat on a foil-lined baking sheet and place over indirect heat on the grill, with the lid closed, for 30 minutes.
7. Remove from the heat and let cool for 15 minutes.
8. While the crab cools, combine the crushed crackers, Dijon mustard, mayonnaise, lemon juice, melted butter, Worcestershire sauce, Old Bay, parsley, ground mustard, and eggs until well incorporated.
9. Fold in the smoked crabmeat, then shape the mixture into 8 (1-inch-thick) crab cakes.
10. In a large skillet or cast-iron pan on the grill, heat 2 tablespoons of olive oil. Add half of the crab cakes, close the lid, and smoke for 4 to 5 minutes on each side, or until crispy and golden brown.
11. Remove the crab cakes from the pan and transfer to a wire rack to drain. Pat them to remove any excess oil.
12. Repeat steps 6 and 7 with the remaining oil and crab cakes.
13. Serve the crab cakes with the remoulade.

Baked Steelhead

Servings: 4
Cooking Time: 20 Minutes

Ingredients:

- 1 steelhead fillet
- 16-oz bottle Italian dressing
- 3 Tablespoon unsalted butter
- Blackened Saskatchewan Rub
- 1/2 shallot, minced
- 2 Clove garlic, minced
- 1 lemon

Directions:

1. Supply your smoker with wood pellets and follow the start-up procedure. Preheat the grill, with the lid closed, to 350° F.
2. Put butter in a small cast iron pan and place inside Traeger while preheating to soften. Pour Italian dressing over fillet to evenly coat.
3. Shake Traeger Blackened Saskatchewan rub evenly in a thin layer to cover dressing. Mince shallot and garlic.
4. Remove butter from pre-heated grill, careful as the cast iron will be hot. Stir in shallots and garlic.
5. Spread a nice thick layer of mixture on the top-middle of the fillet. Cut lemon into thin slices and place on top of butter mix.
6. Place steelhead on the grill and cook for 20 to 30 minutes, until fish is flaky, being careful not to over cook.
7. Remove fillet from the grill. Enjoy!

Delicious Crab Legs

Servings: 4
Cooking Time: 30 Minutes

Ingredients:

- 3 Pound crab legs, thawed and halved
- 1 Cup butter, melted
- 2 Tablespoon fresh lemon juice
- 2 Clove garlic, minced
- 1 Tablespoon Fin & Feather Rub or Old Bay Seasoning, plus more to taste
- lemon wedges
- Italian Parsley, chopped

Directions:

1. If the crab legs are too long to fit in the roasting pan, break them down at the joints by twisting, or use a heavy knife or cleaver. Split the shells open lengthwise. Transfer to the roasting pan.
2. Combine the butter, lemon juice and garlic; whisk to mix. Pour mixture over the crab legs, turning the legs to coat. Sprinkle the Traeger Fin & Feather Rub or Old Bay Seasoning over the legs.
3. Supply your smoker with wood pellets and follow the start-up procedure. Preheat the grill, with the lid closed, to 350° F.

4. Cook the crab legs, basting once or twice with the butter sauce from the bottom of the pan, for 20 to 30 minutes (depending on the size of the crab legs) or until warmed through. Grill: 350 °F

5. Transfer the crab legs to a large platter and divide the sauce and accumulated juices between 4 dipping bowls. Enjoy!

Grilled Lemon Shrimp Scampi

Servings: 4

Cooking Time: 6 Minutes

Ingredients:

- 1 ½ pounds medium shrimp, peeled and deveined
- ¼ cup olive oil
- ¼ cup lemon juice
- 3 tablespoons chopped fresh parsley
- 1 tablespoon minced garlic
- ground black pepper to taste
- ¼ teaspoon crushed red pepper flakes to taste

Directions:

1. In a large, non-reactive bowl, stir together the olive oil, lemon juice, parsley, garlic, and black pepper. Season with crushed red pepper, if desired. Add shrimp, and toss to coat. Marinate in the refrigerator for 30 minutes.
2. Supply your smoker with wood pellets and follow the start-up procedure. Preheat the grill, with the lid closed, to high heat.
3. Thread shrimp onto skewers, piercing once near the tail and once near the head. Discard any remaining marinade.
4. Lightly oil grill grate. Place the shrimp skewers on the grill grates.
5. Grill for 2 to 3 minutes per side, or until opaque.

Dijon-smoked Halibut

Servings: 6

Cooking Time: 120 Minutes

Ingredients:

- 4 (6-ounce) halibut steaks
- ¼ cup extra-virgin olive oil
- 2 teaspoons kosher salt
- 1 teaspoon freshly ground black pepper
- ½ cup mayonnaise
- ½ cup sweet pickle relish
- ¼ cup finely chopped sweet onion
- ¼ cup chopped roasted red pepper
- ¼ cup finely chopped tomato
- ¼ cup finely chopped cucumber
- 2 tablespoons Dijon mustard
- 1 teaspoon minced garlic

Directions:

1. Rub the halibut steaks with the olive oil and season on both sides with the salt and pepper. Transfer to a plate, cover with plastic wrap, and refrigerate for 4 hours.
2. Supply your smoker with wood pellets and follow the start-up procedure. Preheat, with the lid closed, to 200°F.
3. Remove the halibut from the refrigerator and rub with the mayonnaise.
4. Put the fish directly on the grill grate, close the lid, and smoke for 2 hours, or until opaque and an instant-read thermometer inserted in the fish reads 140°F.
5. While the fish is smoking, combine the pickle relish, onion, roasted red pepper, tomato, cucumber, Dijon mustard, and garlic in a medium bowl. Refrigerate the mustard relish until ready to serve.
6. Serve the halibut steaks hot with the mustard relish.

Grilled Lobster Tails With Smoked Paprika Butter

Servings: 4

Cooking Time: 10-12 Minutes

Ingredients:

- 4 lobster tails, each about 8 to 10oz (225 to 285g), thawed if frozen
- 3 lemons, 1 quartered lengthwise, 2 halved through their equators
- for the butter
- 1¼ cup unsalted butter, at room temperature
- 2 garlic cloves, peeled and finely minced
- 3 tbsp chopped fresh parsley
- 2 tbsp chopped fresh chives
- 1 tbsp freshly squeezed lemon juice
- 2 tsp finely chopped lemon zest

- 2 tsp smoked paprika
- 1 tsp coarse salt

Directions:

1. Supply your smoker with wood pellets and follow the start-up procedure. Preheat the grill, with the lid closed, to 450° F.
2. In a medium bowl, make the paprika butter by combining the ingredients. Beat with a wooden spoon until well blended.
3. Use a sharp, heavy knife or sturdy kitchen shears to cut lengthwise through the top shell of each lobster tail in a straight line toward the tail fin. Gently loosen the meat from the bottom shell and sides. Lift the meat through the slit you just made so the meat sits on top of the shell. Slip a lemon quarter underneath the meat (between the meat and the bottom shell) to keep it elevated. Spread 1 tablespoon of paprika butter on top of each lobster. Melt the remaining butter and keep it warm.
4. Place the lobster tails flesh side up and lemon halves cut sides down on the grate. Grill the lobsters until the flesh is white and opaque and the internal temperature of the lobster meat reaches 135 to 140°F (57 to 60°C), about 10 to 12 minutes, basting at least once with some of the melted butter. (Don't overcook or the lobster will become unpleasantly rubbery.)
5. Transfer the lobsters and the lemon halves to a platter. Divide the remaining melted butter between 4 ramekins before serving.

Garlic Blackened Salmon

Servings: 4
Cooking Time: 10 Minutes

Ingredients:

- 1 Tablespoon, Optional Cayenne Pepper
- 2 Cloves Garlic, Minced
- 2 Tablespoons Olive Oil
- 4 Tablespoons Sweet Rib Rub
- 2 Pound Salmon, Fillet, Scaled And Deboned

Directions:

1. Supply your smoker with wood pellets and follow the start-up procedure. Preheat the grill, with the lid closed, to 350° F.
2. Remove the skin from the salmon and discard. Brush the salmon on both sides with olive oil, then rub the salmon fillet with the minced garlic, cayenne pepper and Sweet Rib Rub.
3. Grill the salmon for 5 minutes on one side. Flip the salmon and then grill for another 5 minutes, or until the salmon reaches an internal temperature of 145°F. Remove from the grill and serve.

Whole Vermillion Red Snapper

Servings: 6
Cooking Time: 20 Minutes

Ingredients:

- 1 Whole Vermillion Red Snapper, scaled & gutted
- 4 Clove garlic, chopped
- 1 Whole lemon, thinly sliced
- 2 Sprig rosemary sprigs
- sea salt and freshly ground black pepper

Directions:

1. Supply your smoker with wood pellets and follow the start-up procedure. Preheat the grill, with the lid closed, to High heat.
2. Stuff the cavity of the fish with chopped garlic. Sprinkle the fish with sea salt, pepper, rosemary, and lemon.
3. Grill fish directly on the grill grate. Cook for 20-25 minutes. Serve. Enjoy!

Smoked Lobster Scampi

Servings: 2
Cooking Time: 30 Minutes

Ingredients:

- 1 Lobster Tail
- 1 Handful Pasta, Angel Hair
- 2 Tablespoon butter
- 1 Teaspoon garlic, minced
- 1/2 Teaspoon lemon juice
- 2 Teaspoon Parmesan cheese, grated
- 2 Tablespoon Sun Dried Tomato Pesto

- fresh parsley

Directions:

1. Supply your smoker with wood pellets and follow the start-up procedure. Preheat the grill, with the lid closed, to 180° F.
2. Use kitchen shears to cut along the top of the lobster on both sides to expose the meat. Place the lobster directly on the grill for 20-25 minutes, depending on the size of the lobster. Grill: 180 °F
3. While lobster smokes, cook pasta according to packaged directions.
4. After 20-25 minutes, take lobster off the grill and remove the meat from the tail. Cut meat into chunks.
5. While the pasta is boiling, melt butter over medium high heat. Once butter starts to brown, add the garlic and lobster chunks. Toss in pan a few times then add lemon and parmesan. Set aside.
6. When pasta has finished, place 1 tbsp of the sun dried tomato pesto on the bottom of a bowl or plate. Top with pasta, then finish with the lobster scampi. Garnish with parsley. Enjoy!

Cajun-blackened Shrimp

Servings: 4

Cooking Time: 20 Minutes

Ingredients:

- 1 pound peeled and deveined shrimp, with tails on
- 1 batch Cajun Rub
- 8 tablespoons (1 stick) butter
- ¼ cup Worcestershire sauce

Directions:

1. Supply your smoker with wood pellets and follow the start-up procedure. Preheat the grill, with the lid closed, to 450°F and place a cast-iron skillet on the grill grate. Wait about 10 minutes after your grill has reached temperature, allowing the skillet to get hot.
2. Meanwhile, season the shrimp all over with the rub.
3. When the skillet is hot, place the butter in it to melt. Once the butter melts, stir in the Worcestershire sauce.
4. Add the shrimp and gently stir to coat. Smoke-braise the shrimp for about 10 minutes per side, until opaque and cooked through. Remove the shrimp from the grill and serve immediately.

Honey Balsamic Salmon

Servings: 2

Cooking Time: 25 Minutes

Ingredients:

- 1 Medium salmon fillet
- Fin & Feather Rub
- 1/2 Cup balsamic vinegar
- 1 Tablespoon minced garlic
- 2 Tablespoon honey

Directions:

1. Season the fillet with the Traeger Fin & Feather Rub.
2. Make the glaze: Combine the vinegar, garlic and honey in a small saucepan. Simmer over medium heat until reduced by half. Usually 10 to 15 minutes. The glaze will be properly reduced when it coats the back of a spoon. Using a basting brush, coat the fillet with the glaze.
3. Supply your smoker with wood pellets and follow the start-up procedure. Preheat the grill, with the lid closed, to 350° F.
4. Arrange the salmon fillet on the grill grate. Grill for 25 to 30 minutes, or until the salmon is opaque and flakes easily with a fork. Grill: 350 °F
5. Transfer to a platter or plates and serve immediately. If desired, heat any remaining glaze to a boil and drizzle over top of the salmon. Enjoy!

PORK RECIPES

Smoked Bacon Roses

Servings: 2

Cooking Time: 60 Minutes

Ingredients:

- 1 Pack Bacon, Thick Cut
- 1 Dozen Roses, Fake

Directions:

1. Supply your smoker with wood pellets and follow the start-up procedure. Preheat the grill, with the lid open, to 225° F.
2. Roll each piece of bacon tightly, starting on the thicker side of the strip. Take a toothpick and skewer the middle of the bottom of the bacon roll to keep the bacon from unraveling. With a second toothpick, skewer the bacon roll so that the two toothpicks form an "X" at the bottom of the roll of bacon. Do this to every piece of bacon.
3. Place the bacon rolls directly on the grates of your preheated Grill and smoke for an hour, checking on them every 20 minutes.
4. While the bacon is smoking, rip the petals of the fake roses off of the steams.
5. Once the bacon is fully cooked, remove the toothpicks and pierce the bacon in the head of the steam (where the fake flowers once were). If the bacon isn't staying, you can break a toothpick in half and stick it in the tip of the steam, press firmly and try piercing the bacon again.
6. Place in a nice vase with some babies breath and gift to your Valentine.

Smoked Pork Tenderloin

Servings: 4

Cooking Time: 180 Minutes

Ingredients:

- 1/2 Cup apple juice
- 3 Tablespoon honey
- 3 Tablespoon Pork & Poultry Rub
- 1/4 Cup brown sugar
- 2 Tablespoon thyme leaves
- 1/2 Tablespoon black pepper
- 2 (1-1/2 lb) pork tenderloins, silverskin removed

Directions:

1. For the Marinade: In a large bowl, add the apple juice, honey (warmed), Traeger Pork & Poultry rub, brown sugar, thyme leaves and black pepper. Whisk to combine.
2. Add pork loins to the bowl with the marinade. Turn pork to coat and cover bowl with plastic wrap.
3. Transfer to the refrigerator and marinate for 2 to 3 hours.
4. Supply your smoker with wood pellets and follow the start-up procedure. Preheat the grill, with the lid closed, to 225° F.
5. Place the tenderloins directly on the grill grate and smoke until the internal temperature registers 145°F, about 2-1/2 to 3 hours. Grill: 225 °F Probe: 145 °F
6. Remove from grill and let rest 5 minutes before slicing. Enjoy!

Hawaiian Pulled Pork

Servings: 8-10

Cooking Time: 640 Minutes

Ingredients:

- 2 Cups Aloe Leaf Juice
- 1 Tsp Coriander, Ground
- 2 Tsp Cracked Pepper
- 1 Tsp Cumin
- Dash Of Salt
- 4-6 Garlic, Cloves
- 1 (3-Inch) Ginger, Fresh
- 1-2 Limes
- 4 Cups No Sodium Added Chicken Bone Broth
- ¼ Cup Olive Oil
- 4 Tsp Paprika
- 6-8 Lbs Pork Shoulder/Butt
- 1/2 Sweet Onion
- 2 Packets Truvia To Sweeten Above Aloe Juice

- 2 Tbs Or 2 Tbs Swerve Brown Sugar Truvia – Honey Substitute

Directions:

1. Supply your smoker with wood pellets and follow the start-up procedure. Preheat the grill, with the lid closed, to 300° F. Make sure your flame broiler is closed, you want to use indirect heat for this recipe.
2. Add all spices into a bowl (salt, paprika, cumin, coriander, pepper, onion powder if needed). Set bowl aside.
3. Grate the ginger into a separate bowl (wet ingredients bowl).
4. Mince or smash the garlic cloves into the same bowl.
5. Dice onion and add it to the ginger and garlic (if no onion sub onion powder).
6. Juice 1-2 limes and add to the "wet" ingredients bowl.
7. Add 4 cups chicken bone broth.
8. Add two cups aloe leaf juice w/lemon and add two packets Truvia to sweeten.
9. Add 1-2 tbsp Truvia honey substitute. Mix and set bowl aside.
10. Add the oil to your Cast Iron and coat the bottom and sides. Place the pork in the cast iron roasting pan.
11. Take your dry rub and coat the pork.
12. Pour the wet ingredients around the pork, into the Cast Iron Roasting Pan.
13. Cover the roasting pan with the lid and set it on your grill.
14. Check the pork every couple hours (basting if you prefer). When internal temperature reaches 195°F (after around 6 – 8 hours of cook time), it should easily start to pull apart. Don't pull apart the whole shoulder yet.
15. Remove the Roasting Pan from the grill and set aside to allow it to rest for 1 hour. Remove the lid to help speed cooling.
16. Once cooled, shred the pork into a separate bowl, removing the fat as you go.
17. If you want to add some of the marinade to the pork for additional flavor, make sure you skim the fat off the top first and discard.
18. Viola! Pair with fresh grilled veggies, delicious fruit or make tacos or salads! So many options for this type of protein.

Spiced Grilled Pork Chops

Servings: 4
Cooking Time: 30 Minutes

Ingredients:

- 3 Tbsp Black Peppercorns, Ground
- 1 Tbsp Coriander, Seed
- 1/4 Cup Cumin
- 1 - 2 Tsp Dry Rub
- 1 Tsp Olive Oil
- 4 Pork, Chop Bone-In
- 1 1/2 Tsp Salt
- 2 Tbsp Sugar

Directions:

1. Supply your smoker with wood pellets and follow the start-up procedure. Preheat the grill, with the lid open, to 450° F.
2. Combine the cumin seeds, whole black peppercorns, and coriander seeds in a cast iron skillet. Stir over medium heat for about 8 minutes until toasted. Let them cool slightly. Finely grind toasted spices in a blender and transfer to a small bowl, then mix in sugar and salt.
3. Rub the spices into the pork chops on both sides. Place cast iron skillet inside the grill. Once hot, add the olive oil to the skillet and coat the bottom. Sprinkle the pork chops with salt, and then add to the skillet. Make sure that each pork chop has enough space in between one another. Cook the chops for about 30 minutes. Once pork chops are fully cooked, turn off the grill, remove skillet, plate and enjoy!

3-2-1 Bbq Baby Back Ribs

Servings: 6
Cooking Time: 360 Minutes

Ingredients:

- 2 Rack baby back pork ribs
- 1/3 Cup yellow mustard
- 1/2 Cup apple juice, divided
- 1 Tablespoon Worcestershire sauce

- Pork & Poultry Rub
- 1/2 Cup dark brown sugar
- 1/3 Cup honey, warmed
- 1 Cup 'Que BBQ Sauce

Directions:

1. If your butcher has not already done so, remove the thin silverskin membrane from the bone-side of the ribs by working the tip of a butter knife or a screwdriver underneath the membrane over a middle bone. Use paper towels to get a firm grip, then tear the membrane off.
2. In a small bowl, combine the mustard, 1/4 cup of apple juice (reserve the rest) and the Worcestershire sauce. Spread the mixture thinly on both sides of the ribs and season with Traeger Pork & Poultry Rub.
3. Supply your smoker with wood pellets and follow the start-up procedure. Preheat the grill, with the lid closed, to 180° F.Smoke the ribs, meat-side up for 3 hours.
4. After the ribs have smoked for 3 hours, transfer them to a rimmed baking sheet and increase the grill temperature to 225°F.
5. Tear off four long sheets of heavy-duty aluminum foil. Top with a rack of ribs and pull up the sides to keep the liquid enclosed. Sprinkle half the brown sugar on the rack, then top with half the honey and half the remaining apple juice. Use a bit more apple juice if you want more tender ribs. Lay another piece of foil on top and tightly crimp the edges so there is no leakage. Repeat with the remaining rack of ribs.
6. Return the foiled ribs to the grill and cook for an additional 2 hours.
7. Carefully remove the foil from the ribs and brush the ribs on both sides with Traeger 'Que Sauce. Discard the foil. Arrange the ribs directly on the grill grate and continue to grill until the sauce tightens, 30 to 60 minutes more.
8. Let the ribs rest for a few minutes before serving. Enjoy!

Lynchburg Bacon

Servings: 4

Cooking Time: 20 Minutes

Ingredients:

- 1 Pound country-style bacon
- 1 Cup Tennessee whiskey, such as Jack Daniel's or apple juice
- 1 Tablespoon Pork & Poultry Rub
- 3/4 Cup all-purpose flour
- 1/3 Cup brown sugar
- 1 Teaspoon freshly ground black pepper

Directions:

1. Separate the bacon slices and place them into a large resealable bag.
2. Stir the Traeger Pork & Poultry Rub into the whiskey (or apple juice). Pour the whiskey over the bacon, massaging the bag to coat all the slices.
3. Set aside for at least 30 minutes.
4. On a piece of wax paper, sift together the flour, brown sugar and black pepper. Transfer to a second resealable bag.
5. Drain the bacon and add to the flour mixture a few slices at a time.
6. Shake the bag to coat each piece evenly, then arrange in a single layer on a baking pan.
7. Supply your smoker with wood pellets and follow the start-up procedure. Preheat the grill, with the lid closed, to 375° F.
8. Bake the bacon until it is golden brown and crisp, about 20 to 25 minutes. Enjoy! Grill: 375 °F

Spiced Orange Ribs

Servings: 4

Cooking Time: 180 Minutes

Ingredients:

- 1 Tablespoon Adobo Sauce
- 2 (2 1/2-Pound) Racks Baby Back Rib
- 1/3 Cup Firmly Packed Light Brown Sugar
- 1 Tablespoon Chili Powder
- 5 In Adobo Sauce Chipotle Peppers
- 1/3 Cup Leaves Cilantro, Fresh
- 1 Teaspoon Ground Cumin
- 1/4 Cup Honey
- 1/4 Cup Ketchup

- 2 Tablespoons Lime Juice
- 1 Cup Orange Juice, Fresh
- 5 Tablespoons Sweet Heat Rub

Directions:

1. First, make the barbecue sauce. Into the bowl of a blender, add ¾ cup of orange juice, cilantro, honey, ketchup, lime juice, 2 chipotles in adobo, adobo sauce, and 1 tablespoon of the Sweet Heat Rub. Place the lid on the blender and blend until completely smooth. Pour into a bowl, reserve ½ cup and set aside.
2. Prepare the ribs. Using the paper towels, pull the membrane off of the back of the ribs and discard. In the bowl of a blender, add the orange juice, brown sugar, chipotle peppers, chili powder, ground cumin, and Sweet Heat. Place the lid on the blender and blend until smooth. Pour this mixture over the ribs and massage into the meat. Place the ribs in the refrigerator and marinade for 8 hours.
3. Supply your smoker with wood pellets and follow the start-up procedure. Preheat the grill, with the lid open, to 275° F. Place the ribs, meat side up, and grill for 1 ½ hours. Baste the ribs with the reserved barbecue sauce, then BBQ for another 1 ½ hours, or until the ribs are extremely tender. Remove the ribs from the grill and serve with barbecue sauce.

Simple Smoked Baby Backs

Servings: 4-8
Cooking Time: 360 Minutes

Ingredients:

- 2 (2- or 3-pound) racks baby back ribs
- 2 tablespoons yellow mustard
- 1 batch Pork Rub

Directions:

1. Supply your smoker with wood pellets and follow the start-up procedure. Preheat the grill, with the lid closed, to 225°F.
2. Remove the membrane from the backside of the ribs. This can be done by cutting just through the membrane in an X pattern and working a paper towel between the membrane and the ribs to pull it off.
3. Coat the ribs on both sides with mustard and season them with the rub. Using your hands, work the rub into the meat.
4. Place the ribs directly on the grill grate and smoke until their internal temperature reaches between 190°F and 200°F.
5. Remove the racks from the grill and cut into individual ribs. Serve immediately.

Smoked Curry Ketchup Pork Ribs

Servings: 4
Cooking Time: 205 Minutes

Ingredients:

- 1 Tsp Chili Powder
- 1 Tbsp Curry Powder
- 1/2 Tsp Ground Mustard
- 2 Tsp Honey
- To Taste, Kansas City Barbecue Rub Seasoning
- 1 Cup Ketchup
- 2 Pork Back Rib Racks, Membrane Removed
- 2 Tsp Smoked Paprika
- 2 Tsp Worcestershire Sauce

Directions:

1. Supply your smoker with wood pellets and follow the start-up procedure. Preheat the grill, with the lid open, to 225° F. If using a gas or charcoal grill, set it up for low, indirect heat.
2. Place rib racks on a sheet tray, then season both sides with Kansas City Barbeque Rub. Transfer ribs to the grill and smoke for 1 hour.
3. Meanwhile, prepare the curry ketchup: In a mixing bowl, add ketchup, curry powder, smoked paprika, chili powder, ground mustard, Worcestershire, and honey and whisk to incorporate. Set aside.
4. Rotate the rib racks and increase temperature to 250 F. Cook for another hour, then remove the ribs from the grill and place on butcher paper. Brush ribs with sauce then wrap with paper.
5. Return ribs to the grill. Cook for one more hour, until tender.
6. Remove ribs from the grill, cut open the butcher paper, and baste with remaining curry ketchup. Place

racks back on the grill, increase the temperature to 275 F, then cook for an additional 15 minutes. Remove ribs from the grill, cut open the butcher paper, and baste with remaining curry ketchup. Place racks back on the grill, increase the temperature to 275 F, then cook for an additional 15 minutes.

7. Remove ribs from the grill, rest for 10 minutes, then slice and serve warm.

Grilled Dr. Pepper Ribs

Servings: 4

Cooking Time: 300 Minutes

Ingredients:

- Aluminum Foil
- 2 Racks Baby Back Ribs
- 1 Cup Bbq Sauce
- 1 Stick Butter, Melted
- 1/2 Cup Dark Brown Sugar
- 12 Oz Dr. Pepper Soda
- 1/4 Cup Sweet Rib Rub
- 1/4 Cup Yellow Mustard

Directions:

1. Supply your smoker with wood pellets and follow the start-up procedure. Preheat the grill, with the lid open, to 225° F. If using a gas or charcoal grill, set it up for low, indirect heat.
2. After the grill comes to temp, place the ribs directly on the grill grates, close the lid, and smoke for 2 hours.
3. In a glass measuring cup, whisk together butter, brown sugar, and 8 ounces of Dr. Pepper.
4. Pour half of the mixture on a foil-lined sheet tray.
5. Place ribs, meat-side down, on top of the mixture, then pour remaining mixture on the bone-side. Tent the sheet tray with foil, then return to the grill for another 2 hours.
6. Remove ribs from liquid and set meat-side up directly on the grill grate.
7. Whisk together BBQ sauce and 4 ounces of Dr. Pepper, then brush half of the sauce all over the ribs.
8. Increase temperature to 275°F and cook an additional 30 to 60 minutes until ribs are tender, and meat pulls away from the bones.
9. Place ribs on a sheet tray, allow to rest for 10 minutes, then slice and serve with remaining BBQ sauce.

3-2-1 Spare Ribs

Servings: 4

Cooking Time: 180 Minutes

Ingredients:

- 2 racks of St. Louis–cut pork spare ribs, each about 3lb (1.4kg)
- all-purpose barbecue rub
- 3 tbsp unsalted butter, cut into cubes
- 1 cup apple juice or apple cider
- low-carb barbecue sauce

Directions:

1. Supply your smoker with wood pellets and follow the start-up procedure. Preheat the grill, with the lid closed, to 225° F.
2. Place the ribs on a rimmed sheet pan and dust with the rub. Place the ribs bone side down on the grate and smoke for 3 hours.
3. Tear off 2 large sheets of heavy-duty aluminum foil. Place one rack of ribs bone side down on the foil and top with half the butter cubes. Place the second rack of ribs bone side down on the butter cubes and top with the remaining butter cubes.
4. Bring up all 4 sides of the foil and pour in the apple juice. Crimp the edges of the foil so the ribs are tightly enclosed. Place the foil package on the grate and smoke for 2 hours more.
5. Transfer the ribs to a workspace and carefully open the foil package. (Be careful of escaping steam.) Discard the foil and any accumulated juices. Brush the ribs on both sides with barbecue sauce. Place the ribs on the grate and smoke for 1 hour more to set the sauce and firm up the bark.
6. Transfer the ribs to a cutting board. Use a sharp knife to cut the slabs in half or into individual ribs. Serve immediately.

Maple Baked Ham

Servings: 8
Cooking Time: 60 Minutes

Ingredients:

- 1 (14-16 lb) ham
- whole cloves
- 1/2 Cup pure maple syrup
- 1/2 Cup brown sugar
- 1/2 Cup apple juice
- 1 Tablespoon brown mustard
- ground cinnamon
- ground ginger

Directions:

1. Supply your smoker with wood pellets and follow the start-up procedure. Preheat the grill, with the lid closed, to 325° F.
2. Score the ham all over in a diamond pattern, cutting to a depth of about 3/4 inch. Insert a clove into each intersection or "X" of the diamond pattern.
3. In a saucepan, stir together the maple syrup, brown sugar, apple juice, brown mustard, cinnamon and ginger and simmer over medium heat until brown sugar has melted. Set aside and keep warm.
4. Place ham in large roasting pan lined with aluminum foil. Place pan on grill and cook for 1-1/2 hours. Grill: 325 ˚F
5. Open grill and glaze ham with reserved mixture. Continue cooking for another 30 minutes or until a thermometer inserted into the thickest part of the meat reaches an internal temperatures of 135˚F. Grill: 325 ˚F Probe: 135 ˚F
6. Remove ham from grill and allow to rest covered with foil for 20 minutes before serving. Warm remaining sauce and serve with ham if desired. Enjoy!

Prosciutto Wrapped Dates With Marcona Almonds

Servings: 8
Cooking Time: 5 Minutes

Ingredients:

- 24 Whole medjool dates
- 1 Small container Marcona salted almonds
- 8 Ounce prosciutto
- 2 Tablespoon olive oil
- 2 limes, washed and dried for zesting
- honey, for serving
- flake salt, for serving

Directions:

1. Supply your smoker with wood pellets and follow the start-up procedure. Preheat the grill, with the lid closed, to 400° F.
2. Place a large cast iron pan into the grill to preheat. Using a small paring knife, cut a slit lengthwise across the top of each date. Remove the pit. Replace pits with 1 to 2 Marcona almonds, then press the dates back together with your fingers to seal.
3. Cut the prosciutto into 24 pieces lengthwise. To wrap each date, place one at the bottom of a strip of prosciutto, then roll the prosciutto around the date to cover, leaving a little bit of the date showing on each end.
4. Add 2 Tablespoons olive oil to the preheated cast iron pan. Place the dates in the pan and cook, searing the prosciutto on all sides, turning as needed, about 3 to 5 minutes total. When the prosciutto is crispy, carefully remove the pan from the grill.
5. Zest the limes over the pan so the citrus zest is absorbed into the olive oil and onto the dates. Place the dates on a serving platter. Sprinkle with flake salt, an additional drizzle of olive oil, honey and serve. Enjoy!

Smoked Chorizo & Arugula Pesto

Servings: 4
Cooking Time: 20 Minutes

Ingredients:

- 4 Cup Arugula, fresh
- 1 Clove garlic
- 1/2 Cup Parmesan cheese, grated
- 1/2 Cup pine nuts
- 1/4 Cup extra-virgin olive oil
- 1/4 Cup grapeseed oil
- sea salt
- freshly ground black pepper
- water

Directions:

1. To make the pesto, add arugula, garlic, cheese, and nuts to the bowl of a food processor or blender, and puree. As the processor is running, drizzle in the oil. Season the mixture with salt and pepper, to taste. If the pesto is too thick, thin it out with water.
2. Supply your smoker with wood pellets and follow the start-up procedure. Preheat the grill, with the lid closed, to 375° F.
3. Smoke the sausages whole for 20 minutes, or until it reaches an internal temperature of 170°F. Grill: 375 °F Probe: 170 °F
4. Let rest for 10 minutes, then cut the sausage links into large 1-1/2" chunks. Transfer the sausage to a platter and serve with dollops of the arugula pesto. Enjoy!

Cheese Bacon

Servings: 6-8

Cooking Time: 30 Minutes

Ingredients:

- 2 Teaspoon Applewood Bacon Seasoning
- 1 Pack Cheddar Cheese, Shredded
- 1 Pack Cream Cheese, Softened
- Cut In Half Lengthwise, Destemmed, Deveined And Deseeded Jalapeno Peppers
- 8 Strips Smoked Applewood Bacon, Cut In Half

Directions:

1. In a large bowl, combine cream cheese, Applewood Bacon seasoning and cheddar cheese. Mix until completely combined.
2. Using a spoon, fill the peppers with the cream cheese mixture. Wrap each pepper with a half slice of bacon and secure with a toothpick. Repeat until all jalapeno poppers are finished.
3. Supply your smoker with wood pellets and follow the start-up procedure. Preheat the grill, with the lid open, to 400° F. Place your jalapeno poppers on the grill basket and grill for 15-20 minutes, or until the bacon is cooked and crispy.
4. Serve and enjoy!

Pulled Pork Shoulder And Chicken

Servings: 6 - 8

Cooking Time: 300 Minutes

Ingredients:

- 1/3 Cup Apple Cider Vinegar
- 4 Cups Chicken Broth
- 1/3 Cup Ketchup
- 2 Tbsp Pulled Pork Seasoning
- 4 Lbs. Pork Shoulder, Bone In

Directions:

1. Supply your smoker with wood pellets and follow the start-up procedure. Preheat the grill, with the lid open, to 350° F. In a bowl, combine the chicken broth, ketchup, apple cider vinegar, and 1 tablespoon of Pulled Pork Seasoning. Whisk well to combine and set aside.
2. Generously season the pork shoulder with the remaining 3 tablespoons of Pulled Pork Seasoning on all sides of the pork shoulder, then place on the grill and sear on all sides until golden brown, about 10 minutes.
3. Remove the pork shoulder from the grill and place in the disposable aluminum pan. Pour the chicken broth mixture over the pork shoulder. It should come about 1/3 to ½ way up the side of the pork shoulder. Cover the top of the pan tightly with aluminum foil.
4. Reduce the temperature of your grill to 250°F. Place the foil pan on the grill and grill for four to five hours, or until the pork is tender and falling off the bone.
5. Remove the pork from the grill and allow to cool slightly. Drain the liquid from the pan, reserving about a cup, then shred the pork and cover with the reserved liquid. Serve and enjoy!

Smoked Spare Ribs

Servings: 4-8

Cooking Time: 360 Minutes

Ingredients:

- 2 (2- or 3-pound) racks spare ribs
- 2 tablespoons yellow mustard
- 1 batch Sweet Brown Sugar Rub
- ¼ cup The Ultimate BBQ Sauce

Directions:

1. Supply your smoker with wood pellets and follow the start-up procedure. Preheat the grill, with the lid closed, to 225°F.
2. Remove the membrane from the backside of the ribs. This can be done by cutting just through the membrane in an X pattern and working a paper towel between the membrane and the ribs to pull it off.
3. Coat the ribs on both sides with mustard and season with the rub. Using your hands, work the rub into the meat.
4. Place the ribs directly on the grill grate and smoke until their internal temperature reaches between 190°F and 200°F.
5. Baste both sides of the ribs with barbecue sauce.
6. Increase the grill's temperature to 300°F and continue to cook the ribs for 15 minutes more.
7. Remove the racks from the grill, cut them into individual ribs, and serve immediately.

Pineapple-pepper Pork Kebabs

Servings: 12-15
Cooking Time: 240 Minutes

Ingredients:

- 1 (20-ounce) bottle hoisin sauce
- ½ cup Sriracha
- ¼ cup honey
- ¼ cup apple cider vinegar
- 2 tablespoons canola oil
- 2 teaspoons minced garlic
- 2 teaspoons onion powder
- 1 teaspoon ground ginger
- 1 teaspoon salt
- 1 teaspoon freshly ground black pepper
- 2 pounds thick-cut pork chops or pork loin, cut into 2-inch cubes
- 10 ounces fresh pineapple, cut into chunks
- 1 red onion, cut into wedges
- 1 bag mini sweet peppers, tops removed and seeded
- 12 metal or wooden skewers (soaked in water for 30 minutes if wooden)

Directions:

1. In a small bowl, stir together the hoisin, Sriracha, honey, vinegar, oil, minced garlic, onion powder, ginger, salt, and black pepper to create the marinade. Reserve ¼ cup for basting.
2. Toss the pork cubes, pineapple chunks, onion wedges, and mini peppers in the remaining marinade. Cover and refrigerate for at least 1 hour or up to 4 hours.
3. Supply your smoker with wood pellets and follow the start-up procedure. Preheat, with the lid closed, to 450°F.
4. Remove the pork, pineapple, and veggies from the marinade; do not rinse. Discard the marinade.
5. Use the double-skewer technique to assemble the kebabs (see Tip below). Thread each of 6 skewers with a piece of pork, a piece of pineapple, a piece of onion, and a sweet mini pepper, making sure that the skewer goes through the left side of the ingredients. Repeat the threading on each skewer two more times. Double-skewer the kebabs by sticking another 6 skewers through the right side of the ingredients.
6. Place the kebabs directly on the grill, close the lid, and smoke for 10 to 12 minutes, turning once. They are done when a meat thermometer inserted in the pork reads 160°F.

Barbecued Tenderloin

Servings: 4-6
Cooking Time: 30 Minutes

Ingredients:

- 2 (1-pound) pork tenderloins
- 1 batch Sweet and Spicy Cinnamon Rub

Directions:

1. Supply your smoker with wood pellets and follow the start-up procedure. Preheat the grill, with the lid closed, to 350°F.
2. Generously season the tenderloins with the rub. Using your hands, work the rub into the meat.
3. Place the tenderloins directly on the grill grate and smoke until their internal temperature reaches 145°F.
4. Remove the tenderloins from the grill and let them rest for 5 to 10 minutes, before thinly slicing and serving.

Delicious Cajun Broil

Servings: 8

Cooking Time: 60 Minutes

Ingredients:

- 2 Tablespoon olive oil
- 2 Pound red potatoes
- Old Bay Seasoning
- 6 Corn Ears, each cut into thirds
- 2 Pound smoked kielbasa sausage
- 3 Pound large shrimp with tails, deveined
- 2 Tablespoon butter

Directions:

1. Supply your smoker with wood pellets and follow the start-up procedure. Preheat the grill, with the lid closed, to 450° F.
2. Drizzle potatoes with half of the olive oil and lightly season with Old Bay seasoning. Place directly on the grill grate. Roast 20 minutes or until tender. Grill: 450 ˚F
3. Drizzle corn with remaining olive oil and lightly season with Old Bay seasoning. Place corn and kielbasa directly on the grill grate next to the potatoes. Roast 15 minutes. Grill: 450 ˚F
4. Season shrimp with Old Bay seasoning. Place shrimp directly on grill grate next to the rest of the items and cook for 10 minutes, or until bright pink and cooked through. Grill: 450 ˚F
5. Remove everything from the grill and transfer to a large bowl. Add butter and season with more Old Bay seasoning to taste. Toss to coat and serve immediately. Enjoy!

Apple Bacon Smoked Ham

Servings: 8-12

Cooking Time: 120 Minutes

Ingredients:

- 1 1/2 Cup Apple Cider
- 3 Tablespoon Apple Cider Vinegar
- 2 Apples
- 1 Lb. Bacon
- 2 Tablespoon Butter, Unsalted
- 2 Tablespoon Cornstarch
- 3 Tablespoon Dijon Mustard
- Smoke Infused Applewood Bacon Rub
- 1/2 Cup Pure Maple Syrup
- 1 Large Bone In Spiral Cut Smoked Ham
- 2 Tablespoon Yellow Mustard

Directions:

1. Supply your smoker with wood pellets and follow the start-up procedure. Preheat the grill, with the lid open, to 250° F.
2. Smoke the bacon directly on the grates for 25 minutes, flipping at the 15-minute mark. Thinly slice the apples while the bacon cooks. Once the bacon is done, set your temperature down to 225 degrees F.
3. Put the spiral-sliced ham into an aluminum foil roasting pan. Start by adding apple into the first slice and every other slice after that. Fill in all other slices with the bacon strips. Season with Smoke Infused Applewood Bacon Rub. Add any extra apple cider to the bottom of the pan for added flavor.
4. Place ham in the grill for 60 minutes.
5. Meanwhile, in a saucepan, whisk together apple cider, maple syrup, apple cider vinegar, Dijon mustard, yellow mustard, cornstarch and Smoke Infused Applewood Bacon Rub. Bring to a boil. Reduce to a simmer, stirring often, until the sauce has thickened and reduced (approximately 15-20 minutes). Stir in the butter until it has completely melted. Glaze should thicken more as it stands.
6. After 60 minutes, add carrots into the roasting pan and glaze the entire ham. Glaze again every 30 minutes until done.
7. Remove ham from grill and allow to rest covered with foil for 20 minutes before serving.
8. Serve with remaining warmed up sauce if desired.

Bbq Bacon-wrapped Water Chestnuts

Servings: 6

Cooking Time: 35 Minutes

Ingredients:

- 1 Pound bacon
- 2 Can Water Chestnuts
- 1/3 Cup brown sugar
- 1/3 Cup mayonnaise

- 1/3 Cup Texas Spicy BBQ Sauce

Directions:

1. Supply your smoker with wood pellets and follow the start-up procedure. Preheat the grill, with the lid closed, to 350° F.
2. Line a rimmed baking sheet with aluminum foil. Cut each piece of bacon into thirds or halves. Wrap each water chestnut with a piece of bacon large enough to encircle it and secure the bacon with a toothpick.
3. Arrange the bacon-wrapped chestnuts in a single layer on the prepared baking sheet. Bake for 20 minutes. Leave the grill on. Grill: 350 °F
4. Meanwhile, whisk the mayonnaise, brown sugar, and Traeger Spicy Barbecue Sauce in a mixing bowl. Pour the sauce over the chestnuts and return to the grill to bake for 10 to 15 minutes more. Transfer to a platter for serving. Enjoy!

Spicy Bacon Wrapped Grilled Chicken Skewers

Servings: 6

Cooking Time: 20 Minutes

Ingredients:

- 1/2 Cup Ranch
- 1/2 Teaspoon garlic powder
- 2 Tablespoon Chile Sauce
- 1/2 Teaspoon dried oregano
- 16 Ounce Chicken Breast, cubed
- 1 Whole red onion, sliced
- 1 Whole green bell peppers, sliced
- 8 Strips Bacon, sliced

Directions:

1. In a large bowl, mix together ranch, garlic powder, oregano, and chile sauce. Add in cubed chicken, tossing to thoroughly coat. Allow the chicken to marinate in fridge for 1 to 3 hours.
2. Supply your smoker with wood pellets and follow the start-up procedure. Preheat the grill, with the lid closed, to High heat.
3. Begin assembling Traeger skewers: slide on a wedge of onion, a pepper, a slice of bacon, and chicken. Continue to alternate bacon and chicken, so the bacon weaves around the chicken pieces. Finish off each skewer with a pepper and onion wedge. Be sure to not overcrowd skewer, to allow faster and even cooking. Repeat with all skewers.
4. Place the skewers on the grill grate, keeping a piece of foil under the end of the skewers to prevent them from burning and to make turning them easier.
5. Cook for approximately 5 minutes per side, doing a quarter-turn each time, for a total of 20 minutes, or until the chicken reaches an internal temperature of 165°F. Remove skewers. Enjoy! Grill: 450 °F

Maple Syrup Bacon Wrapped Tenderloin

Servings: 5

Cooking Time: 30 Minutes

Ingredients:

- 1 Package Bacon, Thick Cut
- 1/4 Cup Maple Syrup
- 2 Tbsp Olive Oil
- 3 Tbsp Competition Smoked Rub
- 1 Trimmed With Silver Skin Removed Pork, Tenderloin

Directions:

1. Lay the strips of bacon out flat, with each strip slightly overlapping the other.
2. Sprinkle the pork tenderloin with 1 tablespoon of the Competition Smoked Rub and lay in the center.
3. Wrap with bacon over the tenderloin and tuck in the ends.
4. In a small bowl, mix the olive oil, maple syrup and remaining seasoning together and brush onto the wrapped tenderloin.
5. Supply your smoker with wood pellets and follow the start-up procedure. Preheat the grill, with the lid open, to 350° F.
6. When the grill is ready, place your tenderloin on the grill and cook, turning, for 15 minutes.
7. Increase the grill temperature to 400°F and grill for another 15 minutes or until the internal temperature is 145°F. Serve and enjoy!

Grilled Mac And Cheese Quesadillas

Servings: 4
Cooking Time: 75 Minutes

Ingredients:

- 1/2 Lb Bacon, Sliced And Halved
- 3 Tbsp Butter
- 1 Cup Cheddar Cheese, Shredded
- 1 Cup Cheddar Jack Cheese, Shredded
- 4 Oz Cream Cheese
- 2 Tbsp Flour
- 4 Flour Tortillas
- 1 1/2 Tsp Hickory Bacon Seasoning
- 8 Oz Macaroni, Cooked Al Dente
- 1 Tsp Mustard Powder
- 1/2 Cup Parmesan Cheese, Grated
- 1 2/3 Cups Whole Milk

Directions:

1. Fire up your Platinum Series KC Combo and with the lid open, set your temperature to SMOKE mode.
2. Supply your smoker with wood pellets and follow the start-up procedure. Preheat the grill, with the lid open, to 225° F. If using a gas or charcoal grill, set it up for low, indirect heat.
3. Set a cast iron skillet on the grill. Melt the butter then whisk in flour until smooth. Cook for 1 minute, then whisk in Hickory Bacon and mustard powder.
4. Pour in milk and bring to a boil, whisking constantly. When sauce begins to thicken, whisk in the cream cheese until smooth, then add cheddar and parmesan and stir until melted
5. Add the pasta to the cheese sauce. Close the lid, and smoke for 1 hour.
6. Fire up your griddle to medium-low flame, and cook bacon, turning occasionally, until desired crispness is reached, about 3 to 5 minutes.
7. Set bacon aside, then place 4 tortillas on the griddle. Sprinkle cheddar jack cheese on top of the tortilla, a heaping scoop of smoked mac 'n cheese on one side, topped with bacon.
8. Fold over the tortilla and press down gently with a spatula. Remove from the griddle, rest for 2 minutes, then cut into wedges, and serve warm with an extra side of smoked mac 'n cheese.

Onion Pork Shoulder

Servings: 8 - 10
Cooking Time: 240 Minutes

Ingredients:

- Aluminum Foil
- 1 Diced Apple
- 1 Cup Broth, Chicken
- 2 Tbsp Butter, Salted
- 1 Diced Onion
- 1 Pork Shoulder Or Pork Butt Roast
- 1 Box Or Bag Of Stovetop Stuffing Mix
- Champion Chicken Seasoning

Directions:

1. Prepare the pork shoulder. Place the pork shoulder on the cutting board, and with a sharp knife, trim any very fatty sections of the pork shoulder and remove. Then, butterfly the shoulder. Beginning on one side, carefully cut a slit horizontally into one side of the pork shoulder and carefully continue to slice almost all the way to the right side, rolling the shoulder as you cut, unfolding the meat like a book, until the pork shoulder is one long strip.
2. Began to make the stuffing by using a medium sized pan and adding 2 tbsp of salted butter to the pan. Add in the onion and apple and let cook for about 5 minutes making sure to stir in between. Add 2 tbsp of Champion Chicken Seasoning. Add the 1 cup of chicken broth followed by a bag of stuffing mix. Let reduce and mix together very well and remove from heat. Transfer to a bowl and set aside.
3. Once the pork shoulder is butterflied, place some stuff on the roast making sure to leave enough space to roll and tie the roast as well.
4. Starting on one end of the pork shoulder, roll the pork shoulder up into a tight spiral, and set onto the cutting board, seam side down. Cut four even lengths of butcher's twine, and wiggle under the pork shoulder, two inches apart from each other. Tie tightly to hold the roast together and place on a sheet pan.

5. Supply your smoker with wood pellets and follow the start-up procedure. Preheat the grill, with the lid open, to 250° F. If you're using a gas or charcoal grill, set it up for medium low heat. Place the aluminum pan in the center of the grill and cook for 3-4 hours, or until the temperature of the pork shoulder reaches an internal temperature of 180°F and is very tender.
6. Remove the pork shoulder from the grill and allow to rest for 15 minutes, then slice and serve.

Bbq Pork Short Ribs

Servings: 4
Cooking Time: 360 Minutes

Ingredients:

- 2 Pork Short Rib Racks With At Least 1 1/2-2" of Meat On Bone
- Pork & Poultry Rub

Directions:

1. Clean and trim short ribs. Season generously on all sides with Traeger Pork and Poultry rub.
2. Supply your smoker with wood pellets and follow the start-up procedure. Preheat the grill, with the lid closed, to 250° F.
3. Place ribs directly on the grill grate and cook for 4-6 hours or until the internal temperature reaches 202-204°F when an instant read thermometer is inserted in the thickest part of meat. Spritz with apple juice every hour if desired. Grill: 250 °F Probe: 202 °F
4. Remove from grill and allow to rest 10 minutes before slicing. Cut into individual ribs and serve with your favorite sides. Enjoy!

Hanging St. Louis-style Grilled Ribs

Servings: 4
Cooking Time: 270 Minutes

Ingredients:

- 1 1/3 Cup Apple Juice
- 1 2/3 Cup BBQ Sauce, Divided
- Pulled Pork Rub
- 4 Half Racks Spare Ribs, St. Louis Style

Directions:

1. Supply your smoker with wood pellets and follow the start-up procedure. Preheat the grill, with the lid open, to 250° F. If using a gas or charcoal grill, set it up for low, indirect heat.
2. Using a sharp knife, remove the back membrane from the rib racks and pat dry with paper towel. Cut rib racks in half, then season generously with Pulled Pork Rub.
3. Insert a hanging hook under the top rib, then transfer racks to the smoking cabinet. Smoke for 2 ½ hours.
4. Remove ribs from the smoking cabinet and set on heavy duty foil. Mix together ⅔ cup BBQ sauce and ⅓ cup apple juice, then brush thinned BBQ sauce on both sides of ribs. Pour ¼ cup of apple juice around each of the ribs. Fold over foil, then transfer to the grill, meat side down. Increase temperature to 300° F and continue cooking for an additional 2 hours.
5. Remove ribs from the grill, baste with BBQ, then return to the grill and cook for another 10 to 15 minutes. Allow to rest for 15 minutes, then slice and serve hot.

Smoked Pork Spare Ribs

Servings: 8
Cooking Time: 240 Minutes

Ingredients:

- 2 Rack (6 lb) pork spare ribs, trimmed
- 3 Tablespoon Pork & Poultry Rub
- 1 Cup apple juice, cider or beer
- 9 Ounce BBQ Sauce

Directions:

1. Supply your smoker with wood pellets and follow the start-up procedure. Preheat the grill, with the lid closed, to 250° F.
2. If your butcher hasn't done so already, remove the silver-skin on the back of the ribs and trim off any excess fat.
3. Season the ribs on all sides with Traeger Pork & Poultry rub.
4. Arrange the racks of spare ribs on the grill grate, bone-side down and cook for 3 to 4 hours. After the first

hour, spray the ribs with apple juice. Continue spraying every hour after that with apple juice. Grill: 250 ˚F

5. Start checking the temp after 2 hours. The finished internal temperature should be 203°F, about 3 to 4 hours. Grill: 250 ˚F Probe: 203 ˚F

6. When the internal temperature registers 203°F, brush the ribs on all sides with Traeger BBQ sauce of your choice. Return ribs to the grill and cook for an additional 30 to 60 minutes to tighten the sauce.

7. To serve, cut each slab in half or into individual ribs and serve with additional BBQ sauce on the side. Enjoy!

Smoked Porchetta With Italian Salsa Verde

Servings: 8-12

Cooking Time: 180 Minutes

Ingredients:

- 3 Tablespoon dried fennel seed
- 2 Tablespoon red pepper flakes
- 2 Tablespoon sage, minced
- 1 Tablespoon rosemary, minced
- 3 Clove garlic, minced
- As Needed lemon zest
- As Needed orange zest
- To Taste salt and pepper
- 6 Pound Pork Belly, skin on
- As Needed salt and pepper
- 1 Whole shallot, thinly sliced
- 6 Tablespoon parsley, minced
- 2 Tablespoon freshly minced chives
- 1 Tablespoon Oregano, fresh
- 3 Tablespoon white wine vinegar
- 1/2 Teaspoon kosher salt
- 3/4 Cup olive oil
- 1/2 Teaspoon Dijon mustard
- As Needed fresh lemon juice

Directions:

1. Prepare herb mixture: In a medium bowl, mix together fennel seeds, red pepper flakes, sage, rosemary, garlic, citrus zest, salt and pepper.
2. Place pork belly skin side up on a clean work surface and score in a crosshatch pattern. Flip the pork belly over and season flesh side with salt, pepper and half of the herb mixture.
3. Place trimmed pork loin in the center of the belly and rub with remaining herb mixture. Season with salt and pepper.
4. Roll the pork belly around the loin to form a cylindrical shape and tie tightly with kitchen twine at 1" intervals.
5. Season the outside with salt and pepper and transfer to refrigerator, uncovered and let air dry overnight.
6. When ready to cook, start the smoker grill and set to Smoke.
7. Fit a rimmed baking sheet with a rack and place the pork on the rack seam side down.
8. Place the pan directly on the grill grate and smoke for 1 hour.
9. Increase the grill temperature to 325 degrees F and roast until the internal temperature of the meat reaches 135 degrees, about 2 1/2 hours. If the exterior begins to burn before the desired internal temperature is reached, tent with foil.
10. Remove from grill and let stand 30 minutes before slicing.
11. To make the Italian salsa verde: Combine shallot, parsley, chives, vinegar, oregano and salt in a medium bowl. Whisk in olive oil then stir in mustard and lemon juice.
12. Drizzle slices with Italian salsa verde and enjoy!

Anytime Pork Roast

Servings: 6

Cooking Time: 360 Minutes

Ingredients:

- 6 (4-6 lb) pork roast
- Pork & Poultry Rub
- 1/4 Cup apple juice

Directions:

1. Supply your smoker with wood pellets and follow the start-up procedure. Preheat the grill, with the lid closed, to 180° F.
2. Sprinkle pork roast with Traeger Pork & Poultry Rub on all sides. Place roast in an aluminum foil pan and

pour apple juice on top. Place roast in the grill and smoke the for 1 hour. Grill: 180 °F

3. Remove roast from grill and increase Traeger temperature to 275°F and preheat, lid closed 15 minutes. Grill: 275 °F

4. Cook roast for an additional 2 hours, uncovered. After two hours, wrap pan with aluminum foil and return to grill to cook for an additional 3 hours or until the internal temperature reaches 205°F. Grill: 275 °F Probe: 205 °F

5. Allow to rest for 10 minutes before serving. Serve with roasted onions, potatoes, carrots and apples. Enjoy!

Cheese Potato Stuffed Pork Chops

Servings: 4

Cooking Time: 45 Minutes

Ingredients:

- 4 Bone-In Pork Chops
- 1 Package Frozen Shredded Hash Browns, Thawed
- 1 Tbsp Parsley, Minced Fresh
- Pulled Pork Seasoning
- 1 Cup Shredded Cheddar Cheese
- ¼ Cup Sour Cream
- White Onion, Diced

Directions:

1. Place the pork chops on a flat work surface. Using a sharp knife, cut a pocket into the side of each pork chop, being careful not to cut all the way through the sides of the chop. Season the pork chops generously on both sides with Pulled Pork Seasoning.
2. In a large mixing bowl, mix together the hash browns, shredded cheddar, sour cream, diced onion, parsley, and 1 tablespoon of Pulled Pork seasoning. Stuff each pork chop with about ¼ cup of the potato filling. Use a toothpick to securely close the chop if needed.
3. Supply your smoker with wood pellets and follow the start-up procedure. Preheat the grill, with the lid open, to 350° F. If you're using a gas or charcoal grill, set it up for medium heat. Insert a temperature probe into the thickest part of one of the chops and place the meat on the grill. Grill the chops on one side for 10-15 minutes, then flip and grill for another 10-15, or until the internal temperature of the chops reach 145°F.
4. Remove the chops from the grill, take the toothpicks out of the meat, and serve immediately.

Sweet And Spicy Pork Roast

Servings: 2

Cooking Time: 60 Minutes

Ingredients:

- 2 Pound Pork, Loins
- 2/3 habanero peppers, seeded
- 2/3 Can coconut milk
- 1/3 Teaspoon Chinese five-spice powder
- 2/3 Tablespoon paprika
- 2/3 Teaspoon curry powder
- 2/3 Tablespoon lime juice
- 2/3 Tablespoon garlic, minced
- 2/3 Teaspoon freshly grated ginger

Directions:

1. Mix all ingredients, except pork, in a bowl. Rub the mixture onto your pork and let it sit overnight.
2. Supply your smoker with wood pellets and follow the start-up procedure. Preheat the grill, with the lid closed, to 300° F.
3. Place pork on hot grill. Cook for 1 to 1-1/2 hours, or until it reaches an internal temperature of 145-150°F for medium-rare to medium. Enjoy! Grill: 300 °F Probe: 150 °F

The Dan Patrick Show Baked Chili Cheese Dog Cups

Servings: 6

Cooking Time: 30 Minutes

Ingredients:

- 2 Cup Chili With Beans, Your Choice
- 2 Olympia Provisions Franks
- 1 Can Pillsbury Grands Buttermilk Biscuits

Directions:

1. Supply your smoker with wood pellets and follow the start-up procedure. Preheat the grill, with the lid closed, to 350° F.

2. Combine chili and sliced hot dogs in a medium bowl. Open biscuits and separate into 8 biscuits.
3. Place each biscuit in a lightly greased muffin tin and press down on the sides and bottom to create a cup. Spoon a little bit of the chili hot dog mixture into each cup.
4. Place muffin tin directly on the grill grate and cook 30 minutes until biscuits are golden brown and chili is warmed. Grill: 350 °F
5. Let chili cups cool for five minutes before unmolding. Finish with your choice of toppings. Enjoy!

Delicious Roasted Easter Ham

Servings: 8
Cooking Time: 60 Minutes

Ingredients:

- 1 (6-7 lb) bone-in ham
- 1 Cup Sweet & Heat BBQ Sauce
- 2 Cup brown sugar
- 1/2 Cup pineapple juice

Directions:

1. Supply your smoker with wood pellets and follow the start-up procedure. Preheat the grill, with the lid closed, to 225° F.
2. Place ham in grill and cook for 60 minutes. Grill: 225 °F
3. While the ham is cooking, mix together the Traeger Sweet & Heat BBQ Sauce, brown sugar and pineapple juice.
4. Glaze ham with the sauce every 10 minutes during the last 30 minutes. Remove ham from grill and serve. Enjoy!

Asian-style Pork Tenderloin

Servings: 6
Cooking Time: 15 Minutes

Ingredients:

- 2 Whole Pork Tenderloin, 8-10 oz each
- 2 Tablespoon canola oil
- 2 Tablespoon Sambai Oelek
- 1 Teaspoon sesame oil
- 1 Teaspoon garlic, minced
- 1 Teaspoon fresh ginger
- 1 Teaspoon fish sauce
- 1 Teaspoon soy sauce
- 1/4 Cup brown sugar

Directions:

1. Use a sharp paring knife to remove the silver skin of the pork tenderloin.
2. Combine all the ingredients together. Cover the tenderloins in the mixture and allow them to marinate in the refrigerator for 30 minutes.
3. Supply your smoker with wood pellets and follow the start-up procedure. Preheat the grill, with the lid closed, to 450° F.
4. Place the loins towards the very front of the grill; turn periodically until there are dark grill marks all around. Transfer them to the middle of the grill to finish cooking. Cook for an addition 7-10 minutes for a medium rare tenderloin. When they are done cooking, remove them from the grill and let them rest for 10 minutes before slicing. Enjoy!

Competition Style Bbq Pulled Pork

Servings: 8
Cooking Time: 600 Minutes

Ingredients:

- 1 (8-10 lb) bone-in pork butt
- 1 Cup Pork & Poultry Rub, divided
- 2 3/4 Cup apple juice, divided
- 1/4 Cup Butcher BBQ Pork Injection
- meat injector

Directions:

1. Supply your smoker with wood pellets and follow the start-up procedure. Preheat the grill, with the lid closed, to 225° F.
2. While the grill heats up, trim excess fat from pork.
3. In a small bowl, mix together half the Traeger Pork & Poultry Rub, 2 cups apple juice and butchers pork injection. Thoroughly inject pork butt throughout using an injector.
4. Season the pork with a layer of Traeger Pork & Poultry Rub. Let pork rest for 20 minutes.

5. Place pork on the grill and cook for 4-1/2 to 5-1/2 hours. After 4-1/2 hours, check the internal temperature of the pork. It should be between 155-165°F. If not, check again in 30 minutes. Grill: 225 °F Probe: 155 °F
6. When the temperature reaches 155-165°F, wrap the pork in a double layer of heavy duty aluminum foil. Pour 3/4 cup reserved apple juice in a foil packet with the pork and place back on the grill.
7. Turn the grill temperature up to 250°F and cook for another 3 to 4 hours. Check the internal temperature after 3 hours. The desired temperature is between 204°F and 206°F in the thickest part of the pork. If the pork is not to temperature, check back every 30 minutes until it reaches 204-206°F. The entire cook time should be between 8-10 hours depending on the size of the pork. Grill: 250 °F Probe: 204 °F
8. Remove pork from grill and open the foil packet to vent for 10 minutes. Seal back up and let rest for 45 minutes to one hour.
9. After resting, pour the liquid out of the foil and separate the fat from the broth using a fat separator. Remove the bone and pull the meat. Add 2 cups of the broth to the pulled meat. Add extra broth, if necessary, to achieve desired moisture level. Enjoy!

Egg Sausage Casserole

Servings: 12
Cooking Time: 60 Minutes

Ingredients:

- 12 sausage links
- 30 oz hash browns, thawed
- 1 1/2 c. marble jack cheese, shredded
- 1/2 tsp pepper
- 12 large eggs
- 1 tsp salt
- 1/2 c. yellow onion, chopped
- 1 c. milk

Directions:

1. Supply your smoker with wood pellets and follow the start-up procedure. Preheat the grill, with the lid closed, to 350° F.
2. Grill sausage links on the preheated grill for 10-15 minutes or until heated through.
3. Remove the sausage links from grill and cut them into 1-inch pieces.
4. Spray a 9" ×13" tin pan with non-stick spray. Spread out hash browns on bottom of pan. Top with sausage pieces.
5. Combine eggs, salt, pepper, 1 c. cheese, onions, and milk in a bowl. Pour the mixture over sausage and hash browns. Then top with the remaining 1/2 c. of cheese.
6. Transfer the tin pan to the grill grate, and grill at 350 °F for 45 minutes or until the middle is set.

Bbq Baby Back Ribs With Bacon Pineapple Glaze By Scott Thomas

Servings: 4
Cooking Time: 180 Minutes

Ingredients:

- 2 Rack baby back ribs
- 1 As Needed salt and pepper
- 1 As Needed Your Favorite Spicy Rub
- 6 Slices bacon
- 6 Fluid Ounce pineapple juice
- 1 Teaspoon garlic, minced
- 2 Tablespoon honey

Directions:

1. Remove the membrane from the bone side of the ribs and apply the salt, pepper and rub to that side. Flip the ribs over and season the meat side.
2. Supply your smoker with wood pellets and follow the start-up procedure. Preheat the grill, with the lid closed, to 350° F.
3. While the grill heats up, cook the bacon in a frying pan. As the bacon is cooking, pour the pineapple juice, garlic and honey into an oven safe pot.
4. Remove the bacon from the grease and let the pan and bacon fat cool down. After the pan has cooled for a while, pour the bacon grease in with the pineapple juice, garlic and honey and stir to combine.
5. Place the ribs and the pot on the grill and close the lid. After an hour, the slurry will have reduced down a bit and can be applied to the ribs. Slather the ribs with

the reduction every 15 minutes. When the bones peek out about a quarter to a third of an inch, the ribs are done which is about 2 hours and 15 minutes. Grill: 350 ˚F

6. For fall off the bone ribs, go another 30-45 minutes, continuing to glaze every 15 minutes. Grill: 350 ˚F

7. The sweet and savory of the reduction will temper the heat of the spicy rub forming an outstanding and complex blend of flavors. Enjoy!

Bourbon Chile Glazed Ham

Servings: 8 – 10

Cooking Time: 90 Minutes

Ingredients:

- ¼ Cup Apple Cider Vinegar
- 2 Cups Bourbon
- 1 Cup Brown Sugar
- 2 Canned Chipotle Chiles In Adobo Sauce
- 2 Cups Chicken Stock
- 2 Dried Ancho Chiles
- 1 Dried Arbol Chile
- 2 Dried Guajillo Chiles
- 2 Tbsp Extra Virgin Olive Oil
- 4 Fresh Garlic, Roughly Chopped
- 4 Cloves Roasted Garlic
- Salt
- 2 Shallots, Roughly Chopped
- 1 Spiral Cut Ham

Directions:

1. Supply your smoker with wood pellets and follow the start-up procedure. Preheat the grill, with the lid open, to 450° F.
2. In a large, heavy-bottomed skillet, heat the oil over medium-high heat. Add the shallots and cook for 5 minutes, or until softened.
3. Add the roasted and fresh garlic and cook, stirring occasionally, for 3 to 4 minutes, until the garlic is browned.
4. Remove the skillet from the heat and add the bourbon.
5. Return the skillet to medium-high heat, add the vinegar, and cook until the liquid is reduced by one third, about 10 minutes.
6. Add the ancho, guajillo, árbol, and chipotle chiles and the brown sugar, then add the chicken stock and continue to cook until the mixture reduces by two thirds, about 15 minutes.
7. Strain the reduction through a fine-mesh strainer into a bowl, then pour it into a small saucepan.
8. Return to the heat over medium and reduce until the glaze coats the back off a spoon. Taste and add salt if needed.

Pork Tenderloin With Bourbon Peaches

Servings: 6

Cooking Time: 27 Minutes

Ingredients:

- 2 pork tenderloins, about 2lb (1kg) total, trimmed of silver skin and excess fat
- extra virgin olive oil
- for the rub
- 3 tbsp coarse salt
- 3 tbsp freshly ground black pepper
- 3 tbsp smoked or regular paprika
- 3 tbsp granulated light brown sugar or low-carb substitute
- 2 tbsp instant coffee
- 1 tbsp granulated garlic
- 2 tsp ground cumin
- 1 tsp chili powder
- for the peaches
- 4 freestone peaches, about 1lb (450g) total, peeled, pitted, and sliced
- 1 tbsp freshly squeezed lemon juice
- ¼ cup unsalted butter
- 4 tbsp granulated light brown sugar or low-carb substitute
- 2 tbsp bourbon
- ½ tsp ground cinnamon
- ½ tsp pure vanilla extract
- pinch of coarse salt

Directions:

1. Supply your smoker with wood pellets and follow the start-up procedure. Preheat the grill, with the lid closed, to 400° F.
2. In a small bowl, make the rub by combining the ingredients. Coat the tenderloins in olive oil and season with the rub.
3. Place the peaches and lemon juice in a medium bowl, turning the peaches gently to coat. Measure the other ingredients and then take them and the peaches grill side.
4. Place 1 tablespoon of olive oil in the hot skillet and add the tenderloins. Quickly sear the pork, about 2 to 3 minute per side, turning as needed with tongs. When they're nicely browned, transfer the tenderloins to the grate. Cook until the internal temperature in the thickest part of the meat reaches 145°F (63°C), about 8 minutes. For moist meat, don't cook the tenderloins beyond 155°F (68°C).
5. Transfer the pork to a cutting board and tent with aluminum foil.
6. Replace the cast iron skillet with a clean one and close the grill lid to let it heat. Once hot, make the bourbon peaches by melting the butter. Add the brown sugar, bourbon, cinnamon, vanilla, and salt. Cook the mixture until it bubbles, about 5 to 8 minutes. Add the peaches and cook for 5 to 8 minutes more, turning the peaches carefully with a spoon to coat. Carefully transfer the skillet to a trivet or another heatproof surface.
7. Slice the pork on a diagonal into ½-inch (1.25cm) slices. Shingle the slices on a platter. Spoon the peaches around the pork or serve separately.

Amazing Bacon Cheese Fries

Servings: 2
Cooking Time: 25 Minutes

Ingredients:

- 2 Bacon, Strip
- 1/2 Cup Colby Jack Cheese, Shredded
- 1/2 Package Fries, Frozen
- 1/2 Cup Monterey Jack Cheese, Shredded

Directions:

1. Supply your smoker with wood pellets and follow the start-up procedure. Preheat the grill, with the lid open, to 350° F.
2. Place the bacon on the bacon rack and place on the grill. Cook until crispy, about 15 minutes.
3. Once slightly cooled, crumble the strips into small pieces and set it aside.
4. Grill the frozen French fries based on the package instructions, cooking on a pan in the instead of the oven.
5. Once fries are golden brown, sprinkle cheese and bacon on top of the fries, and return the pan to the grill and barbecue at 450°F for 1 minute. Remove from grill and enjoy!

Old-fashioned Roasted Glazed Ham

Servings: 8
Cooking Time: 60 Minutes

Ingredients:

- 1 (10 lb) fully cooked bone-in spiral cut ham
- 1 Cup pineapple juice
- 1/2 Cup brown sugar
- 1 cinnamon stick
- 14 whole cloves
- 1 Whole Pineapple, fresh
- 10 Cherries, fresh, sweet

Directions:

1. Supply your smoker with wood pellets and follow the start-up procedure. Preheat the grill, with the lid closed, to 325° F.
2. Rinse ham under cold water and pat dry with paper towel.
3. In a saucepan combine pineapple juice, brown sugar, cinnamon stick and four cloves. Bring to a boil. Reduce heat to medium low and simmer for about 15 minutes or until pineapple juice is reduced by half, thick and syrupy.
4. Brush half of the glaze onto the ham and into the folds of the cut slices. Reserve the other half of the glaze for later.
5. Cut pineapple in desired sized pieces, about 2 inch squares, then place on ham with a cherry and a clove to pin in place, repeating all over ham.

6. Put ham in a deep baking dish with fat side up. Place on the Traeger and cook for about 1-¼ hours. Grill: 325 °F
7. Carefully remove from Traeger and brush remaining glaze onto ham.
8. Return ham to Traeger and continue cooking for another 15 to 20 minutes, until internal temperature of ham reaches 160°F. Grill: 325 °F Probe: 160 °F
9. Allow ham to rest for 15 – 20 minutes before serving. Enjoy!

Southern Sugar-glazed Ham

Servings: 12-15

Cooking Time: 300 Minutes

Ingredients:

- 1 (12- to 15-pound) whole bone-in ham, fully cooked
- ¼ cup yellow mustard
- 1 cup pineapple juice
- ½ cup packed light brown sugar
- 1 teaspoon ground cinnamon
- ½ teaspoon ground cloves

Directions:

1. Supply your smoker with wood pellets and follow the start-up procedure. Preheat, with the lid closed, to 275°F.
2. Trim off the excess fat and skin from the ham, leaving a ¼-inch layer of fat. Put the ham in an aluminum foil–lined roasting pan.
3. On your kitchen stove top, in a medium saucepan over low heat, combine the mustard, pineapple juice, brown sugar, cinnamon, and cloves and simmer for 15 minutes, or until thick and reduced by about half.
4. Baste the ham with half of the pineapple–brown sugar syrup, reserving the rest for basting later in the cook.
5. Place the roasting pan on the grill, close the lid, and smoke for 4 hours.
6. Baste the ham with the remaining pineapple–brown sugar syrup and continue smoking with the lid closed for another hour, or until a meat thermometer inserted in the thickest part of the ham reads 140°F.
7. Remove the ham from the grill, tent with foil, and let rest for 20 minutes before carving.

Kodiak Cakes Candied Bacon Crumble Brownies

Servings: 6

Cooking Time: 45 Minutes

Ingredients:

- 1 Box Big Bear Brownie Mix, Kodiak Cakes
- 2 eggs
- 1 Stick butter, melted
- 2 Tablespoon coconut oil
- 2 Tablespoon water
- 2 Cup cooked bacon
- 1/2 Cup Almonds, chopped
- 1/2 Cup sugar

Directions:

1. Supply your smoker with wood pellets and follow the start-up procedure. Preheat the grill, with the lid closed, to 300° F.
2. Spray an 8” baking pan with non-stick spray.
3. Empty Kodiak Cake brownie mix into a medium-size mixing bowl. Add eggs, melted butter, coconut oil, and water. Gently mix, being careful not to overmix. Pour into prepared pan.
4. Place brownies in center of grill grate; bake for 45 minutes. Grill: 300 °F
5. While the brownies are baking, begin assembling bacon crumble. Add honey or sugar to a medium-size saucepan, over high heat. Add bacon and almonds. Stir for 2-3 minutes, or until sugar has dissolved. Remove from heat and let cool.
6. Remove brownies from grill and cool completely. Sprinkle candied bacon crumble over the top of brownies. Enjoy!

Grilled Rosemary Pork Chops

Servings: 4
Cooking Time: 10 Minutes

Ingredients:

- 6 Tbsp Brown Sugar
- 4 Pork, Chop
- 2 Tbsp Dried Rosemary, Springs
- 1 Cup Soy Sauce
- 1/2 Cup Water, Warm

Directions:

1. Supply your smoker with wood pellets and follow the start-up procedure. Preheat the grill, with the lid open, to 350° F.
2. Lightly oil the grate. Remove the pork chops from the marinade, shake off the excess, and discard the marinade.
3. Grill the pork chops until the pork is no longer pink in the center, while brushing occasionally with the reserved marinade, for about 4-5 minutes on each side, or until done.
4. Remove the pork chops from the grill and serve.

Baked Sage & Sausage Stuffing

Servings: 4
Cooking Time: 45 Minutes

Ingredients:

- 1 Pound Sage-Flavored Sausage, Such as Bob Evans Or Jimmy Dean
- 1/2 Cup onion, diced
- 1/2 Cup celery, diced
- 14 Ounce (14 oz) package herb seasoned stuffing
- 1/2 Cup dried sweetened cranberries
- 2 Cup low sodium chicken broth
- 6 Tablespoon butter
- butter

Directions:

1. Brown the sausage in a large frying pan, breaking up the sausage with a wooden spoon.
2. Add the onion and celery and cook until softened. Drain any excess fat. Transfer to a large mixing bowl. Add the stuffing mix and cranberries, if using.
3. Warm the chicken broth over medium-low heat; add butter and cook until melted. Toss with the bread/sausage mixture and mix lightly.
4. Butter a 3-qt casserole or baking dish. Do not compress the mixture or it will be dense.
5. Supply your smoker with wood pellets and follow the start-up procedure. Preheat the grill, with the lid closed, to 350° F.
6. Bake the stuffing, covered, for 35 to 45 minutes; uncover during the last 20 minutes of cooking if you prefer a crunchier texture. Grill: 350 °F
7. Remove from grill and serve. Enjoy!

Bacon Weave Smoked Country Sausage

Servings: 4
Cooking Time: 120 Minutes

Ingredients:

- Pound Sausage, Uncooked
- Pork & Poultry Rub
- 8 Slices bacon

Directions:

1. Using your hands, form sausage into a loaf-shape. Season lightly with Traeger Pork and Poultry Shake.
2. Supply your smoker with wood pellets and follow the start-up procedure. Preheat the grill, with the lid closed, to 180° F.
3. Put the sausage loaf directly on the grill grate and smoke for 1-1/2 hours.
4. While sausage is smoking, assemble the bacon weave on a piece of wax paper. First, lay out 4 pieces of bacon so they are touching each other on the wax paper. Next, lay the 5th piece of bacon so it crosses the others. Tuck every other slice under the 5th piece of bacon. Find the two pieces of bacon that were under the 5th piece of bacon and fold them back on top of themselves.
5. Lay down the 6th piece of bacon and unfold the two that were laid back. Continue folding the bacon back that was most recently under the last piece of bacon, two pieces at a time, laying the next piece of bacon on top until your weave is complete. Set aside. After your sausage has smoked for 1-1/2 hours, take it off the grill

and increase the heat of your Traeger, lid closed to 350°F and preheat. Grill: 350 °F

6. While the grill is heating, wrap your sausage loaf in the bacon weave. Lay the middle of the weave directly on top of the sausage loaf and press the bacon all around the sausage.

7. Flip the sausage and bacon over to finish the weave on the bottom of the sausage. Alternate the bacon ends across the bottom and tuck the ends around each other.

8. Put your sausage back on the grill and cook for 25-30 minutes until the internal temperature of the sausage reaches 160°F. Enjoy! Probe: 160 °F

Grilled Chicago Hot Dog

Servings: 6

Cooking Time: 15 Minutes

Ingredients:

- 8 footlong hot dogs
- 8 footlong hot dog buns
- yellow mustard
- 3/4 Cup sweet pickle relish
- 1 Cup diced white onion
- 2 tomatoes, cored and sliced into wedges
- 8 dill pickle spears
- 16 pickled sport peppers

Directions:

1. Supply your smoker with wood pellets and follow the start-up procedure. Preheat the grill, with the lid closed, to 375° F.
2. Grill footlong hot dogs for 15 minutes, turning every 5 minutes. Grill: 375 °F
3. Place buns on the grill for the last 3 minutes of cooking to warm them. Grill: 375 °F
4. Assemble the Chicago dog with mustard, relish and onions on top. Place the tomato slices on one side of the dog, the pickle spears on the other, and the sport peppers down the middle. Enjoy!

Pork Tenderloin

Servings: 2

Cooking Time: 15 Minutes

Ingredients:

- 1 Pound pork tenderloin
- 1/3 Cup Kentucky bourbon or apple juice
- 1/4 Cup low sodium soy sauce
- 1/4 Cup brown sugar, packed
- 2 Tablespoon Dijon mustard
- 2 Teaspoon Worcestershire sauce
- 1 Teaspoon ground black pepper
- 1 Medium onion, chopped
- 2 Clove garlic, minced

Directions:

1. Trim any silverskin from the tenderloins with a sharp knife. Place meat in a large resealable plastic bag.
2. For the marinade: In a small mixing bowl or resealable bag, combine the bourbon, soy sauce, brown sugar, mustard, Worcestershire sauce and pepper, whisk to mix. Stir in the onion and garlic. Pour over the tenderloins and refrigerate for 8 hours or overnight.
3. Supply your smoker with wood pellets and follow the start-up procedure. Preheat the grill, with the lid closed, to 400° F.
4. Remove the pork from the marinade and scrape off any solid ingredients (onion or bits of garlic). Discard the marinade.
5. Arrange the tenderloins on the grill grate and grill for 6 to 8 minutes per side or until the internal temperature is 145°F. The pork will still be slightly pink in the center. If you prefer your pork well-done, cook it to 160°F. Grill: 400 °F Probe: 145 °F
6. Transfer the tenderloins to a cutting board. Let rest for several minutes before carving on a diagonal into 1/2 inch slices. Enjoy!

Bbq Pork Belly Burnt Ends

Servings: 8

Cooking Time: 240 Minutes

Ingredients:

- 1 (5-7 lb) skinless pork belly, cut into 1 inch cubes
- Meat Church Honey Hog, Honey Hog Hot or The Gospel Rub
- 1 Cup apple juice, for spritzing
- 1 1/2 Cup Apricot BBQ Sauce
- 1/2 Cup clover honey

Directions:

1. Supply your smoker with wood pellets and follow the start-up procedure. Preheat the grill, with the lid closed, to 275° F.
2. Thoroughly coat all sides of the pork belly cubes with your choice of Meat Church Honey Hog, Honey Hog Hot or The Gospel Rub. I prefer a spicier rub because I finish these with a sweet sauce.
3. Allow the rub to adhere on all sides for at least 15 minutes. Place the pork belly in the Traeger fat-side down. I prefer to do this on a wire rack.
4. Cook the pork belly for 3 hours, spritzing with apple juice every 45 minutes or whenever it starts to look dry. Grill: 275 °F
5. Pull the belly when the meat reaches an internal temperature of 190°F to 195°F. Some people pull the belly a lot earlier, but I want it really tender. Grill: 275 °F Probe: 190 °F
6. Place the cubes in the half-size aluminum pan. Season and toss the cubes with more Meat Church rub.
7. Cover the cubes with Traeger Apricot BBQ Sauce. Drizzle clover honey across the top. Finally, toss the cubes thoroughly to ensure they are completely covered.
8. Return the pan (uncovered) to the Traeger and cook for another hour or until all liquid has reduced and caramelized. Grill: 275 °F
9. Allow them to cool for 15 minutes before serving. Enjoy!

Grilled Bacon Dog

Servings: 4

Cooking Time: 25 Minutes

Ingredients:

- 16 hot dogs
- 16 Slices Bacon, sliced
- 2 Vidalia onion, sliced
- 16 hot dog buns
- 'Que BBQ Sauce
- Velveeta cheese

Directions:

1. Supply your smoker with wood pellets and follow the start-up procedure. Preheat the grill, with the lid closed, to 375° F.
2. Wrap bacon strips around the hot dogs, and grill directly on the grill grate for 10 minutes each side. Grill onions at the same time as the hot dogs, and cook for 10 -15 minutes.
3. Open hot dog buns and spread Traeger 'Que sauce, the grilled hot dogs, cheese sauce and grilled onions. Top with vegetables. Serve, enjoy!

Bbq Pulled Pork Grilled Cheese Sandwich

Servings: 8

Cooking Time: 540 Minutes

Ingredients:

- 1 Pork Butt, bone-in, 8-10 lbs.
- 2 Tablespoon Pork & Poultry Rub
- 1 1/2 Cup apple juice
- 4 Tablespoon brown sugar
- 1 Tablespoon salt
- Sweet & Heat BBQ Sauce
- 16 Pieces White Bread
- cheddar cheese
- butter, softened

Directions:

1. Trim pork butt of all excess fat leaving 1/4-inch of the fat cap attached.
2. Combine 2 Tbsp Traeger Pork & Poultry Rub, apple juice, brown sugar and salt in a small bowl stirring until most of the sugar and salt are dissolved.
3. Inject the pork butt every square inch or so with the apple juice mixture. Season the exterior of the pork butt with remaining rub.
4. Supply your smoker with wood pellets and follow the start-up procedure. Preheat the grill, with the lid closed, to 250° F.
5. Place pork butt directly on the grill grate and cook for about 6 hours or until the internal temperature reaches 160 degrees F. Remove pork butt from grill and wrap in two layers of foil. Pour in 1/2 cup of apple juice.

Secure tin foil tightly to contain the apple juice. Grill: 250 °F Probe: 160 °F

6. Increase temperature to 275 degrees F and return to grill in a pan large enough to hold the pork butt in case of leaks. Cook an additional 3 hours or until internal temperature reaches 205 degrees F. Grill: 275 °F Probe: 205 °F

7. Remove from the grill and discard the bone. Shred the pork removing any excess fat or tendons. Season with additional Traeger Pork & Poultry Rub and salt if needed. Add Traeger Sweet & Heat BBQ Sauce and mix to combine. Set pork aside.

8. For the grilled cheese sandwiches: Butter two pieces of bread and place one in a pan warmed over medium heat, butter side down. Place a slice of cheddar cheese on top of the bread and top with pulled pork. Place another slice of cheese on top of pork and finish with the other slice of bread, butter side up.

9. Cook on first side 5-7 minutes until bread is lightly browned. Flip and cook for another 5-7 minutes. Remove from heat and slice in half. Enjoy!

Bbq Pork Shoulder Steaks

Servings: 4

Cooking Time: 120 Minutes

Ingredients:

- 4 (1 to 1-1/4 inch thick) pork shoulder steaks
- 1/2 Cup mustard
- Pork & Poultry Rub
- 1/2 Cup apple juice
- 1 Cup 'Que BBQ Sauce

Directions:

1. Slather the pork steaks on all sides with the mustard and season with the Traeger Pork & Poultry Rub. (The mustard will help keep the pork moist, but the taste will be unnoticeable in the final product.)
2. Supply your smoker with wood pellets and follow the start-up procedure. Preheat the grill, with the lid closed, to 180° F.
3. Arrange the steaks on the grill grate. Smoke for 1-1/2 hours. Grill: 180 °F
4. Remove the pork steaks to a plate and increase temperature to 225°F. Preheat 5 to 10 minutes. Grill: 225 °F
5. Meanwhile, wrap each steak with aluminum foil, adding in a couple tablespoons of apple juice.
6. Cook the steaks for another hour or so or until they are tender (about 160°F on an instant-read meat thermometer). Grill: 225 °F Probe: 160 °F
7. The last 15 minutes, take the pork steaks out of the foil and put them directly on the grill.
8. Brush each steak on both sides with the Traeger 'Que BBQ Sauce or your favorite barbecue sauce.
9. Let the steaks rest for 3 minutes before serving. Enjoy!

Brown Sugar And Bacon Wrapped Lil Smokies

Servings: 6

Cooking Time: 30 Minutes

Ingredients:

- 1 Pound bacon
- 1 (14 oz) cocktail sausages
- 1/2 Cup brown sugar

Directions:

1. Lay strips of bacon out on a clean, flat surface. Roll out bacon strips using a rolling pin, so they are a bit longer with even thickness. Cut bacon strips in half.
2. Wrap each sausage in a 1/2 strip of bacon and secure with a toothpick. Place the bacon-wrapped sausages in a casserole dish in a single layer and cover with brown sugar.
3. Transfer to the fridge and let sit for 30 minutes.
4. Supply your smoker with wood pellets and follow the start-up procedure. Preheat the grill, with the lid closed, to 350° F.
5. Lay the sausages out on a parchment lined sheet tray and place the sheet directly on the grill grate.
6. Cook for 25 to 30 minutes until the bacon is crispy. Enjoy! Grill: 350 °F

Grilled Bratwurst With Apple Slaw

Servings: 2
Cooking Time: 20 Minutes

Ingredients:

- 2 Whole Granny Smith Apples, Unpeeled
- 1/2 Small Red Onion, peeled
- 1/2 Cup mayonnaise
- 1/2 Tablespoon apple cider vinegar
- 1/4 Cup spicy brown mustard
- 1 Teaspoon Veggie Rub
- 1 Stick butter, melted
- 6 Whole bratwurst
- 6 Whole buns

Directions:

1. Supply your smoker with wood pellets and follow the start-up procedure. Preheat the grill, with the lid closed, to 350° F. For the apple slaw: Grate unpeeled Granny Smith apples and red onion into a large bowl. Toss with mayonnaise, apple cider vinegar, spicy brown mustard, Traeger Veggie Rub and melted butter.
2. Place brats directly on the grill grate and cook for 10 minutes per side, or when an instant read thermometer inserted into the thickest part of the meat registers 160 degrees F. Grill: 350 °F Probe: 160 °F
3. Remove from grill, place in bun and top with apple slaw. Enjoy!

Hickory Smoked Pork Shoulder

Servings: 7
Cooking Time: 420 Minutes

Ingredients:

- 1 Cup Apple Cider Vinegar
- 2 Tbsp Hickory Bacon Seasoning
- 5 - 6 Lbs Pork Shoulder, Bone In
- 1 Tbsp Sugar

Directions:

1. Supply your smoker with wood pellets and follow the start-up procedure. Preheat the grill, with the lid open, to 225° F. If you're using a gas or charcoal, set up your grill for low, indirect heat.
2. Rinse the pork shoulder (aka pork butt) under cold running water and make sure to pat dry the entire surface, including any small cracks and crevices.
3. Place the pork shoulder in the aluminum pan, fat side up, and sprinkle a liberal amount of Hickory Bacon seasoning over the top. You want to be very generous with the outer layer of seasoning here, making sure to coat the meat from end to end.
4. In a large bowl, pour the 1 cup of apple cider vinegar, the 2 tablespoons of Hickory Bacon, and 1 tablespoon of sugar. Mix until the sugars are completely dissolved.
5. Fill your marinade injector with the marinade and inject it deep into the meat. For even flavor, inject the marinade all over the pork shoulder at one-inch intervals. Pressing the syringe slowly will help avoid the marinade squirting out.
6. Tightly wrap aluminum foil over the top of the pan, set it on your grill, and close the lid.
7. Smoke the pork shoulder for 6-8 hours, or until the meat is tender and the internal temperature is 195°F to 200°F.
8. Remove from the grill and let it rest on a cutting board for 20-30 minutes with the aluminum foil loosely tented over the top.
9. When you're ready to serve, shred the pork shoulder, discarding any large pieces of fat.

Grilled Lemon Pepper Pork Tenderloin

Servings: 4
Cooking Time: 20 Minutes

Ingredients:

- 2 lemons, zested
- 1 Clove garlic, minced
- 1 Teaspoon freshly minced parsley
- 1 Teaspoon lemon juice
- 1/4 Teaspoon black pepper
- 1/2 Teaspoon kosher salt
- 2 Tablespoon olive oil
- 1 (2 lb) pork tenderloin

Directions:

1. In a small bowl, whisk together everything except the tenderloin.

2. Trim all silverskin and excess fat from the tenderloin.
3. Place pork in a large resealable bag. Pour the marinade over the tenderloin and zip closed. Transfer to the refrigerator and marinate for at least 2 hours but no more than 8.
4. Supply your smoker with wood pellets and follow the start-up procedure. Preheat the grill, with the lid closed, to 375° F.
5. Remove the tenderloin from the bag and discard the marinade.
6. When the grill is hot, place tenderloin directly on the grill grate and cook 15 to 20 minutes, flipping once halfway through until the internal temperature reaches 145˚F. Grill: 375 ˚F Probe: 145 ˚F
7. Remove from the heat and let rest 5 to 10 minutes before slicing. Enjoy!

St. Louis–style Pork Steaks

Servings: 4
Cooking Time: 120 Minutes

Ingredients:

- 1 cup low-carb barbecue sauce
- ¼ cup low-carb beer or sugar-free dark-colored soda or sugar-free root beer
- 4 bone-in pork shoulder steaks, each about 1lb (450g) and at least 1 inch (2.5cm) thick
- for the rub
- 1 tbsp coarse salt
- 1 tbsp freshly ground black pepper
- 1 tbsp granulated light brown sugar or low-carb substitute
- 1 tbsp sweet or smoked paprika
- 1 tsp granulated garlic or garlic powder
- 1 tsp celery salt

Directions:

1. Supply your smoker with wood pellets and follow the start-up procedure. Preheat the grill, with the lid closed, to 250° F.
2. In a small bowl, combine the barbecue sauce and beer. Set aside.
3. In a small bowl, make the rub by combining the ingredients. Mix well. Season the steaks on both sides with some of the rub.
4. Place the steaks on the grate at an angle to the bars and smoke for 30 minutes. Transfer the steaks to an aluminum foil roasting pan. Pour the barbecue mixture over them. Use tongs to turn the steaks, making sure each is coated well with the sauce.
5. Tightly wrap aluminum foil over the top of the pan and place it on the grate. Braise the steaks until they're fork tender, about 1½ hours. (Protect your hands when lifting a corner of the foil because steam will escape.)
6. Remove the pan from the grill and serve the steaks immediately.

Bacon Wrapped Pickles

Servings: 6
Cooking Time: 60 Minutes

Ingredients:

- 13 Strips Bacon
- 3 Bratwursts, Raw
- 1/2 Cup Colby Jack Cheese, Shredded
- 4 Oz Cream Cheese
- 13 Large Dill Pickles, Spears
- Hickory Bacon Rub
- 2 Scallion, Sliced Thin
- 1/4 Cup Sour Cream

Directions:

1. Supply your smoker with wood pellets and follow the start-up procedure. Preheat the grill, with the lid open, to 375° F.
2. Preheat griddle to medium- low flame.
3. In a mixing bowl combine cream cheese, sour cream, and scallions.
4. Use a hand mixer to blend well, then fold in grated cheddar-jack. Set aside.
5. Cook bratwurst on the griddle. Use a metal spatula to chop up sausage into smaller bits and cook until browned.
6. Remove from the griddle and set aside on a sheet tray to cool.

7. Place pickles on a sheet tray. Cut in half, then remove seeds with a small measuring spoon.
8. Stuff one half of each pickle with cream cheese mixture and top with crumbled bratwurst.
9. Top with the other pickle half, then wrap in bacon.
10. Season bacon-wrapped pickles with Hickory Bacon Rub, place in cast iron skillet, then transfer to grill.
11. Grill pickles for 45 to 55 minutes, until bacon starts to crisp on top. Remove from grill. Serve warm.

Jalapeno Cheddar Smoked Sausages

Servings: 6
Cooking Time: 180 Minutes

Ingredients:

- hog casings
- 2 Pound ground pork
- 5 Medium jalapeños, seeded and diced small
- 1/2 Cup shredded sharp cheddar cheese
- 1/2 Tablespoon kosher salt
- 1 Teaspoon black pepper
- 1 Teaspoon granulated garlic
- 1 Teaspoon onion powder

Directions:

1. Soak your hog casings in water according to package directions. While casings are soaking, make your sausage.
2. Place all ingredients in the bowl of a food processor and pulse to combine. Be careful not to overwork, the meat should be a little tacky and all spices fully incorporated.
3. Place sausage mixture in your sausage stuffer and proceed to stuff the casing according to manufacturer's directions. Be sure to stuff the length of the casing, then create the links afterwards. Use caution not to overstuff or they will burst when you go to create the links.
4. Hang the sausages and allow to air dry at room temperature for an hour or so, then transfer to the refrigerator to dry overnight.
5. Supply your smoker with wood pellets and follow the start-up procedure. Preheat the grill, with the lid closed, to 180° F.
6. Place the sausages directly on the grill grate and smoke for 2 to 3 hours, or until they reach an internal temperature of 155°F. Enjoy! Grill: 180 °F Probe: 155 °F

Lip-smackin' Pork Loin

Servings: 8
Cooking Time: 180 Minutes

Ingredients:

- ¼ cup finely ground coffee
- ¼ cup paprika
- ¼ cup garlic powder
- 2 tablespoons chili powder
- 1 tablespoon packed light brown sugar
- 1 tablespoon ground allspice
- 1 tablespoon ground coriander
- 1 tablespoon freshly ground black pepper
- 2 teaspoons ground mustard
- 1½ teaspoons celery seeds
- 1 (1½- to 2-pound) pork loin roast

Directions:

1. Supply your smoker with wood pellets and follow the start-up procedure. Preheat, with the lid closed, to 250°F.
2. In a small bowl, combine the ground coffee, paprika, garlic powder, chili powder, brown sugar, allspice, coriander, pepper, mustard, and celery seeds to create a rub, and generously apply it to the pork loin roast.
3. Place the pork loin on the grill, fat-side up, close the lid, and roast for 3 hours, or until a meat thermometer inserted in the thickest part of the meat reads 160°F.
4. Let the pork rest for 5 minutes before slicing and serving.

Sweet Bacon

Servings: 4
Cooking Time: 60 Minutes

Ingredients:

- 1 Pack Bacon, Thick Cut
- 1/2 Cup Brown Sugar
- 1/2 Cup Maple Syrup
- Mandarin Habanero Seasoning

Directions:

1. Place the bacon in a deep dish. Add the maple syrup, cover and refrigerate 2 - 3 hours or overnight.
2. Supply your smoker with wood pellets and follow the start-up procedure. Preheat the grill, with the lid open, to 225° F.
3. When the grill has preheated, place the bacon directly on the cooking grids and sprinkle with brown sugar and Mandarin Habanero. Check every 15-20. After 30 minutes, flip and rotate bacon and baste with syrup. Allow to hot smoke for another 20 to 30 minutes or until the bacon is done to your desired liking.
4. Allow to cool on a rack and serve.
5. Can be refrigerated in an airtight container.

Texas Grilled Ribs

Servings: 4
Cooking Time: 240 Minutes

Ingredients:

- 1 Cup Apple Cider Vinegar
- 1 Rack Baby Back Rib
- 2 Tablespoons Whole Grain Mustard
- 2 Tablespoons Olive Oil
- 1 Bottle Sweet Heat Rub
- 1 Tablespoons Worcestershire Sauce

Directions:

1. Remove the ribs from their packaging and pat dry.
2. Flip to back of ribs and score the membrane with a knife, then peel off the membrane.
3. Rub the ribs with the olive oil, followed by a generous amount of Sweet Heat Rub & Grill, on both sides.
4. In a small bowl, mix together the mustard, apple cider vinegar, and Worcestershire. Set aside.
5. Supply your smoker with wood pellets and follow the start-up procedure. Preheat the grill, with the lid open, to 225° F. Add the ribs and smoke for 3 hours.
6. Transfer the ribs onto a foil lined sheet pan and brush both sides with the apple cider vinegar mixture. Wrap the ribs tightly in foil and place back on the smoker for 2 more hours.
7. Carefully remove the ribs from the foil and brush with more of the apple cider vinegar mixture. Place the ribs back on the smoker grates and smoke for 1 additional hour.
8. Remove from the smoker and let rest for 5 minutes before serving.

Grilled Lasagna With Cold-smoked Mozzarella

Servings: 8-12
Cooking Time: 70 Minutes

Ingredients:

- 15 Oz. Ricotta Cheese
- 3 Cups Cold-Smoked Mozzarella, Grated Divided
- 2 Eggs
- 6 Garlic Cloves, Chopped
- 1 Tsp Garlic Powder
- 1 Cup Grated Parmesan Cheese, Divided
- 1 Lb. Italian Sausage
- 1 Tbsp Italian Seasoning
- 1 Pkg."No-Bake" Lasagna Noodles
- 48 Oz. Marinara Sauce
- 1 Lb. Mozzarella Block
- 1 Tbsp Olive Oil
- 1 Tbsp Chopped Oregano
- ¼ Cup Italian Parsley, Chopped
- 1 Yellow Onion, Chopped

Directions:

1. In a glass bowl, mix together the eggs, Italian seasoning, garlic powder, ricotta cheese, ½ cup parmesan cheese, and 1 cup of smoked mozzarella, and 2 tablespoons of parsley. Cover and refrigerate for 1 hour.
2. Supply your smoker with wood pellets and follow the start-up procedure. Preheat the grill, with the lid open, to 400° F. If using a gas or charcoal grill, set it up for medium-high heat. Place a cast iron skillet on the grill grates and allow to preheat.
3. Heat olive oil in skillet, then add Italian sausage and cook for 5 minutes, then add in onion and garlic, and cook an additional 3 minutes. Remove from heat and stir in 1 tablespoon of parsley and dried oregano. Set aside and reduce grill temperature to 350° F.
4. To assemble, begin by covering the bottom of a 9x13 pan with 1 cup of sauce. For the first layer, place a single

layer of uncooked noodles over the sauce, followed by ⅓ of the ricotta cheese mixture, half of the Italian sausage, 1 cup of mozzarella cheese, and 1 cup of sauce. Repeat for layer two with a single layer of uncooked lasagna noodles, ⅓ of the ricotta cheese mixture, and 1 ½ cups of sauce. Repeat for layer three with a layer of uncooked lasagna noodles, remaining ricotta mixture, remaining Italian sausage, 1 cup of sauce. For the final layer, add a layer of uncooked lasagna noodles, remaining sauce, and remaining 1 cup mozzarella plus ½ cup parmesan.

5. Transfer lasagna to grill and cook, covered with foil, for 35 minutes. Remove foil and continue cooking for 10 minutes, sprinkle with additional parmesan and parsley, if desired. Remove from grill and let stand 15 minutes before serving.

Pulled Pork Corn Tortillas

Servings: 4

Cooking Time: 15 Minutes

Ingredients:

- Cilantro
- Cilantro, Chopped
- 8 Corn Tortillas
- Jalepeno, Sliced
- 1 Lime, Wedges
- 2 Cups Pulled Pork
- Radishes, Sliced
- White Onion, Diced

Directions:

1. Supply your smoker with wood pellets and follow the start-up procedure. Preheat the grill, with the lid open, to 350° F. Grill the corn tortillas until they are softened and have charred spots, about 30 seconds.
2. To assemble the carnitas, add the pulled pork to the tortillas, and top with radishes, diced onion, cilantro, jalapeno and a squeeze of lime juice, if desired. Serve and enjoy!

Smoky Pork Tenderloin

Servings: 4

Cooking Time: 20 Minutes

Ingredients:

- 2 Pork Tenderloins (3-5 Pounds Total), Trimmed of Excess Fat or Silver Skin
- 1 Tablespoon Olive Oil
- 1-2 Tablespoons Fresh Lime Juice
- 1/4 Cup Light Brown Sugar
- 2 Teaspoons Smoked Paprika
- 1 Teaspoon Onion Powder
- 1 Teaspoon Garlic Powder
- 1 Teaspoon Coarse, Kosher Salt
- Pinch of Coarsely Ground Black Pepper

Directions:

1. Stir together the olive oil, lime juice, brown sugar, paprika, onion powder, garlic powder, salt, and pepper in a small bowl.
2. Rub the mixture over the pork and place the meat in a shallow dish. You can grill right away, but for more flavor, cover the dish and refrigerate up to 24 hours.
3. Supply your smoker with wood pellets and follow the start-up procedure. Preheat the grill, with the lid closed, to 375° F.
4. Grill the pork tenderloin for 10 minutes, flip and continue to cook until internal temperature at the thickest part of the meat registers 145 degrees F on an instant-read thermometer, about 8-10 minutes.
5. Remove the pork from the grill and cover with aluminum foil for 10-15 minutes before slicing and serving.

Big Game Day Bbq Ribs

Servings: 6

Cooking Time: 180 Minutes

Ingredients:

- 2 Rack St. Louis-style ribs
- 1/4 Cup Big Game Rub
- 1 Cup peach nectar
- 1 Cup Apricot BBQ Sauce

Directions:

1. Wash ribs and pat dry. Pull membrane off the back of ribs.
2. Supply your smoker with wood pellets and follow the start-up procedure. Preheat the grill, with the lid closed, to 275° F.

3. Apply a thin coat of rub to the back of the ribs and all sides. Let rest 5 minutes. Turn ribs over, apply a heavy coat of rub to the top and let rest or "sweat" for 15 minutes.
4. Place ribs bone side down directly on the grill grate and cook for 2 to 2-1/2 hours. Check for doneness, the internal temperature should be 160°F and the meat should be pulling away from the bones. Grill: 275 °F Probe: 160 °F
5. Remove ribs from the grill placing them meat side down on top of a piece of foil. Pour 1/2 cup peach nectar over ribs and wrap foil tightly around the ribs creating a packet. Grill: 275 °F
6. Put ribs back on the grill, bone side up and cook for another 30 to 45 minutes or until tender, but not fall-off-the-bone. Grill: 275 °F
7. Remove from the grill and sauce the front and back of the ribs. Place the ribs back on the Traeger for 15 minutes to set the sauce.
8. Remove, let rest for 15 minutes, slice and serve. Enjoy!

Smoked Blt Sandwich

Servings: 4
Cooking Time: 20 Minutes

Ingredients:

- 2 Pound thick-cut bacon
- 1/2 Cup mayonnaise
- 8 Slices Texas toast
- 2 Head butter lettuce
- 3 heirloom tomato, sliced

Directions:

1. Supply your smoker with wood pellets and follow the start-up procedure. Preheat the grill, with the lid closed, to 350° F.
2. When the grill is hot, place the bacon slices directly on the grill grate and cook for 15-20 minutes or until crispy. Grill: 350 °F
3. To build the sandwich, smear mayo on two pieces of toast. Layer lettuce leaves, tomatoes, bacon and top with the other piece of toast. Enjoy!

Baked Honey Glazed Ham

Servings: 8
Cooking Time: 120 Minutes

Ingredients:

- 1 (6-8 lb) Snake River Farms Kurobuta Half Bone-In Ham
- 20 whole cloves
- 1 Stick butter, softened
- 1/4 Cup dark corn syrup
- 1 Cup honey, room temperature

Directions:

1. Supply your smoker with wood pellets and follow the start-up procedure. Preheat the grill, with the lid closed, to 325° F.
2. Score ham. Smear the entire ham with softened butter and stud with the whole cloves and place ham in foil-lined pan.
3. Combine the dark corn syrup and honey. Warm to combine if needed. Pour 3/4 of the glaze over ham, and bake for 1-1/2 to 2 hours on the grill or until the ham reaches 140°F. Grill: 325 °F Probe: 140 °F
4. Baste ham every 20 minutes with remaining honey glaze. Grill: 325 °F Probe: 140 °F
5. Remove from grill and let rest a few minutes.
6. Slice and serve. Enjoy!

Bacon Onion Ring

Servings: 6
Cooking Time: 60 Minutes

Ingredients:

- 16 Slices bacon
- 2 Whole Vidalia onion, sliced
- 1 Tablespoon Chili Garlic Sauce
- 1 Tablespoon yellow mustard
- 1 Teaspoon honey

Directions:

1. Wrap a piece of bacon around an individual onion ring; continue until bacon is gone. Some onion slices may be larger and require 2 pieces of bacon to complete a ring.

2. Place a skewer through the bacon-wrapped onion slice, to keep bacon from unraveling while cooking.
3. Supply your smoker with wood pellets and follow the start-up procedure. Preheat the grill, with the lid closed, to 400° F.
4. Meanwhile, mix chili garlic sauce and yellow mustard in a small bowl until incorporated; add honey.
5. Place skewers on the grill grate and cook for approximately 90 minutes, flipping after 45 minutes. Enjoy! Grill: 400 ˚F

Smoked Pig Shots

Servings: 8
Cooking Time: 45 Minutes

Ingredients:

- 1 (8 oz) block cream cheese, softened
- 2 Large green chile peppers, diced
- 1 Cup shredded cheese
- 1 Tablespoon chile powder
- 2 Tablespoon Meat Church Honey Hog BBQ Rub
- 1 Pound Sausage, Smoked
- 1 Pound thick-cut bacon

Directions:

1. Supply your smoker with wood pellets and follow the start-up procedure. Preheat the grill, with the lid closed, to 350° F.
2. Mix cream cheese, chiles, shredded cheese, chili powder and Honey Hog BBQ Rub thoroughly in a mixing bowl. Set aside.
3. Slice sausage into 1/2 inch slices. Cut bacon strips in half. Wrap bacon around the sausage, creating a bowl and secure with a toothpick.
4. Fill the bowl with the cream cheese mixture. Top with more Honey Hog BBQ Rub.
5. Place the pig shots on the Traeger until the bacon is crispy and golden brown, about 45 to 60 minutes. Grill: 350 ˚F
6. Remove the pig shots from the grill and cool for 10 minutes, the cream cheese may still be hot. Enjoy!

Delicious Pulled Pork Sandwiches

Servings: 8
Cooking Time: 660 Minutes

Ingredients:

- 1 (5-7 lb) bone-in pork shoulder
- Pork & Poultry Rub
- 2 Cup apple juice, in food-grade spray bottle
- BBQ Sauce
- 10 hamburger buns
- coleslaw, for serving

Directions:

1. Generously season pork roast on all sides with Traeger Pork & Poultry rub.
2. Supply your smoker with wood pellets and follow the start-up procedure. Preheat the grill, with the lid closed, to 225° F.
3. Put the roast on the grill grate, fat-side up and smoke for 3 hours. Spray the roast with apple juice every hour after the first hour. Grill: 225 ˚F
4. After 3 hours, transfer pork to a disposable aluminum foil pan large enough to hold the roast. Increase the grill temperature to 250°F, and continue to cook for 6 to 8 additional hours, or until an instant-read meat thermometer inserted in the thickest part, but not touching bone, registers 203°F. If the pork starts to brown too much, cover it loosely with aluminum foil. Grill: 250 ˚F Probe: 203 ˚F
5. Carefully transfer the pork roast to a cutting board and let it rest for 20 minutes. Pour the juices from the bottom of the pan into a gravy separator. Discard any fat that has floated to the top.
6. With your hands (preferably protected from the heat with lined, heavy-duty rubber gloves) pull the pork into chunks. Discard the bone and any lumps of fat, including the cap. Pull each chunk into shreds and transfer to a large mixing bowl.
7. Season with additional rub and moisten with the reserved pork juice. Add your favorite Traeger BBQ sauce to the pulled pork and mix well.
8. Pile the pork mixture on the hamburger buns and serve with coleslaw. Enjoy!

Apple Cider Maple Glazed Ham

Servings: 10 - 14
Cooking Time: 190 Minutes

Ingredients:

- 1 1/2 Cups Apple Cider
- 3 Tbsp Apple Cider Vinegar
- 1/2 Cup Packed Light Brown Sugar
- 2 Tbsp Unsalted Butter
- ¼ Tsp Chili Powder
- 2 Tsp Cornstarch
- 3 Tbsp Dijon Mustard
- ½ Tsp Ground Cinnamon
- ¼ Tsp Ground Cloves
- Large Cast Iron Skillet
- 1/2 Cup Pure Maple Syrup
- 2 Tsp Tennessee Apple Butter Rub
- 1 Spiral-Sliced Ham, Bone-In
- ¼ Tsp Thyme, Dried
- 3 Tbsp Yellow Mustard

Directions:

1. Remove ham from refrigerator and let rest at room temperature for 2-3 hours.
2. Supply your smoker with wood pellets and follow the start-up procedure. Preheat the grill, with the lid open, to 300° F. If using a gas or charcoal grill, set heat to medium-high heat.
3. Create a bed of foil in the bottom of a large cast iron pan, making sure to have enough to seal entire ham. Set ham inside foil and add one cup of water to the bottom of pan. Pour some glaze (about ⅓ of mixture) over ham, making sure to coat in between slices. Wrap ham tightly in foil and grill for 2 hours.
4. Remove ham from grill and increase temperature to 400° F. Carefully unfold foil to expose ham and pour an additional ⅓ of glaze over ham. Leave ham exposed and grill for 30 minutes or until edges are golden brown and caramelized.
5. Remove ham from grill and carefully remove foil from underneath ham, so that ham is directly sitting on cast iron. Return to grill, brush with more glaze, and grill another 15 minutes. Remove ham from grill, let rest for 15 minutes, then carve and serve with remaining glaze.

Spiced Pork Belly

Servings: 4
Cooking Time: 130 Minutes

Ingredients:

- 2lb (1kg) skinless pork belly
- for the rub
- 2 tbsp fine kosher salt
- 2 tbsp granulated white or light brown sugar or low-carb substitute
- 2 tsp freshly ground black pepper
- 2 tsp ground mustard
- 2 tsp Chinese five-spice powder

Directions:

1. In a small bowl, make the rub by combining the ingredients. Mix well. Lightly season the pork belly on all sides with the rub. Cover and refrigerate overnight.
2. Supply your smoker with wood pellets and follow the start-up procedure. Preheat the grill, with the lid closed, to 450° F.
3. Place the pork belly on the grate and roast for 30 minutes, turning once. Lower the temperature to 275°F (135°C). Roast the pork until tender and the internal temperature reaches 185°F (85°C), about 1 to 1½ hours more.
4. Remove the pork belly from the grill and let cool completely. Wrap tightly in plastic wrap and refrigerate until firm and well chilled.
5. Preheat the grill to 450°F (232°C).
6. Cut the pork belly into slices, slabs, or cubes. Place the pork on the grate and grill until the edges crisp, about 8 to 10 minutes, turning as needed.
7. Remove the pork from the grill and serve immediately.

VEGETABLES RECIPES

Portobello Marinated Mushroom

Servings: 2
Cooking Time: 15 Minutes

Ingredients:

- 1 Teaspoon chopped thyme
- 1 Teaspoon rosemary, chopped
- 1 Teaspoon Oregano, chopped
- 3 Tablespoon extra-virgin olive oil
- 1 To Taste Jacobsen Salt Co. Pure Kosher Sea Salt
- 1 To Taste pepper
- 6 Whole Portobello Mushroom
- 2 Whole russet potatoes

Directions:

1. Supply your smoker with wood pellets and follow the start-up procedure. Preheat the grill, with the lid closed, to 450° F.
2. Mix fresh herbs, olive oil, salt, and pepper together in a bowl. Rub over mushrooms. Grill both sides of mushrooms for approximately 2-3 minutes on each side. Grill: 450 ˚F
3. Clean the potatoes and slice into long strips.
4. Heat the oil on the Traeger in a sauce pan; drop the potatoes in the hot oil and fry for 7-8 minutes. Let the potatoes cool slightly on a sheet pan. Enjoy! Grill: 450 ˚F

Baked Stuffed Avocados

Servings: 6
Cooking Time: 15 Minutes

Ingredients:

- 4 avocados, halved and pit removed
- 8 eggs
- 2 Cup shredded cheddar cheese
- 1/4 Cup cherry tomatoes, halved
- 4 Slices Bacon, cooked & chopped
- salt and pepper
- 1 scallion, thinly sliced

Directions:

1. Supply your smoker with wood pellets and follow the start-up procedure. Preheat the grill, with the lid closed, to 450° F.
2. After removing the pit from the avocado, scoop out a little of the flesh to make enough room to fit 1 egg per half.
3. Fill the bottom of a cast iron pan with kosher salt and nestle the avocado halves into the salt, cut side up. The salt helps to keep them in place while cooking, like ice with oysters.
4. Crack one egg into each half, top with shredded cheddar cheese, cherry tomatoes and bacon. Season with salt and pepper to taste.
5. Place the cast iron pan directly on the grill grate and bake the avocados for 12 to 15 minutes until the cheese is melted and the egg is just set. Grill: 450 ˚F
6. Remove from the grill and let rest 5 to 10 minutes. Top with sliced scallions and enjoy!

Roasted Potato Poutine

Servings: 6
Cooking Time: 40 Minutes

Ingredients:

- 4 Large russet potatoes
- Tablespoon olive oil or vegetable oil
- Prime Rib Rub
- Cup chicken or beef gravy (homemade or jarred)
- 1 1/2 Cup white or yellow cheddar cheese curds
- freshly ground black pepper
- 2 Tablespoon scallions

Directions:

1. Supply your smoker with wood pellets and follow the start-up procedure. Preheat the grill, with the lid closed, to 500° F.
2. Scrub the potatoes and slice into fries, wedges or preferred shape.
3. Put potatoes into a large mixing bowl and coat with oil. Season generously with Traeger Prime Rib rub.
4. Tip the potatoes onto a rimmed baking sheet and spread in a single layer, cut sides down.

5. Roast for 20 minutes, then using a spatula, turn the potatoes to the other cut side. Continue to roast until the potatoes are tender and golden brown, about 15 to 20 minutes more.
6. While potatoes cook, warm the gravy on the stovetop or in a heat-proof saucepan on your Traeger.
7. To assemble the poutine, arrange the potatoes in a large shallow bowl or on a serving platter. Distribute the cheese curds on top. Pour the hot gravy evenly over the potatoes and cheese curds.
8. Season with black pepper and garnish with thinly sliced scallions. Serve immediately. Enjoy!

Roasted Fall Vegetables

Servings: 6
Cooking Time: 30 Minutes

Ingredients:

- 1/2 Pound Potatoes, new
- 2 Tablespoon olive oil
- salt and pepper
- 1/2 Pound Butternut Squash, diced
- 1/2 Pound fresh Brussels sprouts
- 1 Pint mushrooms, sliced

Directions:

1. Supply your smoker with wood pellets and follow the start-up procedure. Preheat the grill, with the lid closed, to 200° F.
2. Toss potatoes and squash with olive oil, salt and pepper and spread out on a sheet tray.
3. Place directly on the grill grate and cook for 15 minutes. Add brussels sprouts and mushrooms and toss to coat.
4. Cook another 15-20 minutes until veggies are lightly browned and cooked through.
5. Adjust seasoning as needed. Enjoy!

Smoked Bbq Onion Brussels Sprout

Servings: 4
Cooking Time: 110 Minutes

Ingredients:

- 4 strip bacon
- 1 onion minced
- 2 cloves garlic minced
- 1 lb brussels sprouts stems trimmed and cut in half
- 1 tbsp BBQ Spice Blend
- 1/2 cup Apple Habanero Bar-B-Que Sauce (or other BBQ sauce)

Directions:

1. Supply your smoker with wood pellets and follow the start-up procedure. Preheat the grill, with the lid closed, to High heat. Place a cast iron skillet over the highest heat spot and cook the bacon until crisp.
2. Remove the bacon from pan and drain, reserving the bacon fat in the pan.
3. Reduce the heat on your smoker to 250°F.
4. Add the onions, garlic, and brussels to the pan and toss to coat in the bacon drippings. Sprinkle the BBQ spice blend over top.
5. Cover the lid and allow to smoke for 1 to 1 1/2 hours, until the sprouts are fork tender.
6. For the last 20 minutes of smoking, toss the brussels sprouts in half of the barbecue sauce.
7. Remove the sprouts from the smoker.
8. Chop the bacon and add it and the remaining barbecue sauce to the pan of sprouts, tossing to coat.
9. Serve hot.

Baked Heirloom Tomato Tart

Servings: 4
Cooking Time: 45 Minutes

Ingredients:

- 1 Whole Puff Pastry Sheet
- 2 Pound heirloom tomatoes, various shapes and sizes
- 1/2 Tablespoon kosher salt
- 1/2 Cup Ricotta Cheese
- 5 Whole eggs
- 1 To Taste salt and pepper
- 1/2 Teaspoon thyme leaves
- 1/2 Teaspoon red pepper flakes
- 4 Sprig thyme

Directions:

1. Supply your smoker with wood pellets and follow the start-up procedure. Preheat the grill, with the lid closed, to 350° F.

2. Place the puff pastry on a parchment lined sheet tray, and make a cut ¾ of the way through the pastry, ½" from the edge.
3. Slice the tomatoes and season with salt. Place on a sheet tray lined with paper towels.
4. In a small bowl combine the ricotta, 4 of the eggs, salt, thyme leaves, red pepper flakes and black pepper. Whisk together until combined. Spread the ricotta mixture over the puff pastry, staying within ½" from the edge.
5. In a small bowl whisk the last egg. Brush the egg wash onto the exposed edges of the pastry.
6. Place the sheet tray directly on the grill grate and bake for 45 minutes, rotating half-way through. Grill: 350 °F
7. When the edges are browned and the moisture from the tomatoes has evaporated, remove from the grill and let cool 5-7 minutes before serving. Enjoy!

Parmesan Roasted Cauliflower

Servings: 4
Cooking Time: 40 Minutes

Ingredients:

- 1 Head cauliflower, cut into florets
- 1 Medium onion, sliced
- 4 Clove garlic, unpeeled
- 4 Tablespoon olive oil
- salt
- black pepper
- 1 Teaspoon fresh thyme
- 1/2 Cup Parmesan cheese, grated

Directions:

1. Supply your smoker with wood pellets and follow the start-up procedure. Preheat the grill, with the lid closed, to 400° F.
2. On a baking tray, mix together cauliflower, onion, thyme, garlic, olive oil, salt and pepper.
3. Place tray on preheated grill and cook until cauliflower is firm and almost tender (about 25 minutes). Grill: 400 °F
4. Sprinkle cauliflower with Parmesan cheese and continue to cook on the Traeger for another 10 to 15 minutes. Cauliflower should be tender and the Parmesan crisp. Serve immediately, enjoy!

Steak Fries With Horseradish Creme

Servings: 6
Cooking Time: 25 Minutes

Ingredients:

- 5 Potatoes, Baking
- 2 Tablespoon extra-virgin olive oil
- 1 Teaspoon butter
- 3 Clove garlic, crushed
- 1 Teaspoon onion powder
- 2 Teaspoon Jacobsen Salt Co. Pure Kosher Sea Salt
- 1 Teaspoon black pepper

Directions:

1. Wash the potatoes thoroughly, and cut them in eighths, then toss them in the olive oil, butter, crushed garlic, onion powder, salt, and pepper.
2. Supply your smoker with wood pellets and follow the start-up procedure. Preheat the grill, with the lid closed, to 450° F.
3. In order to get great grill marks, line up the wedges on the front of the grill and the back of the grill, turning to get grill marks on all sides.
4. Once they have been seared, move them to the center of the grill and finish cooking about ten more minutes, serve hot with the horseradish mayo. Enjoy!

Roasted Do-ahead Mashed Potatoes

Servings: 6
Cooking Time: 50 Minutes

Ingredients:

- 5 Pound Yukon Gold or russet potatoes
- 9 Tablespoon butter
- 8 Ounce cream cheese
- 1/2 Cup milk
- salt and pepper

Directions:

1. Peel the potatoes and cut into chunks that are roughly the same size. Cover with cold water and add a teaspoon of salt. Bring to a boil over high heat, then

reduce the heat to medium and simmer the potatoes until they are tender.

2. Drain the potatoes and return them to the pot. Stir over low heat for 2 to 3 minutes to evaporate any excess moisture.

3. Mash the potatoes with a hand-held potato masher. (Alternative, rice the potatoes using a ricer.) Incorporate 8 tbsp butter and cream cheese. Add milk until the potatoes are of a good consistency. Stir in salt and pepper to taste.

4. Butter the inside of a casserole dish. Spread the potatoes out in an even layer in the casserole dish, smoothing the top with a spatula. Cool, cover, and refrigerate if not cooking right away. Before cooking, let the potatoes warm to room temperature (about an hour).

5. Supply your smoker with wood pellets and follow the start-up procedure. Preheat the grill, with the lid closed, to 350° F.

6. Bake the potatoes for 45 to 50 minutes, or until hot through. Grill: 350 ˚F

Grilled Chili-lime Corn

Servings: 8

Cooking Time: 45 Minutes

Ingredients:

- 12 Corn, ears
- 1 Teaspoon chili powder
- 1/2 Teaspoon onion powder
- 1 Teaspoon Leinenkugel's Summer Shandy Rub
- 2 lime, juiced
- 1 Tablespoon lime zest

Directions:

1. Soak the ears of corn, still in their husk, in water for 4 to 8 hours.

2. Supply your smoker with wood pellets and follow the start-up procedure. Preheat the grill, with the lid closed, to 350° F.

3. Place corn directly on grill grates. Turn corn every 15 minutes for 45 minutes total cooking time. Grill: 350 ˚F

4. Combine chili powder, onion powder, Summer Shandy rub, lime juice, lime zest and butter in an oven safe dish and place in grill for 10 minutes. Remove corn and butter from the grill.

5. Pull corn husk back, but not off and remove corn silk. Using the corn husk as a handle, brush the corn with the melted chili-lime butter. Enjoy!

Red Potato Grilled Lollipops

Servings: 4

Cooking Time: 25 Minutes

Ingredients:

- 8 Large red bliss potatoes, halved
- 2 Clove garlic, minced
- 2 Sprig rosemary, minced
- 2 Tablespoon olive oil
- 1 Teaspoon salt
- 1/2 Teaspoon black pepper
- 5 Wooden Skewers, soaked in water
- 1/4 Cup Parmesan cheese, grated

Directions:

1. Supply your smoker with wood pellets and follow the start-up procedure. Preheat the grill, with the lid closed, to 450° F.

2. Halve potatoes and poke each several times with a fork.

3. Put the potatoes in a large bowl and toss with the minced garlic, rosemary leaves, a few tablespoons of olive oil, kosher salt, and pepper. Microwave the potatoes for 4 minutes. Gently toss potatoes and microwave for another 3 minutes.

4. Skewer potato halves threading about 4 or 5 potato halves on each skewer. Brush potatoes with olive oil.

5. Place the potato skewers on the Traeger, cut side down, and grill until the sides begin to brown (4-7 minutes).

6. Flip and grill skin side down for another 7-10 minutes.

7. They are done when a sharp knife tip easily penetrates the sides. Remove potatoes from grill and top with grated parmesan cheese. Enjoy!

Smoked Pickled Green Beans

Servings: 4

Cooking Time: 45 Minutes

Ingredients:

- 1 Pound Green Beans, blanched
- 1/2 Cup salt
- 1/2 Cup sugar
- 1 Tablespoon red pepper flakes
- 2 Cup white wine vinegar
- 2 Cup ice water

Directions:

1. Supply your smoker with wood pellets and follow the start-up procedure. Preheat the grill, with the lid closed, to 180° F.
2. Place the blanched green beans on a mesh grill mat and place mat directly on the grill grate. Smoke the green beans for 30-45 minutes until they've picked up the desired amount of smoke. Remove from grill and set aside until the brine is ready. Grill: 180 ˚F
3. In a medium sized saucepan, bring all remaining ingredients, except ice water, to a boil over medium high heat on the stove. Simmer for 5-10 minutes then remove from heat and steep 20 minutes more. Pour brine over ice water to cool.
4. Once brine has cooled, pour over the green beans and weigh them down with a few plates to ensure they are completely submerged. Let sit 24 hours before use. Enjoy!

Spicy Asian Brussels Sprouts

Servings: 4

Cooking Time: 10 Minutes

Ingredients:

- 2 Cup fresh Brussels sprouts
- 2 Tablespoon vegetable oil
- 1 Tablespoon Asian BBQ Rub
- 1/4 Cup Thai sweet chile sauce

Directions:

1. Supply your smoker with wood pellets and follow the start-up procedure. Preheat the grill, with the lid closed, to 350° F.
2. Spread the halved brussel sprouts in a single layer on a lined cookie sheet. Drizzle with the oil and toss to coat.
3. Sprinkle the brussel sprouts evenly with an Asian BBQ rub and put the cookie sheet on the grill. Close the lid and cook for 7-8 minutes. Grill: 350 ˚F
4. Toss the brussels sprouts in the Thai Chili Sauce and return to the grill for an additional 3-4 minutes, or until the sprouts are crisp-tender. Grill: 350 ˚F
5. Serve immediately. Enjoy!

Carolina Baked Beans

Servings: 12-15

Cooking Time: 180 Minutes

Ingredients:

- 3 (28-ounce) cans baked beans (I like Bush's brand)
- 1 large onion, finely chopped
- 1 cup The Ultimate BBQ Sauce
- ½ cup light brown sugar
- ¼ cup Worcestershire sauce
- 3 tablespoons yellow mustard
- Nonstick cooking spray or butter, for greasing
- 1 large bell pepper, cut into thin rings
- ½ pound thick-cut bacon, partially cooked and cut into quarters

Directions:

1. Supply your smoker with wood pellets and follow the start-up procedure. Preheat, with the lid closed, to 300°F.
2. In a large mixing bowl, stir together the beans, onion, barbecue sauce, brown sugar, Worcestershire sauce, and mustard until well combined
3. Coat a 9-by-13-inch aluminum pan with cooking spray or butter.
4. Pour the beans into the pan and top with the bell pepper rings and bacon pieces, pressing them down slightly into the sauce.
5. Place a layer of heavy-duty foil on the grill grate to catch drips, and place the pan on top of the foil. Close the lid and cook for 2 hours 30 minutes to 3 hours, or until the beans are hot, thick, and bubbly.
6. Let the beans rest for 5 minutes before serving.

Roasted New Potatoes With Compound Butter

Servings: 4
Cooking Time: 45 Minutes

Ingredients:

- 2 Pound Small Red, White or Purple Potatoes (or Combination of All Three)
- 3 Tablespoon olive oil
- salt and pepper
- 2 Stick Butter, unsalted
- 1 Tablespoon shallot, minced
- 3 Tablespoon Finely Chopped Herbs, Such As Tarragon, Parsley, Basil or Combination
- 2 Teaspoon kosher salt

Directions:

1. Supply your smoker with wood pellets and follow the start-up procedure. Preheat the grill, with the lid closed, to 400° F. Cut the potatoes in half and place in a large mixing bowl. Cover with the olive oil, a teaspoon of salt and generous grinding of pepper.
2. Place on a large baking sheet so there is space between the potatoes. Place on the grill and roast for 45 minutes to 1 hour, until crispy skinned. Toss once during cooking. Grill: 400 °F
3. To make the butter: Place it in a medium sized shallow mixing bowl. Use a wooden spoon or strong spatula to break it up and soften it even more. Sprinkle the shallot, herbs, and salt over the butter, then use the spoon to combine the ingredients. Taste, adding more salt or herbs if necessary. Reserve a few tablespoons of the butter to serve on the potatoes.
4. To freeze the butter for future use, place a foot long piece of plastic wrap on the counter. Spread the butter out into a 6" log across the long direction of the plastic wrap towards the bottom. Begin to roll the plastic wrap away from you to roll it into a log, twisting the sides of the plastic wrap like a candy wrapper to secure.
5. Using your hands, shape the log into an even cylinder. Once it's wrapped tightly, place in the freezer. Then when more is needed, simply slice off coins of it to serve over grilled steak, chicken, veggies, or roasted potatoes. The butter holds well in the freezer for up to one month. Enjoy! *Cook times will vary depending on set and ambient temperatures.

Roasted Olives

Servings: 4
Cooking Time: 45 Minutes

Ingredients:

- 2 Cup mixed olives
- 3 Sprig fresh rosemary
- 2 Clove garlic, minced
- 2 Tablespoon orange zest
- 1/3 Cup extra-virgin olive oil
- 2 Tablespoon orange juice
- 1/2 Teaspoon red pepper flakes

Directions:

1. Combine the olives, rosemary, garlic, orange zest, red pepper flakes, olive oil, and orange juice in a glass oven-safe pie plate or baking dish. Cover with foil.
2. Supply your smoker with wood pellets and follow the start-up procedure. Preheat the grill, with the lid closed, to 300° F.
3. Roast the olives for 45 minutes, stirring once or twice. Serve warm in an attractive bowl. Enjoy! Grill: 300 °F

Roasted Garlic Herb Fries

Servings: 4
Cooking Time: 45 Minutes

Ingredients:

- 4 Whole russet potatoes
- 1 Teaspoon salt
- 2 Tablespoon avocado oil
- 1 Teaspoon fresh chopped rosemary
- 1 Teaspoon fresh chopped thyme
- 2 Clove garlic, minced
- 2 Teaspoon flake salt
- 1 Teaspoon chopped parsley, for garnish

Directions:

1. Supply your smoker with wood pellets and follow the start-up procedure. Preheat the grill, with the lid closed, to 425° F.

2. Chop potatoes into fries, (a mandolin works great for this) and place directly into an ice water bath with 1 teaspoon salt for 15 to 30 minutes.
3. Combine oil, rosemary, thyme and garlic in a big bowl. Remove potatoes from ice water and dry thoroughly with paper towels.
4. Toss potatoes in the oil mixture and place them on 2 to 3 parchment-lined baking sheets in a single layer. Sprinkle the flake salt over the fries.
5. Place baking sheets on the grill and roast for 30 minutes, flip the fries, then cook for an additional 15 minutes until golden and crispy. Dust with parsley. Grill: 425 ˚F
6. Serve with your favorite dipping sauce, side dish or as a nacho base.

Grilled Beer Cabbage

Servings: 4
Cooking Time: 50 Minutes

Ingredients:

- 2 Cabbage, head
- 1 Tablespoon extra-virgin olive oil
- 1 Teaspoon salt
- 1 Teaspoon freshly ground black pepper
- 14 Fluid Ounce Guinness Extra Stout

Directions:

1. Clean and core cabbages. Drizzle with olive oil and salt and pepper. Rub into the cabbage.
2. Supply your smoker with wood pellets and follow the start-up procedure. Preheat the grill, with the lid closed, to 180° F.
3. Place cabbages directly on grill grate; smoke for 15 to 20 minutes. Remove from grill and thickly slice cabbage. Grill: 180 ˚F
4. Place sliced cabbage in cast-iron skillet. Pour beer over cabbage and return to grill.
5. Increase temperature to 375˚F and cook for 30 minutes, or until cabbage has reached desired softness. Grill: 375 ˚F
6. Serve with corned beef. Enjoy!

Grilled Asparagus And Hollandaise Sauce

Servings: 4
Cooking Time: 10 Minutes

Ingredients:

- 1 Pound asparagus
- 2 Teaspoon red pepper flakes
- 2 Tablespoon olive oil
- salt and pepper
- 4 egg yolk
- 1 Tablespoon lemon juice
- 1/2 Cup butter, melted
- cayenne pepper
- salt

Directions:

1. Supply your smoker with wood pellets and follow the start-up procedure. Preheat the grill, with the lid closed, to 375° F.
2. In a large bowl, mix asparagus with olive oil, red pepper flakes and salt. Arrange asparagus on a cooking sheet and take to the grill. Cook for approximately 10 to 15 minutes. Grill: 375 ˚F
3. In an aluminum bowl, whisk the egg yolks well. Add the lemon juice and whisk until creamy.
4. Place bowl over a double boiler, over low heat, making sure that it does not touches the water.
5. While whisking, add the melted butter slowly. Whisk until it doubles the volume. Take off the heat, still whisking and add the cayenne pepper and salt.
6. Arrange asparagus over a serving plater. Pour hollandaise sauce over asparagus and serve. Enjoy!

Roasted Beet & Bacon Salad

Servings: 4
Cooking Time: 45 Minutes

Ingredients:

- 2 Medium raw beets, peeled and thinly sliced
- 8 Slices bacon
- 1/4 Cup raw pecans or walnuts
- 2 Medium ripe pears, sliced
- 2 Large avocados, diced
- 1 Head red leaf lettuce or baby spinach, torn into bite-size pieces

- 1/4 Cup champagne vinaigrette

Directions:

1. Supply your smoker with wood pellets and follow the start-up procedure. Preheat the grill, with the lid closed, to 400° F.
2. Place beets on a foil-lined baking sheet and top with bacon. Place baking sheet directly on the grill grate (while preheating) and cook for 25 minutes. Grill: 400 °F
3. Toss to coat beets in rendered bacon fat.
4. Spread everything out in a single layer and continue to cook for another 15 minutes, or until beets are tender and bacon is crispy. Grill: 400 °F
5. Add pecans or walnuts and roast for 5 more minutes. Spoon out nuts and place on paper towels to drain and cool.
6. Once bacon is cool to the touch, roughly chop into medium pieces.
7. Place bacon, beets, nuts, pears, avocado and lettuce in a large salad bowl. Drizzle with champagne vinaigrette, toss to coat, and serve. Enjoy!

Delicious Smoked Coleslaw

Servings: 8

Cooking Time: 20 Minutes

Ingredients:

- 1 Head purple cabbage, shredded
- 1 Head green cabbage, shredded
- 1 Cup shredded carrots
- 2 scallions, thinly sliced
- 1 1/2 Cup mayonnaise
- 1/8 Cup white wine vinegar
- 1 Teaspoon celery seed
- 1 Teaspoon sugar
- salt and pepper

Directions:

1. Supply your smoker with wood pellets and follow the start-up procedure. Preheat the grill, with the lid closed, to 180° F.
2. Spread cabbage and carrots out on a sheet tray and place directly on the grill grates. Smoke for 20 to 25 minutes or until cabbage picks up desired amount of smoke. Grill: 180 °F
3. Remove from grill and transfer to the refrigerator immediately to cool. While cabbage is cooling, make the dressing.
4. For the dressing, combine all ingredients in a small bowl and mix well.
5. Place smoked cabbage and carrots in a large bowl and pour dressing over them. Stir to coat well.
6. Transfer to a serving dish and sprinkle with scallions. Enjoy!

Smoked Beet-pickled Eggs

Servings: 4

Cooking Time: 30 Minutes

Ingredients:

- 6 Eggs, hard boiled
- 1 Red Beets, scrubbed and trimmed
- 1 Cup apple cider vinegar
- 1 Cup Beet, juice
- 1/4 Onion, Sliced
- 1/3 Cup granulated sugar
- 3 Cardamom
- 1 star anise

Directions:

1. Supply your smoker with wood pellets and follow the start-up procedure. Preheat the grill, with the lid closed, to 275° F.
2. Place the peeled hard boiled eggs directly on the grill and smoke for 30 minutes. Grill: 275 °F
3. Put the smoked eggs in a quart size glass jar with the cooked/chopped beets in the bottom.
4. In a medium sauce pan, add the vinegar, beet juice, onion, sugar, cardamom and anise.
5. Bring to a boil and cook, uncovered, until sugar has dissolved and the onions are translucent (about 5 minutes).
6. Remove from the heat and let cool for a few minutes.
7. Pour the vinegar and onions mixture over the eggs and beets in the jar, covering the eggs completely.
8. Securely close with the jar lid. Refrigerate up to a month. Enjoy!

Grilled Fingerling Potato Salad

Servings: 6

Cooking Time: 15 Minutes

Ingredients:

- 10 Whole scallions
- 2/3 Cup extra-virgin olive oil, divided
- 1 1/2 Pound fingerling potatoes, cut in half lengthwise
- pepper
- 2 Teaspoon kosher salt, divided, plus more as needed
- 2 Tablespoon rice vinegar
- 2 Teaspoon lemon juice
- 1 Small jalapeño, sliced

Directions:

1. Supply your smoker with wood pellets and follow the start-up procedure. Preheat the grill, with the lid closed, to 450° F.
2. Brush the scallions with oil and place on the grill.
3. Cook until lightly charred, about 2 to 3 minutes. Remove and let cool. Grill: 450 °F
4. Once the scallions have cooled, slice and set aside.
5. Brush the fingerling potatoes with oil (reserving 1/3 cup for later use), then salt and pepper. Place cut-side down on the grill until cooked through, about 4 to 5 minutes. Grill: 450 °F
6. In a bowl, whisk the remaining 1/3 cup olive oil, 1 teaspoon salt, rice vinegar and lemon juice. Next mix in the scallions, potatoes and sliced jalapeño.
7. Season with salt and pepper, and serve. Enjoy!

Grilled Zucchini Squash Spears

Servings: 4

Cooking Time: 10 Minutes

Ingredients:

- 4 Medium zucchini
- 2 Tablespoon olive oil
- 1 Tablespoon sherry vinegar
- 2 thyme, leaves pulled
- salt and pepper

Directions:

1. Clean the zucchini and cut the ends off. Cut each in half lengthwise, then each half into thirds.
2. Combine remaining ingredients in a medium Ziplock bag and add the spears. Toss and mix well to coat the zucchini.
3. Supply your smoker with wood pellets and follow the start-up procedure. Preheat the grill, with the lid closed, to 350° F.
4. Remove the spears from the bag and place directly on the grill grate cut side down.
5. Cook for 3-4 minutes per side, until grill marks appear and zucchini is tender. Grill: 350 °F
6. Remove from grill and finish with more thyme leaves if desired. Enjoy!

Grilled Cabbage Steaks With Warm Bacon Vinaigrette

Servings: 4

Cooking Time: 10 Minutes

Ingredients:

- 3 Strips thick-cut lean bacon, cut into 1/4 inch strips
- 1 Large shallot, minced
- 2 Tablespoon sherry vinegar
- 1 Tablespoon whole grain mustard
- 1 Teaspoon chopped thyme
- 2 Tablespoon olive oil, plus more as needed
- 1 Head green cabbage, cut into 3/4 inch thick slices (about 6 steaks)
- salt and pepper

Directions:

1. Supply your smoker with wood pellets and follow the start-up procedure. Preheat the grill, with the lid closed, to 450° F.
2. For the Vinaigrette: In a large skillet, cook the bacon in 2 tablespoons olive oil over medium-high heat until browned and crisp. Remove bacon from heat and stir in the shallot, vinegar, mustard and thyme then set aside.
3. Brush cabbage steaks with olive oil and season with salt and pepper. Place cabbage steaks directly on grill grate and grill for 5 minutes per side. Grill: 450 °F
4. Remove cabbage steaks from grill and drizzle with bacon vinaigrette. Enjoy!

Roasted Tomatoes

Servings: 2
Cooking Time: 180 Minutes

Ingredients:

- 3 Large ripe tomatoes
- 1/2 Tablespoon kosher salt
- 1 Teaspoon coarse ground black pepper
- 1/4 Teaspoon sugar
- 1/4 Teaspoon thyme or basil
- olive oil

Directions:

1. Line a rimmed baking sheet with parchment paper.
2. Supply your smoker with wood pellets and follow the start-up procedure. Preheat the grill, with the lid closed, to 225° F.
3. Remove the stem end from each tomato and cut the tomatoes into 1/2 inch thick slices.
4. Combine the salt, pepper, sugar and thyme or basil in a small bowl and mix.
5. Pour olive oil into the well of a dinner plate.
6. Dip one side of each tomato slice in the olive oil and arrange on the baking sheet. Dust the tomato slices with the seasoning mixture.
7. Arrange the pan directly on the grill grate and roast the tomatoes until the juices stop running and the edges have contracted, about 3 hours. Remove from grill and enjoy!

Grilled Corn On The Cob With Parmesan And Garlic

Servings: 6
Cooking Time: 30 Minutes

Ingredients:

- 4 Tablespoon butter, melted
- 2 Clove garlic, minced
- salt and pepper
- 8 ears fresh corn
- 1/2 Cup shaved Parmesan
- 1 Tablespoon chopped parsley

Directions:

1. Supply your smoker with wood pellets and follow the start-up procedure. Preheat the grill, with the lid closed, to 450° F.
2. Place butter, garlic, salt and pepper in a medium bowl and mix well.
3. Peel back corn husks and remove the silk. Rub corn with half of the garlic butter mixture.
4. Close husks and place directly on the grill grate. Cook for 25 to 30 minutes, turning occasionally until corn is tender. Grill: 450 °F
5. Remove from grill, peel and discard husks. Place corn on serving tray, drizzle with remaining butter and top with Parmesan and parsley.

Baked Sweet Potatoes

Servings: 8
Cooking Time: 60 Minutes

Ingredients:

- 1 Cup butter, softened
- 1/4 Cup pure maple syrup
- 1/2 Teaspoon ground cinnamon
- 8 Medium sweet potatoes

Directions:

1. Make the Maple-Cinnamon Butter: In a mixing bowl, combine the butter, maple syrup, and cinnamon and whip with a wooden spoon. (Alternatively, blend the ingredients using a hand-held mixer or a stand mixer.) Transfer to a small bowl, cover, and chill until serving time.
2. Supply your smoker with wood pellets and follow the start-up procedure. Preheat the grill, with the lid closed, to 375° F. Arrange the sweet potatoes on the grill grate and bake until soft, 1 to 1-1/2 hours, depending on the size of the potatoes. Make a slit in the side of each, and squeeze the ends gently to fluff.
3. Serve hot with the Maple-Cinnamon Butter. Enjoy!

Baked Sweet Potato Casserole With Marshmallow Fluff

Servings: 6

Cooking Time: 60 Minutes

Ingredients:

- 3 Pound sweet potatoes
- 1/2 Cup milk
- 1 Cup brown sugar
- 3 eggs
- 4 Tablespoon butter
- 1/2 Teaspoon salt
- 3 egg white
- 1 Pinch salt
- 1 Pinch ground cinnamon

Directions:

1. Supply your smoker with wood pellets and follow the start-up procedure. Preheat the grill, with the lid closed, to 375° F.
2. Rinse, dry and pierce the sweet potatoes and place in grill whole. Cook for 45 minutes or until fork tender. Remove from grill and peel. Grill: 375 °F
3. Once peeled, mash the sweet potatoes in a large bowl with the milk, brown sugar, eggs, butter and salt. Place mashed potatoes in a baking dish and cook for 35 minutes. Grill: 375 °F
4. While the potatoes bake, make the fluff. Make a double boiler by bringing a small pot of water to a simmer, then placing the bowl of your stand mixer or another large stainless steel bowl atop the water.
5. Add the 3 egg whites, 2/3 cup brown sugar, a pinch of salt and a pinch of cinnamon to the bowl and whisk continuously until the sugar dissolves and the liquid is warm to the touch.
6. Transfer the bowl from the stovetop to your stand mixer and use the whisk attachment to whip the whites on medium-high speed until it turns glossy with stiff peaks, about 5-8 minutes.
7. Once the casserole has finished baking, use a rubber spatula to cover the sweet potato mixture with the fluff. Use the back of the spatula to create dramatic peaks.
8. Return to the grill for 5-7 minutes, or until the fluff starts to turn golden and the peaks are just shy of burnt. Remove from grill and enjoy!

Bacon Wrapped Corn On The Cob

Servings: 4

Cooking Time: 21 Minutes

Ingredients:

- 4 Whole Corn, ears
- 8 Slices bacon
- 1 Teaspoon freshly ground black pepper
- 1 Teaspoon chili powder
- 1 To Taste Parmesan cheese, grated

Directions:

1. Peel back the corn husks, remove silk strings and rinse corn under cold water.
2. Wrap 2 pieces of bacon around each ear of corn, securing with toothpicks.
3. Dust each ear of corn with some chili powder and cracked black pepper.
4. Supply your smoker with wood pellets and follow the start-up procedure. Preheat the grill, with the lid closed, to 375° F.
5. Place the ears of corn directly on the Traeger and grill for approximately 20 minutes or until the bacon is cooked crisp. Grill: 375 °F
6. Take the corn off the Traeger. Carefully remove the toothpicks and season with a little more chili powder and a grating of parmesan cheese, if desired. Serve & enjoy!

Sicilian Stuffed Mushrooms

Servings: 6

Cooking Time: 25 Minutes

Ingredients:

- 12 Medium Fresh Mushrooms, about 1-1/2 inches in diameter
- 4 Ounce cream cheese, room temperature
- 1/4 Cup Parmesan cheese, grated
- 1/4 Cup shredded mozzarella cheese
- 8 Whole Pimento Stuffed Green Olives, chopped
- 3 Tablespoon Pepperoni, finely diced

- 1 1/2 Tablespoon Sun Dried Tomatoes, drained & minced
- 1/4 Teaspoon freshly ground black pepper

Directions:

1. Dampen a paper towel and wipe the outside of the mushrooms clean. Remove the stem. Using a small spoon, scoop out the inside of the mushroom leaving a shell.
2. Filling: In a small mixing bowl, beat together the cream cheese, Parmesan, and mozzarella. Stir in olives, pepperoni, tomatoes, basil, and pepper.
3. Mound the filling in the mushroom caps. Set each filled cap into the well of a muffin tin.
4. Supply your smoker with wood pellets and follow the start-up procedure. Preheat the grill, with the lid closed, to 350° F.
5. Arrange the muffin tin on the grill grate and bake the mushrooms for 25 to 30 minutes, or until the mushrooms are tender and the filling is beginning to brown.
6. Transfer to a serving plate or platter. Enjoy!

Double-smoked Cheese Potatoes

Servings: 12

Cooking Time: 35 Minutes

Ingredients:

- 4 large baking potatoes (12 to 14 ounces each—preferably organic)
- 1 1/2 tablespoons bacon fat or butter, melted, or extra virgin olive oil
- Coarse salt (sea or kosher) and freshly ground black pepper
- 4 strips artisanal bacon (like Nueske's), cut crosswise into 1/4-inch slivers
- 6 tablespoons (3/4 stick) cold unsalted butter, thinly sliced
- 2 scallions, trimmed, white and green parts finely chopped (about 4 tablespoons)
- 2 cups coarsely grated smoked or regular white cheddar cheese (about 8 ounces)
- 1/2 cup sour cream
- Spanish smoked paprika (pimentón) or sweet paprika, for sprinkling

Directions:

1. Supply your smoker with wood pellets and follow the start-up procedure. Preheat the grill, with the lid closed, to 400° F.Add enough wood for 1 hour of smoking as specified by the manufacturer.
2. Scrub the potatoes on all sides with a vegetable brush. Rinse well under cold running water and blot dry with paper towels. Prick each potato several times with a fork (this keeps the spud from exploding and facilitates the smoke absorption). Brush or rub the potato on all sides with the bacon fat and season generously with salt and pepper.
3. Place the potatoes on the smoker rack. Smoke until the skins are crisp and the potatoes are tender in the center (they'll be easy to pierce with a slender metal skewer), about 1 hour.
4. Meanwhile, place the bacon in a cold skillet and fry over medium heat until browned and crisp, 3 to 4 minutes. Drain off the bacon fat (save the fat for future potatoes).
5. Transfer the potatoes to a cutting board and let cool slightly. Cut each potato in half lengthwise. Using a spoon, scrape out most of the potato flesh, leaving a 1/4-inch-thick shell. (It's easier to scoop the potatoes when warm.) Cut the potato flesh into 1/2-inch dice and place in a bowl.
6. Add the bacon, 4 tablespoons of the butter, the scallions, and cheese to the potato flesh and gently stir to mix. Stir in the sour cream and salt and pepper to taste; the mixture should be highly seasoned. Stir as little and as gently as possible so as to leave some texture to the potatoes.
7. Spoon the potato mixture back into the potato shells, mounding it in the center. Top each potato half with a thin slice of the remaining butter and sprinkle with paprika. The potatoes can be prepared up to 24 hours ahead to this stage, covered, and refrigerated.
8. Just before serving, preheat your smoker to 400 °F. Add enough wood for 30 minutes of smoking. Place the potatoes in a shallow aluminum foil pan and re-smoke them until browned and bubbling, 15 to 20 minutes.

Roasted Artichokes With Garlic Butter

Servings: 2
Cooking Time: 60 Minutes

Ingredients:

- 2 Large artichokes
- 3 Tablespoon olive oil
- sea salt
- 1 Stick unsalted butter
- 2 Clove garlic, chopped
- 2 Tablespoon chives, parsley, tarragon or cilantro
- 1 lemon

Directions:

1. Supply your smoker with wood pellets and follow the start-up procedure. Preheat the grill, with the lid closed, to 375° F.
2. Meanwhile, break off and discard any small outer leaves on the artichokes. Use a knife to slice off the tops of the artichokes, then using scissors, cut off any thorns on the remaining artichoke leaves. Trim the very bottom of the stem, then peel the tough and fibrous outer layer of the stem. Finally, cut artichokes in half and rinse off.
3. Transfer artichokes to a large mixing bowl, drizzle with olive oil and generously sprinkle with sea salt. Toss to coat the artichokes thoroughly. Grill: 375 °F
4. Add the artichokes to the grill, cut side down, and roast at 375°F until the artichoke bottoms are tender when poked with a fork or knife, about 50 to 60 minutes. Grill: 375 °F
5. When artichokes are almost done, add butter, chopped garlic and a pinch of sea salt to a small sauce pan and melt slowly over medium-low heat. Once the butter melts all the way and starts to bubble slightly, add the herbs.
6. When the artichokes are done, transfer to a butcher paper lined tray with the cut sides up. Drizzle half the garlic butter and squeeze half of the lemon over the artichokes. Add a small sprinkle of sea salt over the artichokes.
7. Serve with a ramekin of the remaining butter for dipping and extra wedges of lemon. Enjoy! Chef Tip: You can also serve with a ramekin of good mayonnaise mixed with a bit of hot sauce.

Roasted Green Beans With Bacon

Servings: 4
Cooking Time: 20 Minutes

Ingredients:

- 1 1/2 Pound green beans, ends trimmed
- 4 Strips bacon, cut into small pieces
- 4 Tablespoon extra-virgin olive oil
- 2 Clove garlic, minced
- 1 Teaspoon kosher salt

Directions:

1. Supply your smoker with wood pellets and follow the start-up procedure. Preheat the grill, with the lid closed, to 350° F.
2. Toss all ingredients together and spread out evenly on a sheet tray.
3. Place the tray directly on the grill grate and roast until the bacon is crispy and beans are lightly browned, about 20 minutes. Enjoy! Grill: 450 °F

Smoked Macaroni Salad

Servings: 4
Cooking Time: 20 Minutes

Ingredients:

- 1 Pound macaroni, uncooked
- 1/2 Small red onion, diced
- 1 green bell pepper, diced
- 1/2 Cup shredded carrot
- 1 Cup mayonnaise
- 3 Tablespoon white wine vinegar
- 2 Tablespoon sugar
- salt
- black pepper

Directions:

1. Bring a large stock pot of salted water to a boil over medium heat and cook pasta according to package directions. Make sure to cook to al dente, strain, and rinse under cold water.
2. Supply your smoker with wood pellets and follow the start-up procedure. Preheat the grill, with the lid closed, to 225° F.

3. Spread cooked pasta out on a sheet tray and place sheet tray directly on the grill grate. Smoke for 20 minutes, remove from heat, and transfer directly to the refrigerator to cool. Grill: 225 °F
4. While the pasta is cooling mix the dressing. Place all ingredients in a medium bowl and whisk to combine.
5. When pasta is cool combine chopped veggies, smoked pasta and dressing in a large bowl.
6. Cover with plastic wrap and place in the fridge for 20 minutes before serving. Enjoy!

Blt Pasta Salad

Servings: 6
Cooking Time: 45 Minutes

Ingredients:

- 1 pound thick-cut bacon
- 16 ounces bowtie pasta, cooked according to package directions and drained
- 2 tomatoes, chopped
- ½ cup chopped scallions
- ½ cup Italian dressing
- ½ cup ranch dressing
- 1 tablespoon chopped fresh basil
- 1 teaspoon salt
- 1 teaspoon freshly ground black pepper
- 1 teaspoon garlic powder
- 1 head lettuce, cored and torn

Directions:

1. Supply your smoker with wood pellets and follow the start-up procedure. Preheat, with the lid closed, to 225°F.
2. Arrange the bacon slices on the grill grate, close the lid, and cook for 30 to 45 minutes, flipping after 20 minutes, until crisp.
3. Remove the bacon from the grill and chop.
4. In a large bowl, combine the chopped bacon with the cooked pasta, tomatoes, scallions, Italian dressing, ranch dressing, basil, salt, pepper, and garlic powder. Refrigerate until ready to serve.
5. Toss in the lettuce just before serving to keep it from wilting.

Baked Loaded Tater Tots

Servings: 6
Cooking Time: 35 Minutes

Ingredients:

- 2 Pound frozen tater tots
- 1 Can Black Beans
- 1 1/2 Cup leftover chili
- 1 Cup leftover queso
- 1 red onion, finely diced
- 1/2 Cup chopped cilantro
- 1/2 Cup sour cream
- 1 jalapeños, sliced

Directions:

1. Supply your smoker with wood pellets and follow the start-up procedure. Preheat the grill, with the lid closed, to 375° F.
2. Spread frozen tots out on a sheet tray and place directly on the grill grate.
3. Cook for 20 to 25 minutes or until tots are crispy. Grill: 375 °F
4. Top with warmed chili, queso and beans. Place back on the grill for 15 minutes. Grill: 375 °F
5. Remove from grill and top with red onion, cilantro, sour cream and jalapeño. Enjoy!

Twice-smoked Potatoes

Servings: 16
Cooking Time: 95 Minutes

Ingredients:

- 8 Idaho, Russet, or Yukon Gold potatoes
- 1 (12-ounce) can evaporated milk, heated
- 1 cup (2 sticks) butter, melted
- ½ cup sour cream, at room temperature
- 1 cup grated Parmesan cheese
- ½ pound bacon, cooked and crumbled
- ¼ cup chopped scallions
- Salt
- Freshly ground black pepper
- 1 cup shredded Cheddar cheese

Directions:

1. Supply your smoker with wood pellets and follow the start-up procedure. Preheat, with the lid closed, to 400°F.
2. Poke the potatoes all over with a fork. Arrange them directly on the grill grate, close the lid, and smoke for 1 hour and 15 minutes, or until cooked through and they have some give when pinched.
3. Let the potatoes cool for 10 minutes, then cut in half lengthwise.
4. Into a medium bowl, scoop out the potato flesh, leaving ¼ inch in the shells; place the shells on a baking sheet.
5. Using an electric mixer on medium speed, beat the potatoes, milk, butter, and sour cream until smooth.
6. Stir in the Parmesan cheese, bacon, and scallions, and season with salt and pepper.
7. Generously stuff each shell with the potato mixture and top with Cheddar cheese.
8. Place the baking sheet on the grill grate, close the lid, and smoke for 20 minutes, or until the cheese is melted.

Roasted Pumpkin Seeds

Servings: 8
Cooking Time: 40 Minutes

Ingredients:

- 1 Whole Pumpkin, seeds
- olive oil or vegetable oil
- Jacobsen Salt Co. Pure Kosher Sea Salt

Directions:

1. As soon as possible after removing the seeds from the pumpkin, rinse pumpkin seeds under cold water in a colander and pick out the pulp and strings.
2. Place the pumpkin seeds in a single layer on an oiled baking sheet, stirring to coat. Supply your smoker with wood pellets and follow the start-up procedure. Preheat the grill, with the lid closed, to 180° F.
3. Place the baking sheet with the seeds on the grill grate, close the lid, and smoke for 20 minutes. Grill: 180 °F
4. Sprinkle your seeds with salt and turn the temperature on your grill up to 325°F. Roast the seeds until toasted, about 20 minutes. Check and stir seeds after the first 10 minutes. Grill: 325 °F
5. Seeds will be brown because they were smoked before being roasted. Enjoy!

Roasted Jalapeno Cheddar Deviled Eggs

Servings: 6
Cooking Time: 30 Minutes

Ingredients:

- 7 Eggs, hard boiled
- 3 Tablespoon mayonnaise
- 1 Teaspoon brown mustard
- 1 Teaspoon apple cider vinegar
- 1 Dash hot sauce
- 1 jalapeño pepper, seeded and minced
- salt and pepper
- 1/2 Cup shredded cheddar cheese
- paprika

Directions:

1. Supply your smoker with wood pellets and follow the start-up procedure. Preheat the grill, with the lid closed, to 180° F.
2. Place your eggs directly on the grill grate and smoke for 30 minutes.
3. Remove from the grill and allow the eggs to cool. Smoking the eggs will give them a slightly yellowed color, but an intense smoky flavor. If a classic white egg is your preference, then skip this step.
4. Slice the eggs lengthwise and scoop the egg yolks directly into a gallon zip top bag.
5. Add the mayo, mustard, vinegar, hot sauce, roasted jalapeños and salt and pepper to the bag.
6. Zip the bag closed and, using your hands, knead all of the ingredients together in the bag until completely smooth.
7. Squeeze the yolk mixture into one corner of the bag and then cut the corner off. Pipe the yolk mixture into the whites.
8. Sprinkle with the finely shredded cheddar or paprika and chill until you are ready to serve. Enjoy!

Roasted Tomatoes With Hot Pepper Sauce

Servings: 4

Cooking Time: 60 Minutes

Ingredients:

- 2 Pound fresh Roma tomatoes
- 3 Tablespoon parsley, chopped
- 2 Tablespoon garlic, chopped
- salt and pepper
- 1/2 Cup extra-virgin olive oil
- 1 Pound Spaghetti
- Hot peppers

Directions:

1. Supply your smoker with wood pellets and follow the start-up procedure. Preheat the grill, with the lid closed, to 400° F.
2. Wash tomatoes and cut them in half, lengthwise. Place them in a baking dish cut side up.
3. Sprinkle with chopped parsley, garlic, add salt and black pepper and pour 1/4 cup (100 mL)of olive oil over them.
4. Place on pre-heated grill and bake for 1 1/2 hours. Tomatoes will shrink and the skins will be partly blackened. Grill: 400 ˚F
5. Remove tomatoes from baking dish and place in a food processor leaving the cooked oil, and puree them.
6. Drop pasta into boiling salted water and cook until tender. Drain and toss immediately with the pureed tomatoes.
7. Add the remaining 1/4 cup (60mL) of raw olive oil and crumbled hot red pepper to taste. Toss and serve. Enjoy!

Smoked Mashed Potatoes

Servings: 6

Cooking Time: 45 Minutes

Ingredients:

- 2 Pound red bliss potatoes, washed and diced medium
- chicken stock or water
- 1/2 Stick salted butter
- 1 Cup whole milk
- 1/2 Cup sour cream
- 1/2 Cup shredded or grated Parmesan cheese
- kosher salt
- freshly ground black pepper
- 1/2 Cup fresh sliced green onions

Directions:

1. Place the diced red potatoes into a small saucepan or stockpot and cover with chicken stock or water.
2. Bring to a boil and cook on a simmer until fork tender, then cook 4 to 5 minutes past that until soft.
3. Supply your smoker with wood pellets and follow the start-up procedure. Preheat the grill, with the lid closed, to 400° F.
4. In a separate ovenproof pan, such as a cast iron skillet, add butter and milk and place in the Traeger during start up, until melted (approximately 7 to 10 minutes). Grill: 400 ˚F
5. Carefully remove the butter/milk mixture from the Traeger using heatproof gloves.
6. Drain the potatoes and place into a large bowl. Add the melted butter/milk mixture and slowly mash.
7. Add sour cream, cheese and green onions, then season to taste with salt and pepper.
8. Place into the cast iron skillet, then place the skillet back into the Traeger and cook until the potatoes have a slight crust and are bubbling, about 15 minutes. Grill: 400 ˚F
9. Carefully remove the mashed potatoes from the Traeger using heatproof gloves. Allow to cool for 5 minutes. Scoop and enjoy!

Potluck Salad With Smoked Cornbread

Servings: 6

Cooking Time: 45 Minutes

Ingredients:

- 1 cup all-purpose flour
- 1 cup yellow cornmeal
- 1 tablespoon sugar
- 2 teaspoons baking powder
- 1 teaspoon salt
- 1 cup milk

- 1 egg, beaten, at room temperature
- 4 tablespoons (½ stick) unsalted butter, melted and cooled
- Nonstick cooking spray or butter, for greasing
- ½ cup milk
- ½ cup sour cream
- 2 tablespoons dry ranch dressing mix
- 1 pound bacon, cooked and crumbled
- 3 tomatoes, chopped
- 1 bell pepper, chopped
- 1 cucumber, seeded and chopped
- 2 stalks celery, chopped (about 1 cup)
- ½ cup chopped scallions

Directions:

1. For the cornbread:
2. In a medium bowl, combine the flour, cornmeal, sugar, baking powder, and salt.
3. In a small bowl, whisk together the milk and egg. Pour in the butter, then slowly fold this mixture into the dry ingredients.
4. Supply your smoker with wood pellets and follow the start-up procedure. Preheat, with the lid closed, to 375°F.
5. Coat a cast iron skillet with cooking spray or butter.
6. Pour the batter into the skillet, place on the grill grate, close the lid, and smoke for 35 to 45 minutes, or until the cornbread is browned and pulls away from the side of the skillet.
7. Remove the cornbread from the grill and let cool, then coarsely crumble.
8. For the salad:
9. In a small bowl, whisk together the milk, sour cream, and ranch dressing mix.
10. In a medium bowl, combine the crumbled bacon, tomatoes, bell pepper, cucumber, celery, and scallions.
11. In a large serving bowl, layer half of the crumbled cornbread, half of the bacon-veggie mixture, and half of the dressing. Toss lightly.
12. Repeat the layering with the remaining cornbread, bacon-veggie mixture, and dressing. Toss again.
13. Refrigerate the salad for at least 1 hour. Serve cold.

Roasted Mashed Potatoes

Servings: 8
Cooking Time: 40 Minutes

Ingredients:

- 5 Pound Yukon Gold potatoes
- 1 1/2 Stick butter, softened
- 1 1/2 Cup heavy whipping cream, room temperature
- kosher salt
- white pepper

Directions:

1. Supply your smoker with wood pellets and follow the start-up procedure. Preheat the grill, with the lid closed, to 300° F.
2. Peel and cut potatoes into 1/2 inch cubes. Place the potatoes in a shallow baking dish with 1/2 cup water and cover. Bake until tender, about 40 minutes. Grill: 300 ˚F
3. In a medium saucepan, combine cream and butter. Cook over medium heat until butter is melted.
4. Remove potatoes from the grill and drain water.
5. Transfer potatoes to a bowl and mash using a potato masher. Gradually add in cream and butter mixture and mix using the masher. Be careful not to overwork or the potatoes will becomes gluey. Season with salt and pepper to taste. Enjoy!

Broccoli-cauliflower Salad

Servings: 4
Cooking Time: 25 Minutes

Ingredients:

- 1½ cups mayonnaise
- ½ cup sour cream
- ¼ cup sugar
- 1 bunch broccoli, cut into small pieces
- 1 head cauliflower, cut into small pieces
- 1 small red onion, chopped
- 6 slices bacon, cooked and crumbled (precooked bacon works well)
- 1 cup shredded Cheddar cheese

Directions:

1. In a small bowl, whisk together the mayonnaise, sour cream, and sugar to make a dressing.

2. In a large bowl, combine the broccoli, cauliflower, onion, bacon, and Cheddar cheese.
3. Pour the dressing over the vegetable mixture and toss well to coat.
4. Serve the salad chilled.

Grilled Asparagus & Honey-glazed Carrots

Servings: 4
Cooking Time: 35 Minutes

Ingredients:

- 1 Bunch asparagus, woody ends removed
- 1 Pound Carrots, peeled
- 2 Tablespoon olive oil
- sea salt
- 2 Tablespoon honey
- lemon zest

Directions:

1. Rinse all vegetables under cold water. Drizzle asparagus with olive oil and a generous sprinkling of sea salt. Generously drizzle carrots with honey and lightly sprinkle with sea salt.
2. Supply your smoker with wood pellets and follow the start-up procedure. Preheat the grill, with the lid closed, to 350° F.
3. Place carrots on the grill first and cook for 10-15 minutes, then add asparagus and cook both for another 15 to 20 minutes, or until they're done to your liking. Grill: 350 ˚F
4. Top the asparagus with some fresh lemon zest. Enjoy!

Roasted New Potatoes

Servings: 4
Cooking Time: 25 Minutes

Ingredients:

- 2 Pound small new potatoes
- 3 Tablespoon butter, melted
- 2 Tablespoon olive oil
- 2 Tablespoon whole mustard seeds
- salt and pepper
- 2 Tablespoon freshly minced chives
- 2 Tablespoon freshly minced parsley

Directions:

1. Place potatoes in a colander and rinse with cold water. Dry on paper towels and transfer to a rimmed baking sheet large enough to hold them in a single layer.
2. Drizzle the potatoes with butter and olive oil, then sprinkle them with the mustard seeds. Season with salt and pepper.
3. Supply your smoker with wood pellets and follow the start-up procedure. Preheat the grill, with the lid closed, to 400° F.
4. Place the baking sheet with the potatoes on the grill grate. Roast for about 25 minutes shaking the pan once or twice, until potatoes are tender and the skins are slightly wrinkled. Grill: 400 ˚F
5. Transfer potatoes to a bowl or platter. Top with fresh chives and parsley. Enjoy!

Roasted Sweet Potato Steak Fries

Servings: 4
Cooking Time: 40 Minutes

Ingredients:

- 3 Whole sweet potatoes
- 4 Tablespoon extra-virgin olive oil
- salt and pepper
- 2 Tablespoon fresh chopped rosemary

Directions:

1. Supply your smoker with wood pellets and follow the start-up procedure. Preheat the grill, with the lid closed, to 450° F.
2. Cut sweet potatoes into wedges and toss with olive oil, salt, pepper and rosemary. Spread on a parchment lined baking sheet and put in the grill. Cook for 15 minutes then flip and continue to cook until lightly browned and cooked through, about 40 to 45 minutes total. Grill: 450 ˚F
3. Serve with your favorite dipping sauce. Enjoy! Grill: 450 ˚F

Tater Tot Bake

Servings: 4

Cooking Time: 15 Minutes

Ingredients:

- 1 Whole frozen tater tots
- salt and pepper
- 1 Cup sour cream
- 1 Cup shredded cheddar cheese, divided
- 1/2 Cup bacon, chopped
- 1/4 Cup green onion, diced

Directions:

1. Supply your smoker with wood pellets and follow the start-up procedure. Preheat the grill, with the lid closed, to 375° F.
2. Line a baking sheet with aluminum foil for easy clean up and spread frozen tater tots onto sheet.
3. Sprinkle with Veggie Shake or salt and pepper to taste.
4. Place the baking sheet on the preheated grill grate and cook the tater tots for 10 minutes.
5. Drizzle sour cream over cooked tater tots.
6. Sprinkle the cheese, bacon bits and green onions on top of the tater tots.
7. Turn heat up to High heat and cook for 5 more minutes until the cheese melts and serve immediately. Enjoy!

Mashed Red Potatoes

Servings: 4

Cooking Time: 40 Minutes

Ingredients:

- 8 Large red potatoes
- salt
- black pepper
- 1/2 Cup heavy cream
- 1/4 Cup butter

Directions:

1. Supply your smoker with wood pellets and follow the start-up procedure. Preheat the grill, with the lid closed, to 180° F.
2. Slice red potatoes in half, lengthwise then cut in half again to make quarters. Season potatoes with salt and pepper.
3. Increase the heat to High and preheat. Once the grill is hot, set potatoes directly on the grill grate. Grill: 450 °F
4. Every 15 minutes flip potatoes to ensure all sides get color. Continue to do this until potatoes are fork tender.
5. When tender, mash potatoes with cream, butter, salt, and pepper to taste. Serve warm, enjoy!

Smoked Jalapeño Poppers

Servings: 4

Cooking Time: 60 Minutes

Ingredients:

- 12 Medium jalapeño
- 6 Slices bacon, cut in half
- 8 Ounce cream cheese
- 2 Tablespoon Pork & Poultry Rub
- 1 Cup grated cheese

Directions:

1. Supply your smoker with wood pellets and follow the start-up procedure. Preheat the grill, with the lid closed, to 180° F. For optimal flavor, use Super Smoke if available.
2. Slice the jalapeños in half lengthwise. Scrape out any seeds and ribs with a small spoon or paring knife. Mix softened cream cheese with Traeger Pork & Poultry rub and grated cheese. Spoon mixture onto each jalapeño half. Wrap with bacon and secure with a toothpick.
3. Place the jalapeños on a rimmed baking sheet. Place on grill and smoke for 30 minutes. Grill: 180 °F
4. Increase the grill temperature to 375°F and cook an additional 30 minutes or until bacon is cooked to desired doneness. Serve warm, enjoy! Grill: 375 °F

Grilled Broccoli Rabe

Servings: 4

Cooking Time: 10 Minutes

Ingredients:

- 4 Tablespoon extra-virgin olive oil
- 4 Bunch broccoli rabe or broccolini

- kosher salt
- 1 lemon, halved

Directions:

1. Supply your smoker with wood pellets and follow the start-up procedure. Preheat the grill, with the lid closed, to 450° F.
2. On a platter or in a mixing bowl, drizzle the olive oil over the broccoli rabe. Use your hands to mix thoroughly, coating the vegetables evenly with the oil. Season with sea salt.
3. Place the broccoli rabe in one layer directly on the lowest grill grate. Close the lid and cook for 5 to 10 minutes. You want there to be some color and slight char on the first side. Flip and cook for a few more minutes. Grill: 450 °F
4. Transfer the broccoli rabe to a serving platter and squeeze the juice of half a lemon evenly over the top.
5. Serve with more lemon wedges on the side. Enjoy!

Christmas Brussel Sprouts

Servings: 6
Cooking Time: 50 Minutes

Ingredients:

- 1/2 Pound thick-cut bacon
- 1 Medium onion, diced
- 2 Pound fresh Brussels sprouts
- 2 Tablespoon olive oil
- salt and pepper

Directions:

1. Supply your smoker with wood pellets and follow the start-up procedure. Preheat the grill, with the lid closed, to 350° F.
2. Place bacon directly on grill grate and cook for 15-20 minutes, or until lightly browned. Remove from grill and set aside on paper towel lined plate.
3. Slice onion in half and then slice into 1⁄4 inch moons and add to large mixing bowl. Slice brussels sprouts in half lengthwise and add to bowl.
4. Cut reserved bacon into 1⁄2 inch pieces and add to bowl. Drizzle with olive oil and sprinkle with salt and pepper. Toss to coat and pour into baking pan.
5. Turn the temperature on grill to 375 and place baking pan on grill. Roast for 30 minutes mixing halfway through cooking. Grill: 375 °F

Baked Sweet And Savory Yams By Bennie Kendrick

Servings: 6
Cooking Time: 60 Minutes

Ingredients:

- 3 Medium Yams
- 3 Tablespoon extra-virgin olive oil
- honey
- Goat Cheese
- 1/2 Cup brown sugar
- 1/2 Cup Pecans, pieces

Directions:

1. Supply your smoker with wood pellets and follow the start-up procedure. Preheat the grill, with the lid closed, to 350° F.
2. While Traeger comes to temperature, wash yams and poke a few holes all over. Wrap yams in foil.
3. Bake for 45-60 minutes or until knife tender. You don't want to overcook and get the yams too soft because you want to be able to cut each yam into rounds.
4. Once yams have cooled to the touch, cut each into 1/4" rounds. Lightly coat each round with oil olive and place on sheet tray.
5. Sprinkle each top with brown sugar. Using a teaspoon, place desired amount of goat cheese on each round. Next top with chopped pecans. Finally, drizzle Bee Local honey over each round.
6. Based on how sweet you like your yams, you can add more brown sugar and honey.
7. After complete, place your sheet tray back in the grill and cook, lid closed, for another 20 minutes. Enjoy!

Roasted Red Pepper White Bean Dip

Servings: 4
Cooking Time: 40 Minutes

Ingredients:

- 4 Whole garlic

- 4 Tablespoon extra-virgin olive oil
- 2 Bell Pepper, Red
- 3 Tablespoon Dill Weed, fresh
- 3 Tablespoon chopped flat-leaf parsley
- 2 Can cannellini beans, mashed
- 4 Teaspoon lemon juice
- 1 1/2 Teaspoon salt

Directions:

1. Roasting the garlic and red peppers:
2. Supply your smoker with wood pellets and follow the start-up procedure. Preheat the grill, with the lid closed, to 400° F.
3. Peel away the outside layers of the garlic husk. Cut off the top of the garlic bulb, exposing each of the individual cloves. Drizzle olive oil over the top of the head of garlic and rub it in. Wrap the garlic in foil, completely covering it. Put the head of garlic and the two red peppers (washed and dried) on the Traeger.
4. Roast the garlic for 25-30 minutes and the peppers for about 40 minutes. Rotate the peppers a quarter-turn every 10 minutes until the exterior is blistered and blackened. Grill: 400 °F
5. Pull the peppers off the grill and put them in a bowl. Cover the bowl with plastic wrap and leave them for 15 minutes. The steam will loosen the skins so that they slip off like a drumstick covered in barbecue sauce.
6. Peel off the pepper skin. Cut off the stems and scrape out the seeds and they're ready to use.
7. As for the garlic, let it cool and then pull out the individual cloves as needed.
8. The dip:
9. In a blender put the roasted red peppers, 4 cloves of roasted garlic, dill, parsley, drained and rinsed beans, olive oil, lemon juice and salt.
10. Blend until the dip is smooth and creamy. You may need to scrape down the sides of the blender a couple of times. If it's having difficulty blending or looks too thick add more olive oil or lemon juice. (Add more lemon juice if it tastes like it needs more acid or brightness.) Enjoy!

Green Bean Casserole

Servings: 6
Cooking Time: 25 Minutes

Ingredients:

- 1/2 Stick butter
- 1 Small onion
- 1/2 Cup sliced button mushrooms
- 4 Can green beans, drained
- 2 Can cream of mushroom soup
- 1 Teaspoon Lawry's Seasoned Salt
- pepper
- 1 Can French's Original Crispy Fried Onions
- 1 Cup grated sharp cheddar cheese

Directions:

1. Supply your smoker with wood pellets and follow the start-up procedure. Preheat the grill, with the lid closed, to 375° F.
2. Melt butter in a cast iron skillet and add onions and mushrooms, stirring occasionally until softened.
3. Add drained green beans and cream of mushroom soup and stir gently to combine.
4. Season with seasoned salt and pepper and sprinkle the top with grated cheddar cheese and fried onions.
5. Bake for 25 minutes. Serve warm, enjoy! Grill: 375 °F

Baked Breakfast Mini Quiches

Servings: 8
Cooking Time: 15 Minutes

Ingredients:

- cooking spray
- 1 Tablespoon extra-virgin olive oil
- 1/2 yellow onion, diced
- 3 Cup Spinach, fresh
- 10 eggs
- 4 Ounce shredded cheddar, mozzarella or Swiss cheese
- 1/4 Cup fresh basil
- 1 Teaspoon kosher salt
- 1/2 Teaspoon black pepper

Directions:

1. Spray a 12-cup muffin tin generously with cooking spray.
2. In a small skillet over medium heat, warm the oil. Add the onion and cook, stirring frequently, until softened, about 7 minutes. Add the spinach and cook until wilted, about 1 minute longer.
3. Transfer to a cutting board to cool, then chop the mixture so the spinach if broken up a little.
4. Supply your smoker with wood pellets and follow the start-up procedure. Preheat the grill, with the lid closed, to 350° F.
5. In a large bowl, whisk the eggs until frothy. Add the cooled onions and spinach, cheese, basil, 1 tsp salt and 1/2 tsp pepper. Stir to combine. Divide egg mixture evenly among the muffin cups.
6. Place tray on the grill and bake until the eggs have puffed up, are set, and are beginning to brown, about 18 to 20 minutes. Grill: 350 ˚F
7. Serve immediately, or allow to cool on a wire rack, then refrigerate in an air tight container for up to 4 days. Enjoy!

Whole Roasted Cauliflower With Garlic Parmesan Butter

Servings: 4
Cooking Time: 45 Minutes

Ingredients:

- 1 Whole head cauliflower
- 1/4 Cup olive oil
- salt and pepper
- 1/2 Cup butter, melted
- 1/4 Cup shredded Parmesan cheese
- 2 Clove garlic, minced
- 1/2 Tablespoon chopped parsley

Directions:

1. Supply your smoker with wood pellets and follow the start-up procedure. Preheat the grill, with the lid closed, to 450° F.
2. Brush the cauliflower with olive oil and season liberally with salt and pepper.
3. Put cauliflower in a cast iron skillet, place directly on the grill grate and cook for 45 minutes until golden brown and the center is tender.
4. While the cauliflower is cooking, combine the melted butter, parmesan, garlic and parsley in a small bowl.
5. During the last 20 minutes of cooking, baste the cauliflower with the melted butter mixture.
6. Remove the cauliflower from the grill and top with extra parmesan and parsley if desired. Enjoy!

Cast Iron Potatoes

Servings: 4
Cooking Time: 60 Minutes

Ingredients:

- 4 Tablespoon butter, cut into cubes
- 2 1/2 Pound potatoes, peeled and cut into 1/8 inch slices
- 1/2 Large sweet onion, thinly sliced
- salt
- black pepper
- 1 1/2 Cup grated mild cheddar or jack cheese
- 2 Cup milk
- paprika

Directions:

1. Butter the inside of a cast iron skillet and layer half the potato slices on the bottom. Top with half the onions. Season with salt and pepper.
2. Sprinkle 1 cup of the cheese over the potatoes and onions and dot with half the butter. Layer the remaining potatoes and onions on top. Dot with remaining butter.
3. Pour the milk into the skillet. Cover the skillet tightly with aluminum foil.
4. Supply your smoker with wood pellets and follow the start-up procedure. Preheat the grill, with the lid closed, to 350° F.
5. Bake for 1 hour, or until the potatoes are very tender. Grill: 350 ˚F
6. Remove the foil and top with the remaining 1/2 cup of cheese. Bake for 30 minutes more (uncovered) until the cheese is lightly browned. Dust the top with paprika and serve immediately.

Smoked Asparagus Soup

Servings: 4

Cooking Time: 40 Minutes

Ingredients:

- Pound Asparagus Spears
- 1 Tablespoon olive oil
- salt and pepper
- 1/2 yellow onion, diced
- 1 Tablespoon butter
- 2 Clove garlic, minced
- 1 1/2 Cup chicken stock
- 1 1/2 Cup cream
- 2 Stalk Raw Asparagus, Shaved

Directions:

1. Supply your smoker with wood pellets and follow the start-up procedure. Preheat the grill, with the lid closed, to 180° F.
2. Drizzle 1 pound of asparagus with olive oil and season with salt and pepper. Place directly on the grill grate and smoke for 20-30 minutes. Taste along the way to assess smoke level pulling earlier if needed. Grill: 180 ˚F
3. Place 1 Tbsp butter in a saucepan and melt over medium heat. Add onion and garlic and saute for 2-3 minutes or until onion is translucent.
4. Remove asparagus from the grill and cut into 1" pieces. Place asparagus in the pan with the onions and add stock and cream. Bring to a simmer.
5. Remove from heat and puree using a blender or immersion blender until smooth.
6. Season with salt and pepper and serve. Top with fresh shaved asparagus, sprinkle with salt, pepper, and smoked paprika if desired. Enjoy!

Sweet Potato Marshmallow Casserole

Servings: 6

Cooking Time: 60 Minutes

Ingredients:

- 5 Yams
- 1 1/2 Stick butter
- 1/2 Cup brown sugar
- 1 Teaspoon vanilla
- 1 Teaspoon kosher salt
- 1 Teaspoon cracked black pepper
- 1 Marshmallows, miniature
- 1/4 Unsalted Butter, Softened

Directions:

1. Supply your smoker with wood pellets and follow the start-up procedure. Preheat the grill, with the lid closed, to 375° F.
2. Pierce the skin of the yams with a fork a few times. Place on a baking sheet or foil tin inside the grill and let roast for 50 minutes or until extremely softened. Grill: 375 ˚F
3. Remove yams from the grill and set aside until cool enough to handle. While the potatoes cool, with a stiff whisk, whip together 1/2 cup softened butter, the brown sugar, vanilla, salt and pepper.
4. Remove and discard skins from sweet potatoes and mash until smooth. Fold in the butter mixture and transfer to a cast iron pan.
5. Place cast iron on the grill and bake for 15-20 minutes. Remove from the grill, top with marshmallows and dot with remaining 1/4 cup butter.
6. Place back in the grill for 15 minutes until warm and the marshmallows are golden. Enjoy! Grill: 375 ˚F

Smoked Pico De Gallo

Servings: 4

Cooking Time: 30 Minutes

Ingredients:

- 3 Cup diced Roma tomatoes
- 1 jalapeño, diced
- 1/2 red onion, diced
- 1/2 Bunch cilantro, finely chopped
- 2 lime, juiced
- salt
- olive oil

Directions:

1. Supply your smoker with wood pellets and follow the start-up procedure. Preheat the grill, with the lid closed, to 180° F.
2. Place the diced tomatoes on a small sheet pan spreading them into a thin layer. Place the sheet pan

directly on the grill and smoke for 30 minutes. Grill: 180 °F

3. When the tomatoes are finished, toss all ingredients in a medium bowl and finish with lime juice, salt and olive oil to taste. Serve and enjoy!

Grilled Street Corn

Servings: 6

Cooking Time: 10 Minutes

Ingredients:

- 6 ears corn, husked
- 1 As Needed extra-virgin olive oil
- 1/4 Cup mayonnaise
- 1 Tablespoon ancho or guajillo chile powder
- 1/2 Cup chopped cilantro, plus more for serving
- 1 lime, zested and juiced
- salt
- 1/2 Cup Cotija cheese
- 1 As Needed cilantro, finely chopped

Directions:

1. Supply your smoker with wood pellets and follow the start-up procedure. Preheat the grill, with the lid closed, to 450° F.
2. Brush corn with oil and place on grill, turning occasionally.
3. While corn is on the grill, mix mayonnaise with chile powder, cilantro, lime juice and zest in a bowl. Season with salt.
4. After about 10 minutes corn should be cooked through and slightly charred on the outside. Remove from grill.
5. Top corn with chile mayonnaise then sprinkle on the Cotija cheese and chopped cilantro. Enjoy!

Baked Artichoke Parmesan Mushrooms

Servings: 8

Cooking Time: 30 Minutes

Ingredients:

- 8 Cremini Mushroom Caps
- 6 1/2 Ounce artichoke hearts
- 1/3 Cup Parmesan cheese, grated
- 1/4 Cup mayonnaise
- 1/2 Teaspoon garlic salt
- your favorite hot sauce
- paprika

Directions:

1. Clean the mushrooms with a damp paper towel. Remove the stems and discard or save for another use.
2. Using a small spoon, scoop out the inside (gills, etc.). Combine the artichoke hearts, parmesan, mayonnaise, garlic salt, and hot sauce and mix well.
3. Mound the filling in the mushroom caps. Dust the tops with paprika.
4. Arrange the mushrooms in an oven-safe baking dish.
5. Supply your smoker with wood pellets and follow the start-up procedure. Preheat the grill, with the lid closed, to 350° F.
6. Bake the mushrooms (uncovered) until the filling is bubbling and just beginning to brown, about 25 to 30 minutes. Serve immediately. Grill: 350 °F
7. For a simple variation, stuff the mushrooms with your favorite bulk sausage and bake on your Traeger as directed above. Enjoy!

Butter Braised Green Beans

Servings: 6

Cooking Time: 60 Minutes

Ingredients:

- 24 Ounce thin fresh green beans, trimmed or whole frozen green beans, thawed
- 8 Tablespoon butter, melted
- Veggie Rub or coarse salt
- freshly ground black pepper

Directions:

1. Supply your smoker with wood pellets and follow the start-up procedure. Preheat the grill, with the lid closed, to 325° F.
2. Put the green beans in a pile on a rimmed baking sheet and pour the melted butter over them. Using tongs, spread the beans out in the pan and season with Traeger Veggie Rub and black pepper.
3. Roast the beans for about 1 hour, stirring and lifting with tongs every 20 minutes or so. The beans should be very tender, shriveled, and lightly browned in places. Transfer to a serving bowl and serve while hot. Enjoy!

Skillet Potato Cake

Servings: 4
Cooking Time: 40 Minutes

Ingredients:

- 8 Tablespoon butter, melted
- 2 Pound russet potatoes, peeled and thinly sliced
- 3 Tablespoon kosher salt
- 2 Tablespoon freshly ground black pepper
- thyme

Directions:

1. Supply your smoker with wood pellets and follow the start-up procedure. Preheat the grill, with the lid closed, to 375° F.
2. Brush the bottom of a cast iron skillet with part of the melted butter. Place potato slices vertically around the outer edges then fill in the middle in the same fashion.
3. Pour additional melted butter over the top of the layers and sprinkle with salt and pepper.
4. Place skillet in grill and cook for 35 to 40 minutes or until potatoes are fork tender and golden brown.
5. Garnish with a sprinkle of fresh thyme over the top of the potatoes. Enjoy!

Grilled Asparagus And Spinach Salad

Servings: 8
Cooking Time: 10 Minutes

Ingredients:

- 4 Fluid Ounce apple cider vinegar
- 8 Fluid Ounce Honey Bourbon BBQ Sauce
- 2 Bunch asparagus, ends trimmed
- 3 Fluid Ounce extra-virgin olive oil
- 2 Ounce Beef Rub
- 24 Ounce Spinach, fresh
- 4 Ounce candied pecans
- 4 Ounce feta cheese

Directions:

1. Combine apple cider vinegar and Traeger Apricot BBQ Sauce to create salad dressing.
2. Supply your smoker with wood pellets and follow the start-up procedure. Preheat the grill, with the lid closed, to High heat.
3. Toss the asparagus with Olive Oil and the Beef Shake. Put asparagus in the Traeger Grilling Basket and move the basket to the grill grate.
4. Grill for about 10 minutes. Remove the asparagus once it is cooked. Grill: 350 ˚F
5. Place the hot asparagus right on top of the bowl of spinach.
6. Add candied pecans, feta cheese & salad dressing then toss and serve. Enjoy!

Smoked & Loaded Baked Potato

Servings: 4
Cooking Time: 60 Minutes

Ingredients:

- 6 Yukon Gold or russet potatoes
- 8 Slices bacon
- 1/2 Cup butter, melted
- 1 Cup sour cream
- 1 1/2 Cup shredded cheddar cheese, divided
- salt and pepper
- 1 Bunch green onions, thinly sliced

Directions:

1. Supply your smoker with wood pellets and follow the start-up procedure. Preheat the grill, with the lid closed, to 375° F.
2. Poke potatoes with a fork, then place straight onto the grill. Cook for 1 hour. Grill: 375 ˚F
3. At the same time, cook bacon on a baking sheet on the grill for about 20 minutes; remove, cool and crumble. Grill: 375 ˚F
4. Once potatoes are done, remove and allow to cool for 15 minutes.
5. Cut each potato lengthwise, creating long halves. Use a small spoon to scoop out about 70% of the potato to make a boat, keeping a thick layer of potato near skin.
6. Place excess potato in a bowl and reserve. Lightly mash extra potato with a fork; add butter, sour cream, 1/2 cup cheese and season with salt and pepper.

7. Take the potato skins and fill with potato mixture, then sprinkle with extra cheese and bacon.
8. Place back on grill for about 10 minutes or until warm and cheese has melted. Garnish with green onions and extra sour cream. Enjoy! Grill: 375 °F

Stuffed Jalapenos

Servings: 8
Cooking Time: 60 Minutes

Ingredients:

- 40 Whole jalapeño
- 8 Ounce cream cheese, room temperature
- 1 Cup Sharp Cheddar Grated
- 1 1/2 Teaspoon Pork & Poultry Rub
- 2 Tablespoon sour cream
- 1 Whole (14 oz) cocktail sausages
- 20 Whole Slices of Smoked Bacon, Cut in Half

Directions:

1. Wash and dry the peppers. Cut the stem ends off with a paring knife, and using the same knife or a small metal spoon, carefully scrape the seeds and ribs out of each pepper. Set aside.
2. In a small bowl, combine the cream cheese, grated cheese, Traeger Pork and Poultry Rub, and the sour cream.
3. Transfer the mixture to a sturdy resealable plastic bag and trim 1/2-inch off one of the lower corners with a scissors. Squeeze the cream cheese mixture into each pepper, filling each a little over the halfway point.
4. Stuff one sausage into each pepper. Wrap the outside of each with a piece of bacon, securing with 1 or 2 toothpicks.
5. Arrange the peppers on a foil-lined baking sheet. Supply your smoker with wood pellets and follow the start-up procedure. Preheat the grill, with the lid closed, to 180° F, and smoke the peppers for 1 to 1-1/2 hours.
6. Increase the heat to 350 degrees F and continue to cook for 20 to 30 minutes, or until the bacon begins to render its fat and crisp. Enjoy! Grill: 350 °F

Smoked Parmesan Herb Popcorn

Servings: 2
Cooking Time: 15 Minutes

Ingredients:

- 4 Tablespoon butter
- 2 Teaspoon Italian Seasoning
- 1 Teaspoon garlic powder
- 1 Teaspoon salt
- 1/4 Cup popcorn kernels
- 1/2 Cup Parmesan cheese, grated

Directions:

1. Supply your smoker with wood pellets and follow the start-up procedure. Preheat the grill, with the lid closed, to 250° F.
2. In a small saucepan, melt the butter over medium heat. Add Italian seasoning, garlic powder, and salt and stir to combine. Remove from heat and set aside.
3. Add 1/4 cup of popcorn to a brown paper lunch bag. Fold the top of the bag over twice to close. Place the bag in the microwave and microwave on high for 1 to 2 minutes, or until there are about 5 seconds between pops. Open the bag with care and dump into a large mixing bowl.
4. Pour butter mixture of popcorn in a bowl and toss to combine. Dump popcorn onto a baking sheet and place in grill.
5. Smoke for 10 minutes; remove from grill. Toss with parmesan cheese to serve. Enjoy! Grill: 250 °F

Roasted Jalapeño Poppers

Servings: 2
Cooking Time: 30 Minutes

Ingredients:

- 8 Slices Bacon, Center Cut
- 2 Cup cream cheese
- 2 Ounce Cheese, sharp cheddar
- 1/2 Cup green onions, minced
- 2 Teaspoon fresh squeezed lime juice
- 4 Tablespoon Seeded Tomato, Chopped
- 4 Tablespoon cilantro, chopped
- 1/2 Teaspoon kosher salt
- 2 Small garlic clove, minced
- 12 Whole Jalapeños

Directions:

1. Supply your smoker with wood pellets and follow the start-up procedure. Preheat the grill, with the lid closed, to 350° F.
2. Place 2 bacon slices directly on the grill grate and cook 10-15 minutes until cooked through and crispy flipping halfway through. Remove from grill, but leave the grill on. When cool enough to handle, coarsely chop the bacon and reserve. Grill: 350 ˚F
3. In the bowl of a stand mixer, combine cream cheese, cheddar cheese, green onions, chopped bacon, lime juice, tomatoes, cilantro, salt and garlic. Mix on medium speed with a paddle until combined. Transfer mixture to a piping bag.
4. Cut the tops off the jalapeños and remove the seeds and ribs with a small paring knife.
5. Pipe the filling into each pepper so that the filling comes up a 1/4" over the top of the pepper. Place the tops back on each pepper.
6. With a rolling pin, flatten out the remaining six slices of bacon until they are 1/8" thick. Cut each slice in half. Wrap 1/2 a bacon slice around each pepper and secure with a toothpick.
7. Place the peppers in the Traeger Jalapeno Popper Tray. Place the tray directly on the grill grate and cook for 30-40 minutes until the peppers are tender, bacon is crispy, and cheese is melted. Enjoy! Grill: 350 ˚F

Chef Curtis' Famous Chimichurri Sauce

Servings: 4
Cooking Time: 5 Minutes

Ingredients:

- 2 Whole lemon, halved
- 2 Medium flat-leaf Italian parsley, washed and chopped with the majority of stems cut off
- 4 Clove garlic, diced
- 1/4 Cup red wine vinegar
- 1/2 Teaspoon black pepper
- 1/4 Cup extra-virgin olive oil
- 1 Teaspoon salt

Directions:

1. Supply your smoker with wood pellets and follow the start-up procedure. Preheat the grill, with the lid closed, to 450° F.
2. Place lemon halves directly on the grill grate and cook for 5 minutes or until grill marks appear. Grill: 450 ˚F
3. Take lemons off grill and juice. Combine all of the ingredients in a food processor or blender and purée until smooth, or leave slightly chunky for some texture.
4. Add additional olive oil to taste for a milder flavor if preferred. Serve on protein or as a dip. Enjoy!

Baked Kale Chips

Servings: 4
Cooking Time: 20 Minutes

Ingredients:

- 2 Bunch kale, leaves washed and stems removed
- 1 As Needed extra-virgin olive oil
- 1 To Taste sea salt

Directions:

1. Dry the kale leaves well and lay them out on a sheet tray. Drizzle lightly with olive oil and sprinkle with sea salt.
2. Supply your smoker with wood pellets and follow the start-up procedure. Preheat the grill, with the lid closed, to 250° F.
3. Place the sheet tray directly on the grill grate and cook until kale is lightly browned and crispy, about 20 minutes. Enjoy! Grill: 250 ˚F

Roasted Vegetable Napoleon

Servings: 4
Cooking Time: 30 Minutes

Ingredients:

- 2 Whole sweet potatoes
- 2 Whole zucchini
- 2 Whole Squash
- 1 Whole red onion
- 2 Whole Bell Pepper, Red
- salt and pepper

Directions:

1. Supply your smoker with wood pellets and follow the start-up procedure. Preheat the grill, with the lid closed, to High heat.
2. Salt and pepper all vegetables and grill them on both sides. Begin with the peppers and onions as they will take a little longer to cook. Grill: 450 ˚F

Delicious Grilled Whole Corn

Servings: 4
Cooking Time: 25 Minutes

Ingredients:

- 3 green onions
- 6 Tablespoon butter, softened
- 1 Teaspoon chile powder
- 1 Teaspoon toasted sesame seeds
- 4 ears corn, in husk

Directions:

1. Supply your smoker with wood pellets and follow the start-up procedure. Preheat the grill, with the lid closed, to 325° F.
2. Place green onions directly on the grill grate and cook 15 minutes until lightly charred. Remove from grill and set aside.
3. Sesame-Chile Butter: Take butter out of fridge and let soften. Chop up charred green onions and add to butter along with chile powder and sesame seeds. Mash all ingredients together.
4. Grill corn, rotating occasionally, until husks are blackened (some will flake and fall off) and kernels are tender with some browned and charred spots, about 25 to 35 minutes. Grill: 325 ˚F
5. Let corn cool slightly, then shuck. Serve with the Sesame-Chile Butter. Enjoy

POULTRY RECIPES

Flavoured Hibachi Chicken

Servings: 4
Cooking Time: 10 Minutes

Ingredients:

- To Taste, Blackened Sriracha Rub Seasoning
- To Taste, Blackened Sriracha Rub Seasoning (For Vegetables)
- 2 Cups Broccoli Florets, Blanched
- 1 Tbsp Brown Sugar
- 1 Tbsp Butter, Unsalted
- 1 1/2 Lbs Chicken Breast, Boneless, Skinless, Sliced Thin
- 1 Tbsp Cilantro, Chopped
- 3 Garlic Cloves, Minced
- 2 Garlic Cloves, Minced (For Vegetables)
- 1 Tsp Ginger, Grated
- 1 Tsp Ginger, Grated (For Vegetables
- 1/2 Lime, Juiced
- 1/2 Red Bell Pepper, Sliced Thin
- For Serving, Rice Noodles, Cooked
- 2 Scallions, Chopped
- 1 Tbsp Sesame Oil
- 2 Tbsp Sesame Oil, Divided
- 1 Cup Snap Peas, Blanched
- 1/4 Cup Tamari
- For Serving, Toasted Sesame Seeds
- 1 Tbsp Vegetable Oil
- 1 Tbsp Vegetable Oil (For Vegetables)
- For Serving, Yum-Yum Sauce

Directions:

1. Supply your smoker with wood pellets and follow the start-up procedure. Preheat the grill, with the lid open, to medium-high heat. When hot, add 1 tablespoon of sesame oil and vegetable oil. Immediately add the chicken and season with Blackened Sriracha. When the chicken starts to brown, flip it over to brown the other side.
2. Add the garlic, ginger, soy sauce, brown sugar, butter, and the remaining tablespoon of sesame oil and stir. Turn the heat down to medium-low and let the mixture simmer for 3 minutes, until it thickens and adheres to the chicken. Add lime juice, cilantro, and scallions, then remove the mixture from the griddle.
3. After starting the sauce for the chicken, sauté the vegetables: Add sesame oil and vegetable oil to the other side of the griddle. Quickly sauté broccoli, snap peas, and red bell pepper with garlic and ginger. Season with Blackened Sriracha. Remove from the griddle after 2 minutes.
4. Serve hibachi chicken warm with sautéed vegetables, toasted sesame seeds, rice noodles, and Yum-Yum sauce if desired.

Roasted Stuffed Turkey Breast

Servings: 6
Cooking Time: 40 Minutes

Ingredients:

- 1 (4-5 lb) boneless turkey breast
- 5 Slices thick-cut bacon, chopped
- 3/4 Cup assorted mushrooms
- 1 Bunch scallions, chopped
- 1/8 Cup white wine
- 3 Tablespoon panko breadcrumbs
- salt
- black pepper

Directions:

1. Supply your smoker with wood pellets and follow the start-up procedure. Preheat the grill, with the lid closed, to 375° F.
2. Slice the turkey breast horizontally, making sure not to slice all the way through. Lay breast open flat.
3. Cook bacon in a skillet over medium heat until crispy. Remove bacon and set aside. Sauté mushrooms in the bacon grease until browned. Add scallions and cook for an additional two minutes. Add white wine and cook down until no wine remains. Stir in breadcrumbs and bacon, adding salt and pepper to taste.
4. Transfer filling to fridge to cool for 15 to 20 minutes. Once chilled, spread the filling onto the turkey breast,

pressing lightly to make sure it adheres. Roll the turkey breast tightly and tie with butcher's twine at about 1 inch intervals. Tuck the ends of the turkey breast under and tie with twine lengthwise.

5. Season the outside of the turkey breast with salt and pepper. Place in grill for 40 minutes. Check the internal temperature, desired temperature is 165°F. Once the finished temperature is reached, remove turkey from the grill and let rest for 10 minutes. Slice and serve. Enjoy! Grill: 375 °F Probe: 165 °F

Lemon Rosemary Beer Can Chicken

Servings: 4

Cooking Time: 60 Minutes

Ingredients:

- 1 (3 to 3-1/2 lb) whole chicken
- 1 lemon, halved
- 1 Teaspoon kosher salt
- 1 Teaspoon ground black pepper
- 1 Teaspoon fresh finely chopped rosemary
- 1 (12 oz) can beer

Directions:

1. Supply your smoker with wood pellets and follow the start-up procedure. Preheat the grill, with the lid closed, to 400° F.
2. Coat the chicken inside and out with the juice from one lemon. In a small bowl, combine salt, pepper and rosemary, and sprinkle on the inside and outside of chicken.
3. Empty half of the beer from the can and place the can on a solid surface. Place the chicken atop the beer can, tucking the legs in the front.
4. Carefully place the chicken directly on the grill grate using the legs to support if needed. Alternatively, place the chicken atop the beer can on a sheet tray for a more stable surface, then place the sheet tray directly on the grill grate.
5. Cook the chicken until an instant-read thermometer reads 165°F when inserted in the thickest part of the breast, about 60 minutes. Grill: 400 °F Probe: 165 °F
6. Let the chicken rest 10 minutes before carving. Serve with Chardonnay or any of your favorite medium body red or white wines. Enjoy!

Smoking Duck With Mandarin Glaze

Servings: 4

Cooking Time: 240 Minutes

Ingredients:

- 1 quart buttermilk
- 1 (5-pound) whole duck
- ¾ cup soy sauce
- ½ cup hoisin sauce
- ½ cup rice wine vinegar
- 2 tablespoons sesame oil
- 1 tablespoon freshly ground black pepper
- 1 tablespoon minced garlic
- Mandarin Glaze, for drizzling

Directions:

1. With a very sharp knife, remove as much fat from the duck as you can. Refrigerate or freeze the fat for later use.
2. Pour the buttermilk into a large container with a lid and submerge the whole duck in it. Cover and let brine in the refrigerator for 4 to 6 hours.
3. Supply your smoker with wood pellets and follow the start-up procedure. Preheat, with the lid closed, to 250°F.
4. Remove the duck from the buttermilk brine, then rinse it and pat dry with paper towels.
5. In a bowl, combine the soy sauce, hoisin sauce, vinegar, sesame oil, pepper, and garlic to form a paste. Reserve ¼ cup for basting.
6. Poke holes in the skin of the duck and rub the remaining paste all over and inside the cavity.
7. Place the duck on the grill breast-side down, close the lid, and smoke for about 4 hours, basting every hour with the reserved paste, until a meat thermometer inserted in the thickest part of the meat reads 165°F. Use aluminum foil to tent the duck in the last 30 minutes or so if it starts to brown too quickly.
8. To finish, drizzle with glaze.

Jalapeño- & Cheese-stuffed Chicken

Servings: 4

Cooking Time: 30 Minutes

Ingredients:

- 4 boneless, skinless chicken breasts, each about 6 to 8oz (170 to 225g)
- 8 strips of thin-sliced bacon
- for the filling
- 4oz (110g) light cream cheese, at room temperature
- ⅓ cup shredded pepper Jack or Cheddar cheese
- 2 jalapeños, destemmed, deseeded, and minced
- 2 tbsp reduced-fat mayo
- 1 tsp chili powder
- ½ tsp coarse salt

Directions:

1. Supply your smoker with wood pellets and follow the start-up procedure. Preheat the grill, with the lid closed, to 375° F.
2. In a large bowl, make the filling by combining the ingredients. Mix well.
3. Use a sharp, thin-bladed knife to cut a deep pocket in the side of each chicken breast, angling the knife toward the opposite side. (Don't cut all the way through.) Spoon ¼ of the cheese filling into the pocket of each breast and gently press the edges of the pocket together to enclose. Wrap 2 slices of bacon in a spiral pattern around each breast.
4. Place the chicken on the grate at an angle to the bars. Grill until the chicken is cooked through, the filling melts, and the bacon is golden brown, about 25 to 30 minutes.
5. Transfer the pockets to a platter. Let rest for 2 minutes before serving.

Grilled Beantown Chicken Wings

Servings: 8

Cooking Time: 50 Minutes

Ingredients:

- 3 Pound chicken wings
- 1/4 Cup vegetable oil
- 1 1/2 Tablespoon Pork & Poultry Rub
- 1 Cup Irish Stout
- 1/2 Cup butter
- 2 Tablespoon apple jelly
- 1 Cup Frank's RedHot Sauce

Directions:

1. Rinse the chicken wings under cold running water and pat dry. With a sharp knife, cut the wings into three pieces through the joints. Discard the wing tips, or save for chicken stock.
2. Transfer the remaining "drumettes" and "flats" to a large a bowl. Add the oil and the Traeger Pork and Poultry shake, and toss with your hands to coat the wings evenly.
3. Make the beer sauce: In a small saucepan, bring the beer to a boil over high heat and reduce by half. Reduce the heat to medium-low and add the butter, stirring until melted. Stir in the apple jelly and the hot sauce. Keep warm.
4. Supply your smoker with wood pellets and follow the start-up procedure. Preheat the grill, with the lid closed, to 350° F.
5. Arrange the wings on the grill grate. Cook for 45 to 50 minutes, or until the chicken is no longer pink at the bone, turning once halfway through. Transfer the wings to a large clean bowl and pour the beer sauce over the wings, tossing to coat. Serve immediately. Grill: 350 °F

Smoked Turkey Breast

Servings: 2-4

Cooking Time: 120 Minutes

Ingredients:

- 1 (3-pound) turkey breast
- Salt
- Freshly ground black pepper
- 1 teaspoon garlic powder

Directions:

1. Supply your smoker with wood pellets and follow the start-up procedure. Preheat the grill, with the lid closed, to 180°F.
2. Season the turkey breast all over with salt, pepper, and garlic powder.
3. Place the breast directly on the grill grate and smoke for 1 hour.

4. Increase the grill's temperature to 350°F and continue to cook until the turkey's internal temperature reaches 170°F. Remove the breast from the grill and serve immediately.

Red Onion Chicken Fajita Omelet

Servings: 4

Cooking Time: 12 Minutes

Ingredients:

- 1 Cup Bell Pepper, Sliced Thin
- To Taste, Blackened Sriracha Rub Seasoning
- 2 Tbsp Butter
- 1 Cup Cheddar Jack Cheese, Shredded
- 8 Oz Chicken Breast, Boneless, Skinless, Sliced Thin
- 6 Eggs, Beaten
- 1 Tbsp Heavy Cream
- 1 Jalapeño, Minced
- 1/2 Lime
- 1 Cup Red Onion, Sliced Thinly
- 1/3 Cup Salsa Roja
- 2 Tbsp Sour Cream
- 1 Tbsp Vegetable Oil, Divided

Directions:

1. Supply your smoker with wood pellets and follow the start-up procedure. Preheat the grill, with the lid open, to medium heat. If using a gas or charcoal grill, preheat a cast iron skillet.
2. Drizzle sliced chicken breast with 1 teaspoon oil, then season with Blackened Sriracha.
3. Drizzle the remaining oil on the griddle, then add the chicken. Sauté for 2 minutes, then add the bell peppers and onions. Season with additional Blackened Sriracha and continue to sauté another 2 minutes, then deglaze with fresh squeezed lime juice. Remove mixture from the griddle, set aside.
4. Turn the griddle down to low, then whisk the eggs (3 per omelet) and heavy cream.
5. Melt 1 tablespoon of butter on the griddle. Quickly pour the eggs over the melted butter.
6. Flip the eggs, then add ¼ cup of cheese and divide all but ½ cup of the reserved filling into the middle of each egg. Add additional cheese and some minced jalapeño. Fold the egg over to shape the omelet.
7. Transfer the omelet to a plate and top with additional filling, cheese, salsa, sour cream, and jalapeño. Serve warm.

Cheese Buffalo Chicken Wings

Servings: 4-6

Cooking Time: 25 Minutes

Ingredients:

- Bleu Cheese Dip
- ⅔ Cup Buffalo Sauce
- Celery
- 2 Lbs. Chicken Wings
- ½ Cup Sweet Heat Rub

Directions:

1. Supply your smoker with wood pellets and follow the start-up procedure. Preheat the grill, with the lid open, to 450° F. If using a gas or charcoal grill, set heat to high heat.
2. Rub wings generously with Sweet Heat Rub and transfer to wing rack.
3. Place rack on grill and cook for 20 minutes, rotating after 10 minutes.
4. Baste with sauce, then cover and grill an additional 5 to 7 minutes. Note: your cooking time will vary depending on the size of the wings. When done, wings should have an internal temperature of 165°F.
5. Remove wings from grill and transfer to a baking sheet and let rest for about 5 minutes.
6. Transfer wings to a large bowl and coat with the Buffalo Sauce. Shake the bowl around gently to combine or use a spatula to ensure every wing is coated.
7. Serve hot with extra sauce, celery, and bleu cheese dip.

Smoked Quarters

Servings: 2-4

Cooking Time: 120 Minutes

Ingredients:

- 4 chicken quarters
- 2 tablespoons olive oil

- 1 batch Chicken Rub
- 2 tablespoons butter

Directions:

1. Supply your smoker with wood pellets and follow the start-up procedure. Preheat the grill, with the lid closed, to 180°F.
2. Coat the chicken quarters all over with olive oil and season them with the rub. Using your hands, work the rub into the meat.
3. Place the quarters directly on the grill grate and smoke for 1½ hours.
4. Baste the quarters with the butter and increase the grill's temperature to 375°F. Continue to cook until the chicken's internal temperature reaches 170°F.
5. Remove the quarters from the grill and let them rest for 10 minutes before serving.

Smoked Bourbon & Orange Brined Turkey

Servings: 8

Cooking Time: 180 Minutes

Ingredients:

- 1 Orange Brine and Turkey Rub Kit
- 4 Quart water
- 1 Cup bourbon
- 1 (12-14 lb) turkey, fresh or thawed
- 1 Tablespoon butter, melted
- 1 Tablespoon Grand Mariner or other orange-flavored liquor

Directions:

1. Mix Orange Brine seasoning (from Traeger Orange Brine & Turkey Rub Kit) with one quart of water. Boil for 5 minutes. Remove from heat, add 3 quarts of cold water and bourbon. Refrigerate until completely cooled.
2. Place turkey breast side down in a large container. Pour cooled brine mix over bird. Add cold water until bird is submerged. Refrigerate for 24 hours.
3. Remove turkey and discard brine. Blot turkey dry with paper towels.
4. Combine butter and Grand Marnier and coat outside of turkey. Season outside of turkey with Traeger Turkey Rub (from Orange Brine & Turkey Rub Kit).
5. Supply your smoker with wood pellets and follow the start-up procedure. Preheat the grill, with the lid closed, to 225° F.
6. Smoke turkey, breast up, for 2 hours. Grill: 225 °F
7. Increase grill temperature to 350°F and roast turkey until the internal temperature of the thickest part of the thigh reaches 165F, 2 to 3 hours, depending on size of turkey. Grill: 350 °F Probe: 165 °F
8. Let rest 20 to 30 minutes before serving. Enjoy!

Bbq Spatchcocked Chicken

Servings: 2

Cooking Time: 45 Minutes

Ingredients:

- 1 whole chicken
- 1/4 Cup Chicken Rub
- olive oil
- 1/2 Cup Sweet & Heat BBQ Sauce

Directions:

1. Supply your smoker with wood pellets and follow the start-up procedure. Preheat the grill, with the lid closed, to 375° F.
2. With a large knife or shears, cut the bird open along the backbone on both sides, through the ribs, and remove the backbone.
3. Brush chicken with olive oil and season both sides with Traeger Chicken rub.
4. Place the poultry on the Traeger, breast side up and cook for 35 to 40 minutes or until a thermometer inserted into the breast registers 160°F. Grill: 375 °F Probe: 160 °F
5. Remove from the grill and let rest 5 minutes before slicing. Enjoy!

Lemon Cajun Chicken Carbonara

Servings: 2

Cooking Time: 20 Minutes

Ingredients:

- 2 Slices Thick-Cut Bacon
- 1 Tbsp Cajun Seasoning
- 8 Oz. Chicken Breast
- 4 Egg, Yolk

- 1 Tbsp Garlic Clove, Minced
- 1 ¼ Cup Heavy Cream
- 2 Tbsp + 1 Tbsp Divided Italian Parsley
- 1 ½ Tbsp Divided Olive Oil
- ½ Cup Grated Parmesan Cheese
- ½ Tbsp Hickory Bacon Seasoning
- ¼ Tbsp Red Chili Flakes
- 1 Tbsp Scallions
- ½ Lb. Spaghetti

Directions:

1. Supply your smoker with wood pellets and follow the start-up procedure. Preheat the grill, with the lid open, to 400° F. If using a gas or charcoal grill, set the temp to medium-high heat. In a medium bowl, combine chicken, Hickory Bacon Seasoning, Cajun seasoning, and ½ tablespoon of olive oil. Toss to combine. Set aside or place in a bag and marinate in the refrigerator for 30 minutes to 1 hour.
2. Place tenders on preheated grill and cook for 3 minutes per side. Remove from grill and place on a cutting board to rest for 5 minutes. Slice thinly on the diagonal and set aside.
3. In a large stock pot, boil pasta per package instructions. Drain and set aside.
4. In a large skillet heat 1 tablespoon of oil over medium heat. Sauté bacon, stirring frequently, for 3 minutes or until crisp. Add garlic and cook for one minute. Lower heat to low and add in drained pasta. Using tongs, gently toss pasta to coat in oil and bacon.
5. In a mixing bowl, whisk together heavy cream, parmesan, egg yolks, and 2 tablespoons of parsley. Slowly pour over pasta, continuously stirring, as to not scramble eggs. After 2 minutes, the sauce will thicken. Add in chicken and lemon zest, and gently stir another minute. Transfer to serving dishes and garnish with additional parsley and red chili flakes.

Gen's Old-fashioned Barbecued Chicken

Servings: 6

Cooking Time: 90 Minutes

Ingredients:

- 2 whole chickens, each about 4 to 4½lb (1.8 to 2kg)
- 6 tbsp unsalted butter, melted
- seasoned salt
- low-carb barbecue sauce

Directions:

1. Supply your smoker with wood pellets and follow the start-up procedure. Preheat the grill, with the lid closed, to 350° F.
2. Cut each chicken into 8 pieces: 2 wings, 2 breasts, 2 legs, 2 thighs. Rinse under cold running water and pat dry with paper towels. Place on a rimmed sheet pan. Brush with butter and season with seasoned salt.
3. Place the chicken skin side down on the grate and grill for 30 minutes. Turn and continue to grill until the internal temperature in the thickest part of a breast or a thigh reaches 165°F (74°C), about 45 minutes to 1 hour. During the last 10 minutes, brush the chicken with barbecue sauce.
4. Transfer the chicken to a platter. Serve with additional barbecue sauce.

Smoked Honey Chicken Drumsticks

Servings: 4

Cooking Time: 30 Minutes

Ingredients:

- 1/2 Cup Apple Cider Vinegar
- 12 Chicken Drumsticks
- 2 Tablespoons Dijon Mustard
- 1/4 Cup Honey
- 1/4 Cup Ketchup
- 1 Tablespoon Sweet Heat Rub
- 1/2 Cup Soy Sauce

Directions:

1. Supply your smoker with wood pellets and follow the start-up procedure. Preheat the grill, with the lid open, to 225° F. Remove the wings from the marinade and place the drumsticks into the Buffalo Wing Rack.
2. Smoke for 60 minutes, or until a thermometer inserted into the thickest part of the drumstick registers at 170°F.
3. Turn the heat up to 350°F and cook for 5 to 10 minutes to make the skin crisp.
4. Remove from the smoker, serve immediately and enjoy!

Smo-fried Chicken

Servings: 4-6

Cooking Time: 55 Minutes

Ingredients:

- 1 egg, beaten
- ½ cup milk
- 1 cup all-purpose flour
- 2 tablespoons salt
- 1 tablespoon freshly ground black pepper
- 2 teaspoons freshly ground white pepper
- 2 teaspoons cayenne pepper
- 2 teaspoons garlic powder
- 2 teaspoons onion powder
- 1 teaspoon smoked paprika
- 8 tablespoons (1 stick) unsalted butter, melted
- 1 whole chicken, cut up into pieces

Directions:

1. Supply your smoker with wood pellets and follow the start-up procedure. Preheat, with the lid closed, to 375°F.
2. In a medium bowl, combine the beaten egg with the milk and set aside.
3. In a separate medium bowl, stir together the flour, salt, black pepper, white pepper, cayenne, garlic powder, onion powder, and smoked paprika.
4. Line the bottom and sides of a high-sided metal baking pan with aluminum foil to ease cleanup.
5. Pour the melted butter into the prepared pan.
6. Dip the chicken pieces one at a time in the egg mixture, and then coat well with the seasoned flour. Transfer to the baking pan.
7. Smoke the chicken in the pan of butter ("smo-fry") on the grill, with the lid closed, for 25 minutes, then reduce the heat to 325°F and turn the chicken pieces over.
8. Continue smoking with the lid closed for about 30 minutes, or until a meat thermometer inserted in the thickest part of each chicken piece reads 165°F.
9. Serve immediately.

Asian Bbq Chicken

Servings: 4

Cooking Time: 60 Minutes

Ingredients:

- 1 Whole whole chicken
- Asian BBQ Rub
- 1 Whole ginger ale

Directions:

1. Rinse chicken in cold water and pat dry with paper towels. Cover the chicken all over with Traeger Asian BBQ rub; make sure to drop some in the inside too. Place in large bag or bowl and cover and refrigerate for 12 to 24 hours.
2. Supply your smoker with wood pellets and follow the start-up procedure. Preheat the grill, with the lid closed, to 375° F.
3. Open your can of ginger ale and take a few big gulps. Set the can of soda on a stable surface. Take the chicken out of the fridge and place the bird over top of the soda can. The base of the can and the two legs of the chicken should form a sort of tripod to hold the chicken upright.
4. Stand the chicken in the center of your hot grate and cook the chicken till the skin is golden brown and the internal temperature is about 165°F on a instant-read thermometer, approximately 40 minutes to 1 hour.
5. De-throne chicken. Enjoy!

Smoked Chicken Fajita Quesadillas

Servings: 4

Cooking Time: 45 Minutes

Ingredients:

- 2 Chicken, Boneless/Skinless
- 1 Tsp Chilli, Powder
- 1 Tsp Garlic Powder
- 1/2 Green Bell Pepper, Sliced
- 1 Cup Mexican Cheese, Shredded
- 1/2 Onion, Sliced
- 1/2 Tsp Oregano
- 1 Tsp Paprika, Powder
- 1/4 Tsp Pepper
- 1/2 Red Bell Peppers
- Salsa
- Sour Cream
- 4 Tortilla

- 1/2 Yellow Bell Pepper, Sliced

Directions:

1. Supply your smoker with wood pellets and follow the start-up procedure. Preheat the grill, with the lid open, to 350° F.
2. Combine spices in a bowl and season chicken breasts. Leave a little bit of seasoning for the vegetables.
3. Place chicken on the grates and cook for 30 minutes, flipped halfway through.
4. In a Vegetable Basket, combine all vegetables and season with the remaining spice mixture.
5. Open up the flame broiler and saute over the open flame for about 15 minutes, or until the vegetables are cooked to your liking.
6. On a tortilla, layer cheese, vegetables, sliced chicken and more cheese. Fold the tortilla and place over the open flame on your Grill. Sear until the tortilla is nicely toasted and the cheese is melted. Cut and serve with salsa and sour cream.

Whole Smoked Honey Chicken

Servings: 4

Cooking Time: 40 Minutes

Ingredients:

- 1 Tablespoon Honey
- 1 ½ Lemon
- 4 Tablespoons Champion Chicken Seasoning
- 4 Tablespoons Unsalted Butter
- 1, 4 Pound Chicken, Giblets Removed And Patted Dry

Directions:

1. Supply your smoker with wood pellets and follow the start-up procedure. Preheat the grill, with the lid open, to 225° F.
2. In a small saucepan, melt together the butter and honey over low heat. Squeeze ½ lemon into the honey mixture and remove from the heat.
3. Smoke the chicken, skin side down until the chicken is lightly browned and the skin releases from the grate without ripping, about 6-8 minutes.
4. Turn the chicken over and baste with the honey butter mixture.
5. Continue to smoke the chicken, basting every 45 minutes, until the thickest part of the chicken reaches 160°F.

Bbq Chicken Thighs

Servings: 4

Cooking Time: 35 Minutes

Ingredients:

- 6 bone-in, skin-on chicken thighs
- salt and ground black pepper
- Big Game Rub

Directions:

1. Supply your smoker with wood pellets and follow the start-up procedure. Preheat the grill, with the lid closed, to 350° F.
2. While grill is heating, trim excess fat and skin from chicken thighs. Season with a light layer of salt and pepper then a layer of Traeger Big Game Rub.
3. Place chicken thighs on the grill grate and cook for 35 minutes. Check internal temperature, chicken is done at 165°F, but there is enough fat that they will stay moist at an internal temperature of 180°F and the texture is better. Grill: 350 °F Probe: 165 °F
4. Remove from the grill and let rest for 5 minutes before serving. Enjoy!

Lollipop Drumsticks

Servings: 4-6

Cooking Time: 75 Minutes

Ingredients:

- 1 Cup Barbecue Sauce
- 10 Tablespoons Butter, Salted
- 12 Chicken Drumsticks
- 1 Cup Hot Sauce
- Champion Chicken Seasoning
- Blue Cheese Or Ranch Dressing

Directions:

1. Supply your smoker with wood pellets and follow the start-up procedure. Preheat the grill, with the lid open, to 300° F.
2. Rinse chicken and pat dry with a paper towel.

3. Chop the very top of the drumstick on the larger, meaty side so the lollipops sit flatly. On the small end of the drumstick, about an inch above the knuckle, use a sharp knife or kitchen shears to cut the skin and tendons all the way down to the bone and pull the skin and cartilage off the knuckle.
4. Remove the tiny, sharp bone that sits right against the exposed chicken leg. Then, push all the meat and skin down to form the lollipop ball. Use your knife or shears to remove any excess tendons.
5. Season each lollipop generously with Champion Chicken seasoning and place in the aluminum pan with the flat side done and bones standing straight up. Then, cut 10 tablespoons of butter into cubes of 1 tablespoon each and place evenly throughout the rows of lollipops.
6. Cook lollipop drumsticks on your at 300°F for 1 hour; checking back every 20 minutes to baste the meat with the melted butter on the bottom of the pan.
7. For the Sauce: add your favorite bbq sauce into one aluminum loaf pan. Then, add 1 cup of hot sauce and 10 tablespoons of butter into the other aluminum loaf pan. Place them on the grill 5 minutes before your chicken is done. Stir well once it's warm and the butter has melted.
8. After 1 hour, use a thermometer to check the internal temperature of the lollipops. They will be ready to glaze when the temperature reaches 165°F.
9. Once ready, dip 6 lollipops in the bbq sauce and 6 in the buffalo sauce making sure to hold the leg and cover the meat entirely. Then, place the lollipops on the wing rack and put back on the grill for 15 more minutes or until the sauce is set.

Jalapeno Chicken Sliders

Servings: 8-10

Cooking Time: 180 Minutes

Ingredients:

- 3 Pounds Boneless Skinless Chicken Breasts
- 8-10 Slices Cheese Of Choice
- 1/2 Cup Chicken Broth
- Pickled Jalapeños
- 1 Tsp Smoked Infused Sweet Mesquite Jalapeno Sea Salt
- 1/2 Cup Salsa Verde
- 1 Package Slider Buns
- 3 Tablespoons Sweet Heat Rub

Directions:

1. Add the chicken breasts, chicken broth, and salsa verde to a disposable aluminum foil pan. Season everything generously with Sweet Heat and 1 tsp of Smoked Infused Sweet Mesquite Jalapeno Sea Salt. Cover tightly with aluminum foil.
2. Supply your smoker with wood pellets and follow the start-up procedure. Preheat the grill, with the lid open, to 275° F. Place the aluminum foil pan on the grill and cook for 3-4 hours, or until the chicken is completely cooked (165°F internal temperature), tender, and falling apart. Remove from the grill and let cool slightly.
3. Shred the chicken with the meat claws and toss with the Sweet Heat rub. Then, build the sliders: top the slider buns with a scoop of the pulled chicken, a slice cheese, and a few slices of pickled jalapeños. Serve immediately.

Bell Pepper Chicken Sliders

Servings: 5

Cooking Time: 20 Minutes

Ingredients:

- 16 Oz Chicken, Ground
- 1 Pepper, Anaheim
- Jalapeno Brat Burger Seasoning
- 1 Red Bell Peppers
- Spinach

Directions:

1. Supply your smoker with wood pellets and follow the start-up procedure. Preheat the grill, with the lid closed, to 400° F.
2. Put the ground chicken into a bowl and generously add the Jalapeno Brat Burger seasoning to the mixture.
3. Dice the Anaheim pepper and add it to the bowl as well.
4. Mix with your hands until the meat looks evenly coated.

5. Separate the meat out into 3oz balls, disperse or toss the remnants.
6. Use the 3-in-1 Burger press to create the perfect patty! If your chicken is too sticky to use the burger press, we put the 3oz balls into a tinfoil covered pan and placed that on the grill. Allow to cook 20-25 minutes, do not flip.
7. Add the buns to the grill if you'd like them toasted!
8. Remove the chicken sliders (and the buns) from the grill, add spinach, red peppers and whatever else you enjoy!

Smoked Spatchcocked Cornish Game Hens

Servings: 2
Cooking Time: 45 Minutes

Ingredients:

- 4 Cornish game hens
- 2 Ounce Big Game Rub

Directions:

1. Place the game hen breast side down on a cutting board. Using poultry shears, cut from the neck to the tailbone to remove the backbone.
2. Once backbone is removed, you will be able to see the inside of the bird. Make a small slit in the cartilage at the base of the breastbone to reveal the keel bone. Grab the bird with both hands on the ribs and open like a book, facing down towards the cutting board. Remove the keel bone. Cut small slits in the skin of the bird behind the legs and tuck the drumsticks into them to hold them in place.
3. Season on both sides with Traeger Big Game Rub.
4. Supply your smoker with wood pellets and follow the start-up procedure. Preheat the grill, with the lid closed, to 275° F.
5. Place the game hens on the Traeger skin side up and cook until internal temperature reaches 160°F (about 45 minutes). Grill: 275 °F Probe: 160 °F
6. Remove from Traeger and place on a cutting board; tent with foil. Let stand 10 minutes, then serve. Enjoy!

Oktoberfest Pretzel Mustard Chicken

Servings: 4
Cooking Time: 25 Minutes

Ingredients:

- 1/4 Pound pretzel sticks
- 3 Tablespoon Dijon mustard
- 3 Tablespoon apple cider or brown ale
- 1 Tablespoon honey
- 1 1/2 Teaspoon fresh thyme, plus more for garnish
- 4 boneless, skinless chicken breasts

Directions:

1. Pulse the pretzel sticks in a food processor or crush by hand in a resealable bag until they've turned into a powder the texture of panko breadcrumbs.
2. Transfer the crumbs to a wide, shallow bowl.
3. In separate shallow bowl, whisk mustard, beer or cider, honey and thyme together.
4. Spray a wire rack with cooking spray and place atop a sheet tray. Dip each chicken breast in the mustard mixture, then dredge in the pretzel crumbs to coat evenly and place on the wire rack. Spray the top of each chicken breast lightly with cooking spray.
5. Supply your smoker with wood pellets and follow the start-up procedure. Preheat the grill, with the lid closed, to 375° F.
6. Place the pan on the Traeger and bake for about 20 to 25 minutes, until the chicken breasts are fully cooked and register 165°F on an instant-read thermometer. Grill: 375 °F Probe: 165 °F
7. Let chicken rest for 5 minutes. Garnish with fresh thyme if desired. Enjoy!

Buffalo Chicken Wings

Servings: 4
Cooking Time: 20 Minutes

Ingredients:

- 1 1/2 Tbsp Apple Cider Vinegar
- 1/2 Cup Butter, Unsalted, Cubed
- 1/4 Tsp Cayenne Pepper
- 3 Lbs Chicken Wings, Split
- 2 Tsp Chives, Minced (Garnish)
- 1/8 Tsp Garlic, Granulated

- 2/3 Cup Hot Pepper Sauce
- 1 Tbsp Ranch Seasoning
- To Taste, Sweet Heat Rub
- 1/2 Tsp Sweet Heat Rub (For Sauce)
- 1/4 Tsp Worcestershire Sauce

Directions:

1. Supply your smoker with wood pellets and follow the start-up procedure. Preheat the grill, with the lid open, to 425° F. If using a gas or charcoal grill, set it up for medium-high heat.
2. Place chicken wings in a large mixing bowl. Season with Sweet Heat.
3. Prepare sauce: Set a small cast iron pan or saucepan on the grill. Add the hot pepper sauce, apple cider vinegar, Worcestershire sauce, Sweet Heat, cayenne, and granulated garlic to the skillet, and whisk to combine. When the sauce begins to bubble, remove the skillet from the grill and whisk in butter. Transfer the sauce to a mason jar.
4. Combine 1 cup of the buffalo sauce with ranch seasoning. Set aside.
5. Place wings on the grill and cook for 20 minutes, flipping and rotating every 3 to 5 minutes.
6. Remove wings from the grill when an internal temperature of 165° F is reached. Transfer to a mixing bowl, then pour sauce over. Toss to evenly coat. Garnish with fresh chives and serve warm.

Grilled Chipotle Chicken Skewers

Servings: 4

Cooking Time: 25 Minutes

Ingredients:

- BBQ Sauce
- 1 cup spicy BBQ sauce
- 3 chipotle peppers
- 1 Tbsp adobo sauce
- Skewers
- Olive oil
- 2 lbs boneless skinless chicken breasts
- 10 thick-cut bacon strips
- 1 large green bell pepper, cut into 3/4 to 1 inch pieces
- 1 medium red onion, peeled and cut into 3/4 to 1 inch pieces
- Bamboo skewers
- Garnish: freshly chopped garnish

Directions:

1. Supply your smoker with wood pellets and follow the start-up procedure. Preheat the grill, with the lid closed.
2. Soak the wooden skewers in water for at least 10 to 15 minutes before skewering to avoid them burning as much.
3. Add all ingredients for the sauce to a blender. Blend until they are combined well.
4. Cut chicken into 3/4-inch bite-sized pieces. Cut bacon into 3/4-inch strips.
5. Thread bacon (folding the bacon in half before skewering), chicken, peppers, and onion onto the skewers, alternating as you go.
6. Arrange the skewers on the grill grate and cook for 10 minutes, turning every few minutes. Baste the skewers with BBQ sauce on all sides. Continue to baste and turn the skewers every minute or so to caramelize.
7. The chicken is cooked through when it reaches an internal temperature of 165 °F. The bacon should be nice and crispy at this point.
8. Remove the skewers from the grill and sprinkle with freshly chopped parsley.

Juicy Jerk Chicken Kebabs

Servings: 4

Cooking Time: 12 Minutes

Ingredients:

- 1 Tablespoon All Spice, Ground
- 2 Lbs Chicken, Boneless/Skinless
- 1 Tablespoon Cinnamon, Ground
- 1/4 Cup Extra-Virgin Olive Oil
- 3 Garlic, Cloves
- 2 Inch Piece Ginger, Fresh
- 3 Green Onion
- 1 Lime, Juiced
- 1 Tablespoon Nutmeg, Ground
- 1 Cup Orange Juice, Fresh

- Pepper
- 1 Red Onion, Chopped
- Salt
- Skewers
- 1/4 Cup Soy Sauce
- 1/4 Cup Thyme, Fresh Sprigs

Directions:

1. Soak the bamboo skewers in water for about 30 minutes (the longer the better).
2. In a food processor, combine orange juice, oil, soy sauce, thyme, allspice, nutmeg, cinnamon, garlic, onions, ginger, lime juice, salt and pepper. Puree until smooth.
3. In a large resealable bag, pour all but 1/4 cup of the mixture in along with the sliced up chicken breasts. Seal the bag and marinate in the fridge for 2 - 3 hours.
4. Supply your smoker with wood pellets and follow the start-up procedure. Preheat the grill, with the lid open, to 450° F. Skewer the chicken and grill for about 7 minutes. Flip and continue grilling for about 5 minutes, or until the chicken is cooked through and grill marks appear. Serve with the remaining 1/4 cup of marinade.

Roasted Christmas Goose

Servings: 8

Cooking Time: 120 Minutes

Ingredients:

- 5 1/2 Pound Goose
- 2 lemons
- 2 limes
- 2 Teaspoon salt
- 2 thyme sprigs
- 2 sage sprigs
- 1 Medium Apple, green
- 3 Tablespoon honey

Directions:

1. Supply your smoker with wood pellets and follow the start-up procedure. Preheat the grill, with the lid closed, to High heat.
2. Lightly score the breast and leg skin in a criss-cross pattern. This will help the fat to render down more quickly during cooking.
3. Grate the lemon and limes. Mix citrus zest with 2 teaspoons fine sea salt. Cut the lemons and lime into wedges.
4. Season cavity of the goose generously with salt, then rub the citrus mix well into the skin and sprinkle some inside the cavity.
5. Stuff goose with sage, thyme, lemons, limes and apples wedges. Place goose directly on the grill grate and cook for 40 minutes. Brush goose with honey and reduce temperature to 325℉.
6. Cook for 1-1/2 to 2 hours or until an instant read thermometer inserted in the thickest part of the breast reads 160℉. Grill: 325 °F Probe: 160 °F
7. Remove from grill, tent with foil and allow to rest for 30 minutes. Final internal temperature should be 165℉ in the thickest part of the breast. Enjoy!

Bacon Weaved Stuffed Turkey Breast

Servings: 8

Cooking Time: 60 Minutes

Ingredients:

- 1/2 Cup celery, diced
- 14 Ounce Stuffing Mix
- 2 Tablespoon chopped sage
- 4 Tablespoon Chicken Rub
- 1/2 Cup dried sweetened cranberries
- 2 Cup apple cider
- 20 Strips thick-cut bacon

Directions:

1. Prepare the stuffing: Add all stuffing ingredients into a large bowl and toss to mix together.
2. Create a bacon weave and lay it out in a 5x5 pattern on cutting board.
3. Using a long, thin knife, butterfly each of the turkey breasts. Stuff each breast with a generous amount of stuffing and close.
4. Place turkey breast on prepared bacon weave, carefully wrap turkey, and secure with tooth picks. Repeat for the second breast.
5. Supply your smoker with wood pellets and follow the start-up procedure. Preheat the grill, with the lid closed, to 375° F.

6. Place the breasts seam side down on a rimmed baking sheet. Transfer directly to grill.
7. Place the bacon wrapped turkey breasts directly to the Traeger and cook for approximately 45 mins to 1 hour or until an instant read thermometer inserted into the center of the stuffing reaches 165 degrees F. Grill: 375 °F Probe: 165 °F
8. If the bacon gets too dark, cover with foil. Slice and enjoy!

Smoked Whiskey Peach Pulled Chicken

Servings: 6-8
Cooking Time: 45 Minutes

Ingredients:

- 3-4 pound whole chicken
- 1 cup peach juice
- 1/4 cup whiskey
- 1/4 cup melted butter
- 1/4 cup Hey Grill Hey's Sweet BBQ Rub
- 1/2 cup Whiskey Peach BBQ sauce

Directions:

1. Supply your smoker with wood pellets and follow the start-up procedure. Preheat the grill, with the lid closed, to 225°F, using a mild fruit wood like a peach.
2. Remove any giblets or neck from inside of the chicken and pat dry.
3. In a jar, combine the peach juice, whiskey, and melted butter. Inject this mixture into your chicken in several spots. Be sure to inject in at least 3 different places in each breast, 2 places in the thighs, and 1 time in each leg.
4. Season your chicken generously on all sides with the Sweet BBQ Rub. Place in the middle of your grill and close the lid. Smoke for 45 minutes per pound of chicken.
5. Brush liberally with the whiskey peach BBQ sauce once the internal temperature of your meat reaches 150 degrees.
6. Check the temperature in both the thighs and the breasts and when your internal temperature reads consistently 160 degrees F, remove the chicken to a rimmed serving platter or baking sheet and cover tightly with foil to allow the chicken to come up to 165 degrees F and rest for 20 minutes.
7. Shred the chicken and set it onto your serving platter. Discard the carcass or save for homemade stock. Drizzle your smoked pulled chicken with more of the Whiskey Peach Barbecue Sauce and serve on toasted buns.

Glazed Bbq Half Chicken

Servings: 6
Cooking Time: 120 Minutes

Ingredients:

- Meat Church Bird Bath Poultry Brine
- 1/2 Gallon water or chicken stock
- 1 Whole chicken
- 1 Whole whole chicken
- Meat Church Holy Gospel BBQ Rub
- 1 Stick butter
- Cup favorite BBQ sauce
- 2 Teaspoon blackberry jelly, pepper jelly or your favorite jelly

Directions:

1. Mix the Meat Church Bird Bath Poultry Brine thoroughly in a 1/2 gallon of water or chicken stock. Feel free to be creative and add ingredients to enhance the flavor profile to your liking. Completely submerge the chicken in the brine mixture and place in the refrigerator overnight. We recommend 12 to 24 hours for this brine.
2. Remove the bird from the brine. Rinse off and pat dry with a paper towel.
3. Supply your smoker with wood pellets and follow the start-up procedure. Preheat the grill, with the lid closed, to 275° F.
4. Using a pair of chicken shears or a very sharp knife, remove the backbone. Do this by trimming along one side of the backbone from one end of the chicken to the other. Then repeat the process on the other side of the backbone and remove it completely. Open the chicken once the backbone is removed. At this point you can remove the breastbone if you like. Slice the bird in half using a sharp knife. Now you have 2 half chickens.
5. Apply Meat Church Holy Gospel BBQ Rub to all sides of the chicken; underneath and on top of the skin.

We also recommend working your hands underneath the chicken skin and applying rub directly on the meat. This will ensure a really flavorful bite even if they don't get any skin.

6. Place the chicken halves and butter in a half steam pan and put the pan on the Traeger. Baste the chicken with the butter periodically throughout the cook.
7. Using an instant-read thermometer, remove the chicken from the grill when they reach an internal temperature of at least 165°F in the deepest part of the breast, about 1-1/2 to 2 hours. Grill: 275 °F Probe: 165 °F
8. For the glaze, mix the BBQ sauce, honey and jelly and heat in a small sauce pan.

Cheesy Buffalo Chicken Pinwheels

Servings: 8

Cooking Time: 10 Minutes

Ingredients:

- 2 T Bleu Cheese, Crumbled
- ½ Cup Buffalo Wing Sauce, Divided
- 1-2, Boneless And Skinless Chicken Breast
- ½ Cup Colby Cheese, Shredded
- 4 Oz. Cream Cheese
- 4, 10" Diameter Flour Tortillas
- 2 Scallions, Thinly Sliced [Reserve 1 Tsp Of Green For Garnish]

Directions:

1. Supply your smoker with wood pellets and follow the start-up procedure. Preheat the grill, with the lid closed, to 375° F. If you're using a gas or charcoal grill, set it up for medium heat. Remove chicken from refrigerator place on grill. Grill chicken for 10 min, turning once. Allow to rest 10 minutes, then shred.
2. In a food processor, add remaining buffalo wing sauce, cream cheese, Colby cheese, bleu cheese, and scallions. Process on low for 20 seconds. Add shredded chicken breast to mixture and pulse about 8 times, or until mixture is fully combined.
3. Place tortillas on a flat work surface and divide filling into quarters. Spread mixture evenly over each tortilla with a rubber spatula.
4. Roll up tortillas and place seam side down on cutting board. Refrigerate for 10 minutes, then slice into ½ inch pieces. Transfer to serving platter and garnish with remaining scallions. Serve with extra buffalo sauce or ranch dressing.

Roasted Rosemary Orange Chicken

Servings: 4

Cooking Time: 45 Minutes

Ingredients:

- 1 (3-4 lb) chicken, backbone removed
- 1/4 Cup olive oil
- 2 oranges, juiced
- 1 orange, zested
- 2 Teaspoon Dijon mustard
- 3 Tablespoon chopped rosemary leaves
- 2 Teaspoon kosher salt

Directions:

1. Rinse the chicken and pat dry with paper towels.
2. For the Marinade: In a medium bowl, combine olive oil, juice from the oranges (about 1/4 cup of freshly squeezed juice), orange zest, Dijon mustard, rosemary and salt. Whisk to combine.
3. Place the chicken in a shallow baking dish large enough for chicken to be fully opened in one piece. Pour marinade over the chicken ensuring it is covered with the marinade.
4. Cover with plastic wrap and refrigerate for a minimum of 2 hours or up to overnight, turning once during the process.
5. Supply your smoker with wood pellets and follow the start-up procedure. Preheat the grill, with the lid closed, to 350° F.
6. Remove the chicken from the marinade and place on the Traeger, skin-side down.
7. Cook for 25 to 30 minutes until the skin is well-browned, then flip. Continue to grill chicken until the internal temperature of the breast reaches 165°F and the thigh reaches 175°F, about 5 to 15 minutes longer. Grill: 350 °F Probe: 165 °F
8. Let rest 10 minutes before carving. Enjoy!

Crispy Chicken Quarters

Servings: 4
Cooking Time: 55 Minutes

Ingredients:

- 2 Cups Alabama White Sauce
- 1 Tbsp Champion Chicken
- 4 Chicken Leg Quarters
- 1 Tbsp Olive Oil

Directions:

1. Place chicken leg quarters on a sheet tray lined with aluminum foil. Gently pull away the skin from the chicken leg quarters, then drizzle inside and out with olive oil. Season the chicken leg quarters all over and under the skin with Champion Chicken. Let chicken sit out at room temperature for 1 hour.
2. Supply your smoker with wood pellets and follow the start-up procedure. Preheat the grill, with the lid open, to 450° F. If using a gas or charcoal grill, set it up for medium-high heat and direct heat.
3. Sear the leg quarters on all sides over direct flame until crispy and golden brown. Transfer to indirect heat and close the sear slide. Reduce temperature to 350° F and grill the chicken for 45 minutes, turning occasionally, until chicken registers an internal temperature of 165° F.
4. Remove chicken from grill and allow to rest for 10 minutes. Serve chicken hot with a generous drizzling of Alabama white sauce*.

Tandoori Chicken Leg Quarters

Servings: 4
Cooking Time: 40 Minutes

Ingredients:

- 4 skinless chicken leg quarters, about 2½lb (1.2kg) total
- juice of 2 lemons
- ¼ cup cold distilled water
- 1½ tsp coarse salt
- ½ tsp ground turmeric
- 3 tbsp vegetable oil, plus more
- 3 garlic cloves, peeled and minced
- 1½-inch (3.75cm) piece of fresh ginger, peeled and minced
- 2 tsp sweet paprika
- 1 tsp chili powder, preferably Kashmiri
- 1 tsp ground coriander
- 1 tsp ground cumin
- ½ tsp ground cayenne
- ¼ tsp ground nutmeg
- ½ cup plain Greek yogurt
- 4 tbsp unsalted butter, melted
- for serving
- 1 large red onion, peeled and thinly sliced crosswise
- ½ cup cilantro leaves
- lemon wedges

Directions:

1. Use a sharp, thin-bladed knife to cut several deep slashes in the fleshy side of each leg quarter to increase the surface area exposed to the marinade and to help the chicken cook faster. Place the chicken legs in a resealable plastic bag.
2. In a small bowl, combine the lemon juice, water, salt, and turmeric. Stir until the salt dissolves. Pour the mixture over the chicken legs and massage the bag to thoroughly coat the chicken, forcing the liquid into the slashes. Refrigerate for 15 minutes.
3. In a medium bowl, combine the vegetable oil, garlic, ginger, paprika, chili powder, coriander, cumin, cayenne, and nutmeg. Whisk in the yogurt. Add this mixture to the plastic bag and again massage the bag to thoroughly coat the chicken legs. Refrigerate for 4 to 8 hours.
4. Supply your smoker with wood pellets and follow the start-up procedure. Preheat the grill, with the lid closed, to 400° F.
5. Remove the chicken from the plastic bag and discard the marinade. Place the leg quarters fleshy side down on the grate and grill until the chicken is nicely browned and the temperature in the thickest part of the thigh reaches 170°F (77°C), about 35 to 40 minutes, turning once or twice.
6. Remove the chicken leg quarters from the grill and let rest for 2 minutes. Brush on both sides with butter. Place the legs on a platter. Scatter the red onion, cilantro leaves, and lemon wedges on the platter. Serve immediately.

Easy Rapid-fire Roast Chicken

Servings: 4
Cooking Time: 120 Minutes

Ingredients:

- 1 (4-pound) whole chicken, giblets removed
- Extra-virgin olive oil, for rubbing
- 3 tablespoons Greek seasoning
- Juice of 1 lemon
- Butcher's string

Directions:

1. Supply your smoker with wood pellets and follow the start-up procedure. Preheat, with the lid closed, to 450°F.
2. Rub the bird generously all over with oil, including inside the cavity.
3. Sprinkle the Greek seasoning all over and under the skin of the bird, and squeeze the lemon juice over the breast.
4. Tuck the chicken wings behind the back and tie the legs together with butcher's string or cooking twine.
5. Put the chicken directly on the grill, breast-side up, close the lid, and roast for 1 hour to 1 hour 30 minutes, or until a meat thermometer inserted in the thigh reads 165°F.
6. Let the meat rest for 10 minutes before carving.

Smoked Turkey

Servings: 6
Cooking Time: 420 Minutes

Ingredients:

- 1 (12-16 lb) fresh or frozen turkey, thawed, giblets removed
- 1 Cup Rub
- 1 1/2 Tablespoon minced garlic
- 1 Cup sugar
- 1/2 Cup Worcestershire sauce
- 2 Tablespoon canola oil

Directions:

1. Ensure the turkey is fully thawed and remove any giblets. Pour 3 gallons of water in a 5 gallon non-metal bucket.
2. Add Traeger rub, garlic, sugar, and Worcestershire sauce and mix until sugars are completely dissolved.
3. Place the turkey, breast side down, into the bucket with the brine. Make sure the turkey is completely submerged.
4. Cover bucket and place in refrigerator overnight.
5. Remove turkey from brine and pat dry. Rub canola oil over entire outside of turkey and place breast side up into disposable aluminum roasting pan.
6. Supply your smoker with wood pellets and follow the start-up procedure. Preheat the grill, with the lid closed, to 225° F.
7. Place the turkey on the grill and smoke for 2 1/2 to 3 hours Grill: 180 °F
8. Increase grill temperature to 350°F and cook for 3-1/2 to 4 hours, or until the internal temperature reaches 165°F in the thickest part of the breast. Grill: 350 °F Probe: 165 °F
9. Remove from grill and allow to rest for 30 minutes before carving. Enjoy!

Chicken Lollipops

Servings: 8
Cooking Time: 60 Minutes

Ingredients:

- 18 Pieces chicken drumsticks
- Cajun Shake
- 1 Stick butter
- 'Que BBQ Sauce
- Louisiana Brand Hot Sauce (Optional)

Directions:

1. To turn regular chicken legs into lollipops, you'll need a sharp knife and a pair of kitchen shears. Start by making a cut all of the way around the leg just below the knuckle, cutting through the skins and tendons using either a sharp knife or a pair of kitchen shears. Push the meat down to the large end and pull/cut the remaining skin and cartilage off the knuckle. You might want to also remove the tiny bone right against the leg. Remove this bone with your fingers or the shears, and trim away the tendons sticking out the top.

2. Season the chicken with the Cajun Shake. Wrap the bones of the drumsticks with a small piece of aluminum foil to keep them from turning too black. Let the chicken sit for an hour in the fridge to allow the flavor to permeate.
3. Supply your smoker with wood pellets and follow the start-up procedure. Preheat the grill, with the lid closed, to 180° F.
4. Place the chicken lollipops on the grill grate and let them smoke for 30 minutes.
5. After you remove the chicken, increase the grill temperature to 350°F and let it preheat, lid closed for 15 minutes. Place the stick of butter in a baking pan or aluminum pan and put it on the grill to allow the butter to melt while the grill is coming to temperature. (The butter doesn't need to cover the chicken. It just keeps the drumstick moist and of course, gives it a little added buttery finish.)
6. Arrange the lollipops in the pan with the bones sticking up straight. Let the chicken cook for about 40 minutes or until the internal temperature registers 165F on an instant-read thermometer. Grill: 350 °F Probe: 165 °F
7. Meanwhile, warm up the barbecue sauce in a small saucepan on the stove over low heat. If you want it to have that Louisiana kick, add in a few squirts of the hot sauce, to your taste. Once it starts to thin, turn down the heat to just keep it warm. If the sauce needs to be thinned, pour in a little bit of the butter used in the pan until it reaches a thickness that is thick enough to adhere to the drumsticks but not gluey.
8. Dip the lollipops into the barbecue sauce so that it is completely covered. You can also brush the barbecue sauce on the bones if you want a uniform look and sheen on the lollipops.
9. Increase the temperature to 450F. Place the chicken directly on the grill grate and cook until the internal temperature registers 175F, about 10 more minutes. Keep an eye on the lollipops to make sure that the glaze doesn't burn. You're looking for that perfect caramelization of the barbecue sauce on the outside with a crisp skin to give a little texture. Grill: 450 °F Probe: 175 °F

Whole Smoked Chicken

Servings: 6
Cooking Time: 180 Minutes

Ingredients:

- 1/2 Cup kosher salt
- 1 Cup brown sugar
- 1 (3 to 3-1/2 lb) whole chicken
- 1 Teaspoon minced garlic
- Chicken Rub
- 1 lemon, halved
- 1 Medium yellow onion, quartered
- 3 Whole garlic cloves
- 5 thyme sprigs

Directions:

1. For the Brine: Dissolve the kosher salt and brown sugar in 1 gallon of water. Once dissolved, place the chicken in the brine and refrigerate overnight. Make sure chicken is fully submerged weighing it down if necessary.
2. Supply your smoker with wood pellets and follow the start-up procedure. Preheat the grill, with the lid closed, to 225° F.
3. While the grill preheats, remove the chicken from the brine and pat dry. Rub with the minced garlic and Traeger Chicken Rub. Next, stuff the cavity with the lemon, onion, garlic and thyme. Tie the legs together.
4. Place chicken directly on the grill grate and smoke for 2-1/2 to 3 hours or until an instant-read thermometer reads 160°F when inserted into the thickest part of the breast. The finished internal temperature will rise to 165°F in the breast as the chicken rests. Let rest for 15 minutes before carving. Enjoy! Probe: 160 °F

Smoked Pulled Chicken

Servings: 6
Cooking Time: 65 Minutes

Ingredients:

- To Taste, Ale House Beer Can Chicken Seasoning
- 1 Lb Chicken Breasts, Boneless, Skinless
- 1 Tbsp Cilantro, Chopped
- 1 Tsp Cumin, Ground
- 2 Jalapeños, Chopped

- 2 Tsp Olive Oil
- 1 Bag Tortilla Chips
- 1 Lb White American Cheese, Cubed
- 1 Cup Milk

Directions:

1. Supply your smoker with wood pellets and follow the start-up procedure. Preheat the grill, with the lid open, to 350° F. If using a gas or charcoal grill, preheat to medium heat.
2. Score the chicken, rub with olive oil, then season with Ale House Beer Can Chicken.
3. Transfer the chicken to the grill and cook for 8 to 10 minutes, turning occasionally.
4. Remove chicken from the grill, and reduce the temperature to 225° F. Allow the chicken to rest for 10 minutes, then pull apart with 2 forks. Set aside.
5. While the chicken is resting, heat a cast iron skillet on the grill. Partially open the sear slide, then to the skillet add the cubed cheese, jalapeño, milk, and cumin. Stir occasionally, for 5 minutes, until the cheese melts. Fold in the pulled chicken, then close the lid and allow the dip to smoke for 30 to 45 minutes.
6. Remove from grill and let rest for 5-10 minutes to thicken. Serve warm with fresh cilantro and tortilla chips.

County Fair Turkey Legs

Servings: 4

Cooking Time: 90 Minutes

Ingredients:

- 4 turkey legs, each about 1lb (450g)
- for the brine
- ½ gallon (1.9 liters) distilled water
- ½ cup kosher salt
- ¼ cup light brown sugar or low-carb substitute
- 2½ tsp pink curing salt #1
- 1 tsp liquid smoke (optional)

Directions:

1. In a stockpot on the stovetop over medium-high heat, make the brine by combining the ingredients. Bring the mixture to a boil. Stir until the salts and sugar dissolve. Remove the pot from the stovetop and let the brine cool to room temperature. Cover and refrigerate until cool.
2. Submerge the turkey legs in the brine. If they float, place a resealable bag of ice on top. Refrigerate for 24 hours, turning from time to time so the legs cure evenly.
3. Supply your smoker with wood pellets and follow the start-up procedure. Preheat the grill, with the lid closed, to 325° F.
4. Remove the turkey legs from the brine and discard the liquid. Rinse the legs under cold running water and pat dry with paper towels.
5. Place the turkey legs on the grate and grill for 45 minutes. Turn and continue to cook until the turkey skin is nicely browned and the internal temperature in a leg reaches 170 to 175°F (77 to 79°C), about 45 minutes. (Turkey legs have a lot of connective tissue and they seem to turn out better when cooked to a slightly higher temperature.)
6. Remove the legs from the grill and serve warm or cold.

Grilled Garlic Chicken Kabobs

Servings: 6

Cooking Time: 15 Minutes

Ingredients:

- 3 (Cut Into 1 Inch Cubes) Chicken Breast, Raw
- 2 Cloves Garlic, Minced
- 2 Tablespoons Honey
- 1 Pound Of Button (Destemmed And Cut In Half) Mushroom
- 1/2 Cup Olive Oil
- 1 Red (Cut Into Quarters And Seperated) Onion
- 1 Green (Cut Into Large Chunks) Bell Pepper
- 2 Tablespoons Competition Smoked Seasoning
- 2 Tablespoons Soy Sauce

Directions:

1. To make the marinade: In a large bowl, combine the olive oil, soy sauce, honey, garlic and Competition Smoked. Add the chicken and mix well. When the chicken is covered completely, allow it to marinate for 2-12 hours.

2. In a large, shallow baking dish, soak the kabob skewers for a minimum of 2 hours and up to 12 hours.
3. Once the chicken has finished marinating and the skewers are finished soaking, drain the water from the skewers and remove the chicken from the marinade.
4. Supply your smoker with wood pellets and follow the start-up procedure. Preheat the grill, with the lid closed, to 350° F.
5. Thread a piece of chicken, followed by a piece of pepper, mushroom, and onion. Repeat until the skewers are full.
6. Grill the kabobs for 5 minutes on one side, then flip and grill for 5 more minutes or until the chicken reaches an internal temperature of 180°F. Remove from the grill and serve.

Savory Smoked Turkey Legs

Servings: 4
Cooking Time: 150 Minutes

Ingredients:

- 1 Cup Chicken Stock
- 2 Tbsp Blackened Sriracha Rub
- 4 Turkey Legs (Drumsticks)

Directions:

1. Fire up your pellet grill on SMOKE mode. With the lid open, let it run for 10 minutes.
2. Supply your smoker with wood pellets and follow the start-up procedure. Preheat the grill, with the lid closed, to 225° F. If using a gas or charcoal grill, set it up for low, indirect heat.
3. Combine turkey stock with 2 teaspoons of Blackened Sriracha Rub.
4. Place turkey legs on a sheet tray, then inject each with seasoned stock. Season the outside of the legs with remaining Blackened Sriracha.
5. Place turkey legs directly on the grate of the smoking cabinet, and cook for 1 ½ hours.
6. Increase temperature to 325°F, then transfer turkey legs to the bottom grill and cook for another 45 to 60 minutes, until the internal temperature reaches 170°F.
7. Remove turkey from the grill, allow to rest for 10 minutes, then serve warm.

Teriyaki Apple Cider Turkey

Servings: 8-10
Cooking Time: 180 Minutes

Ingredients:

- 1/2 Cup Apple Cider
- 1/4 Cup Melted Butter, Unsalted
- 1 Teaspoon Cornstarch
- 2 Finely Chopped Garlic, Cloves
- 1/2 Teaspoon Ginger, Ground
- 2 Tablespoon Honey
- 2 Tablespoon Champion Chicken Seasoning
- 1 Shady Brook Farms® Whole Turkey, Thawed
- 2 Tablespoon Soy Sauce
- 1 Tablespoon Water, Cold

Directions:

1. Supply your smoker with wood pellets and follow the start-up procedure. Preheat the grill, with the lid closed, to 300° F.
2. In a saucepan, whisk together melted butter, garlic, soy sauce, apple cider, ground ginger, and honey. Bring to a boil then reduce to a simmer.
3. Place the turkey in an aluminum roasting pan.
4. With a marinade injector, fill with the mixture and pierce the meat with the needle while pushing on the plunger, injecting the flavor. You want to inject into the thickest part of the breast, thigh, and wings.
5. Next, rub entire turkey with your favorite poultry seasoning or the Champion Chicken seasoning. For added flavor, throw some extra garlic gloves into the cavity and apple cider in the aluminum pan.
6. Place the turkey in the grill and cook until the internal temperature reaches 165-170°F.
7. In a separate bowl, mix cornstarch and cold water together and add to the leftover original mixture to create a glaze. Glaze the turkey with the remaining mixture with approximately 15-20 minutes left. Skin will darken because of the sugar in the glaze.
8. Let the turkey rest 20-25 minutes before carving and enjoy!

Chicken Tenders

Servings: 2-4
Cooking Time: 80 Minutes

Ingredients:

- 1 pound boneless, skinless chicken breast tenders
- 1 batch Chicken Rub

Directions:

1. Supply your smoker with wood pellets and follow the start-up procedure. Preheat the grill, with the lid closed, to 180°F.
2. Season the chicken tenders with the rub. Using your hands, work the rub into the meat.
3. Place the tenders directly on the grill grate and smoke for 1 hour.
4. Increase the grill's temperature to 300°F and continue to cook until the tenders' internal temperature reaches 170°F. Remove the tenders from the grill and serve immediately.

Roasted Tingle Wings

Servings: 6
Cooking Time: 30 Minutes

Ingredients:

- 3 Whole jalapeño
- 1 Tablespoon Trappey's Red Devil Cayenne Pepper Sauce
- 1/2 Cup Texas Spicy BBQ Sauce
- 2 Tablespoon Blackened Saskatchewan Rub
- 1/2 Cup honey
- 1 Tablespoon Worcestershire sauce
- 1/4 Cup water

Directions:

1. For the sauce, place all ingredients except the wings into a blender and mix until smooth.
2. Pour the sauce into a resealable plastic bag and place the wings in the bag, turning to coat thoroughly. Marinate for 1 hour to overnight.
3. Supply your smoker with wood pellets and follow the start-up procedure. Preheat the grill, with the lid closed, to 350° F.
4. Place wings directly on the gill grate and cook for 30 minutes or until wings reach an internal temperature of 165 degrees F. Enjoy!

Savory Smoked Chicken Breasts

Servings: 2
Cooking Time: 30 Minutes

Ingredients:

- 1 lb Boneless Skinless Chicken Breasts
- 2-3 Tbsp BBQ Chicken Rub

Directions:

1. Supply your smoker with wood pellets and follow the start-up procedure. Preheat the grill, with the lid closed, to 250° F.
2. Pound chicken breasts flat, about 1/2" thick. Rub the dry rub all over chicken breasts.
3. Place chicken breasts on the grill grate. Close pellet grill lid and cook at 250 °F for about 30 minutes or until the chicken reaches an internal temperature of 165 °F.
4. Remove from pellet grill and let rest 5-10 minutes.

Onion Turkey Burger Sliders

Servings: 5
Cooking Time: 30 Minutes

Ingredients:

- 1 Sweet Onion, Chopped
- 1 Pepper, Anaheim
- Bacon Cheddar Burger Seasoning
- Spinach
- 16 Oz Turkey, Ground

Directions:

1. Supply your smoker with wood pellets and follow the start-up procedure. Preheat the grill, with the lid closed, to 400° F.
2. Put the ground turkey into a bowl and generously add the Bacon Cheddar Burger seasoning to the mixture.
3. Dice the Anaheim pepper and add it to the bowl as well.
4. Dice about 1/3 of the sweet onion and add it to the bowl.

5. Mix with your hands until the meat looks evenly coated in seasoning and the veggies are evenly mixed.
6. Separate the meat out into 3oz balls, disperse or toss the remnants.
7. Use the 3-in-1 Burger press to create the perfect patty! Place the patties on the grill and cook for 15-20 minutes depending on their thickness. Flip every 5ish minutes.
8. Add the buns to the grill if you'd like them toasted!
9. Remove the turkey sliders (and the buns) from the grill, add spinach, and whatever you think will taste good!

Smoked Avocado Turkey Tamale Pie

Servings: 6
Cooking Time: 240 Minutes

Ingredients:

- 1 Avocado, Diced (For Topping)
- 15 Oz Black Beans, Drained (For Filling)
- To Taste, Blackened Sriracha Rub Seasoning
- 2 Tsp Blackened Sriracha Rub Seasoning (For Filling)
- To Taste, Blackened Sriracha Rub Seasoning (For Polenta)
- 2 Tbsp Butter (For Polenta)
- 2 Tbsp Cilantro, Chopped (For Topping)
- 1 Cup Corn Kernels (For Filling)
- 2 Cups Enchilada Sauce (For Filling)
- 1/2 Jalapeño, Minced (For Topping)
- 2 Cups Milk Or Water (For Polenta)
- 1 Cup Polenta, Or Fine Cornmeal (For Polenta)
- 2 Scallions, Sliced (For Topping)
- 2 Cups Smoked Turkey Breast, Shredded (For Filling)
- 2 1/2 Lbs Split Turkey Breast , Bone-In
- 2 Cups Turkey Stock (For Polenta)
- 4 Oz White Cheddar, Shredded (For Polenta)
- 4 Oz White Cheddar, Shredded (For Topping)

Directions:

1. Supply your smoker with wood pellets and follow the start-up procedure. Preheat the grill, with the lid closed, to 225° F. If using a gas or charcoal grill, set it up for low, indirect heat.
2. Season the turkey breast with Blackened Sriracha, then transfer to the grill, on a rack, over indirect heat.
3. Smoke the turkey breast for 2 ½ to 3 hours, until an internal temperature of 160° F. Remove the turkey from the grill, allow to rest for 20 minutes, then shred with 2 forks.
4. While the turkey is resting, prepare the polenta:
5. Place a deep, cast iron skillet on the grill, then increase the temperature to 375° F. Add chicken broth and milk to a skillet and bring to a boil.
6. Whisk in the polenta, then reduce the heat to a simmer, stirring often for 5 minutes. Season with Blackened Sriracha, then stir in cheese and butter. Remove the skillet from the grill and smooth out the polenta in an even layer.
7. In a large glass measuring cup or mixing bowl, combine the turkey, enchilada sauce, black beans, corn and Blackened Sriracha.
8. Spoon the turkey mixture over the polenta, then top with 4 ounces of shredded cheese. Place on the grill, over indirect heat and bake for 20 to 25 minutes, until the filling is bubbling along the edge and the cheese is melted.
9. Remove the skillet from the grill and allow it to rest for 10 minutes. Serve warm, garnished with avocado, scallions, jalapeño, and fresh cilantro.

Bbq Cheese Chicken Stuffed Bell Peppers

Servings: 4
Cooking Time: 15 Minutes

Ingredients:

- ½ Cup Barbecue Sauce
- 4 Bell Pepper
- ½ Cup Cheddar Cheese, Shredded
- 2 Cups Leftover Chicken, Chopped
- 2 Tablespoons Champion Chicken Seasoning

Directions:

1. Wash and slice the bell peppers in half, long ways. Deseed them and set aside.
2. Supply your smoker with wood pellets and follow the start-up procedure. Preheat the grill, with the lid open, to 350° F.

3. In a large bowl, mix together the cheese, chicken, Champion Chicken Seasoning, and barbecue sauce, then stuff inside the pepper halves.
4. Grill the peppers for 7-10 minutes or until the peppers are softened and the filling is heated through and melted. Remove from the grill and serve.

Texas Style Black Pepper Turkey

Servings: 6
Cooking Time: 240 Minutes

Ingredients:

- 1/2 Cup Coarse Black Pepper
- 1Lb Butter
- 1/2 Cup Salt, Kosher
- 1 Brined Turkey

Directions:

1. Supply your smoker with wood pellets and follow the start-up procedure. Preheat the grill, with the lid closed, to 300° F.
2. Liberally season Turkey with equal parts kosher salt and coarse black pepper.
3. Cook on grill until Internal temp reaches approximately 145°F or the skin has darkened to your liking.
4. Place turkey in a roasting pan topped with a pound of chopped butter and cover.
5. Return to the grill until internal temp of the thigh and breast reaches 165°F
6. Let rest for 30 minutes, carve and serve.

Garlic Sriracha Buffalo Chicken Wings

Servings: 6-8
Cooking Time: 160 Minutes

Ingredients:

- 1 Cup Buffalo Sauce
- 6 Lbs Chicken Wings
- 2 Tbsp Garlic Powder
- 1 Tsp Pepper
- Divided By 2 Tbsp And ½ Tbsp Sweet Heat Rub
- 1 Tsp Salt
- ⅓ Cup, Divided Sriracha Sauce

Directions:

1. In a non-stick sauce pot, add the remaining Sriracha and buffalo sauce. Stir to combine and set aside.
2. Supply your smoker with wood pellets and follow the start-up procedure. Preheat the grill, with the lid open, to 250° F. If using a gas or charcoal grill, set it to low heat with indirect heat. Place marinated wings directly on grill grate and cook (covered) for 1 hour 15 minutes.
3. Flip wings and baste each piece with Sriracha sauce. Season with additional Sweet Heat Rub, cover, and continue to grill for an additional 1 hour 15 minutes.
4. Remove wings from grill and place on sheet tray. Baste with additional sauce, then open Sear Slide and return wings to the grill. Grill for 3-5 minutes, rotating often, until wings begin to char lightly.
5. Transfer wings to a serving tray, baste with remaining sauce and serve!

Green Chile Chicken Enchiladas

Servings: 6
Cooking Time: 45 Minutes

Ingredients:

- 2 Cups Chicken, Shredded
- 1 (12 Oz) Package Colby Jack Cheese, Shredded
- 1 Enchilada Sauce, Can
- 1 Can Green Chile, Drained
- 1 Onion, Diced
- 1 Tablespoon Sweet Rib Rub
- 1 Cup Sour Cream
- 1 Package Flour Tortilla

Directions:

1. Supply your smoker with wood pellets and follow the start-up procedure. Preheat the grill, with the lid open, to 300° F.
2. In a bowl, mix - the chicken, green chiles, Sweet Heat seasoning, sour cream, diced onion, and half the bag of shredded cheese.
3. Place a large spoonful of the chicken mixture in the center of a tortilla and roll it up. Repeat with the remaining tortillas, then place in the baking pan, and pour the enchilada sauce over the tortilla pans. Top with the remainder of the shredded cheese.

4. Wrap the top of the pan tightly in aluminum foil and grill for 45 minutes or until the enchilada sauce is bubbly. Remove from the grill and serve.

Lemon & Herb Chicken

Servings: 3-4

Cooking Time: 75 Minutes

Ingredients:

- 1 roaster chicken, about 4lb (1.8kg), preferably organic
- 1 large sweet onion, peeled and sliced lengthwise into 8 wedges
- ½ cup chicken stock or broth
- sprigs of fresh rosemary, thyme, parsley, tarragon, or chives (or a mix)
- lemon wedges
- for the butter
- 4 tbsp unsalted butter, at room temperature
- 1 garlic clove, peeled and finely minced
- 2 tbsp chopped fresh herbs, such as rosemary, thyme, parsley, tarragon, or chives (or a mix)
- 2 tsp lemon zest
- 2 tsp freshly squeezed lemon juice
- ½ tsp coarse salt
- ½ tsp freshly ground black pepper

Directions:

1. Supply your smoker with wood pellets and follow the start-up procedure. Preheat the grill, with the lid closed, to 400° F.
2. In a small bowl, make the herb butter by combining the ingredients.
3. Place the chicken on a rimmed sheet pan and tuck the lemon rinds from the butter into the main cavity. Rub the outside of the chicken with the herb butter. (Reserve any remainder.) Tuck the wings behind the back and tie the legs together with butcher's twine. Place the onion wedges in a shallow roasting pan to help form a natural rack for the chicken. (Alternatively, place several large carrots, trimmed and peeled, on the bottom of the pan.) Place the chicken on the onion rack. Add the chicken stock and any remaining herbed butter and lemon juice.
4. Place the roasting pan on the grate, roast the chicken for 30 minutes, and then baste with the juices from the bottom of the pan. Baste every 15 minutes until the chicken is golden brown and the internal temperature reaches 165°F (74°C), about 45 minutes more.
5. Transfer the chicken to a cutting board and let rest for 10 minutes. Carve the chicken and place the slices on a platter with a deep well. Spoon some of the juices over the chicken. Scatter fresh herbs over the top. Serve with the lemon wedges.

Smoked Apple Chicken Leg Quarters

Servings: 8

Cooking Time: 120 Minutes

Ingredients:

- 8 leg quarters
- 1 bottle marinade
- Pork & chicken rub
- 1 cup of apple juice or water

Directions:

1. Rinse chicken and pat dry.
2. Marinade chicken in the fridge for at least 30 minutes or overnight (preferred).
3. Once the chicken is marinated, sprinkle both sides with the rub.
4. Supply your smoker with wood pellets and follow the start-up procedure. Preheat the grill, with the lid closed, to 225° F.
5. Place a small stainless steel pot of apple juice or water in the inside corner to help keep moist.
6. Place chicken on your grill, skin side up, with lid closed.
7. Smoke for 2 hours or until the internal temperature in the thickest part of a thigh is 165 °F.
8. Remove chicken from the grill and let it rest for 5 minutes before serving. Enjoy!

Roasted Prosciutto Stuffed Chicken

Servings: 2
Cooking Time: 35 Minutes

Ingredients:

- 2 Whole boneless, skinless chicken breast
- salt and pepper
- 2 Tablespoon Dijon mustard
- 2 Slices Prosciutto Ham
- 4 Pieces mozzarella cheese
- 1 Large Tomatoes, sliced
- 4 Large basil leaves
- 2 Tablespoon olive oil
- Toothpicks

Directions:

1. Supply your smoker with wood pellets and follow the start-up procedure. Preheat the grill, with the lid closed, to 225° F.
2. While grill heats up, use a sharp knife to fillet each chicken breast in two. Open up each half, by pounding with a meat tenderizer.
3. Season each breast half with salt and pepper to taste. Rub mustard on both sides. Place a slice of proscuitto on the inside of the breast followed by a slice of mozzarella, a slice of tomato and a basil leaf. Drizzle olive oil on top.
4. Fold chicken breast back in half and secure with toothpicks. Brush outside of stuffed breast with olive oil.
5. Place directly on the grill grate. Cook for 6 to 7 minutes per side, or until chicken reaches an internal temperature of 160 degrees F.

Bbq Chicken Drumsticks

Servings: 4
Cooking Time: 120 Minutes

Ingredients:

- 8 chicken drumsticks
- 2 Tablespoon Chicken Rub
- 1/2 Cup 'Que BBQ Sauce

Directions:

1. Season each drumstick and let rest for 20 minutes.
2. Supply your smoker with wood pellets and follow the start-up procedure. Preheat the grill, with the lid closed, to 275° F.
3. Hang the drumsticks on the leg hanger (alternatively, place directly on the grill grate flipping halfway through) and cook for 1 hour. Grill: 275 ˚F
4. Remove the drumsticks from the hanger (or grate) and place in a pan. Grill: 275 ˚F Probe: 190 ˚F
5. Cover with foil and cook for 45 more minutes or until meat reaches an internal temperature of 190 degrees F. Grill: 275 ˚F Probe: 190 ˚F
6. Remove the foil and sauce all drumsticks in the pan.
7. Cook for an additional 15 minutes so sauce can set. Grill: 275 ˚F
8. Remove from Traeger and let rest for 15 minutes before serving. Enjoy!

Bbq Game Day Chicken Wings And Thighs

Servings: 6
Cooking Time: 50 Minutes

Ingredients:

- 10 chicken thighs
- 30 chicken wings
- 1/2 Cup olive oil
- 1/2 Cup Chicken Rub

Directions:

1. Place thighs and wings in a large bowl. Add the olive oil and Traeger Chicken Rub and mix well. Cover bowl and refrigerate for 3 to 8 hours.
2. Supply your smoker with wood pellets and follow the start-up procedure. Preheat the grill, with the lid closed, to 375° F.
3. Place chicken directly on the grill grate and cook for 45 minutes. Check the internal temperature of the chicken, it is considered done at 165℉, however, a finished temperature of 175 to 180℉ results in a better texture in dark meat. Grill: 375 ˚F Probe: 165 ˚F
4. Once the finished temperature is reached, remove chicken from the grill and let rest for 5 to 10 minutes before serving. Enjoy!

Smoked Buffalo Fries

Servings: 4

Cooking Time: 30 Minutes

Ingredients:

- 4 Chicken Breast
- salt
- black pepper
- 2 Cup Blue Cheese Dressing
- 1/2 Cup Frank's RedHot Sauce
- 1 Celery, stalks
- 6 russet potatoes
- Oil, For Frying

Directions:

1. Supply your smoker with wood pellets and follow the start-up procedure. Preheat the grill, with the lid closed, to 325° F.
2. Season chicken breast with salt and pepper. Smoke for 25-30 minutes or until 165 degrees. Pull and set aside.
3. Whisk blue cheese dressing and hot sauce together in a bowl; set aside.
4. Soak cut celery (2" long sticks) in cold water until serving
5. Cut potatoes into ¼ in sticks, resembling French fries.
6. Heat oil to 375 degrees in a Dutch oven or deep pot and gently place in potatoes. Fry until golden brown, drain on a sheet pan lined with paper towels. Season with kosher or sea salt. Repeat until all the potatoes are cooked. Keep them warm in an oven until you are ready to serve.
7. To assemble, place fries on a platter or wood board lined with butchers paper. Drizzle with franks sauce mixture, then the pulled chicken. Garnish with celery and serve immediately. Enjoy!

Nashville Spiced Smoked Chicken

Servings: 6

Cooking Time: 40 Minutes

Ingredients:

- 6 drumsticks
- 1 quart Butter Milk
- 1 tbsp Louisiana Hot Sauce
- 1 tbsp Ground Cumin
- 1/2 tbsp Chili powder
- 1 tbsp Onion Powder
- 1 tbsp Garlic Powder
- 1/2 tbsp White Pepper
- 1 tbsp Red Cayenne Pepper
- 1 tbsp Black Pepper
- 2 tbsp Brown Sugar

Directions:

1. Soak wings overnight in marinade.
2. Remove chicken from marinade.Dry off chicken and wash off buttermilk.
3. Drizzle chicken with olive oil.
4. Apply dry rub to drumsticks by rubbing thoroughly.
5. Let drumsticks rest in dry rub for at least 30 minutes.
6. Supply your smoker with wood pellets and follow the start-up procedure. Preheat the grill, with the lid closed, to 325° F, using Apple Wood Pellets.
7. Cook chicken on 325 degrees for 30-40 minutes or until internal temperature reach 160 degrees F.
8. Let chicken rest for 10 minutes before serving.

Carrot Celery Chicken Drumsticks

Servings: 4

Cooking Time: 30 Minutes

Ingredients:

- Buffalo Style Dry Rub
- Carrot, Stick
- Celery, Stick
- 12 Chicken, Drumsticks

Directions:

1. Supply your smoker with wood pellets and follow the start-up procedure. Preheat the grill, with the lid closed, to 350° F.
2. Generously sprinkle the Buffalo Wing Rub all over the drumsticks. Hang each drumstick by the bone on the Wing Rack. Place in the for about 30 minutes.
3. Serve hot with celery and carrot sticks. Enjoy!

Chile Cilantro Lime Chicken Wings

Servings: 4

Cooking Time: 20 Minutes

Ingredients:

- 1 Tsp Ancho Chili Powder
- 2 Tsp Blackened Sriracha Rub Seasoning
- 2 Lbs Chicken Wings, Split
- 2 Tbsp Cilantro, Chopped, Divided
- 1 Tsp Cumin
- 1 Lime, Zest & Juice
- 1 1/2 Tbsp Olive Oil

Directions:

1. In a medium bowl, combine 1 tablespoon of cilantro, lime juice and zest, olive oil, Blackened Sriracha, ancho chili powder, and cumin.
2. Place chicken wings in a resealable gallon bag and add cilantro mixture. Transfer to the refrigerator and marinate for 1 hour, turning occasionally.
3. Supply your smoker with wood pellets and follow the start-up procedure. Preheat the grill, with the lid closed, to 350° F. If using a gas or charcoal grill, set it up for medium heat.
4. Remove chicken wings from the marinade and place on the grill over indirect heat. Grill for 15 to 18 minutes, turning and rotating every 3 to 5 minutes.
5. Remove chicken wings from the grill, garnish with remaining cilantro, and serve warm.

Grilled Honey Chicken Wings

Servings: 4 - 8

Cooking Time: 30 Minutes

Ingredients:

- 2 Chipotles Chopped In Adobo
- 1 Apple Cider Vinegar
- 2 Tablespoons Balsamic Vinegar
- ¼ Cup Brown Sugar
- 2 ½ Lbs Chicken Wings, Trimmed And Patted Dry
- ¼ Cup Honey
- ½ Cup Ketchup
- ¼ Cup Adobo Sauce
- 2 Tablespoons Sweet Rib Rub
- 2 Teaspoons Worcestershire Sauce

Directions:

1. Supply your smoker with wood pellets and follow the start-up procedure. Preheat the grill, with the lid open, to 350° F. If you're using a charcoal or gas grill, set up the grill for medium high heat.
2. In a large bowl, whisk together the apple cider vinegar, ketchup, brown sugar, honey, chopped chipotle peppers with adobo sauce, balsamic vinegar, Worcestershire sauce, and Sweet Rib Rub. Whisk the glaze until it's well combined.
3. Add the wings to the glaze and place the bowl in the refrigerator. Marinade the chicken wings for up to 12 hours. Once the wings have finished marinating, remove the chicken wings from the marinade and place the chicken wings onto the wing rack.
4. Once all the wings have been placed on the wing rack, place the wing rack on the grill. Insert a temperature probe into the thickest part into one of the wings and grill the wings for 5 minutes, and then rotate the rack 180° and grill for another 5 minutes. Remove the wings once they have an internal temperature of 165°F and the juice from the chicken runs clear.
5. Remove the wings from the grill and serve immediately.

Duck Breast With Pomegranate Sauce

Servings: 4

Cooking Time: 13 Minutes

Ingredients:

- 4 duck breasts, each about 6oz (170g), skin on
- for the rub
- 2 tsp coarse salt
- 1 tsp ground cumin
- 1 tsp ground coriander
- 1 tsp freshly ground black pepper
- ½ tsp ground cinnamon
- ½ tsp ground fennel
- for the sauce
- 1 shallot, peeled and minced
- 1 cup pomegranate juice
- 1 tbsp sherry vinegar or balsamic vinegar
- 1 tsp cornstarch

- ¼ cup chicken stock or chicken broth
- 1 tbsp chilled unsalted butter, cut into 4 pieces
- ¼ cup fresh pomegranate seeds (optional)
- 1 tbsp minced fresh chives

Directions:

1. Place a cast iron skillet on the grate. Supply your smoker with wood pellets and follow the start-up procedure. Preheat the grill, with the lid closed, to 400° F.
2. In a small bowl, make the rub by combining the ingredients. Use a sharp knife to diagonally score the skin of each duck breast—but don't nick the flesh. Lightly season the scored side of each breast.
3. Place the duck breasts skin side down in the skillet and sear until the skin is crisp and golden brown, about 8 to 10 minutes. Turn the breasts and cook until the internal temperature in the thickest part of a breast reaches 130°F (54°C), about 2 to 3 minutes more. Transfer the breasts to a plate.
4. In a large saucepan on the stovetop over medium heat, make the sauce by heating 1 tablespoon of duck fat from the skillet. (Reserve the remainder for another use.) Add the shallot and sauté until soft, about 2 to 3 minutes.
5. Add the pomegranate juice and bring the mixture to a boil over medium-high heat. Reduce the sauce by half, about 3 to 5 minutes. Add the vinegar and lower the heat to medium low.
6. Whisk together the cornstarch and chicken stock until smooth. Whisk into the sauce and cook until the sauce thickens, about 1 to 2 minutes. Whisk in the butter and stir in the pomegranate seeds (if using).
7. Place the duck breasts on a warm platter. Drizzle the pomegranate sauce over the top. Scatter the chives around the platter before serving.

Buffalo Chicken Wraps

Servings: 4

Cooking Time: 20 Minutes

Ingredients:

- 2 teaspoons poultry seasoning
- 1 teaspoon freshly ground black pepper
- 1 teaspoon garlic powder
- 1 to 1½ pounds chicken tenders
- 4 tablespoons (½ stick) unsalted butter, melted
- ½ cup hot sauce (such as Frank's RedHot)
- 4 (10-inch) flour tortillas
- 1 cup shredded lettuce
- ½ cup diced tomato
- ½ cup diced celery
- ½ cup diced red onion
- ½ cup shredded Cheddar cheese
- ¼ cup blue cheese crumbles
- ¼ cup prepared ranch dressing
- 2 tablespoons sliced pickled jalapeño peppers (optional)

Directions:

1. Supply your smoker with wood pellets and follow the start-up procedure. Preheat, with the lid closed, to 350°F.
2. In a small bowl, stir together the poultry seasoning, pepper, and garlic powder to create an all-purpose rub, and season the chicken tenders with it.
3. Arrange the tenders directly on the grill, close the lid, and smoke for 20 minutes, or until a meat thermometer inserted in the thickest part of the meat reads 170°F.
4. In another bowl, stir together the melted butter and hot sauce and coat the smoked chicken with it.
5. To serve, heat the tortillas on the grill for less than a minute on each side and place on a plate.
6. Top each tortilla with some of the lettuce, tomato, celery, red onion, Cheddar cheese, blue cheese crumbles, ranch dressing, and jalapeños (if using).
7. Divide the chicken among the tortillas, close up securely, and serve.

Jamaican Jerk Chicken Quarters

Servings: 4

Cooking Time: 120 Minutes

Ingredients:

- 4 chicken leg quarters, scored
- ¼ cup canola oil
- ½ cup Jamaican Jerk Paste
- 1 tablespoon whole allspice (pimento) berries

Directions:

1. Supply your smoker with wood pellets and follow the start-up procedure. Preheat, with the lid closed, to 275°F.
2. Brush the chicken with canola oil, then brush 6 tablespoons of the Jerk paste on and under the skin. Reserve the remaining 2 tablespoons of paste for basting.
3. Throw the whole allspice berries in with the wood pellets for added smoke flavor.
4. Arrange the chicken on the grill, close the lid, and smoke for 1 hour to 1 hour 30 minutes, or until a meat thermometer inserted in the thickest part of the thigh reads 165°F.
5. Let the meat rest for 5 minutes and baste with the reserved jerk paste prior to serving.

Crispy Spiced Chicken Wings

Servings: 10
Cooking Time: 75 Minutes

Ingredients:

- 5 pounds of chicken wings (flats and drumettes)
- 2 1/2 Tablespoons baking powder
- 1 teaspoon salt

Directions:

1. Dry your chicken wings thoroughly on all sides with a paper towel. Place them in a zip-top bag.
2. Add the baking powder and salt to the wings, close the bag, and toss to coat evenly.
3. Supply your smoker with wood pellets and follow the start-up procedure. Preheat the grill, with the lid closed, to 250° F, using your favorite wood. Place the wings directly on the grill grates, close the lid, and smoke for 30 minutes.
4. Increase the heat in your smoker to 425 degrees F and continue cooking for 45 more minutes, or until the internal temperature of the wing reads 175 degrees F. You can rotate or flip the wings as needed to maintain even cooking and avoid any hot spots on the grill.
5. Remove the wing from the grill and serve. You can serve plain, toss in your favorite BBQ seasoning, or hot sauce.

Roasted Buffalo Wings

Servings: 4
Cooking Time: 30 Minutes

Ingredients:

- 4 Pound chicken wings
- 1 Tablespoon corn starch
- Chicken Rub
- kosher salt
- 1/2 Cup Frank's RedHot Sauce
- 1/4 Cup spicy mustard
- 6 Tablespoon unsalted butter

Directions:

1. Supply your smoker with wood pellets and follow the start-up procedure. Preheat the grill, with the lid closed, to 375° F.
2. While grill is preheating, dry off chicken wings with a paper towel. Place wings in a large bowl and sprinkle with cornstarch, Traeger Chicken Rub and salt to taste. Mix to coat both sides of the chicken wings.
3. When the grill is hot, place the wings on the grill and cook for 35 minutes total, turning halfway through cook time. Grill: 375 °F
4. Check the internal temperature of the wings at 35 minutes. The internal temperature should be at least 165°F . However, an internal temperature of 175-180°F will yield a better texture. Grill: 375 °F Probe: 175 °F
5. For the Buffalo Sauce: In a saucepot, add the Franks Red Hot, mustard and butter. Whisk to combine and heat through on the stove top. Keep sauce warm while the wings are cooking.
6. When wings are done, remove from grill and place into a medium bowl Pour the buffalo sauce over the wings, turning with tongs to coat. Grill: 375 °F
7. Cook for an additional 10-15 minutes on the grill for the sauce to set. Serve wings with ranch or blue cheese dressing. Enjoy!

Thai Chicken Satays

Servings: 4
Cooking Time: 10 Minutes

Ingredients:

- 1½lb (680g) boneless, skinless chicken breasts

- for the marinade
- ½ cup unsweetened canned light coconut milk
- 2 garlic cloves, peeled and coarsely chopped
- ¼ cup loosely packed fresh cilantro leaves
- 1-inch (2.5cm) piece of fresh ginger, peeled and coarsely chopped
- 2 tbsp light soy sauce
- 1 tbsp Asian fish sauce
- 1 tbsp light brown sugar or low-carb substitute
- 2 tsp sambal oelek (optional)
- 1 tsp Thai-style curry powder
- 1 tsp ground cumin
- 1 tsp ground turmeric
- 1 tsp coarse salt
- 2 tbsp vegetable oil
- for serving
- butter lettuce leaves, washed and dried
- cherry tomatoes
- Peanut Sauce

Directions:

1. Use a sharp knife to slice the chicken breasts lengthwise into strips, each about 1 inch (2.5cm) wide. (If the chicken breasts are unusually thick, butterfly them before cutting them into strips.) Place the breasts in a resealable plastic bag.
2. In a blender, make the marinade by combining the ingredients. Blend until fairly smooth. Pour the marinade over the chicken, turning and massaging the bag to thoroughly coat the chicken. Refrigerate for 2 hours.
3. Supply your smoker with wood pellets and follow the start-up procedure. Preheat the grill, with the lid closed, to 450° F.
4. Remove the chicken from the marinade and let any excess drip off. (Discard the marinade.) Thread each chicken strip on a bamboo skewer, pushing the point in one side of the chicken and out the other as if sewing. Leave very little of the tip exposed because it will burn easily.
5. Place the skewers on the grate perpendicular to the bars. Grill until the chicken has grill marks and is fully cooked, about 3 to 5 minutes per side.
6. Remove the skewers from the grill. Place the lettuce leaves on a platter. Place the satays atop the leaves. Scatter cherry tomatoes over the top. Serve with the peanut sauce.

Italian Grilled Chicken Saltimbocca

Servings: 4
Cooking Time: 30 Minutes

Ingredients:

- 6 Chicken Breast
- olive oil
- Pork & Poultry Rub
- 6 Slices Prosciutto Slices
- 10 Sage, Leaves
- 1 Cup Parmesan cheese

Directions:

1. Supply your smoker with wood pellets and follow the start-up procedure. Preheat the grill, with the lid closed, to 350° F.
2. Using a sharp knife, carefully butterfly each chicken breast.
3. Oil the outside of each breast and season lightly with Traeger Pork and Poultry rub.
4. Wrap with a slice of prosciutto. Top with fresh sage and Parmesan cheese.
5. Arrange the chicken on a baking sheet or directly on the grill grate at an angle to the bars.
6. Roast until the chicken is cooked through, about 25 to 30 minutes or until it reaches an internal temperature of 165˚F (75 C). Grill: 350 ˚F Probe: 165 ˚F
7. Let rest for 2 minutes before serving. Top with more fresh sage and parmesan. Enjoy!

Marinated Grilled Honey Chicken Wings

Servings: 4-6
Cooking Time: 30 Minutes

Ingredients:

- 1/2 Bottle Beer, Any Brand
- 2 Lbs Chicken Wings, Whole
- 2 Tablespoon Honey
- 1 Tablespoon Sweet Heat Rub
- 2 Tablespoon Rice Wine Vinegar

- 1/2 Tablesoon Sesame Oil
- 1/4 Cup Soy Sauce
- 1 Tablespoon Sriracha Hot Sauce

Directions:

1. In a large glass or plastic bowl, combine the beer, soy sauce, honey, rice wine vinegar, sriracha, sesame oil and Sweet Heat Seasoning. Whisk well to combine.
2. Add the chicken wings to the marinade and toss well to combine. Cover with plastic wrap and refrigerate for 2 hours and up to 24 hours.
3. Remove chicken wings from refrigerator, drain marinade and pat dry. Supply your smoker with wood pellets and follow the start-up procedure. Supply your smoker with wood pellets and follow the start-up procedure. Preheat the grill, with the lid open, to 350° F. Place the wings on a grill pan and grill for 20-25 minutes, or until the wings' internal temperature is 165F. Remove from the grill, serve and enjoy!

Bbq Chicken Breasts

Servings: 6
Cooking Time: 25 Minutes

Ingredients:

- 6 boneless, skinless chicken breast
- 1 1/2 Cup Sweet & Heat BBQ Sauce
- salt and pepper
- 1 Tablespoon chopped parsley, for garnish

Directions:

1. Place chicken breasts and 1 cup of Traeger Sweet & Heat BBQ Sauce in a resealable bag or large bowl, and gently turn to cover chicken evenly in the sauce. Marinate in the refrigerator overnight.
2. Supply your smoker with wood pellets and follow the start-up procedure. Preheat the grill, with the lid closed, to 450° F.
3. Remove chicken from marinade and season with salt and pepper.
4. Place chicken directly on the grill grate and cook for 10 minutes on each side flipping once or until internal temperature reaches 150℉.
5. Brush on remaining 1/2 cup of Traeger Sweet & Heat BBQ Sauce while chicken is still on the grill, and continue to cook 5 to 10 minutes longer or until a finished internal temperature of 165℉.
6. Remove chicken from grill and let rest 5 minutes before serving. Sprinkle with chopped parsley. Enjoy!

Savory Jerk Chicken Wings

Servings: 4
Cooking Time: 20 Minutes

Ingredients:

- 1 Tsp Allspice, Ground
- 3 Lbs Chicken Wings, Split
- 1/2 Tsp Cinnamon, Ground
- 4 Garlic Cloves, Smashed
- 2 Tsp Ginger, Grated
- 1 Habanero Pepper, Chopped
- 2 Tbsp Honey
- 2 Tbsp Lemon Juice
- 1/3 Cup Lime Juice
- 1/2 Tsp Nutmeg, Ground
- 1/2 Cup Olive Oil
- 1/4 Cup Poblano Pepper, Chopped
- 1 Tbsp Tamari
- 2 Tsp Thyme, Dried
- 1/2 Cup Yellow Onion, Chopped

Directions:

1. Add chicken to a large resealable plastic bag.
2. In the bowl of a food processor, add the garlic, onion, ginger, peppers, tamari, honey, lime juice, lemon juice, thyme, allspice, cinnamon, nutmeg, and oil. Process on low for 1 minute, then transfer marinade to the bag. Seal the bag and place in the refrigerator for at least 2 hours, up to overnight.
3. Supply your smoker with wood pellets and follow the start-up procedure. Preheat the grill, with the lid open, to 425° F. If using a gas or charcoal grill, set it up for medium-high heat.
4. Remove wings from the marinade, and discard remaining marinade. Place wings on the grill and cook for 15 to 20 minutes, flipping every 5 minutes, until an internal temperature of 165 F is reached.
5. Remove wings from the grill and serve warm.

BEEF LAMB AND GAME RECIPES

Slow Smoked And Roasted Prime Rib

Servings: 8

Cooking Time: 240 Minutes

Ingredients:

- 1 (8-10 lb) 4-bone prime rib roast
- 5 Tablespoon kosher salt
- 5 Tablespoon ground black pepper
- 3 Tablespoon fresh chopped thyme
- 3 Tablespoon fresh chopped rosemary

Directions:

1. Supply your smoker with wood pellets and follow the start-up procedure. Preheat the grill, with the lid closed, to 250° F.
2. While grill preheats, trim excess fat off roast. Combine remainder of ingredients and coat the entire roast with the mixture.
3. Place roast on grill and cook until the internal temperature reaches 120°F, about 4 hours. Begin checking the internal temperature every hour or so until it reaches 120°F. Pull roast off the grill and allow to rest for 20 minutes. Grill: 250 °F Probe: 120 °F
4. While roast rests, increase grill temperature to 450°F and preheat. Once the grill is hot, place the roast back on for 15 minutes, flipping halfway through or until the internal temperature registers 130°F for medium rare. Grill: 450 °F Probe: 130 °F
5. Remove roast from grill and allow to rest for 30 minutes before slicing. Enjoy!

Easy Breakfast Cheeseburger

Servings: 2

Cooking Time: 10 Minutes

Ingredients:

- 4 Bacon, Strip
- 6 Ounce Lean Beef, Ground
- 2 Burger Buns
- 2 Cheese, Sliced
- 2 Egg
- Pepper
- Salt

Directions:

1. Supply your smoker with wood pellets and follow the start-up procedure. Preheat the grill, with the lid closed, to 400° F.
2. Take the ground beef and divide it into two thin patties. Brush the grate with oil, then add the patties and grill them on about 2-5 minutes on each side, or until the desired doneness, pressing down to get a good sear.
3. Remove the burgers from the grill, then build your burger. Starting with the bottom bun or bread slice, add the patty, then a slice of American cheese, top with bacon, hash browns, an egg over easy, and finish with the top bun or bread slice. Now it's ready to serve!

Reverse Seared Rib-eye Steaks

Servings: 2

Cooking Time: 50 Minutes

Ingredients:

- 2 (1-1/2 inch thick) rib-eye steaks
- Meat Church Holy Cow BBQ Rub
- Meat Church Gourmet Garlic and Herb Seasoning
- butter, preferably high-quality

Directions:

1. Supply your smoker with wood pellets and follow the start-up procedure. Preheat the grill, with the lid closed, to 225° F.
2. Season both sides of steak with Meat Church Holy Cow BBQ Rub, and Meat Church Garlic and Herb Seasoning. Place steaks on grill and cook for 30 to 45 minutes or until an instant read thermometer inserted in the thickest part of the meat reads 120°F for medium-rare. Grill: 225 °F Probe: 120 °F
3. Remove steaks from grill and increase grill temperature to 500°F. Allow steaks to rest while grill preheats.
4. Place steaks back on grill and sear on both sides for 3 minutes.
5. Remove from grill, top with butter and lightly tent with foil to allow the butter to melt and the steaks to rest before slicing, about 5 minutes. Enjoy!

Roasted Mustard Crusted Prime Rib

Servings: 6

Cooking Time: 180 Minutes

Ingredients:

- 1 3-bone prime rib roast
- 1 Tablespoon black pepper
- 2 Tablespoon kosher salt
- 2 Tablespoon garlic, minced to a paste
- 1 Cup whole grain mustard

Directions:

1. Combine salt, black pepper, whole grain mustard and garlic in a small bowl and mix well. Rub mixture all over the exterior of the roast making sure each section is evenly coated.
2. Supply your smoker with wood pellets and follow the start-up procedure. Preheat the grill, with the lid closed, to 450° F.
3. Place the roast directly on the grill grate with the ribs facing the back of the grill. Close the lid and cook for 45 minutes or until the exterior of the roast has an even layer of browning. Grill: 450 ˚F
4. Reduce the temperature to 325 degrees F and continue to cook for 2.5 hours or until the internal temperature reaches 125 degrees F. Grill: 325 ˚F Probe: 125 ˚F
5. Remove roast from grill and allow to rest 15 minutes before slicing. After roast has rested, remove trussing and bones and slice into 1" inch sections. Enjoy!

Smoked Beer Brisket

Servings: 16

Cooking Time: 420 Minutes

Ingredients:

- 1 15 lb brisket
- Brisket Baste:
- 1 cup beer
- 1/4 cup apple cider vinegar
- 1/4 cup beef stock
- 5 tbsp butter, melted
- Brisket Rub:
- 2 tbsp garlic powder
- 2 tbsp onion powder
- 2 tbsp paprika
- 2 tbsp chili powder
- 2 tbsp kosher salt
- 2 tbsp coarse ground black pepper
- 1 tbsp brown sugar

Directions:

1. Supply your smoker with wood pellets and follow the start-up procedure. Preheat the grill, with the lid closed, to 225 ˚F.
2. In a small bowl, mix together garlic powder, onion powder, paprika, chili pepper, kosher salt, and pepper.
3. Rub the seasonings on all sides of the brisket.
4. Place the brisket on the grill grate, fat side down.
5. Cook the brisket until it reaches an internal temperature of 160 ˚F(about 3 to 4 hours).
6. When brisket reaches an internal temperature of 160 ˚F, remove it from the grill.
7. Double wrap the meat in aluminum foil and add the beef broth to the foil packet.
8. Return brisket to the grill grate and cook until it reaches an internal temperature of 204 ˚F(about 3 hours more).
9. Once finished, remove the brisket from the grill, unwrap from foil and let it rest for 15 minutes.
10. Cut against the grain and serve. Enjoy!

Spiced Lamb Burgers With Tzatziki

Servings: 4

Cooking Time: 10 Minutes

Ingredients:

- 1½lb (680g) ground lamb or a mixture of lamb and beef, well chilled
- 1⁄3 cup grated red onion
- 1 to 2 garlic cloves, peeled and minced
- 2 tbsp chopped fresh dill or fresh mint
- 1 tsp ground cumin
- ½ tsp ground cinnamon
- ½ tsp crushed red pepper flakes (optional)
- extra virgin olive oil
- coarse salt
- freshly ground black pepper
- for the tzatziki

- 1/3 hothouse cucumber, unpeeled and coarsely grated
- coarse salt
- 1½ cups plain Greek yogurt, drained
- 1 to 2 garlic cloves, peeled
- 1 tbsp freshly squeezed lemon juice or white distilled vinegar
- 1½ tbsp extra virgin olive oil
- 1 tbsp chopped fresh dill or fresh mint

Directions:

1. Supply your smoker with wood pellets and follow the start-up procedure. Preheat the grill, with the lid closed, to 450° F.
2. Make the tzatziki by placing the cucumber in a sieve and lightly sprinkle with salt. After 15 minutes, rinse with cold running water. Drain and then squeeze the cucumber dry with paper towels. Transfer the cucumber to a large bowl. Add the yogurt, garlic, and lemon juice. Stir to mix. Season with salt to taste. Transfer to a serving bowl. Set aside. Just before serving, drizzle with the olive oil and scatter the fresh dill over the top.
3. In a large bowl, combine the lamb, red onion, garlic, dill, cumin, cinnamon, and red pepper flakes (if using). Wet your hands with cold water and mix thoroughly but gently. (Try not to overhandle the meat.) Form the meat into 4 patties of equal size, each about ¾ inch (2cm) thick. Use your thumbs to make a shallow depression in the top of each burger. Lightly oil the outsides of the burgers with olive oil. Season with salt and pepper.
4. Place the burgers on the grate and grill until the internal temperature reaches 160°F (71°C), about 4 to 5 minutes per side, turning once.
5. Transfer the burgers to a platter. On a separate platter, place thinly sliced red onions, thinly sliced tomatoes, thinly sliced cucumbers, crumbled feta, and Kalamata olives. Serve with the tzatziki and pita bread.

Beer Braised Beef Sandwiches

Servings: 4

Cooking Time: 180 Minutes

Ingredients:

- 12 oz beer, porter or stout
- 1/2 black pepper
- 2 1/2 lbs chuck roast
- 4 hoagie rolls, sliced lengthwise
- 1/4 cup horseradish sauce
- 1 tbsp kosher salt
- 1 tbsp parsley, chopped
- 1 red onion, cut into thick rings
- 1/2 tbsp worcestershire sauce
- 1 yellow onion, cut into thick rings

Directions:

1. Supply your smoker with wood pellets and follow the start-up procedure. Preheat the grill, with the lid open, to 450° F. If using a gas or charcoal grill, set it up for high heat.
2. Set the chuck roast on a sheet tray, then season with salt and pepper. Place onions in a cast iron skillet or Dutch oven with a lid. Set aside.
3. Sear the chuck roast on the grill, 3 minutes per side, then transfer to the skillet set on top of the onions. Add the Worcestershire sauce and beer to the skillet, along the side of the roast. Cover and reduce the temperature to 325°F. Braise the roast for 2 ½ to 3 hours, until tender.
4. Remove the roast from the grill, add parsley, then pull apart and toss in reduced pan jus and onions.
5. Serve warm on hoagie rolls with horseradish sauce.

Breakfast Brisket Hash Recipe

Servings: 4

Cooking Time: 20 Minutes

Ingredients:

- 3 Tablespoon canola oil
- 1/2 Cup yellow onion, diced
- 1/2 Cup green bell pepper, diced
- 1/2 Cup red bell pepper, diced
- 1 Clove garlic, minced
- 2 Cup Hashbrown Potatoes, Cooked
- 2 Cup brisket, cooked and shredded
- 3 Whole eggs
- salt and pepper

Directions:

1. Supply your smoker with wood pellets and follow the start-up procedure. Preheat the grill, with the lid closed, to 450° F.

2. Place oil, peppers, and onion in the skillet; sauté until they are translucent. Grill: 450 °F

3. Add garlic and cook 3 more minutes. Add cooked potatoes, brisket, and eggs. Cook until the brisket is heated through, about 10 minutes. Sprinkle salt and pepper and stir. Enjoy!

Cheese Onion Steak Sandwiches

Servings: 4

Cooking Time: 10 Minutes

Ingredients:

- 2 tbsp, divided butter
- 4 hoagie rolls, sliced lengthwise
- 2 tbsp olive oil
- 1-2 tbsp chop house steak rub
- 8 slices provolone cheese, sliced
- 2 lbs, sliced thinly rib-eye steaks
- 1 yellow onion, sliced

Directions:

1. Supply your smoker with wood pellets and follow the start-up procedure. Preheat the grill, with the lid closed, to 375° F. If using a gas or charcoal grill, set heat to medium heat. For all other grills, preheat cast iron skillet on grill grates.
2. Melt 1 tablespoon of butter and 1 tablespoon of olive oil on griddle. With a serrated knife, slice rolls 3/4 of the way through, then place facedown onto griddle and cook until toasted. Set aside.
3. Melt remaining tablespoon of butter and olive oil on the griddle. Add sliced onions and cook for 2 minutes, or until lightly caramelized. Move to the lower-right corner of griddle to keep warm.
4. Season steak generously with Chop House Steak Rub, then place on griddle and cook for 3 minutes, stirring to brown all sides. Mix in caramelized onions.
5. Divide steak and onions into 4 portions on the griddle, then top each with 2 slices of provolone cheese. Let cheese melt slightly and transfer to a toasted hoagie roll using a bench scraper or metal spatula. Serve hot and enjoy!

Santa Maria Tri-tip With Pico De Gallo

Servings: 4

Cooking Time: 68 Minutes

Ingredients:

- 1 tri-tip roast, about 2 to 2½lb (1 to 1.2kg)
- coarse salt
- freshly ground black pepper
- granulated garlic or garlic powder
- for the pico de gallo
- 8 Roma tomatoes, decored, deseeded, and diced
- 1 white onion, peeled and diced
- 1 serrano pepper, destemmed, deseeded, and minced, plus more
- 1 garlic clove, peeled and minced
- juice of 1 lime
- ½ cup loosely packed cilantro leaves, chopped
- 1 tsp coarse salt

Directions:

1. In a medium bowl, make the pico de gallo by combining the tomatoes, onion, serrano, garlic, lime juice, and cilantro. Stir gently with a rubber spatula and season with salt to taste. Cover and refrigerate for 2 hours.
2. Approximately 45 minutes before you're ready to cook, season the roast on all sides with salt and pepper and granulated garlic.
3. Supply your smoker with wood pellets and follow the start-up procedure. Preheat the grill, with the lid closed, to 180° F.
4. Place the roast on the grate and smoke until the internal temperature in the thickest part of the roast reaches 115°F (46°C), about 45 minutes to 1 hour. Transfer the roast to a plate.
5. Raise the temperature to 450°F (232°C). Place the roast on the grate and sear until the internal temperature in the thickest part of the roast reaches 130 to 135°F (54 to 57°C), about 3 to 4 minutes per side. For best results, don't cook beyond medium rare. (The thinner tail should satisfy any diner who prefers beef to be more well done.)
6. Remove the roast from the grill and thinly slice on a sharp diagonal against the grain. Serve with the pico de gallo.

Georgia Smoked Onion Brisket Sandwich

Servings: 4

Cooking Time: 450 Minutes

Ingredients:

- ½ Cup Barbecue Sauce
- ¼ Cup Beef Broth
- 2 Tablespoons Bourbon
- 1, 3 Pound Brisket Flat, Trimmed
- 4 Kaiser Rolls
- ½ Cup Peach Preserves
- Sliced Pickles
- 4 Tablespoons Pulled Pork Rub
- Sliced White Onions

Directions:

1. Supply your smoker with wood pellets and follow the start-up procedure. Preheat the grill, with the lid closed, to 225° F.
2. Generously rub the brisket with the Pulled Pork Rub. Set aside.
3. In a bowl, mix together the barbecue sauce, peach preserves and bourbon. Set aside.
4. Place the brisket in the smoker and smoke for 5 hours, or until the internal temperature reaches 170°F. Once the brisket reaches temperature, remove from the smoker, place the brisket in foil and pour the beef broth over the top. Wrap the brisket tightly in aluminum foil and return to the smoker for another 2 hours, or until the internal temperature reaches 190°F.
5. Remove the brisket from the grill, unwrap the brisket, discard the foil, and brush the brisket generously with the peach glaze mixture. Place the brisket back on the smoker and smoke for 30 minutes, or until the brisket is shiny and glazed. Remove the brisket from the grill and rest for 10 minutes, covered in foil.
6. Once the brisket has rested, slice thickly against the grain and top the Kaiser rolls with the brisket slices, onion slices and pickle slices. Serve immediately.

Bbq Sweet Pepper Meatloaf

Servings: 8

Cooking Time: 180 Minutes

Ingredients:

- 5 Pound ground beef, 80% lean
- 2 eggs
- 1 Cup plain panko breadcrumbs
- 1 Tablespoon kosher salt
- 1 Tablespoon black pepper
- 2 Tablespoon Rub
- 1 Cup diced sweet red peppers
- 1 Cup green onion, finely chopped
- 1 Cup ketchup

Directions:

1. Thoroughly mix together the ground beef, eggs, plain panko bread crumbs, kosher salt, black pepper, Traeger Rub, red sweet peppers and green onion.
2. Supply your smoker with wood pellets and follow the start-up procedure. Preheat the grill, with the lid closed, to 225° F.
3. Mold the meat mixture into a loaf and season exterior with the Traeger Rub.
4. Place meatloaf directly on the grill grate and cook for 2 hours and 15 minutes. Grill: 225 °F
5. Increase the grill temperature to 375°F and cook until an internal temperature of 155°F. Grill: 375 °F Probe: 155 °F
6. Glaze the meatloaf with ketchup and cook an additional 15 minutes. Grill: 375 °F
7. Allow to rest for 15 minutes before slicing. Enjoy!

Bistecca Alla Fiorentina With Mushroom Ragout

Servings: 3

Cooking Time: 25 Minutes

Ingredients:

- 2 sprigs of fresh sage
- 2 sprigs of fresh rosemary
- 2 sprigs of fresh thyme
- 1 porterhouse steak, about 2½lb (1.25kg)
- extra virgin olive oil
- coarse salt
- fresh coarsely ground black pepper
- for the ragout
- 3 tbsp unsalted butter
- 3 shallots or 1 white onion, peeled and chopped

- 2 garlic cloves, peeled and minced
- 2lb (1kg) wild mushrooms, cleaned, destemmed, and sliced or chopped
- coarse salt
- freshly ground black pepper
- 2 tbsp Cognac or brandy
- ½ cup low-salt beef broth, plus more
- 2 tsp light soy sauce
- 2 tsp chopped fresh thyme or 1 tsp dried thyme
- ½ cup heavy whipping cream, plus more
- freshly squeezed lemon juice
- freshly chopped chives

Directions:

1. Place a cast iron skillet or cast iron griddle on the grate. Supply your smoker with wood pellets and follow the start-up procedure. Preheat the grill, with the lid closed, to 450° F.
2. In a large skillet on the stovetop over medium heat, begin making the ragout by melting the butter. Add the shallots and sauté until they soften, about 2 to 3 minutes, stirring often. Add the garlic and mushrooms. Season with salt and pepper. Cook until the mushrooms give up their liquid and begin to brown, about 5 minutes. Add the Cognac and cook for 1 minute. Stir in the broth, soy sauce, and thyme. Cook until the liquid reduces slightly, about 5 minutes. Remove the skillet from the stovetop and set aside.
3. Tie the sprigs of sage, rosemary, and thyme together with butcher's twine. Place the steak on a rimmed sheet pan and use the herb brush to generously brush both sides with olive oil. Season with salt and pepper.
4. Place the steak on the skillet and grill until the internal temperature reaches 125°F (52°C), about 8 to 10 minutes per side, occasionally using the herb brush to brush the steak with olive oil. If your grill has enough clearance, stand the porterhouse upright, resting on the bone, and continue to cook for a few minutes more.
5. Transfer the meat to a cutting board and brush it one final time with olive oil. Let rest for 5 minutes.
6. Add the cream to the ragout and reheat over medium-high heat until the mixture boils. Taste for seasoning, adding salt and pepper. If the ragout seems dry, add more cream or broth. If the flavors need brightening, stir in 1 or 2 teaspoons of lemon juice. Transfer the ragout to an attractive serving bowl and top with chives.
7. Carve off the strip steak and filet mignon. Slice them on a diagonal, keeping the slices in order. Place the bone on a platter and then place the slices around the bone. Serve immediately with the mushroom ragout.

Duck Fat Fries (confit)

Servings: 6

Cooking Time: 180 Minutes

Ingredients:

- 1/4 Cup sea salt
- 12 Whole black peppercorn
- 2 Sprig thyme sprigs
- 2 Clove garlic, crushed
- 1 Whole bay leaves
- 6 Whole Duck Leg Quarters, (leg with thigh attached), preferallb moulard
- olive oil

Directions:

1. Combine the salt and the water in a large resealable plastic bag (or a large bowl) and stir until the salt crystals dissolve.
2. Add the peppercorns, thyme, garlic, bay leaf, coriander, if using, and duck leg quarters. Seal the bag, put in a pan or bowl (to contain any potential leaks) and refrigerate for 24 hours.
3. Drain the duck leg quarters (discard the brine) and rinse under cold running water. Pat dry with paper towels. Prick the skin all over with a darning needle or sharp fork, being careful not to nick the meat. (It helps if you go in at an angle.) This creates channels for the fat to escape, making for crispier skin.
4. Supply your smoker with wood pellets and follow the start-up procedure. Preheat the grill, with the lid closed, to 400° F.
5. Meanwhile add enough olive oil to a large cast iron skillet or roasting pan to film the bottom. Arrange the duck leg quarters in the skillet or roasting pan in a single layer, skin-side down.

6. Put the skillet or roasting pan on the grill grate. Roast the duck for 30 minutes, or until the duck fat begins to render. Reduce the temperature to 300F (150C). Turn the duck legs so they are skin-side up. Cover the skillet or roasting pan tightly with foil. Grill: 300 °F
7. Continue to roast the duck for 2 hours. Uncover the duck and roast for an additional hour, or until the skin is crisp and golden brown. Remove the duck, shred, and serve immediately. (Alternatively, you can refrigerate the duck for up to a week. Re-crisp the skin by grilling the duck, skin-side down, in a hot cast iron skillet or on your Traeger.) Serve with brown butter french fries.
8. Strain the remaining duck fat through cheesecloth or a fine-mesh kitchen strainer and transfer to a covered container; refrigerate for up to 6 months. Use the flavorful fat to saut potatoes or sturdy greens.

Kalbi-style Steak Wraps

Servings: 4
Cooking Time: 8 Minutes

Ingredients:

- 1 flat iron steak, about 1½lb (680g)
- 1 tbsp toasted sesame seeds
- 2 scallions, trimmed, white and green parts thinly sliced on a sharp diagonal
- for the marinade
- 1 small white onion, peeled and coarsely grated
- 4 garlic cloves, peeled and smashed with a chef's knife
- ½ Asian pear, decored and coarsely grated
- ½ cup light soy sauce
- ½ cup low-carb beer or distilled water
- 2 tbsp light brown sugar or low-carb substitute
- 2 tbsp rice vinegar or apple cider vinegar
- 2 tbsp toasted sesame oil
- 1 tbsp peeled and grated fresh ginger
- 1 tsp freshly ground black pepper

Directions:

1. In a large bowl, make the marinade by combining the ingredients. Stir until the sugar dissolves. Place the steaks in a resealable plastic bag and add the marinade, massaging the bag to thoroughly coat the meat. Refrigerate for 8 hours or overnight, turning the bag once or twice.
2. Supply your smoker with wood pellets and follow the start-up procedure. Preheat the grill, with the lid closed, to 450° F.
3. Remove the steaks from the marinade and remove any solids. (Discard the marinade.) Pat dry with paper towels. Place the steaks on the cast iron pan and grill until the internal temperature reaches 125 to 130°F (52 to 54°C), about 3 to 4 minutes per side, turning once.
4. Transfer the steaks to a cutting board and let rest for 2 minutes. Thinly slice each steak on a sharp diagonal and place on a platter. Scatter the sesame seeds and scallions over the top.
5. Place leaf lettuce, thinly sliced jalapeños, fresh cilantro leaves, kimchi (optional), and thinly sliced garlic on a separate platter. Place gochujang (Korean chili paste) in a small ramekin and add that to the platter.
6. Place the two platters on the table. Advise each diner to assemble the lettuce wraps to their desire. Serve with Asian beer, sake, or Korean soju.

Perfect Roast Prime Rib

Servings: 8-12
Cooking Time: 300minutes

Ingredients:

- 1 (3-bone) rib roast
- Salt
- Freshly ground black pepper
- 1 garlic clove, minced

Directions:

1. Supply your smoker with wood pellets and follow the start-up procedure. Preheat the grill, with the lid closed, to 360°F.
2. Season the roast all over with salt and pepper and, using your hands, rub it all over with the minced garlic.
3. Place the roast directly on the grill grate and smoke for 4 or 5 hours, until its internal temperature reaches 145°F for medium-rare.
4. Remove the roast from the grill and let it rest for 15 minutes, before slicing and serving.

Roasted Duck

Servings: 4

Cooking Time: 180 Minutes

Ingredients:

- 1 (5-6 lb) duck, defrosted
- Pork & Poultry Rub
- 1 Small onion, peeled and quartered
- 1 orange, quartered
- fresh herbs, such as parsley, sage or rosemary

Directions:

1. Remove the giblets and discard or save for another use. Trim any loose skin at the neck and remove excess fat from around the main cavity. Remove the wing tips if desired.
2. Rinse the duck under cold running water, inside and out, and dry with paper towels.
3. Prick the skin all over with the tip of a knife or the tines of a fork; do not pierce the meat. This helps to render the fat and crisp the skin.
4. Season the bird, inside and out, with Traeger Pork and Poultry Rub. Tuck the onion, orange, and fresh herbs into the cavity.
5. Tie the legs together with butcher's string.
6. Supply your smoker with wood pellets and follow the start-up procedure. Preheat the grill, with the lid closed, to 225° F.
7. Place the duck directly on the grill grate. Roast for 2-1/2 to 3 hours, or until the skin is brown and crisp. The internal temperature should register 160°F in the thigh (be sure to avoid the bone as this will give you an inaccurate reading). Grill: 225 °F Probe: 160 °F
8. If the duck is not browned to your liking, increase the grill temperature to 375°F and roast for several minutes at the higher temperature. Grill: 375 °F
9. Tent the duck loosely with foil and allow it to rest for 30 minutes.
10. Remove the butcher's twine and carve. Enjoy!

Hickory Smoked Prime Rib

Servings: 6

Cooking Time: 240 Minutes

Ingredients:

- 1 (8-10 lb) 4-bone prime rib roast
- 3 Tablespoon Dijon mustard
- 2 Tablespoon Worcestershire sauce
- 4 Clove garlic, mashed to a paste
- 2 Teaspoon dried thyme
- 2 Teaspoon dried rosemary
- Prime Rib Rub or coarse salt and freshly ground black pepper
- prepared horseradish, for serving

Directions:

1. If the roast has a fat cap more than 1/4 inch thick, trim it with a sharp knife or ask your butcher to do it for you. Tie the roast between the bones with butcher's twine. This discourages the eye of the meat from separating from the cap.
2. In a small bowl, whisk together the Dijon mustard, Worcestershire sauce, garlic, thyme and rosemary. If the dried rosemary needles are long, finely chop them before adding.
3. Slather the outside of the roast with the mustard paste and season generously with Traeger Prime Rib Rub on all sides. Refrigerate uncovered for up to 8 hours.
4. Supply your smoker with wood pellets and follow the start-up procedure. Preheat the grill, with the lid closed, to 250° F.Place the prime rib directly on the grill grate, fat-side up. Roast for 3-1/2 to 4 hours, or until the internal temperature of the meat (the tip of the temperature probe should be in the center of the meat) reaches 125°F to 130°F for rare or for medium-rare, 135°F. Grill: 250 °F Probe: 125 °F
5. Transfer meat to a cutting board, preferably one with a deep well so you don't lose the juices, and loosely tent the meat with foil. Allow meat to rest for 30 minutes. Grill: 250 °F Probe: 135 °F
6. To carve, remove the twine. Use a sharp knife to remove the rack of bone following the curvature of the meat. Carve the meat across the grain into 1/2 inch thick slices. Serve with horseradish, if desired. Enjoy!

Italian Beef Pinwheels

Servings: 6
Cooking Time: 45 Minutes

Ingredients:

- 3 Pound skirt steak
- Prime Rib Rub
- 2 Cup spinach
- 4 Slices havarti cheese
- 4 Slices provolone cheese
- 1 Cup sun-dried tomatoes

Directions:

1. Supply your smoker with wood pellets and follow the start-up procedure. Preheat the grill, with the lid closed, to 375° F.
2. Season skirt steak generously with Traeger Prime Rib Rub. Lay your skirt steak flat and add a layer of spinach. Depending on the size of the steak, add up to the full 2 cups. Then add a layer of cheese and lastly the sun-dried tomatoes.
3. Tightly roll the meat up and insert toothpicks to hold it together.
4. Place meat roll directly on the grill grate and cook for 45 minutes. After 45 minutes, remove from the grill and let rest for 10 minutes before slicing. Grill: 375 °F
5. Serve with a large helping of mashed potatoes or your favorite side dish. Enjoy!

Braised Onion Chuck Roast Beef Sandwiches

Servings: 4
Cooking Time: 540 Minutes

Ingredients:

- 3 cups beef stock, divided
- 2 lbs chuck roast
- 4 hoagie rolls, sliced lengthwise
- to taste, lone star brisket rub
- 1 yellow onion

Directions:

1. Place chuck roast in a glass baking dish. Season with Lone Star Brisket Rub, then cover with plastic wrap and refrigerate overnight.
2. The next day, remove chuck roast from the refrigerator. Supply your smoker with wood pellets and follow the start-up procedure. Preheat the grill, with the lid closed, to 225° F. If using a gas or charcoal grill, set it up for low, indirect heat.
3. Place chuck roast directly on the grill grate, then close the lid and smoke for 3 hours, spraying with 1 cup of beef stock every hour.
4. Slice the onion and place in a cast iron skillet, then pour the remaining cup of stock over the onions and set roast on top of onions.
5. Increase temperature to 275° F and cook an additional 2 ½ to 3 hours, or until internal temperature reaches 165° F.
6. Cover the roast with a cast iron lid or aluminum foil, and cook for another 2 ½ to 3 hours, or until the internal temperature reaches 200° F.
7. Remove chuck roast from the grill. Allow the roast to rest for 10 minutes, then remove from the skillet and shred.
8. Serve pulled roast beef in a hoagie roll with braised onions and pan jus.

Bbq Bacon Meatballs

Servings: 4
Cooking Time: 60 Minutes

Ingredients:

- 1 Pound ground beef
- 1 egg
- 1/4 Cup milk
- 1/2 Cup breadcrumbs
- 2 Tablespoon Beef Rub
- 4 Strips bacon, cut in half
- 1/4 Cup Rub
- 1/2 Cup Apricot BBQ Sauce

Directions:

1. Mix beef, egg, milk, breadcrumbs and Traeger Beef Rub in a large bowl by hand. Once well mixed, make 2 ounce meatballs until complete.
2. Wrap each meatball with a half slice of bacon and slide toothpick all the way through.

3. Put Traeger Rub in a small bowl and roll each meatball in the rub until well coated.
4. Supply your smoker with wood pellets and follow the start-up procedure. Preheat the grill, with the lid closed, to 180° F.
5. Place the meatballs on the grate, close the lid and smoke for 1 hour. Grill: 180 °F
6. Increase the Traeger temperature to 350°F and preheat, lid closed for 15 minutes. Cook meatballs for another 20 to 30 minutes or until the internal temperature reaches 160°F to 165°F. Grill: 350 °F Probe: 160 °F
7. About 10 minutes before the meatballs are ready, brush with Traeger Apricot BBQ Sauce and allow it to caramelize.
8. Remove from grill and allow to rest for 5 minutes. Enjoy!

Spiced Leg Of Lamb Gyros

Servings: 8 – 10
Cooking Time: 180 Minutes

Ingredients:

- 1 Tbsp Black Pepper
- 4 Oz. Cremini Mushrooms
- ¼ Cup Dijon Mustard
- 8, Smashed Garlic Cloves
- 1 Cup + 1 Tbsp Grapeseed Oil, Divided
- 5 Lb, Bone-In Sirloin Leg Of Lamb
- ⅓ Cup Lemon Juice
- ½ Tbsp + 1 Tsp Dried, Divided Oregano
- 8-10 Pita
- Large Wedge Chop Red Onion
- 1 Tbsp Rosemary Leaves, Dried
- ⅔ Cup Scallions, Chopped
- 3 Tbsp, Coarse Sea Salt
- ½ Tbsp Thyme, Dried
- Tzatziki Sauce
- 1 Vine-Ripe Tomato, Chopped

Directions:

1. Fire up your grill and preheat to "Smoke" mode. If using a gas or charcoal grill, set it up for low, indirect heat.
2. In a food processor, combine grapeseed oil, lemon juice, mustard, scallions, garlic, rosemary, thyme, salt and pepper. Process until it forms a thick marinade.
3. Score the fat cap of the lamb, then truss with butcher's twine. Pour two-thirds of the marinade onto the leg of lamb to cover completely. Set remaining marinade aside for vegetables. Wrap the lamb in foil and marinate at room temperature for 1 hour.
4. Place the lamb in the smoking cabinet by hanging truss from S hooks. Insert temperature probe and smoke for 45 minutes. Increase the temperature to 400°F.
5. Supply your smoker with wood pellets and follow the start-up procedure. Preheat the grill, with the lid closed, to 225 to 250° F. (If you're using a grill or vertical smoker, set your temperature to 225°F). Once it has reached this temperature, make sure the upper chimney caps are fully open, and you can lower the grill temp to 300°F. As long as the cabinet doors remain closed this should maintain temperature in the upper cabinet.
6. Smoke the lamb until the internal temperature of the meat reaches 135°F, about 3 hours.
7. While the lamb is cooking, skewer together red onion and mushrooms. Brush with remaining marinade, then transfer to grill with sear slide open, 3 to 5 minutes. In a small bowl combine 1 tbsp of grape seed oil and 1 tsp of oregano and brush lightly over pita breads. Grill pita bread to warm while skewers are on the grill.
8. Remove the leg of lamb from the smoker and loosely cover with aluminum foil. Rest the meat for 30 minutes before slicing.
9. Thinly slice the lamb, and serve in warm pita with grilled mushrooms and onions, and chopped tomatoes, and tzatziki, if desired.

Flavour Smoked Tri Tip

Servings: 4
Cooking Time: 90 Minutes

Ingredients:

- 3 Tbsp Olive Oil
- 2 Tbsp Java Chophouse Seasoning
- 1 - 3 Pound Fat Cap And Silver Skin Removed Tri-Tip Roast

Directions:

1. Supply your smoker with wood pellets and follow the start-up procedure. Preheat the grill, with the lid closed, to 225° F.
2. Rub the tri-tip with olive oil and generously season on all sides with Java Chop House.
3. Place the tri-tip on the smoker rack and smoke until the internal temperature reads 140°F, or about 1 ½ hours.
4. Remove the tri-tip from the smoker and allow to rest for 10 minutes. Slice the tri-tip against the grain and serve.

Grilled Garlic Tri Tip

Servings: 2

Cooking Time: 20 Minutes

Ingredients:

- 4 Tablespoons Beef & Brisket Rub
- 1/3 Cup Brown Sugar
- 1 Stick Unsalted Softened Butter
- 1/2 Tsp Cayenne Pepper
- 1 Garlic Clove, Minced
- 2 Tablespoons Olive Oil
- Juice From 1 Orange
- 1 Tbsp Paprika, Powder
- 1/3 Cup Soy Sauce
- 3 - 4 Pounds Trimmed Tri Tip Roast
- 2 Tablespoons Worcestershire Sauce

Directions:

1. Add the brown sugar, orange juice, Worcestershire sauce, minced garlic and soy sauce to a resealable plastic bag. Add the tri tip to the bag, seal it, and massage the meat to help coat it evenly with the marinade. Place the bag in the refrigerator and allow the tri tip to marinate for 2 hours.
2. Remove the bag from the refrigerator and drain the marinade. Remove the steak from the bag and pat dry with paper towels.
3. In a small mixing bowl, combine the softened butter with 2 tablespoons of Beef & Brisket Seasoning, paprika, and cayenne. Mix the butter until well combined. Set aside.
4. Rub the tri tip down with the olive oil and season generously with the remaining Beef & Brisket Seasoning.
5. Supply your smoker with wood pellets and follow the start-up procedure. Preheat the grill, with the lid closed, to 450° F. If you're using a gas or charcoal grill, set it up for high heat. Insert a temperature probe into the thickest part of the steak and place it on the grill. Sear the tri tip on the grill for 3-5 minutes, then flip it and sear for another 3-5 minutes.
6. Turn the temperature down to 250°F, then grill the tri tip for 15 more minutes until the internal temperature reaches 135°F.

Baked Venison Tater Tot Casserole

Servings: 4

Cooking Time: 40 Minutes

Ingredients:

- 2 Pound Venison, ground
- 2 Can Peas, canned
- 2 Can cream of mushroom soup
- 28 Ounce frozen tater tots

Directions:

1. Cook ground venison in a medium sauté pan over medium high until browned. Drain off excess fat and set venison aside.
2. In a 13x9 pan, combine venison, peas and soup. Top with tater tots.
3. Supply your smoker with wood pellets and follow the start-up procedure. Preheat the grill, with the lid closed, to 350° F.
4. Place casserole dish directly on grill grate and cook for 30 minutes. Serve hot, enjoy!

Savory Bacon Wrapped Hot Dogs

Servings: 6

Cooking Time: 10 Minutes

Ingredients:

- 1 - 2 Green Bell Pepper, Diced
- 1 Per Hot Dog Bacon, Strip
- 6 - 8 Hot Dog Bun(S)
- 6 - 8 Hot Dog(S)
- Smoke Infused Applewood Bacon Rub

- 2 Tbsp Vegetable Oil

Directions:

1. Supply your smoker with wood pellets and follow the start-up procedure. Preheat the grill, with the lid closed, to 400° F. Before placing anything on the grill, generously oil the cooking grids, using a cloth and vegetable oil.
2. Heat your grill to medium-high heat.
3. Lay a slice of bacon on a cutting board.
4. Roll the bacon and hot dog around until the bacon covers the whole hot dog. Secure with a toothpick on each end.
5. Repeat steps 3 and 4 again, by wrapping each hot dog with one strip of bacon, and secure with a toothpick on each end.
6. Cook the bacon wrapped hot dogs on the grill. When the bacon is lightly crisp, remove from the heat. This takes about 4-6 minutes.
7. Toast the buns by turning the grill up to high. Open the flame broiler. Place bun face down on cooking grids. Toast until desired done.
8. As soon as the hot dogs are done, place them on a toasted bun, pile on the chopped green peppers, and serve.

Teriyaki Deer Jerky

Servings: 4

Cooking Time: 240 Minutes

Ingredients:

- 1/2 Cup soy sauce
- 1/4 Cup mirin
- 2 Tablespoon sugar
- 3 coins fresh ginger, each ¼ inch thick
- 1 Clove garlic, crushed
- 1/2 Teaspoon onion powder
- 1/2 Teaspoon black pepper
- 2 Pound venison, trimmed

Directions:

1. In a mixing bowl, combine the soy sauce, mirin, sugar, ginger, garlic, onion powder and pepper.
2. With a sharp knife, slice the venison into 1/4 inch thick slices. Trim any fat or connective tissue.
3. Put the meat slices in a large resealable plastic bag. Pour the marinade mixture over the venison and massage the bag so that all the slices get coated with the marinade. Seal the bag and refrigerate for several hours, or overnight.
4. Supply your smoker with wood pellets and follow the start-up procedure. Preheat the grill, with the lid closed, to 180° F. Remove the venison from the marinade; discard marinade. Dry the meat slices between paper towels.
5. Arrange the meat in a single layer directly on the grill grate. Smoke for 3 hours or until the jerky is dry but still chewy and somewhat pliant when you bend a piece. Grill: 180 ˚F
6. Transfer to a resealable plastic bag while the jerky is still warm leaving the top open. Let the jerky rest for an hour at room temperature.
7. Squeeze any air from the bag and refrigerate the jerky. It will keep for several weeks. Enjoy!

Cheesy French Dip Sliders

Servings: 8 - 12

Cooking Time: 60 Minutes

Ingredients:

- 1 ¾ cup beef stock
- 3 lbs. beef top round roast, boneless
- 1 tbsp olive oil
- 2 tbsp chop house steak rub
- 1 8 oz. block of provolone cheese
- 1 red onion, sliced thinly
- ¼ cup sherry
- 1 dozen slider rolls, sliced

Directions:

1. Supply your smoker with wood pellets and follow the start-up procedure. Preheat the grill, with the lid closed, to 400° F.If using a gas or charcoal grill, set it up for medium-high heat.
2. Rub roast with olive oil, then season with Chop House Steak Rub.
3. Place red onion in the bottom of a cast iron skillet and set roast on top. Transfer to grill and roast for 15 minutes. Reduce grill temperature to 325°F then add

beef stock and sherry, and continue to cook another 30 minutes, or until 125 to 130°F internal temperature is reached.

4. Remove from grill and allow the roast to rest for 10 minutes, then slice thinly.

5. Assemble sliders on sheet tray by placing sliced beef on the bottom half of each roll. Top with onion and provolone cheese, then place top half of roll on top of cheese. Transfer jus into a metal gravy boat or porcelain ramekin and reserve for serving.

6. Transfer rolls back into cast iron skillet and return to grill for 5 minutes, until cheese melts. Serve hot with jus for dipping

Reverse Sear Tomahawk Chop

Servings: 4

Cooking Time: 60 Minutes

Ingredients:

- 2 Tbsp Coarsely Ground Black Peppercorns
- 1 Melted Stick Butter, Salted
- 2 Tablespoons Chophouse Steak Seasoning
- 2 Tbsp Sea Salt
- 2 Tsp Sprigs Fresh Thyme, Minced
- 2 Steaks, Tomahawk

Directions:

1. In a small mixing bowl, add the black peppercorns, sea salt, Chophouse Seasoning, and fresh thyme. Mix together and reserve half the seasoning.

2. Place your Tomahawk Steaks onto a sheet pan covered with butcher paper, foil, or parchment paper. Generously season the steaks with the seasoning mixture and rub it into the steaks. Let steaks sit for 1-2 hours if you would like the seasoning to penetrate the meat.

3. Supply your smoker with wood pellets and follow the start-up procedure. Preheat the grill, with the lid closed, to 225° F. If you're using a gas or charcoal grill, set it up for low, indirect heat. Insert a temperature probe into the thickest part of one of the tomahawk chops and place them in the center of the grill. If you have 2 temperature probes insert another into the other steak. Grill until the internal temperature of the steaks reaches 110°F, about 30-40 minutes.

4. Once the steaks reach their internal temperature, remove them from the grill and set aside. Increase the grill temperature to 450-500°F. While the grill is heating up melt one stick of butter and add the reserved seasoning to the melted butter. Mix together and brush the steaks with the butter making sure to evenly coat both sides of the steaks.

5. Place the steaks back on the grill over an open flame and sear for 3-5 min per side to reach 130°F-140°F. Remove the steaks from the grill, let them rest for 5 minutes and slice and serve immediately.

Spicy Smoked Chili Beef Jerky

Servings: 6

Cooking Time: 240 Minutes

Ingredients:

- 1 Cup chili sauce
- 1/3 Cup beer
- 2 Tablespoon soy sauce
- 1 Tablespoon Worcestershire sauce
- 2 Tablespoon Morton Tender Quick Home Meat Cure
- 1 Tablespoon minced pickled jalapeño peppers
- 2 Pound flank steak, cut into 1/4 inch thick slices

Directions:

1. In a mixing bowl, combine the chili sauce, beer, soy sauce, Worcestershire sauce, curing salt and pickled jalapeño peppers.

2. Put the beef slices in a large resealable bag. Pour the marinade mixture over the beef, and massage the bag so that all the slices get coated with the marinade. Seal the bag and refrigerate for several hours, or overnight.

3. Supply your smoker with wood pellets and follow the start-up procedure. Preheat the grill, with the lid closed, to 165° F.

4. Remove the beef from the marinade, discarding the marinade. Dry beef slices between paper towels.

5. Arrange the meat in a single layer directly on the grill grate or smoke shelf.

6. Smoke for 4 to 5 hours, or until the jerky is dry but still chewy and somewhat pliant when bending a piece.

Grill: 165 °F

7. Transfer to a resealable bag while the jerky is still warm.
8. Let the jerky rest for an hour at room temperature. Squeeze any air from the bag, and refrigerate the jerky.
9. Pro Tip: you can use this recipe for any cut of beef or wild game. Enjoy!

Marinated Flank Steak

Servings: 6
Cooking Time: 10 Minutes

Ingredients:

- 2lb (1kg) flank steak
- coarse salt
- freshly ground black pepper
- for the marinade
- ¼ cup red wine vinegar
- 2 tbsp Worcestershire sauce
- 1½ tsp coarse salt
- ½ cup extra virgin olive oil
- 2 garlic cloves, peeled and smashed with a chef's knife
- 1 small white onion, coarsely chopped
- 2 tbsp finely chopped fresh rosemary leaves
- sprigs of fresh rosemary

Directions:

1. In a jar with a tight-fitting lid, make the marinade by combining the vinegar, Worcestershire sauce, salt, and olive oil. Shake vigorously. Stir in the garlic, onion, and rosemary leaves.
2. Place the flank steak in a resealable plastic bag and pour the marinade over it. Turn the steak to thoroughly coat. Refrigerate for 8 to 24 hours, turning the bag periodically to thoroughly marinate the steak.
3. Supply your smoker with wood pellets and follow the start-up procedure. Preheat the grill, with the lid closed, to 232° F.
4. Remove the steak from the marinade and pat dry with paper towels. (Discard the marinade.) Season on both sides with salt and pepper.
5. Place the steak on the grate and grill until the internal temperature reaches 125 to 135°F (52 to 54°C), about 4 to 5 minutes per side.
6. Remove the steak from the grill and let rest for 5 minutes. Slice thinly against the grain with a knife held on a sharp diagonal. Transfer the slices to a platter and scatter rosemary sprigs over the top before serving.

Roasted Prime Rib

Servings: 8
Cooking Time: 105 Minutes

Ingredients:

- 1 four-bone prime rib roast, about 8lb (3.6kg), trimmed
- extra virgin olive oil
- 1 cup beef stock or broth
- fresh coarsely ground black pepper
- Horseradish Sauce
- for the seasoned salt
- ¼ cup coarsely chopped fresh rosemary leaves
- 5 fresh sage leaves, coarsely chopped
- 1 tbsp granulated garlic or 2 tsp garlic powder
- 2 tsp whole black peppercorns or fresh coarsely ground black pepper
- 1¼ cups coarse salt, divided

Directions:

1. Supply your smoker with wood pellets and follow the start-up procedure. Preheat the grill, with the lid closed, to 450° F.
2. In a coffee grinder, make the seasoned salt by combining the rosemary, sage, granulated garlic, peppercorns, and ½ cup of salt. Pulse until the herbs and peppercorns are finely ground and the coarse salt resembles table salt. (The mixture will be damp from the moisture in the herbs.)
3. Transfer the mixture to a bowl and stir in the remaining ¾ cup of salt. Reserve 3 to 4 teaspoons of the seasoned salt for the prime rib. Spread the remaining mixture on a rimmed sheet pan and let dry completely, stirring occasionally, before storing at room temperature in a covered jar. Set aside. (Place the mixture in a dehydrator or low-temperature oven or your smoker to hasten the drying time.)
4. Carve the bones off the roast in a single slab. Set aside. Use butcher's twine to tie the roast at 1½-inch

(3.75cm) intervals. Lightly coat on all sides with olive oil and season with the reserved seasoned salt.

5. Place the bones convex (rounded) side up in an aluminum foil roasting pan. Place the prime rib atop the bones. Add the beef stock to the bottom of the pan.

6. Place the pan on the grate and roast until the exterior is nicely browned, about 30 minutes. Lower the temperature to 350°F (177°C) and continue to roast the meat until the internal temperature reaches 125°F (52°C) to 130°F (54°C), about 60 to 75 minutes, basting with the drippings every 20 minutes. (To avoid overcooking, check the internal temperature of the roast every 20 minutes.)

7. Transfer the roast to a cutting board and loosely tent with aluminum foil. Let rest for 15 minutes. Carve the prime rib into ¾-inch (2cm) slices and serve with the horseradish sauce.

Ancho Pepper Rubbed Brisket

Servings: 12

Cooking Time: 720 Minutes

Ingredients:

- 2 ancho peppers, dried
- 1/2 cup apple cider vinegar
- 9 arbol chilies, dried
- 12 lbs beef brisket, packer cut
- 2 tsp coriander
- 1 tbsp cumin seed, whole
- 2 tsp garlic, granulated
- 1/4 cup kosher salt
- 2 tsp oregano, dried
- 2 tsp smoked paprika
- 3 cups water

Directions:

1. Supply your smoker with wood pellets and follow the start-up procedure. Preheat the grill, with the lid closed, to 350° F. Let it come to temperature. If using a gas or charcoal grill, set it up for medium heat.

2. Place the dried peppers in a large cast iron skillet, then transfer to the grill and cook for 5 minutes, or until fragrant and hot to the touch. Remove from the skillet, and set aside to cool.

3. Add cumin and coriander to the hot skillet, and toast for 1 minute. Remove seeds from the skillet and cool.

4. Remove stems from ancho peppers, then transfer all chilies to a food processor. Pulse a few times to get going, then process on high for 2 minutes, until coarse-ground.

5. Add in garlic, oregano, smoked paprika, and salt. Pulse 10 times to incorporate, then transfer mixture to a bowl.

6. Remove brisket from packaging, set on a cutting board, and blot dry with paper towels.

7. Use a sharp knife to trim the brisket. Start trimming with the fat side down. Trim the silver skin from the flat side, then remove the sides and corners. Remove the fat from around the point. Turn the brisket over and trim any excess fat, leaving around ¼-inch fat thickness.

8. Season the whole brisket with chili pepper rub, then set aside.

9. Fire up your and preheat to Smoke setting. If using a gas or charcoal grill, set it up for low, indirect heat.

10. Place the brisket on the grill, then increase the temperature to 250 F, and smoke until the internal temperature reaches 165°F. After 2 hours, start spraying the brisket every 30 minutes to help retain moisture.

11. Wrap the brisket tightly in butcher paper, then return to the grill and continue to smoke until the internal temperature reaches 200°F.

12. Remove the brisket from the gill and rest for 1 to 2 hours in an insulated cooler before slicing.

Standing Venison Rib Roast

Servings: 6

Cooking Time: 30 Minutes

Ingredients:

- 1 (2 To 2-1/2 Lb) 8-Bone Venison Roast
- 1 Tablespoon extra-virgin olive oil
- Prime Rib Rub
- Blackened Saskatchewan Rub
- Coffee Rub

Directions:

1. Supply your smoker with wood pellets and follow the start-up procedure. Preheat the grill, with the lid closed, to 375° F.
2. Rub the olive oil over the roast coating evenly. Then season with Traeger Prime Rib Rub liberally.
3. Place the roast directly on the grill grate bone side down.
4. Cook for 20-25 minutes or until the internal temperature reaches 125˚F when an instant read thermometer is inserted into the thickest part of the roast. Grill: 375 ˚F Probe: 125 ˚F
5. Remove from the grill and let rest 5-10 minutes before carving. Enjoy!

The Perfect T-bones

Servings: 4
Cooking Time: 30 Minutes

Ingredients:

- 4 (1½- to 2-inch-thick) T-bone steaks
- 2 tablespoons olive oil
- 1 batch Espresso Brisket Rub or Chili-Coffee Rub

Directions:

1. Supply your smoker with wood pellets and follow the start-up procedure. Preheat the grill, with the lid closed, to 500°F.
2. Coat the steaks all over with olive oil and season both sides with the rub. Using your hands, work the rub into the meat.
3. Place the steaks directly on a grill grate and smoke until their internal temperature reaches 135°F for rare, 145°F for medium-rare, and 155°F for well-done. Remove the steaks from the grill and serve hot.

Bbq Burnt Ends

Servings: 6
Cooking Time: 540 Minutes

Ingredients:

- 1 (4-6 lb) point cut brisket
- 2 Cup beef broth
- 12 Ounce Texas Spicy BBQ Sauce
- Beef Rub

Directions:

1. Supply your smoker with wood pellets and follow the start-up procedure. Preheat the grill, with the lid closed, to 250° F.
2. Combine broth and sauce in small bowl and set aside. Trim excess fat off brisket point and rub brisket with Traeger Beef Rub.
3. Place brisket on the grill grate and cook until the internal temperature reaches 190˚F (approximately 6 to 7 hours). Remove brisket from grill and cut into 1 inch cubes. Grill: 250 ˚F Probe: 190 ˚F
4. Toss brisket cubes with sauce mixture in a pan and cover the pan with aluminum foil. Place pan in grill and cook for 1 hour. Grill: 250 ˚F
5. Stir the burnt ends and cook for an additional hour. Enjoy!

Roasted Venison Steaks By The Bowmars

Servings: 4
Cooking Time: 25 Minutes

Ingredients:

- 10 Whole Venison Steaks, 6oz
- 1 L Diet Sprite
- 6 Ounce Big Game Rub
- 2 Pound asparagus
- 3 Tablespoon Rub

Directions:

1. The night before, marinade the steaks with sprite and big game rub.
2. Supply your smoker with wood pellets and follow the start-up procedure. Preheat the grill, with the lid closed, to 350° F.
3. Remove steaks from marinade and pat dry. Place steaks directly on the grill grate and cook 10-15 minutes flipping once until the internal temperature reaches 125 degrees for medium rare. Grill: 350 ˚F
4. Sprinkle asparagus with Traeger Rub and add to Traeger. Cook for 10 minutes turning once.
5. Let steaks rest ten minutes before serving. Enjoy!

Spicy Beer Beef Jerky

Servings: 4-6

Cooking Time: 240 Minutes

Ingredients:

- 1 12 Oz Bottle Dark Beer
- 1/4 Cup Brown Sugar
- 2 Tbsp Coarse Black Pepper
- 4 Tbsp Garlic Salt
- 2 Tbsp Hot Sauce
- 2 Tablespoons, Divided Sweet Heat Rub
- 1 Tablespoon Quick Curing Salt
- 1 Cup Soy Sauce
- 2 Pounds Trimmed Flank Steak
- ¼ Worcestershire Sauce

Directions:

1. When you are ready to smoke your jerky, remove the beef from the marinade and discard the marinade.
2. Supply your smoker with wood pellets and follow the start-up procedure. Preheat the grill, with the lid closed, to 200° F. If using a sawdust or charcoal smoker, set it up for medium low heat.
3. Arrange the meat in a single layer directly on the smoker grate. Smoke the beef for 4-5 hours, or until the jerky is dry but still chewy and still bends somewhat.
4. Remove the jerky from the grill with tongs and transfer to a resealable plastic bag while still warm. Let the jerky rest for 1 hour at room temperature.
5. Squeeze any air out of the resealable plastic bag and refrigerate the jerky. It will keep for several weeks. Enjoy!

Citrus Grilled Lamb Chops

Servings: 4 - 6

Cooking Time: 15 Minutes

Ingredients:

- 2 Tablespoons Chophouse Steak Seasoning
- 4 Finely Garlic Clove, Minced
- 2 Pounds Thick Cut Rib Chops Or Lamb Loin
- Juice From 1/2 Lemon
- Juice From 1/2 Lime
- ¼ Cup Olive Oil
- 3 Tablespoons Orange Juice
- ¼ Cup Red Wine Vinegar

Directions:

1. In a mixing bowl, whisk together all the ingredients and 2 tbsp Chophouse Steak. Place the lamb chops in a glass baking pan and pour the marinade over the top. Flip the chops over a few times to make sure that they are completely coated.
2. Cover the glass pan in aluminum foil and allow the lamb chops to marinade for 4-12 hours. Once the meat has finished marinating, drain off the excess marinade and discard.
3. Supply your smoker with wood pellets and follow the start-up procedure. Preheat the grill, with the lid closed, to 400° F. If you're using a gas or charcoal grill, set it up for medium high heat. Grill the chops for 5-7 minutes per side, then lower the temperature to 350°F or medium heat, and flip and grill for another 5-7 minutes.
4. Remove the lamb chops from the grill, cover in foil, and allow to rest for 5 minutes before serving.

Smoked Bacon Brisket Flat

Servings: 4

Cooking Time: 480 Minutes

Ingredients:

- 1/2 lbs bacon
- 4 lbs brisket flat, trimmed
- tt lonestar brisket rub

Directions:

1. Supply your smoker with wood pellets and follow the start-up procedure. Preheat the grill, with the lid open, to 250° F. If using a gas or charcoal grill, set it up for low, indirect heat.
2. Place the brisket in a foil-lined aluminum pan. Season the fat side of the brisket with Lonestar Brisket Rub, then flip and season the meat side with additional rub.
3. Transfer the brisket to the grill and smoke for 1 hour.
4. Use tongs to flip the brisket over, so the fat side is up, then drape half the bacon slices over the brisket. Smoke for 2 hours, then remove the browned bacon, and set aside.
5. Lay the remaining raw bacon strips over the brisket, and continue cooking until these new bacon strips are

browned and the internal temperature of the brisket reads 202°F, which will likely take an additional 3 to 4 hours cook time.

6. Remove the brisket from the grill, and rest for 1 hour, then slice thin. Serve warm.

Lime Carne Asada Tacos

Servings: 4

Cooking Time: 10 Minutes

Ingredients:

- 1/2 Tsp Black Pepper
- 1 Tsp Garlic Powder
- 2 Lime, Juiced
- 1 Tsp Salt
- 1 1/2 Lbs Steak, Skirt
- 8 Tortilla

Directions:

1. Supply your smoker with wood pellets and follow the start-up procedure. Preheat the grill, with the lid closed, to 400° F. Place the steaks on the grill, and grill them for 4-8 minutes, then flip the steaks and grill for an additional 4-8 minutes.
2. Remove steaks from the grill, loosely cover them with foil, and let them sit for 5-10 minutes. Next chop the steaks into pieces and serve with tortillas and any desired toppings.

Korean Bbq Garlic Short Ribs

Servings: 4

Cooking Time: 240 Minutes

Ingredients:

- 1 Tbsp Beef & Brisket Rub
- 1 Cup Beef Broth
- 2 Tbsp Brown Sugar
- 3 Garlic Cloves, Peeled
- 1 Tbsp Ginger, Minced
- 3- 6 Meaty Beef Short Ribs
- ½ Cup Soy Sauce
- 1 Tbsp Sriracha Sauce
- 1 Tsp Toasted Sesame Seeds

Directions:

1. First, prepare the short ribs. Using a paper towel, remove the silvery membrane on the back of the short ribs and discard if they're not cleaned already.
2. In a medium bowl, add beef broth, soy sauce, brown sugar, garlic, ginger, sriracha, sesame, and Beef & Brisket Rub. Mix well, set aside.
3. In a baking dish, place the beef short ribs and pour the marinade over the top. Marinade for 4-12 hours. Cover and refrigerate.
4. Supply your smoker with wood pellets and follow the start-up procedure. Preheat the grill, with the lid closed, to 250° F. If you're using a gas or charcoal grill, set it up for medium heat. Remove the short ribs from the marinade and place on the grill. Grill for 3-4 hours, brushing leftover marinade juice over occasionally, until the meat from the short ribs begins to pull away from the bone.
5. Take off the grill and let rest for 15 min. Serve with rice and kimchi if desired.

Smoked Seed Pastrami

Servings: 16

Cooking Time: 480 Minutes

Ingredients:

- For the brisket and brine:
- 1 beef brisket flat with plenty of fat intact (6 to 8 pounds)
- 2 quarts hot water and 2 quarts ice water
- 2/3 cup coarse salt (sea or kosher)
- 2 teaspoons pink curing salt (Prague Powder No. 1 or Insta Cure No. 1)
- 1 small onion, peeled and cut in half widthwise
- 8 cloves garlic, peeled and cut in half widthwise
- For the spice rub:
- 1/2 cup cracked black peppercorns
- 1/2 cup coriander seeds
- 2 tablespoons mustard seeds
- 1 tablespoon light or dark brown sugar
- 1 teaspoon ground ginger
- Beer (optional)

Directions:

1. Trim the brisket, leaving a fat cap on top at least 1/4 inch thick.
2. Make the brine: Place the hot water, coarse salt, and pink salt in a large bowl or plastic tub and whisk until the salt crystals are dissolved. Stir in the ice water, onion, and garlic. Place the brisket in a jumbo heavy-duty resealable plastic bag. Add the brine and seal the top, squeezing out the air as you go. Place in a second bag and seal, then place in an aluminum foil pan or roasting pan to contain any leaks. Brine the brisket in the refrigerator for 12 days, turning it over once a day.
3. Make the rub: Place the peppercorns, coriander seeds, mustard seeds, brown sugar, and ginger in a spice mill and grind to a coarse powder, running the machine in short bursts, working in batches as needed. The final rub should feel gritty like coarse sand.
4. Drain the brisket, rinse well under cold running water, and blot dry with paper towels. Place it on a rimmed baking sheet or in a roasting pan and thickly crust it on all sides with the rub.
5. Supply your smoker with wood pellets and follow the start-up procedure. Preheat the grill, with the lid closed, to 225 °F-250 °F. Fill an aluminum foil pan with water or beer to a depth of 3 inches and place it below the rack on which you'll be smoking the ribs.
6. Place the pastrami fat side up in the smoker, directly on the rack. Smoke the pastrami until crusty and black on the outside and cooked to 175 °F on an instant-read thermometer, 7 to 8 hours.
7. Wrap the pastrami in butcher paper. Return it to the smoker. Continue cooking until the internal temperature is 200 °F and the meat is tender enough to pierce with a gloved finger or wooden spoon handle, an additional 1 to 2 hours, or as needed. (You'll need to unwrap it to check it.)
8. Transfer the wrapped pastrami to an insulated cooler and let rest for 1 to 2 hours. Unwrap and slice crosswise (across the grain) for serving.

Pulled Beef

Servings: 5-8
Cooking Time: 840 Minutes

Ingredients:

- 1 (4-pound) top round roast
- 2 tablespoons yellow mustard
- 1 batch Espresso Brisket Rub
- ½ cup beef broth

Directions:

1. Supply your smoker with wood pellets and follow the start-up procedure. Preheat the grill, with the lid closed, to 225°F.
2. Coat the top round roast all over with mustard and season it with the rub. Using your hands, work the rub into the meat.
3. Place the roast directly on the grill grate and smoke until its internal temperature reaches 160°F and a dark bark has formed.
4. Pull the roast from the grill and place it on enough aluminum foil to wrap it completely.
5. Increase the grill's temperature to 350°F.
6. Fold in three sides of the foil around the roast and add the beef broth. Fold in the last side, completely enclosing the roast and liquid. Return the wrapped roast to the grill and cook until its internal temperature reaches 195°F.
7. Pull the roast from the grill and place it in a cooler. Cover the cooler and let the roast rest for 1 or 2 hours.
8. Remove the roast from the cooler and unwrap it. Pull apart the beef using just your fingers. Serve immediately.

Smoked Tri-tip

Servings: 4
Cooking Time: 300 Minutes

Ingredients:

- 1½ pounds tri-tip roast
- Salt
- Freshly ground black pepper
- 2 teaspoons garlic powder
- 2 teaspoons lemon pepper
- ½ cup apple juice

Directions:

1. Supply your smoker with wood pellets and follow the start-up procedure. Preheat the grill, with the lid closed, to 180°F.
2. Season the tri-tip roast with salt, pepper, garlic powder, and lemon pepper. Using your hands, work the seasoning into the meat.
3. Place the roast directly on the grill grate and smoke for 4 hours.
4. Pull the tri-tip from the grill and place it on enough aluminum foil to wrap it completely.
5. Increase the grill's temperature to 375°F.
6. Fold in three sides of the foil around the roast and add the apple juice. Fold in the last side, completely enclosing the tri-tip and liquid. Return the wrapped tri-tip to the grill and cook for 45 minutes more.
7. Remove the tri-tip roast from the grill and let it rest for 10 to 15 minutes, before unwrapping, slicing, and serving.

Reverse-seared Tri-tip

Servings: 4
Cooking Time: 180 Minutes

Ingredients:

- 1½ pounds tri-tip roast
- 1 batch Espresso Brisket Rub

Directions:

1. Supply your smoker with wood pellets and follow the start-up procedure. Preheat the grill, with the lid closed, to 180°F.
2. Season the tri-tip roast with the rub. Using your hands, work the rub into the meat.
3. Place the roast directly on the grill grate and smoke until its internal temperature reaches 140°F.
4. Increase the grill's temperature to 450°F and continue to cook until the roast's internal temperature reaches 145°F. This same technique can be done over an open flame or in a cast-iron skillet with some butter.
5. Remove the tri-tip roast from the grill and let it rest 10 to 15 minutes, before slicing and serving.

Philly Cheese Onion Steaks

Servings: 6
Cooking Time: 45 Minutes

Ingredients:

- 2 Green Bell Pepper, Sliced
- 6 Hot Dog Bun(S)
- 2 Cups Mozzarella Cheese, Shredded
- 1 Quart Mushroom
- 1 Onion, Sliced
- Pepper
- Salt
- 2 Thick Steak, Flank

Directions:

1. Supply your smoker with wood pellets and follow the start-up procedure. Preheat the grill, with the lid closed, to 250° F.
2. Season both sides of your steaks with salt and pepper to your liking. We're going to reverse sear these steaks, so place on the grates of your preheated Grill. You'll want to cook the steaks until the internal temperature reaches 130°F (for medium-rare). Follow these internal temperatures if you'd like to cook your steak more/less done:
3. Rare: 125°F
4. Medium Rare: 130°F
5. Medium: 140°F
6. Well Done: 160°F
7. If you're cooking your steaks medium rare, it will take around 45 minutes depending on how thick the steaks are.
8. While the steaks are cooking, slice up the onion, mushrooms, and peppers thinly and sauté until soft.
9. When the steaks have reached your desired internal temperature, remove steaks from the grill and let them rest for 15 minutes. In the meantime, open up your flame broiler and crank up the grill to HIGH. Sear each side of the steak for about 1 minutes each.
10. Rest steaks again for 10 minutes.
11. Slice steak thinly, combine with the sautéed vegetables and fill a hot dog bun generously with the mixture.

Garlic Pigs In A Blanket

Servings: 10

Cooking Time: 15 Minutes

Ingredients:

- 1 Crescent Dough, Can
- 1 Egg
- 1 Tsp Garlic, Minced
- 20 Hot Dog, Mini
- 1/4 Cup Mustard, Dijon
- 1 Tbsp Onion, Diced
- 2 Tbsp Poppy Seeds
- 1 Tsp Salt, Coarse

Directions:

1. Supply your smoker with wood pellets and follow the start-up procedure. Preheat the grill, with the lid closed, to 350° F. Combine the poppy seeds, dried minced onion, minced garlic, and salt in a bowl.
2. Unroll the crescent roll dough, pull apart the triangles and slice each segment into three little triangle pieces. Try to get 3 strips for each roll for the mini hot dogs.
3. After the strips are cut, spread some Dijon mustard on each piece of dough. Roll the dough around mini hot dogs. Lay the pigs in a blanket on a greased cookie sheet. Brush with egg wash and sprinkle with the prepared seasoning.
4. Bake for 15 minutes, serve hot and enjoy!

Garlic Prime Rib Roast

Servings: 8

Cooking Time: 30 Minutes

Ingredients:

- 2 tsps black pepper
- 10 cloves garlic, minced
- steak seasoning
- 2 lbs prime rib roast
- 2 tsps salt

Directions:

1. Supply your smoker with wood pellets and follow the start-up procedure. Preheat the grill, with the lid closed, to 400° F.
2. Rub roast garlic, salt, pepper and some Chop House Steak Rub.
3. Insert meat thermometer sideways into the center of the roast so that the shaft is not visible, avoiding fat and bone.
4. Cook in a closed grill, maintaining constant heat, until the thermometer reads 145°F(63°C) for medium-rare for about 50 minutes, or cook until desired doneness.
5. Remove roast to cutting board; tent with foil for 5 to 10 minutes. Serve with mashed potatoes and asparagus on the side.

Smoked Garlic Prime Rib Roast

Servings: 12

Cooking Time: 60 Minutes

Ingredients:

- 1 10 pounds Prime Rib Roast (the bones cut off and tied back on)
- 1/2 cup horseradish mustard
- 2 tablespoons Worcestershire sauce
- 4 cloves garlic (minced)
- Coarse ground salt and black pepper (to taste)

Directions:

1. Supply your smoker with wood pellets and follow the start-up procedure. Preheat the grill, with the lid closed, to 225 °F.
2. Prepare your roast while the grill is heating. Trim any excess fat from the top of the roast down to 1/4 inch thick.
3. In a small bowl, combine the mustard, Worcestershire sauce,and garlic. Slather the entire roast with the mustard mixture and season liberally with salt and pepper.
4. Place the roast on the grill grate and close the lid. Smoke until the internal temperature of the roast reaches 120 °F for Rare or 130 °F for Medium. For a rare, bone-in roast, plan on 35 minutes per pound of prime rib.
5. Remove the roast to a cutting board, cover the roast with foil, and allow it to rest for 20 minutes.
6. While the roast is resting, increase the temperature of your grill to 400 °F.

7. Once the grill temperature reaches 400 °F, return the roast to the grill and sear until it reaches your desired internal temperature. Pull the roast off at 130 °F for rare, 135 °F for medium rare, 140 °F for medium. This process should go quickly, so keep an eye on your temperature.
8. Remove your roast to the cutting board and let the meat rest for at least 15 minutes.
9. Slice and serve.

Bourbon-braised Beef Short Ribs

Servings: 4
Cooking Time: 180 Minutes

Ingredients:

- 1/2 Cup yellow mustard
- 2 Tablespoon Worcestershire sauce
- 1 Tablespoon molasses
- 12 beef short ribs, preferably from the chuck or plate
- Prime Rib Rub
- 1 Cup beef broth
- 3 Tablespoon soy sauce or Bragg Liquid Aminos
- 2 Tablespoon bourbon

Directions:

1. Supply your smoker with wood pellets and follow the start-up procedure. Preheat the grill, with the lid closed, to 250° F.
2. In a small mixing bowl, combine mustard, Worcestershire sauce and molasses; whisk to mix.
3. Coat each rib on all sides with the mustard slather sauce. Season with Traeger Prime Rib Rub.
4. Make the mop sauce: Combine the beef broth, soy sauce and bourbon in a food-safe spray bottle.
5. Place the short ribs, bone-side down, directly on the grill grate. Cook for 2 to 2-1/2 hours, or until the internal temperature of each rib is 165°F when read on an instant-read meat thermometer, spraying with the mop sauce every 30 minutes. Grill: 250 °F Probe: 165 °F
6. Transfer the ribs to a large sheet of heavy-duty aluminum foil. Bring up the edges of the foil and add whatever remains of the mop sauce. Bring the opposite sides of the foil together and fold several times, tightly enclosing the ribs. Return the foil-enclosed ribs to the grill grate.
7. Continue to cook the ribs until the internal temperature is 195°F, about 1 hour more. Grill: 250 °F Probe: 195 °F
8. Let the ribs rest for 15 minutes, still enclosed in the foil, then open carefully. (Watch out for escaping steam.) Transfer the ribs to a platter or plates, then drizzle with the juices.

K.i.s.s Texas Bbq Style Brisket

Servings: 8
Cooking Time: 240 Minutes

Ingredients:

- 1 1/2 Tablespoon coarse kosher or sea salt
- 1 1/2 Tablespoon medium grind black pepper
- 2 Teaspoon chili powder
- 1 (6 lb) flat cut brisket, trimmed
- 2 Cup beer, preferably Lone Star or other Texas beer
- 1/4 Cup bacon grease, lard or melted butter
- 2 Tablespoon Worcestershire sauce
- 1 Tablespoon garlic salt
- 1 Teaspoon red pepper flakes

Directions:

1. Supply your smoker with wood pellets and follow the start-up procedure. Preheat the grill, with the lid closed, to 225° F.
2. Combine rub ingredients in a small bowl and stir to mix. Season the brisket generously on both sides.
3. Put a wire cooling rack in a rimmed baking sheet or other shallow pan, then place the brisket, fat-side up, on the cooling rack. Place pan and brisket on the grill grate. Grill: 225 °F
4. Combine all the ingredients for the mop sauce in a nonreactive saucepan over medium heat. Bring to a simmer and stir until the salt dissolves. Re-warm before mopping the brisket so the fat (bacon grease, lard or butter) liquefies.
5. After the first hour, mop the brisket with the mop sauce; continue to mop every hour for the first 4 hours.
6. When the internal temperature of the meat reaches 165°F, wrap the meat tightly in butcher paper. (Note:

Butcher paper is more permeable, but if you don't have access to any, use foil.) Grill: 225 °F Probe: 165 °F
7. Return the meat to the grill and continue to cook until the internal temperature reaches 203°F. (Total cooking time will vary, but plan on 6 to 8 hours total.) Grill: 225 °F Probe: 203 °F
8. Transfer the wrapped meat to an insulated cooler thickly lined with newspapers or bath towels.
9. Let the meat rest for at least 30 minutes. Reserve any juices that have accumulated in the baking sheet.
10. Unwrap the brisket. Thinly slice across the grain using an electric knife or sharp carving knife. Shingle the slices of brisket on a platter and pour the pan juices on top. Enjoy!

Tuscan Cheesesteaks

Servings: 8
Cooking Time: 20 Minutes

Ingredients:

- 2 tbsp extra virgin olive oil, plus more
- 12oz (340g) mixed wild or cremini mushrooms, cleaned and chopped
- 1 red bell pepper, trimmed, deseeded, and cut into ¼-inch (.5cm) strips
- 1 green bell pepper, trimmed, deseeded, and cut into ¼-inch (.5cm) strips
- 1 white onion, peeled and diced
- 3 garlic cloves, peeled and minced
- 1 center-cut beef tenderloin, about 4lb (1.8kg), trimmed
- coarse salt
- freshly ground black pepper
- ½ cup pesto, plus more
- 1 cup grated or shaved Parmigiano-Reggiano cheese
- 12 sun-dried tomatoes packed in olive oil, roughly chopped
- 12oz (340g) thinly sliced provolone cheese, preferably aged

Directions:

1. Supply your smoker with wood pellets and follow the start-up procedure. Preheat the grill, with the lid closed, to 450° F.
2. In a large skillet on the stovetop over medium heat, warm the olive oil. Add the mushrooms and sauté until tender, about 8 minutes, stirring as needed. Transfer the mushrooms to a bowl.
3. Add the bell peppers, onion, and garlic to the skillet and cook until softened, about 5 to 6 minutes. Stir the mushrooms into the vegetable mixture. Remove the skillet from the heat and let the vegetables cool.
4. Place the tenderloin on a rimmed sheet pan. Make a lengthwise cut from one end to the other, but don't cut all the way through. (This is called "butterflying.") Open like a book and season the inside with salt and pepper. Spread the pesto on the inside of the meat with a small rubber spatula. Sprinkle the Parmigiano-Reggiano over the sauce. Place the tomatoes in a line in the center. Top with the vegetable mixture and provolone.
5. Cut five 12-inch (30.5cm) lengths of butcher's twine and place them at evenly spaced intervals under and perpendicular to the tenderloin. Bring the meat up over the stuffing and tie the pieces of twine together, snipping any loose ends. Coat the outside of the tenderloin with olive oil and season with salt and pepper.
6. Place the tenderloin on the grate at an angle to the bars. Grill until the cheese oozes out and the internal temperature reaches 125 to 130°F (52 to 54°C), about 4 to 5 minutes per side, turning with tongs.
7. Transfer the tenderloin to a cutting board and let rest for 3 minutes. Slice the tenderloin into 1-inch-thick (2.5cm) slices before serving.

Smoked Black Pepper Beef Cheeks

Servings: 6
Cooking Time: 240 Minutes

Ingredients:

- 4 beef cheeks, trimmed and with silver skin removed
- Beef Rub:
- 2 parts ground black pepper
- 1 part kosher salt
- 1 part brown sugar (optional)

Directions:

1. Supply your smoker with wood pellets and follow the start-up procedure. Preheat the grill, with the lid closed, to 275 °F.
2. Trim silver skin and excess fat from the beef cheeks.
3. In a bowl combine beef rub ingredients and apply generously to all sides of the beef, including crevices.
4. Transfer to grill grates. Leave to smoke for 4 hours, lid closed.
5. Remove from smoker and wrap in aluminum foil, or place in an aluminum tray and cover with foil.
6. Transfer back to the smoker and leave to smoke for one more hour.
7. Allow to cook until the internal temperature has reached 210 °F.
8. Remove from smoker and leave wrapped in foil. Let it rest for about 10 minutes.
9. Slice and serve, or pulled for beef cheek tacos or sandwiches.

Bourbon Beef And Pork Meatballs

Servings: 4

Cooking Time: 25 Minutes

Ingredients:

- 1 cup cubed stuffing, unseasoned
- 2 , beaten eggs
- 3 garlic cloves, minced
- 1 lb ground beef
- 1 lb. ground pork
- 2.5 cups maple bourbon glaze
- 1 tbsp sweet heat rub
- 1, grated yellow onion
- 2 tbsp milk

Directions:

1. Supply your smoker with wood pellets and follow the start-up procedure. Preheat the grill, with the lid closed, to 350° F. If using a gas or charcoal grill, set it up for medium heat.
2. Put the stuffing in a food processor and pulse to process into small crumbs. Pour the crumbs out into a mixing bowl, then add the onion, garlic, eggs, milk, and Sweet Heat. Let the mixture sit for 10 minutes, then add the ground meat. Using your hands, combine the mixture together until fully incorporated.
3. Form mixture into 2 ounce balls and place on cast iron skillet, evenly spaced apart.
4. Transfer skillet to preheated grill and cook for 15 minutes, then generously glaze with sauce. Cook an additional 5 minutes, then glaze again and cook for 2 more minutes.
5. Remove meatballs from grill and serve hot with remaining sauce (about ⅓ cup).

Smoked Beef Plate Ribs

Servings: 4

Cooking Time: 480 Minutes

Ingredients:

- 1 1/3 cup apple cider vinegar
- 4 lbs beef plate ribs
- 1/3 cup beef stock
- 1/2 tsp black pepper
- 1/4 tsp cayenne pepper
- 4 garlic cloves, peeled and smashed
- 2 tbsp honey
- 1/2 tsp kosher salt
- 1/4 cup molasses
- tbsp olive oil
- 2 tsp paprika
- beef and brisket rub
- 1 tbsp spicy brown mustard
- 2 lbs tomato, cubed
- 1 white onion, quartered

Directions:

1. Fire up your Grill and set it to Smoke. If using a gas or charcoal grill, set it up for low, indirect heat.
2. Prep ribs: remove the top portion of the fat cap from the rib rack. Rub with mustard, then season with Beef Brisket rub. Inject beef stock in meat, in between bones, and along sides.
3. Place the rib rack in the center of the grill, making sure the sear slide is closed. Supply your smoker with wood pellets and follow the start-up procedure. Preheat the grill, with the lid closed, to 250° F. Smoke ribs for 3 hours.

4. Meanwhile, prepare the BBQ sauce: line a sheet tray with foil and place tomatoes, onion, and garlic on top. Drizzle with olive oil, then season with ¼ teaspoon of salt and ¼ teaspoon of black pepper. Transfer to the smoke cabinet for 2 hours.
5. Place a quart mixture of apple cider vinegar and water in a grill-safe pan. Move the rib rack to the right side of the grill, then place the other pan in the middle. Increase temperature to 275°F.
6. Remove tomatoes for the smoke cabinet and place in a blender. Add paprika, cayenne, ¼ teaspoon of salt, ¼ teaspoon of black pepper, 1/3 cup apple cider vinegar, molasses, and honey. Blend until smooth and no lumps remain. Transfer sauce to a cast iron pan and place on grill. Simmer sauce for 1 hour, stirring occasionally, while the ribs continue to cook. When sauce is done, spoon sauce over ribs, then remove remaining sauce to serve when ribs are done.
7. Continue to cook ribs an additional 2-3 hours, or until internal temperature reaches 204°F, and a metal skewer goes through like butter.

New York Strip Steaks With Blue Cheese Butter

Servings: 4
Cooking Time: 8 Minutes

Ingredients:

- 4 boneless New York strip steaks, each about 12oz (340g) and 1 inch (2.5cm) thick
- coarse salt
- freshly ground black pepper
- for the butter
- 8 tbsp unsalted butter, at room temperature
- 1 garlic clove, peeled and finely minced
- ⅓ cup crumbled blue cheese, mashed with a fork
- 1 tbsp minced chives
- 1 tsp Worcestershire sauce
- ½ tsp fresh coarsely ground black pepper

Directions:

1. Approximately 45 minutes before you're ready to cook, lightly season the steaks on both sides with salt and pepper. Place the steaks on a wire rack on a rimmed sheet pan.
2. Supply your smoker with wood pellets and follow the start-up procedure. Preheat the grill, with the lid closed, to 450° F.
3. In a small bowl, make the blue cheese butter by combining the ingredients. Mix thoroughly. Set aside.
4. Place the steaks on the grate at an angle to the bars. Sear until the internal temperature reaches 130°F (54°C), about 3 to 4 minutes per side, turning once.
5. Transfer the steaks to a platter and immediately top with a spoonful of room temperature blue cheese butter. Tent the steaks with aluminum foil for 2 to 3 minutes to encourage the butter to melt before serving.

Grilled Beef Shawarma

Servings: 4
Cooking Time: 10 Minutes

Ingredients:

- arugula
- 1/2 tsp cayenne pepper
- 1/2 tsp cinnamon, ground
- 1/2 tsp cloves, ground
- 1 1/2 tsp coriander, ground
- 1 1/2 lbs flank steak
- 2 garlic cloves, minced
- 2 tsp olive oil
- 1 tsp paprika
- 4 pita
- red onion
- tt salt and pepper
- tahini
- tomatoes
- 1/2 tsp turmeric, powder

Directions:

1. Use a meat mallet to tenderize the steak, then transfer to a glass baking dish and season with salt and pepper. Drizzle with olive oil, then rub minced garlic on steak. Season with spice rub. Cover with plastic wrap and refrigerate overnight.
2. Remove steak from the refrigerator, 1 hour prior to grilling. Supply your smoker with wood pellets and

follow the start-up procedure. Preheat the grill, with the lid closed, to 450° F. If using a gas or charcoal grill, set it up for medium-high heat.

3. Grill steak 3 to 5 minutes per side, then remove from grill and rest for 10 minutes. While steak is grilling, place pitas in the upper smoke cabinet of the Lockhart to warm. Slice steak thinly, against the grain and wrap in flatbread or pita with arugula, tomatoes, onion, and tahini.

Smoked Spiced Rump Roast

Servings: 8

Cooking Time: 60 Minutes

Ingredients:

- 3 pounds rump roast (or bottom round roast)
- 1 ½ teaspoons coarse ground pepper
- 1 teaspoon kosher salt
- ¼ teaspoon garlic powder
- ¼ teaspoon onion powder

Directions:

1. Supply your smoker with wood pellets and follow the start-up procedure. Preheat the grill, with the lid closed, to 250 °F.
2. Combine the seasonings in a small bowl and coat the rump roast evenly with seasonings on all sides.
3. Place roast into the smoker.
4. Cook for 1 hour and 45 minutes, or until the internal temperature reaches 135 degrees (or your desired level of doneness; rare: 135 °F, medium rare: 145 °F, medium: 155 °F, well done: 170 °F)
5. Remove rump roast from the smoker and let it rest for 10 minutesbefore slicing.
6. Slice thinly and serve.

Smoked Brisket With Delicious Coffee Rub

Servings: 8

Cooking Time: 540 Minutes

Ingredients:

- 1 (15 lb) beef brisket
- 1/4 Cup Coffee Rub, divided
- 15 Ounce beef broth
- 4 Tablespoon salt, divided

Directions:

1. Supply your smoker with wood pellets and follow the start-up procedure. Preheat the grill, with the lid closed, to 225° F.
2. Trim brisket of all excess fat.
3. To make the beef broth injection, combine 2 tablespoons Traeger Coffee Rub, beef broth and 2 tablespoons salt in a small bowl, stirring until the salt is dissolved. Inject the brisket by inserting the needle parallel to the grain about 1 inch apart in a checker pattern over the entire brisket. Pull it back out as you press the plunger. Inject in a high-sided aluminum pan or bus tub and hold your hand over where you are injecting to contain the mess.
4. Season the exterior of the brisket with remaining rub and remaining salt.
5. Place brisket directly on the grill grate and cook for about 6 hours or until the internal temperature reaches 160℉ . Grill: 225 °F Probe: 160 °F
6. Wrap the brisket tightly in two layers of foil or butcher paper. Return to grill.
7. Cook an additional 3 hours or until the internal temperature reaches 204℉ . Remove brisket from the grill and make a small opening in the foil to let steam escape. Grill: 225 °F Probe: 204 °F
8. Close the opening after 10 minutes and allow meat to rest 60 minutes before slicing. Slice and enjoy!

Bacon-wrapped Elk Steaks

Servings: 2

Cooking Time: 15 Minutes

Ingredients:

- 1/4 Cup red wine
- 2 Tablespoon soy sauce
- 2 Tablespoon honey
- 2 Clove garlic, minced
- 1/4 Teaspoon freshly cracked black pepper
- 2 Tablespoon rosemary, chopped
- 1/8 Teaspoon red pepper flakes
- 2 Pound Elk Steak

- 1/2 Pound thick-cut bacon

Directions:

1. Make the marinade by whisking together the wine, soy sauce, honey, minced garlic cloves, black pepper, chopped rosemary and red pepper flakes. Slowly drizzle in the olive oil while whisking
2. Add the elk steaks into the marinade and marinate overnight, up to a day or two.
3. Supply your smoker with wood pellets and follow the start-up procedure. Preheat the grill, with the lid closed, to 450° F.
4. Take the steaks out of the marinade; wrap each steak with several pieces of bacon and secure with toothpicks.
5. Place the bacon-wrapped elk steaks directly on the grill grate and cook for 10 to 15 minutes, or until it has reached an internal temperature of 135 degrees F. Rotate halfway through for a good caramelized exterior. Enjoy!

Delicious Blt Burgers

Servings: 6

Cooking Time: 45 Minutes

Ingredients:

- 2 Pound ground chuck, 80% lean
- Beef Rub
- 1/2 Cup mayonnaise
- 1/3 Cup 'Que BBQ Sauce
- 1 pickle juice
- 1 Pound Pastrami, Sliced
- 8 Slices Cheese, sharp cheddar
- 8 hamburger buns
- Desired Toppings: Lettuce, Tomatoes, Red Onions, Etc.

Directions:

1. Supply your smoker with wood pellets and follow the start-up procedure. Preheat the grill, with the lid closed, to 180° F.
2. Divide ground beef into 8 equal sized patties; season with Traeger's Beef Rub. Place directly on the grill grate, close the lid, and smoke for 30 minutes. Grill: 180 °F
3. While the burgers smoke, make the fry sauce. In a small bowl, combine the mayo, BBQ sauce, and pickle juice. Stir to combine, cover, and keep in the refrigerator until ready to use.
4. Remove the burgers from the grill and increase the temperature to 450 degrees F. Allow the grill to preheat for 10-15 minutes before returning the burgers to the grill grate. Grill: 450 °F
5. Cook for 4-5 minutes on one side, then flip burgers. When you flip the burgers, add the pastrami to the grill in 8 individually portioned piles. Close the lid and cook for an additional 4-5 minutes. Grill: 450 °F
6. Carefully transfer the pastrami to the top of the burgers and place a slice of cheese on each. If desired, you can also add the buns to the grill so they can get toasted. Close the lid again and cook until the cheese is melted and the burgers reach a desired level of doneness. The recommended internal temperature for a well-done burger is 175 degrees F.
7. Transfer the pastrami topped burgers to the bottom bun. Slather the top bun with the fry sauce, adorn with the burger toppings of your choosing and serve. Enjoy!

Savory Chili Mac And Cheese

Servings: 4

Cooking Time: 25 Minutes

Ingredients:

- 4 Cups Beef Stock
- 2 Teaspoons Chili Powder
- 2 Tbsp Chopped Fresh Parsley Leaves
- 2 Cloves Garlic, Minced
- 1 1/2 Teaspoon Cumin
- 10 Oz. Elbow Macaroni / Noodles
- 8 Oz Ground Beef
- 3/4 Cup Kidney Beans, Drained And Rinsed
- And Freshly Ground Black Pepper Kosher Salt
- 1 Tbs Olive Oil
- 1 Onion, Diced
- 1 Tbs Sweet Heat Rub
- 3/4 Cup Shredded Cheddar Cheese
- 1 (14.5-Ounce) Tomatoes, Canned And Diced

Directions:

1. Supply your smoker with wood pellets and follow the start-up procedure. Preheat the grill, with the lid

open, to 350° F. If you're using a gas or charcoal grill, set it up for medium heat.
2. Heat olive oil in a Dutch oven or cast iron pan over medium-high heat. Add garlic, onion and ground beef, and cook until browned, about 3-5 minutes. Break up the beef as it cooks with a large wooden spoon or fork.
3. Stir in beef broth, tomatoes, beans, Sweet Heat, chili powder and cumin. Add salt and pepper to taste. Bring to a simmer and stir in pasta.
4. Transfer pot to the preheated grill and cover. Cook until pasta is cooked through, about 15-20 minutes. Remove from heat and top generously with shredded cheese, replace the cover to allow cheese to melt, about 2 minutes. Garnish with fresh parsley and serve immediately!

Dry Brined Texas Beef Ribs By Doug Scheiding

Servings: 8
Cooking Time: 360 Minutes

Ingredients:

- 2 (9-12 Lb) Uncut Prime Or Choice Beef Short Ribs
- Kosher Salt
- Worcestershire Sauce
- Prime Rib Rub
- Blackened Saskatchewan Rub
- 8 Ounce Apple Juice, For Spritzing
- 8 Ounce Beef Broth

Directions:

1. Purchase a package of uncut short ribs from your favorite grocer or butcher store – recommended Prime or Choice quality. Usually 9-12 lbs for 2 racks of 4 bones each for 8 total.
2. Trim as much fat as possible from the top of the ribs with a sharp knife. Remove the membrane from the bottom of each rack of 4 bones.
3. Sprinkle with kosher salt for the dry brine and wrap in plastic wrap for at least 6 hours or overnight in your refrigerator.
4. Supply your smoker with wood pellets and follow the start-up procedure. Preheat the grill, with the lid closed, to 275° F.
5. Wipe the excess salt mixture from the top of the ribs. Coat with a light amount of Worcestershire sauce before putting on a medium coat of Traeger Prime Rib.
6. Follow with a lighter coat of Traeger Saskatchewan rub. Spritz with apple juice and let set for 15-20 minutes.
7. Place on the Traeger with the thicker portion of the ribs (if applicable) to the back of the grill.
8. Smoke the ribs for 4-5 hours with a light spritz every 30 minutes to keep moist until internal temperature reaches approximately 180℉ or the color has a nice deep char. Grill: 275 ˚F Probe: 180 ˚F
9. Like a brisket, take the ribs off the grill and wrap in 2 sheet of heavy duty foil along with 4 oz of broth for each rack of ribs.
10. Place back on the smoker for another 1 to 1-1/2 hours until internal temperature of the meat is around 203℉ . Remove and cut. Serve immediately. Enjoy! Grill: 275 ˚F Probe: 203 ˚F

Smoked Beer Corned Beef

Servings: 6
Cooking Time: 240 Minutes

Ingredients:

- 6 lb corned beef brisket raw
- 2 tbsp black pepper
- 8 oz light beer

Directions:

1. Supply your smoker with wood pellets and follow the start-up procedure. Preheat the grill, with the lid closed, to 275 ˚F.
2. Cut open packaging of corned beef and drain off liquid. Be sure to grab the spice packet included with the brisket. Gently rinse off corned beef and then pat dry with a paper towel.
3. Open the spice packet included with your corned beef and sprinkle contents over the brisket, then sprinkle a light dusting of black pepper according to your preference.

4. Once pellet grill has reached temperature, insert probes into corned beef brisket pieces. If you only have a single probe, insert that probe in the center of the smallest piece because it will cook the fastest.
5. Smoke for 3 to 4 hours until corned beef reaches an internal temperature of 175 degrees F. Next transfer briskets to an aluminum pan and pour just enough beer in to cover the bottom of the pan. Cover with foil leaving one corner open to let out steam.
6. Continue cooking for another 2-3 hours until internal temperature reaches about 205 degrees F. Use an instant read thermometer and poke different parts of the brisket checking for tenderness. If probe goes into the meat with very little tension than it is done. If not, continue cooking until it becomes tender.
7. Once meat is tender and fully cooked, remove pan from pellet grill and let the corned beef rest for about 30 minutes still covered with one corner open to prevent overcooking.
8. Slice corned beef into 1/8 inch slices cutting against the grains of the brisket. If brisket crumbles make slices a little thicker.

Smoked Pot Roast Brisket

Servings: 6
Cooking Time: 240 Minutes

Ingredients:

- 1 Coca-Cola, can
- 1 Heinz Chili Sauce, bottle
- 1 Dry Onion Soup Mix, package
- 4 Pound flat cut beef brisket

Directions:

1. Mix the Coke, Heinz chili sauce (you can find it in the condiment aisle of the grocery store) and dry onion soup mix in a bowl.
2. You'll want to trim the fat on the brisket, leaving only about 1/4 inch on top.
3. Put the brisket into a large baking pan and pour the Coke-chili sauce mixture over top. (If you use a larger piece of brisket, or the whole brisket you may need to double the sauce mixture.)
4. Supply your smoker with wood pellets and follow the start-up procedure. Preheat the grill, with the lid closed, to 300° F.
5. Put the pan of brisket on the grill and cook for 3 to 4 hours or until the brisket is tender. (Stick a fork in it and when it twists with little effort, it's ready!) Grill: 300 °F
6. Let the brisket rest, covered in its juices for 30 minutes to an hour before you slice her up and serve.

Venison Steaks

Servings: 4
Cooking Time: 80 Minutes

Ingredients:

- 4 (8-ounce) venison steaks
- 2 tablespoons extra-virgin olive oil
- 4 garlic cloves, minced
- 1 tablespoon ground sage
- 2 teaspoons sea salt
- 2 teaspoons freshly ground black pepper

Directions:

1. Supply your smoker with wood pellets and follow the start-up procedure. Preheat, with the lid closed, to 225°F.
2. Rub the venison steaks well with the olive oil and season with the garlic, sage, salt, and pepper.
3. Arrange the venison steaks directly on the grill grate, close the lid, and smoke for 1 hour and 20 minutes, or until a meat thermometer inserted in the center reads 130°F to 140°F, depending on desired doneness. If you want a better sear, remove the steaks from the grill at an internal temperature of 125°F, crank up the heat to 450°F, or the “High” setting, and cook the steaks on each side for an additional 2 to 3 minutes.

Bbq Beef Sandwich

Servings: 4
Cooking Time: 360 Minutes

Ingredients:

- 1 (4-6 lb) chuck roast
- 1/4 Cup Coffee Rub
- 1 Cup beef broth

- 6 hamburger buns
- 1 white onion, sliced
- dill pickles
- 1/2 Cup Special Sauce
- Sweet & Heat BBQ Sauce

Directions:

1. Supply your smoker with wood pellets and follow the start-up procedure. Preheat the grill, with the lid closed, to 250° F.
2. Trim excess fat from chuck roast. Rub roast with Traeger Coffee Rub. Place roast on Traeger and cook for 3-1/2 hours or until roast reaches an internal temperature of 160℉. Grill: 250 °F Probe: 160 °F
3. Remove roast from grill and wrap in a double layer of aluminum foil, add beef broth and place roast back in grill. Continue to cook for 1-1/2 hours while checking the temperature. The roast is done when the internal temperature reaches 204℉. Check every 30 minutes if internal temperature has not been reached. Grill: 250 °F Probe: 204 °F
4. Remove roast from grill and pull or shred the meat. Add the drippings back into the meat to help keep it moist.
5. Serve pulled roast in buns and top with sliced onions, pickles Traeger Special Sauce and Traeger Sweet & Heat BBQ Sauce.

Bbq Burnt End Sandwich

Servings: 2

Cooking Time: 480 Minutes

Ingredients:

- 1 point cut brisket
- Beef Rub
- 1/2 Cup beef broth
- 1 Cup Texas Spicy BBQ Sauce
- 4 Slices Monterey Jack cheese
- 4 burger buns

Directions:

1. Supply your smoker with wood pellets and follow the start-up procedure. Preheat the grill, with the lid closed, to 250° F.
2. Trim excess fat off brisket point. Season brisket point liberally with Traeger Beef rub.
3. Place brisket point directly on the grill grate. Cook until it reaches an internal temperature of 170℉, approximately 4 to 5 hours. Grill: 250 °F
4. Remove brisket from grill and cut into 1-inch cubes. Add the beef broth to the pan with the cubed brisket. Cover pan with aluminum foil.
5. Place pan in grill and cook for 90 minutes. Grill: 250 °F
6. Remove the foil and add Traeger Texas Spicy BBQ sauce. Stir and put back on the grill, uncovered, for an additional 45 minutes. Remove from grill. Grill: 250 °F
7. Top each bun with the burnt ends, cheese, and additional BBQ sauce. Enjoy!

Beer Barbecue Burgers

Servings: 4

Cooking Time: 60 Minutes

Ingredients:

- 8 bacon slices
- beer, can
- 1/2 lb cheddar jack, cubed
- 2 1/2 lbs ground beef
- 1 jalapeno pepper, minced
- kansas city barbecue rub
- 1 white onion, caramelized

Directions:

1. Supply your smoker with wood pellets and follow the start-up procedure. Preheat the grill, with the lid closed, to 300° F. If using a gas or charcoal grill, set it up for medium-low heat.
2. Place ground beef in a mixing bowl, season with Kansas City Barbecue Rub, then mix by hand. Form 4, 10 ounce balls, then use a can (any 12 ounce aluminum can will work), and press the can down the center of each ball, creating a small beef bowl. Press along the sides and roll to create a beef bowl, approximately 3 ½ inches tall.
3. Wrap beef with 2 pieces of bacon, then fill with cheese, caramelized onion, and minced jalapeño. Set filled burgers in a large cast iron skillet, then transfer to the grill. Cook for 25 minutes in the skillet, then transfer

burgers to the top rack. Increase the temperature to 325°F, and cook an additional 25 to 30 minutes, rotating halfway. Remove from the grill, top with extra jalapeño, rest for 5 minutes, then serve warm.

Carne Asada Recipe

Servings: 4

Cooking Time: 15 Minutes

Ingredients:

- 2 Pound Flank Steak, or substitute skirt steak
- 1 Cup Carne Asada Marinade
- 1 lime, juiced
- 2 Clove garlic, minced
- 1 Teaspoon cumin
- 1 Teaspoon dried oregano, preferably Mexican
- 1 Chile Pepper in Adobo Sauce, minced

Directions:

1. Lay the flank steak in a baking dish large enough to hold it. In a small bowl, combine the Carne Asada Marinade, the lime juice, garlic, cumin, oregano, and chile in adobo sauce, if using. Pour the marinade over the steak, turning to coat, then cover with plastic wrap and refrigerate for 2 to 4 hours.
2. Supply your smoker with wood pellets and follow the start-up procedure. Preheat the grill, with the lid closed, to High heat.
3. Lift the flank steak from the marinade (discard the marinade) and pat dry with paper towels.
4. Arrange the steak at a diagonal directly on the grill grate. Grill for 6 minutes, then turn with tongs. Continue grilling for 4 to 6 minutes more. (The exact time will depend on the thickness of your steak, but flank steak is best medium-rare.) Grill: 500 °F
5. Transfer the steak to a cutting board and let rest for 5 minutes. Slice thinly on the diagonal across the grain. Arrange on a platter. Serve immediately with the tortillas and salsa. Enjoy!

Smoked Chicken Steak Sandwiches

Servings: 6

Cooking Time: 270 Minutes

Ingredients:

- 1 1/2 tsp black pepper, ground
- 3 lbs brisket flat
- 1 tbsp butter
- 1 1/2 cups chicken stock
- 1/4 cup chop house steak rub
- for topping, dill pickles
- 2 tsp garlic powder
- 8 oz maple cure
- 2 tsp mustard powder
- 1 onion, sliced
- 1 1/2 tbsp pickling spice
- pumpernickel rye, sliced
- to taste, sauerkraut
- to taste, spicy brown mustard
- 6 swiss cheese, sliced
- 2 qts water, cold

Directions:

1. Set the brisket flat on a cutting board, then trim off excess fat and silver skin.
2. Whisk together water and maple cure, until dissolved.
3. Lay brisket in a large container, season with pickling spice, then cover with brine/cure. The meat must be completely immersed. Cover and place in the refrigerator for 3 to 4 days.
4. Remove brisket flat from brine/cure. It will be pale grey in color, which is normal. Discard the cure and replace with plain water. Allow brisket to soak 1-2 hours.
5. Combine all ingredients for the rub in a bowl. Remove the brisket from the water and blot dry with paper towel.
6. Season the brisket well with the rub, pushing and massaging it into the surface. Place the brisket back into the refrigerator, uncovered, overnight.
7. Supply your smoker with wood pellets and follow the start-up procedure. Preheat the grill, with the lid closed, to 250° F. If using a gas or charcoal grill, set it up for low, indirect heat.
8. Transfer the brisket flat directly on the grill grate, fat side down, over indirect heat. Smoke for 2 hours, flipping after 1 hour.
9. Remove the brisket from the grill and place it in a cast iron skillet, or foil-lined aluminum pan with chicken

stock and onions. Cover with a lid, or foil and return to the grill.

10. Increase temperature to 275° F, and cook an additional 1 hour, then check the brisket to see if enough liquid remains. If reducing too quickly, add 1 cup of water. Cook the brisket for another 1 hour, or until the brisket is probe tender

11. Remove from the grill and rest for at least 30 minutes, prior to slicing thin.

12. Preheat the griddle over low flame.

13. Grease griddle with 1 tablespoon of butter, then spread mustard on 4 slices of rye, then set on griddle. Add 2 portions of sliced pastrami. Warm pastrami 1 to 2 minutes, then flip. Top pastrami with sauerkraut and cheese, then close the griddle lid for 1 minute to crisp up the underside of the pastrami and melt the cheese.

14. Brush rye with mustard then set pastrami on every other slice. Set remaining toasted rye on top complete the smoked pastrami sandwich.

15. Remove from the griddle, then repeat. Slice each sandwich on the bias and serve warm with dill pickles.

Mustard Garlic Crusted Prime Rib

Servings: 8

Cooking Time: 195 Minutes

Ingredients:

- 1 (3 Rib) Beef, Prime Rib Roast
- 1 Tbsp Black Pepper
- 2 Tbsp Garlic, Crushed
- 1 Cup Mustard, Whole Grain
- 2 Tbsp Salt, Kosher

Directions:

1. Supply your smoker with wood pellets and follow the start-up procedure. Preheat the grill, with the lid closed, to 450° F.

2. Combine salt, black pepper, mustard and garlic in a bowl. Evenly rub the seasoning all over coating the entire surface of the roast.

3. Once your grill is preheated, place the roast on the grates, ensuring the ribs are facing the back end of the grill. Once the roast is placed on the grill, shut the lid to the grill.

4. After 45 minutes, lower the temperature of the grill to 325°F. Cook for an additional 2.5 hours or until the internal temperature reaches 125°F. Remove the roast, letting it rest for about 15 minutes. Slice and enjoy!

Beef Tenderloin With Tomato Vinaigrette

Servings: 6

Cooking Time: 40 Minutes

Ingredients:

- 1 Whole (1-1/4 to 1-1/2 inch thick) beef tenderloin steaks
- 1 Bottle Prime Rib Rub
- 2/3 Cup extra-virgin olive oil
- salt and pepper
- 1 Teaspoon fresh thyme
- 6 Whole plum tomatoes
- 1 Teaspoon Thyme, minced
- 2 Tablespoon balsamic vinegar

Directions:

1. Supply your smoker with wood pellets and follow the start-up procedure. Preheat the grill, with the lid closed, to 450° F.

2. Tuck the thin end of the tenderloin underneath the roast and secure it with butcher's string. Rub the meat with olive oil and season it with the Prime Rib Rub or salt and pepper. Place the meat on a rack in a shallow roasting pan.

3. Roast in the preheated Traeger for 20 minutes. Adjust the heat to 350F. Roast 20 minutes longer, or to desired degree of doneness (130F for rare; 145F for medium; 155F or higher for well-done). Grill: 350 °F

4. Let rest for 5 minutes before slicing thinly. (If serving cold, thoroughly chill the tenderloin before slicing.) Garnish with sprigs of thyme.

5. To make the vinaigrette, combine the tomatoes, olive oil, balsamic vinegar, and thyme leaves in a blender jar or food processor; puree until smooth. Season to taste with Traeger Prime Rib Rub or salt and pepper.

6. Transfer to a gravy boat and serve with the tenderloin. (Best served the day it's made.)

Smoked Black Pepper Beef Back Ribs

Servings: 2 – 4

Cooking Time: 260 Minutes

Ingredients:

- 2 racks beef back ribs
- ½ tbsp black pepper
- ⅓ cup chop house steak seasoning

Directions:

1. Supply your smoker with wood pellets and follow the start-up procedure. Preheat the grill, with the lid closed, to 250° F. If using a gas or charcoal grill, set it up for low heat.
2. Place the ribs on a sheet tray, then remove the membrane from the back of the ribs: Take a butter knife and wedge it just underneath the membrane to loosen it. Using your hands, or a paper towel to grip, pull the membrane up and off the bone. Rub each rack generously with Chop House Steak seasoning and black pepper.
3. Place the ribs on the grill and smoke for 2 hours. Increase the temperature to 300°F and cook an additional 45 to 60 minutes, or until the ribs reach an internal temperature of 205° F. Be sure and flip the ribs halfway to achieve good bark.
4. Remove ribs from the grill and wrap in butcher paper. Allow ribs to rest for 20 minutes, then slice and serve hot.

APPETIZERS AND SNACKS

Bayou Wings With Cajun Rémoulade

Servings: 8

Cooking Time: 40 Minutes

Ingredients:

- 16 large whole chicken wings or 32 drumettes and flats, about 3lb (1.4kg) total
- for the rub
- 1 tbsp kosher salt
- 1 tsp freshly ground black pepper
- 1 tsp paprika
- ½ tsp ground cayenne, plus more
- ½ tsp garlic powder
- ½ tsp celery salt
- ½ tsp dried thyme
- 2 tbsp vegetable oil
- for the rémoulade
- 1¼ cups reduced-fat mayo
- ¼ cup Creole-style or whole grain mustard
- 2 tbsp horseradish
- 2 tbsp pickle relish
- 1 tbsp freshly squeezed lemon juice
- 1 tsp paprika, plus more
- 1 tsp hot sauce, plus more
- 1 tsp Worcestershire sauce
- coarse salt
- for serving
- lemon wedges
- pickled okra (optional)

Directions:

1. Supply your smoker with wood pellets and follow the start-up procedure. Preheat the grill, with the lid closed, to 350° F.
2. If using whole wings, cut through the two joints, separating them into drumettes, flats, and wing tips. (Discard the wing tips or save them for chicken stock.) Alternatively, leave the wings whole. Place the chicken in a resealable plastic bag.
3. In a small bowl, make the rub by combining the ingredients. Mix well. Pour the rub over the wings and toss them to thoroughly coat. Refrigerate for 2 hours.
4. In a small bowl, make the Cajun rémoulade by whisking together the mayo, mustard, horseradish, pickle relish, lemon juice, paprika, hot sauce, and Worcestershire. Season with salt to taste. The mixture should be highly seasoned. Transfer to a serving bowl and lightly dust with paprika. Cover and refrigerate until ready to serve.
5. Remove the wings from the refrigerator and allow the excess marinade to drip off. Place the wings on the grate at an angle to the bars. Grill for 20 minutes and then turn. (They'll brown more evenly but will also have less of a tendency to stick.) Continue to cook until the wings are nicely browned and the meat is no longer pink at the bone, about 20 minutes more.
6. Remove the wings from the grill and pile them on a platter. Serve with the Cajun rémoulade, lemon wedges, and pickled okra (if using).

Pulled Pork Loaded Nachos

Servings: 4

Cooking Time: 10 Minutes

Ingredients:

- 2 cups leftover smoked pulled pork
- 1 small sweet onion, diced
- 1 medium tomato, diced
- 1 jalapeño pepper, seeded and diced
- 1 garlic clove, minced
- 1 teaspoon salt
- 1 teaspoon freshly ground black pepper
- 1 bag tortilla chips
- 1 cup shredded Cheddar cheese
- ½ cup The Ultimate BBQ Sauce, divided
- ½ cup shredded jalapeño Monterey Jack cheese
- Juice of ½ lime
- 1 avocado, halved, pitted, and sliced
- 2 tablespoons sour cream
- 1 tablespoon chopped fresh cilantro

Directions:

1. Supply your smoker with wood pellets and follow the start-up procedure. Preheat, with the lid closed, to 375°F.
2. Heat the pulled pork in the microwave.
3. In a medium bowl, combine the onion, tomato, jalapeño, garlic, salt, and pepper, and set aside.
4. Arrange half of the tortilla chips in a large cast iron skillet. Spread half of the warmed pork on top and cover with the Cheddar cheese. Top with half of the onion-jalapeño mixture, then drizzle with ¼ cup of barbecue sauce.
5. Layer on the remaining tortilla chips, then the remaining pork and the Monterey Jack cheese. Top with the remaining onion-jalapeño mixture and drizzle with the remaining ¼ cup of barbecue sauce.
6. Place the skillet on the grill, close the lid, and smoke for about 10 minutes, or until the cheese is melted and bubbly. (Watch to make sure your chips don't burn!)
7. Squeeze the lime juice over the nachos, top with the avocado slices and sour cream, and garnish with the cilantro before serving hot.

Chuckwagon Beef Jerky

Servings: 6

Cooking Time: 300 Minutes

Ingredients:

- 2½lb (1.2kg) boneless top or bottom round steak, sirloin tip, flank steak, or venison
- 1 cup sugar-free dark-colored soda
- 1 cup cold brewed coffee
- ½ cup light soy sauce
- ¼ cup Worcestershire sauce
- 2 tbsp whiskey (optional)
- 2 tsp chili powder
- 1½ tsp garlic salt
- 1 tsp onion powder
- 1 tsp pink curing salt

Directions:

1. Slice the meat into ¼-inch-thick (.5cm) strips, trimming off any visible fat or gristle. (Slice against the grain for more tender jerky and with the grain for chewier jerky.) Place the meat in a large resealable plastic bag.
2. In a small bowl, whisk together the soda, coffee, soy sauce, Worcestershire sauce, whiskey (if using), chili powder, garlic salt, onion powder, and curing salt (if using). Whisk until the salt dissolves. Pour the mixture over the meat and reseal the bag. Refrigerate for 24 to 48 hours, turning the bag several times to redistribute the brine.
3. Supply your smoker with wood pellets and follow the start-up procedure. Preheat the grill, with the lid closed, to 150° F.
4. Drain the meat and discard the brine. Place the strips of meat in a single layer on paper towels and blot any excess moisture.
5. Place the meat in a single layer on the grate and smoke for 4 to 5 hours, turning once or twice. (If you're aware of hot spots on your grate, rotate the strips so they smoke evenly.) To test for doneness, bend one or two pieces in the middle. They should be dry but still somewhat pliant. Or simply eat a piece to see if it's done to your liking.
6. For the best texture, when you remove the meat from the grill, place the still-warm jerky in a resealable plastic bag and let rest for 30 minutes. (You might see condensation form on the inside of the bag, but the moisture will be reabsorbed by the meat.) Or let the meat cool completely and then store in a resealable plastic bag or covered container. The jerky will last a few days at room temperature but will last longer (up to 2 weeks) if refrigerated.

Smoked Cashews

Servings: 6

Cooking Time: 60 Minutes

Ingredients:

- 1 pound roasted, salted cashews

Directions:

1. Supply your smoker with wood pellets and follow the start-up procedure. Preheat the grill, with the lid closed, to 120°F.

2. Pour the cashews onto a rimmed baking sheet and smoke for 1 hour, stirring once about halfway through the smoking time.
3. Remove the cashews from the grill, let cool, and store in an airtight container for as long as you can resist.

Pigs In A Blanket

Servings: 4-6
Cooking Time: 15 Minutes

Ingredients:

- 2 Tablespoon Poppy Seeds
- 1 Tablespoon Dried Minced Onion
- 2 Teaspoon garlic, minced
- 2 Tablespoon Sesame Seeds
- 1 Teaspoon salt
- 8 Ounce Original Crescent Dough
- 1/4 Cup Dijon mustard
- 1 Large egg, beaten

Directions:

1. When ready to cook, start your smoker at 350 degrees F, and preheat with lid closed, 10 to 15 minutes.
2. Mix together poppy seeds, dried minced onion, dried minced garlic, salt and sesame seeds. Set aside.
3. Cut each triangle of crescent roll dough into thirds lengthwise, making 3 small strips from each roll.
4. Brush the dough strips lightly with Dijon mustard. Put the mini hot dogs on 1 end of the dough and roll up.
5. Arrange them, seam side down, on a greased baking pan. Brush with egg wash and sprinkle with seasoning mixture.
6. Bake in smoker until golden brown, about 12 to 15 minutes.
7. Serve with mustard or dipping sauce of your choice. Enjoy!

Cold-smoked Cheese

Servings: 6
Cooking Time: 180 Minutes

Ingredients:

- 2lb (1kg) well-chilled hard or semi-hard cheese, such as:
- Edam
- Gouda
- Cheddar
- Monterey Jack
- pepper Jack
- goat cheese
- fresh mozzarella
- Muenster
- aged Parmigiano-Reggiano
- Gruyère
- blue cheese

Directions:

1. Unwrap the cheese and remove any protective wax or coating. Cut into 4-ounce (110g) portions to increase the surface area.
2. If possible, move your smoker to a shady area. Place 1 resealable plastic bag filled with ice on top of the drip pan. This is especially important on a warm day because you want to keep the interior temperature of the grill between 70 and 90°F (21 and 32°C) or below.
3. Place a grill mat on one side of the grate. Place the cheese on the mat and allow space between each piece.
4. Fill your smoking tube or pellet maze (see Cast Iron Skillets and Grill Pans) with pellets or sawdust and light according to the manufacturer's instructions. Place the smoking tube on the grate near—but not on—the grill mat. When the tube is smoking consistently, close the grill lid.
5. Smoke the cheese for 1 to 3 hours, replacing the pellets or sawdust and ice if necessary. Monitor the temperature and make sure the cheese isn't beginning to melt. Carefully lift the mat with the cheese to a rimmed baking sheet and let the cheese cool completely before handling.
6. Package the smoked cheese in cheese storage paper or bags or vacuum-seal the cheese, labeling each. (While you can wrap the cheese tightly in plastic wrap, the cheese will spoil faster.) Let the cheese rest for at least 2 to 3 days before eating. It will be even better after 2 weeks.

Smoked Turkey Sandwich

Servings: 1
Cooking Time: 15 Minutes

Ingredients:

- 2 slices sourdough bread
- 2 tablespoons butter, at room temperature
- 2 (1-ounce) slices Swiss cheese
- 4 ounces leftover Smoked Turkey
- 1 teaspoon garlic salt

Directions:

1. Supply your smoker with wood pellets and follow the start-up procedure. Preheat the grill, with the lid closed, to 375°F.
2. Coat one side of each bread slice with 1 tablespoon of butter and sprinkle the buttered sides with garlic salt.
3. Place 1 slice of cheese on each unbuttered side of the bread, and then put the turkey on the cheese.
4. Close the sandwich, buttered sides out, and place it directly on the grill grate. Cook for 5 minutes. Flip the sandwich and cook for 5 minutes more. Remove the sandwich from the grill, cut it in half, and serve.

Smoked Cheese

Servings: 4
Cooking Time: 150 Minutes

Ingredients:

- 1 (2-pound) block medium Cheddar cheese, or your favorite cheese, quartered lengthwise

Directions:

1. Supply your smoker with wood pellets and follow the start-up procedure. Preheat the grill, with the lid closed, to 90°F.
2. Place the cheese directly on the grill grate and smoke for 2 hours, 30 minutes, checking frequently to be sure it's not melting. If the cheese begins to melt, try flipping it. If that doesn't help, remove it from the grill and refrigerate for about 1 hour and then return it to the cold smoker.
3. Remove the cheese, place it in a zip-top bag, and refrigerate overnight.
4. Slice the cheese and serve with crackers, or grate it and use for making a smoked mac and cheese.

Pig Pops (sweet-hot Bacon On A Stick)

Servings: 24
Cooking Time: 30 Minutes

Ingredients:

- Nonstick cooking spray, oil, or butter, for greasing
- 2 pounds thick-cut bacon (24 slices)
- 24 metal skewers
- 1 cup packed light brown sugar
- 2 to 3 teaspoons cayenne pepper
- ½ cup maple syrup, divided

Directions:

1. Supply your smoker with wood pellets and follow the start-up procedure. Preheat, with the lid closed, to 350°F.
2. Coat a disposable aluminum foil baking sheet with cooking spray, oil, or butter.
3. Thread each bacon slice onto a metal skewer and place on the prepared baking sheet.
4. In a medium bowl, stir together the brown sugar and cayenne.
5. Baste the top sides of the bacon with ¼ cup of maple syrup.
6. Sprinkle half of the brown sugar mixture over the bacon.
7. Place the baking sheet on the grill, close the lid, and smoke for 15 to 30 minutes.
8. Using tongs, flip the bacon skewers. Baste with the remaining ¼ cup of maple syrup and top with the remaining brown sugar mixture.
9. Continue smoking with the lid closed for 10 to 15 minutes, or until crispy. You can eyeball the bacon and smoke to your desired doneness, but the actual ideal internal temperature for bacon is 155°F
10. Using tongs, carefully remove the bacon skewers from the grill. Let cool completely before handling.

Sriracha & Maple Cashews

Servings: 10

Cooking Time: 60 Minutes

Ingredients:

- 2 tbsp unsalted butter
- 3 tbsp pure maple syrup
- 1 tbsp sriracha
- 1 tsp coarse salt (use only if nuts are unsalted)
- 2½ cups unsalted cashews

Directions:

1. Supply your smoker with wood pellets and follow the start-up procedure. Preheat the grill, with the lid closed, to 250° F.
2. In a small saucepan on the stovetop over low heat, melt the butter. Add the maple syrup, sriracha, and salt (if using). Stir until combined. Add the nuts and stir gently to coat thoroughly.
3. Spread the nuts in a single layer in an aluminum foil roasting pan coated with cooking spray. Place the pan on the grate and smoke the nuts until they're lightly toasted, about 1 hour, stirring once or twice.
4. Remove the pan from the grill and let the nuts cool for 15 minutes. They'll be sticky at first but will crisp up. Break them up with your fingers and store at room temperature in an airtight container, such as a lidded glass jar.

Bacon-wrapped Jalapeño Poppers

Servings: 12

Cooking Time: 30 Minutes

Ingredients:

- 8 ounces cream cheese, softened
- ½ cup shredded Cheddar cheese
- ¼ cup chopped scallions
- 1 teaspoon chipotle chile powder or regular chili powder
- 1 teaspoon garlic powder
- 1 teaspoon salt
- 18 large jalapeño peppers, stemmed, seeded, and halved lengthwise
- 1 pound bacon (precooked works well)

Directions:

1. Supply your smoker with wood pellets and follow the start-up procedure. Preheat, with the lid closed, to 350°F. Line a baking sheet with aluminum foil.
2. In a small bowl, combine the cream cheese, Cheddar cheese, scallions, chipotle powder, garlic powder, and salt.
3. Stuff the jalapeño halves with the cheese mixture.
4. Cut the bacon into pieces big enough to wrap around the stuffed pepper halves.
5. Wrap the bacon around the peppers and place on the prepared baking sheet.
6. Put the baking sheet on the grill grate, close the lid, and smoke the peppers for 30 minutes, or until the cheese is melted and the bacon is cooked through and crisp.
7. Let the jalapeño poppers cool for 3 to 5 minutes. Serve warm.

Bacon Pork Pinwheels (kansas Lollipops)

Servings: 4-6

Cooking Time: 20 Minutes

Ingredients:

- 1 Whole Pork Loin, boneless
- To Taste salt and pepper
- To Taste Greek Seasoning
- 4 Slices bacon
- To Taste The Ultimate BBQ Sauce

Directions:

1. When ready to cook, start the smoker and set temperature to 500F. Preheat, lid closed, for 10 to 15 minutes.
2. Trim pork loin of any unwanted silver skin or fat. Using a sharp knife, cut pork loin length wise, into 4 long strips.
3. Lay pork flat, then season with salt, pepper and Cavender's Greek Seasoning.
4. Flip the pork strips over and layer bacon on unseasoned side. Begin tightly rolling the pork strips, with bacon being rolled up on the inside.
5. Secure a skewer all the way through each pork roll to secure it in place. Set the pork rolls down on grill and cook for 15 minutes.
6. Brush BBQ Sauce over the pork. Turn each skewer over, then coat the other side. Let pork cook for another 5-10 minutes, depending on thickness of your pork. Enjoy!

Delicious Deviled Crab Appetizer

Servings: 30
Cooking Time: 10 Minutes

Ingredients:

- Nonstick cooking spray, oil, or butter, for greasing
- 1 cup panko breadcrumbs, divided
- 1 cup canned corn, drained
- ½ cup chopped scallions, divided
- ½ red bell pepper, finely chopped
- 16 ounces jumbo lump crabmeat
- ¾ cup mayonnaise, divided
- 1 egg, beaten
- 1 teaspoon salt
- 1 teaspoon freshly ground black pepper
- 2 teaspoons cayenne pepper, divided
- Juice of 1 lemon

Directions:

1. Supply your smoker with wood pellets and follow the start-up procedure. Preheat, with the lid closed, to 425°F.
2. Spray three 12-cup mini muffin pans with cooking spray and divide ½ cup of the panko between 30 of the muffin cups, pressing into the bottoms and up the sides. (Work in batches, if necessary, depending on the number of pans you have.)
3. In a medium bowl, combine the corn, ¼ cup of scallions, the bell pepper, crabmeat, half of the mayonnaise, the egg, salt, pepper, and 1 teaspoon of cayenne pepper.
4. Gently fold in the remaining ½ cup of breadcrumbs and divide the mixture between the prepared mini muffin cups.
5. Place the pans on the grill grate, close the lid, and smoke for 10 minutes, or until golden brown.
6. In a small bowl, combine the lemon juice and the remaining mayonnaise, scallions, and cayenne pepper to make a sauce.
7. Brush the tops of the mini crab cakes with the sauce and serve hot.

Chicken Wings With Teriyaki Glaze

Servings: 4
Cooking Time: 50 Minutes

Ingredients:

- 16 large chicken wings, about 3lb (1.4kg) total
- 1 to 1½ tbsp toasted sesame oil
- for the glaze
- ½ cup light soy sauce or tamari
- ¼ cup sake or sugar-free dark-colored soda
- ¼ cup light brown sugar or low-carb substitute
- 2 tbsp mirin or 1 tbsp honey
- 1 garlic clove, peeled, minced or grated
- 2 tsp minced fresh ginger
- 1 tsp cornstarch mixed with 1 tbsp distilled water (optional)
- for serving
- 1 tbsp toasted sesame seeds
- 2 scallions, trimmed, white and green parts sliced sharply diagonally

Directions:

1. Supply your smoker with wood pellets and follow the start-up procedure. Preheat the grill, with the lid closed, to 350° F.
2. Place the chicken wings in a large bowl, add the sesame oil, and turn the wings to coat thoroughly.
3. Place the wings on the grate at an angle to the bars. Grill for 20 minutes and then turn. Continue to cook until the wings are nicely browned and the meat is no longer pink at the bone, about 20 minutes more.
4. To make the glaze, in a saucepan on the stovetop over medium-high heat, combine the ingredients and bring the mixture to a boil. Reduce the glaze by 1/3, about 6 to 8 minutes. If you prefer your glaze to be glossy and thick, add the cornstarch and water mixture to the glaze and cook until it coats the back of a spoon, about 1 to 2 minutes more.
5. Transfer the wings to an aluminum foil roasting pan. Pour the glaze over them, turning to coat thoroughly. Place the pan on the grate and cook the wings until the glaze sets, about 5 to 10 minutes.
6. Transfer the wings to a platter. Scatter the sesame seeds and scallions over the top. Serve with plenty of napkins.

Simple Cream Cheese Sausage Balls

Servings: 5

Cooking Time: 30 Minutes

Ingredients:

- 1 pound ground hot sausage, uncooked
- 8 ounces cream cheese, softened
- 1 package mini filo dough shells

Directions:

1. Supply your smoker with wood pellets and follow the start-up procedure. Preheat, with the lid closed, to 350°F.
2. In a large bowl, using your hands, thoroughly mix together the sausage and cream cheese until well blended.
3. Place the filo dough shells on a rimmed perforated pizza pan or into a mini muffin tin.
4. Roll the sausage and cheese mixture into 1-inch balls and place into the filo shells.
5. Place the pizza pan or mini muffin tin on the grill, close the lid, and smoke the sausage balls for 30 minutes, or until cooked through and the sausage is no longer pink.
6. Plate and serve warm.

COCKTAILS RECIPES

Grilled Frozen Strawberry Lemonade

Servings: 4
Cooking Time: 15 Minutes

Ingredients:

- 1 Pound fresh strawberries
- 1/2 Cup turbinado sugar
- 8 lemon, halved
- 1/4 Cup Cointreau
- 1/4 Cup simple syrup
- 2 Cup ice
- 1 Cup Titos Vodka

Directions:

1. Supply your smoker with wood pellets and follow the start-up procedure. Preheat the grill, with the lid closed, to High heat.
2. Dip the lemon halves in turbinado sugar and place directly on the grill grate. Toss the strawberries with remaining sugar and place next to the lemons.
3. Cook until grill marks develop on both, about 15 min for lemons and 10 min for strawberries.
4. Remove from heat and let cool.
5. Juice grilled lemons straining out any seeds or pulp. Pour into a blender pitcher.
6. Remove stems from grilled strawberries and place in blender pitcher with lemon juice. Add simple syrup, vodka, cointreau, and 2 cups of ice.
7. Puree until smooth and transfer to 4-6 glasses. Garnish with grilled strawberries and grilled lemon slices if desired. Enjoy!

Fig Slider Cocktail

Servings: 2
Cooking Time: 15 Minutes

Ingredients:

- 2 peach, halved
- 4 oranges
- honey
- sugar
- 2 Teaspoon orange fig spread
- 1 Ounce fresh lemon juice
- 4 Ounce bourbon
- 3 Ounce honey glazed grilled orange juice

Directions:

1. Supply your smoker with wood pellets and follow the start-up procedure. Preheat the grill, with the lid closed, to 325° F.
2. Pit the peach and cut in half. Cut one of the oranges in half. Glaze the peach and orange cut sides with honey and set directly on the grill grate until the honey caramelizes and fruit has grill marks. Grill: 325 ˚F
3. Cut the second orange into wheels and coat with granulated sugar on both sides. Place directly on the grill grate and cook 15 minutes each side or until grill marks form. Grill: 325 ˚F
4. In a mixing tin, add grilled peaches, bourbon, orange fig spread, fresh lemon juice and honey glazed orange juice.
5. Shake vigorously to blend the juices and fig spread. Strain over clean ice. Garnish with grilled orange wheel. Enjoy!

Smoked Texas Ranch Water

Servings: 4
Cooking Time: 60 Minutes

Ingredients:

- 3 Whole limes
- 1 Tablespoon Blackened Saskatchewan Rub
- 12 Ounce blanco tequila
- 24 Ounce Topo Chico or other sparkling mineral water
- 8 Slices jalapeño, optional

Directions:

1. Supply your smoker with wood pellets and follow the start-up procedure. Preheat the grill, with the lid closed, to 225° F.
2. Cut two of the limes in half and sprinkle with Traeger Blackened Saskatchewan Rub. Place the four lime halves on the edge of the grill grate and smoke for 1

hour. Remove from grill and set aside to cool. Grill: 225 °F

3. Pour some of the rub onto a small plate. Cut the third lime into 1/4 wedges and use the lime to rub the rim of 4 cocktail glasses, turn the glasses upside down, and into the rub to salt the rim.

4. Place several ice cubes into your rimmed glasses and pour 3 ounces tequila, 6 ounces Topo Chico, squeeze the juice of one smoked lime (discard after squeezing), and add one fresh lime wedge to each. If using the jalapeño, add one or two slices to each glass (muddle if desired).

5. Stir to combine and enjoy!

Grilled Rabbit Tail Cocktail

Servings: 2

Cooking Time: 25 Minutes

Ingredients:

- 1 1/2 Ounce lemon juice
- 4 Ounce Apple Brandy
- 1 Ounce orange juice
- 1 Ounce Smoked Simple Syrup

Directions:

1. Supply your smoker with wood pellets and follow the start-up procedure. Preheat the grill, with the lid closed, to 350° F.

2. Place lemon halves directly on the grill grate and cook for 20-25 minutes or until grill marks appear. Remove from grill and let cool. Once cool enough to handle, juice the lemons then chill and reserve the juice. Grill: 350 °F

3. Using the proportions listed above and considering the size and consumption rate of your tailgate crew or party, mix all the above ingredients in a large thermos and top with a bit of ice.

4. Using 6-8 oz glasses or cups, guests can serve themselves from the thermos and garnish each drink with a grilled apple slice. Enjoy!

Smoked Berry Cocktail

Servings: 2

Cooking Time: 15 Minutes

Ingredients:

- 1/2 Cup strawberries, stemmed
- 1/2 Cup blackberries
- 1/2 Cup blueberries
- 8 Ounce bourbon or iced tea
- 2 Ounce lime juice
- 3 Ounce simple syrup
- soda water
- fresh mint, for garnish

Directions:

1. Supply your smoker with wood pellets and follow the start-up procedure. Preheat the grill, with the lid closed, to 180° F.

2. Wash berries well, spread them on a clean cookie sheet and place on the grill. Smoke berries for 15 minutes. Grill: 180 °F

3. Remove berries from grill and transfer to a blender. Puree berries until smooth then pass through a fine mesh strainer to remove seeds.

4. To create a layered cocktail, pour 2 ounces of berry puree in the bottom of a glass. Next, pour 2 ounces of bourbon or iced tea over the back of a spoon into the glass, then 1/2 ounce lime juice and 1/2 ounce simple syrup, top with soda water and ice. Finish with mint or extra berries for garnish.

5. Repeat the same process for 3 more servings. Enjoy!

Grilled Peach Sour Cocktail

Servings: 2

Cooking Time: 15 Minutes

Ingredients:

- 2 peach, sliced
- 2 Tablespoon sugar
- 1 1/2 Ounce Smoked Simple Syrup
- 4 Ounce bourbon
- 6 Dash Bitters Lab Apricot Vanilla Bitters
- 2 Sprig fresh thyme, for garnish

Directions:

1. Supply your smoker with wood pellets and follow the start-up procedure. Preheat the grill, with the lid closed, to 325° F.

2. Toss peach slices with granulated sugar and place directly on grill grate. Cook for 20 minutes or until grill marks form. Remove from grill and let cool. Grill: 325 °F
3. Place peaches and Traeger Smoked Simple Syrup into tin and muddle. Peaches should form about an ounce of juice during the muddling. Once completed, add remaining ingredients and shake.
4. Pour contents into glass over fresh ice and garnish with fresh thyme. Enjoy!

Grilled Peach Mint Julep

Servings: 2
Cooking Time: 45 Minutes

Ingredients:

- 2 Whole peach
- 4 Ounce whiskey
- 2 Cup sugar
- 4 Tablespoon pink peppercorns
- 20 Whole fresh mint leaves, plus more for garnish
- 2 lime wedge, for garnish
- 4 Ounce bourbon

Directions:

1. For the Grilled Whiskey Peaches: cut peach into slices, then soak peach slices in whiskey in the refrigerator for 4 to 6 hours.
2. For the Pink Peppercorn Simple Syrup: In a shallow pan, combine sugar, 1 cup water and pink peppercorns.
3. Supply your smoker with wood pellets and follow the start-up procedure. Preheat the grill, with the lid closed, to 180° F.
4. Cook syrup down on the grill for 30 minutes, or until desired smoke flavor has been reached. Remove from the grill. Grill: 180 °F
5. Increase Traeger temperature to 350°F and preheat. Place the whiskey peach slices directly on the grill grate and cook 10 to 12 minutes or until peaches soften and get grill marks. Grill: 350 °F
6. To make the Julep: Muddle 1/2 ounce Pink Peppercorn Simple Syrup with 10 fresh mint leaves and 4 slices of grilled whiskey peaches.
7. Add crushed ice over the rim of the glass. Pour bourbon over the crushed ice and stir. Garnish with 1 large sprig of mint and fresh lime. Enjoy!

Batter Up Cocktail

Servings: 2
Cooking Time: 60 Minutes

Ingredients:

- 2 whole nutmeg
- 4 Ounce Michter's Bourbon
- 3 Teaspoon pumpkin puree
- 1 Ounce Smoked Simple Syrup
- 2 Large egg

Directions:

1. Supply your smoker with wood pellets and follow the start-up procedure. Preheat the grill, with the lid closed, to 180° F.
2. Place whole nutmeg on a sheet tray and place in the grill. Smoke 1 hour. Remove from grill and let cool. Grill: 180 °F
3. Add everything to a shaker and shake without ice. Add ice, then shake and strain into a chilled highball glass.
4. Garnish with grated, smoked nutmeg. Enjoy!

Delicious Smoked Daiquiri

Servings: 2
Cooking Time: 25 Minutes

Ingredients:

- 2 limes, sliced
- 2 Tablespoon granulated sugar
- 3 Ounce Rum
- 1 Ounce Smoked Simple Syrup
- 1 1/2 Ounce lime juice

Directions:

1. Supply your smoker with wood pellets and follow the start-up procedure. Preheat the grill, with the lid closed, to 350° F.
2. Toss the lime slices with granulated sugar and place directly on the grill grate. Cook 20-25 minutes or until grill marks form. Remove from grill and cool. Grill: 350 °F

3. In a mixing glass add rum, Traeger Simple Syrup, and fresh lime juice. Add ice to the mixing glass and shake. Strain contents into a chilled glass.
4. Garnish with a grilled lime wheel. Enjoy!

Smoked Irish Coffee

Servings: 2
Cooking Time: 15 Minutes

Ingredients:

- 10 Ounce hot coffee
- 1/2 Cup heavy cream
- 1 Tablespoon sugar
- 2 Ounce Irish whiskey
- freshly grated nutmeg, for garnish (optional)

Directions:

1. Supply your smoker with wood pellets and follow the start-up procedure. Preheat the grill, with the lid closed, to 180° F.
2. Place the coffee and cream in separate shallow baking dishes and place both directly on the grill grate. Smoke for 10 to 15 minutes until the liquids pick up a slight smoke flavor. Grill: 180 ˚F
3. Remove from the grill and cool the cream. When the cream is cool, add sugar and whip in a stand mixer or by hand to soft peaks.
4. Pour the hot coffee into two mugs then add 2 ounces of whiskey to each.
5. Top with smoked whipped cream and finish with freshly grated nutmeg, if desired. Enjoy!

Sunset Margarita

Servings: 2
Cooking Time: 55 Minutes

Ingredients:

- 4 oranges
- 2 Cup plus 1 teaspoon agave
- 1/2 Cup water
- 1 Ounce burnt orange agave
- 3 Ounce reposado tequila
- 1 1/2 Ounce fresh squeezed lime juice
- Jacobsen Salt Co. Cherrywood Smoked Salt

Directions:

1. Supply your smoker with wood pellets and follow the start-up procedure. Preheat the grill, with the lid closed, to 350° F.
2. For the Burnt Orange Agave Syrup: Cut one orange in half and brush cut side with agave. Place cut side down directly on the grill grate and grill for 15 minutes or until grill marks develop. Grill: 350 ˚F
3. While the orange halves are grilling, slice the other orange and brush both sides of the slices with agave. Place slices directly on the grill grate next to the halves and cook for 15 minutes or until grill marks develop. Grill: 350 ˚F
4. Remove orange halves from grill grate and let cool. After they have cooled, juice halves and strain. Set aside.
5. Combine 1/4 cup water and agave in a shallow dish and mix well. Remove orange slices from the grill and place in the agave mixture, reserving a few for garnish.
6. Reduce the grill temperature to 180 degrees F and place the shallow dish with agave and oranges directly on the grill grate. Smoke for 40 minutes. Remove from heat and strain. Set aside. Grill: 180 ˚F
7. To Mix Drink: Rim glass with Jacobsen Smoked Salt. Combine tequila, fresh lime juice, grilled orange juice and burnt orange agave syrup in a glass. Add ice and shake well.
8. Strain into a rimmed glass over clean ice. Garnish with a grilled orange slice. Enjoy!

Cran-apple Tequila Punch With Smoked Oranges

Servings: 2
Cooking Time: 15 Minutes

Ingredients:

- 6 Cup apple juice, chilled
- 6 Cup light cranberry cocktail
- 1 Cup cranberries, fresh or thawed
- 3 Large oranges, halved
- 1 Cup sugar, for rimming glasses
- 2 Tablespoon lemon juice
- 2 Cup reposado tequila
- 1 Cup orange-flavored liqueur, such as Grand Marnier or Cointreau

- 2 Bottle sparkling wine (such as prosecco) or sparkling water

Directions:

1. Combine 1 cup each of the apple and cranberry juices, then pour into ice cube trays. If the cube molds are big enough, place a few cranberries into each cube. Freeze for 6 hours to overnight.
2. Supply your smoker with wood pellets and follow the start-up procedure. Preheat the grill, with the lid closed, to 180° F.
3. Place the orange halves cut-side down on the grill and smoke for 15 minutes. Remove from the grill and juice oranges. Reserve smoked orange juice. Grill: 180 ˚F
4. When ready to serve, place the sugar on a flat plate. Pour the lemon juice into a bowl that will fit the rim of each glass.
5. Carefully dip the rim of each glass in the lemon juice, then dip in the sugar to create a 1/8" sugar rim. Turn the glass right-side up and allow to dry for a few minutes before using.
6. Just before serving, mix the remaining apple juice, cranberry cocktail and smoked orange juice with the tequila, orange liqueur, and sparkling wine in a large bowl or pitcher. Taste, adding more of any ingredient to meet your preference.
7. When ready to serve, place a few ice cubes in each glass, then pour a cup of the punch over the top. Alternatively, place all of the ice cubes in the punch bowl and allow guests to help themselves. Enjoy!

Smoked Sangria

Servings: 6

Cooking Time: 45 Minutes

Ingredients:

- 1 (750 ml) medium-bodied red wine
- 1/4 Cup Grand Marnier
- 1/4 Cup Smoked Simple Syrup
- 1 Cup fresh cranberries
- 1 Whole apple, sliced
- 2 Whole limes, sliced
- 4 cinnamon stick
- soda water

Directions:

1. Supply your smoker with wood pellets and follow the start-up procedure. Preheat the grill, with the lid closed, to 180° F.
2. In a shallow dish, combine red wine, Grand Marnier, Traeger Smoked Simple Syrup and cranberries, and place directly on the grill grate.
3. Smoke for 30 to 45 minutes or until the liquid picks up desired amount of smoke. Remove from grill and place in the fridge to cool. Grill: 180 ˚F
4. When the mixture has cooled, place in a large pitcher. Add sliced apples, limes, cinnamon sticks and ice to pitcher.
5. Top with soda water, if desired. Enjoy!

Smoked Raspberry Bubbler Cocktail

Servings: 2

Cooking Time: 45 Minutes

Ingredients:

- 2 Cup fresh raspberries
- Smoked Simple Syrup
- 8 Ounce sparkling wine

Directions:

1. Supply your smoker with wood pellets and follow the start-up procedure. Preheat the grill, with the lid closed, to 180° F.
2. Smoked Raspberry Syrup: Place 1 cup fresh raspberries on a grill mat and smoke for 30 minutes. Grill: 180 ˚F
3. After the raspberries have been smoked, set a few aside for garnish. Place the remainder into a shallow sheet pan with Traeger Smoked Simple Syrup. Place back on the grill grate and let smoke for 45 minutes. Remove from heat and allow to cool. Strain and refrigerate until ready to use. Grill: 180 ˚F
4. Place 1 ounce of the smoked raspberry syrup in the bottom of a champagne flute and top off with sparkling white wine or champagne.
5. Garnish with smoked raspberries. Enjoy!

A Smoking Classic Cocktail

Servings: 2
Cooking Time: 60 Minutes

Ingredients:

- 2 Bottle Angostura orange bitters
- 10 sugar cubes
- 8 Ounce Champagne
- lemon twist

Directions:

1. Supply your smoker with wood pellets and follow the start-up procedure. Preheat the grill, with the lid closed, to 180° F.
2. For the Smoked Orange Bitters: In a small skillet, combine 1 bottle of Angostura orange bitters with a splash of water and 4 sugar cubes.
3. Place skillet on the grill grate and smoke for 60 minutes. Cool the smoked bitters and put back into the bottle. Grill: 180 °F
4. Add a sugar cube to each Champagne flute and soak the sugar cubes with the smoked bitters.
5. Add champagne and a lemon twist in a flute glass. Enjoy!

Smoked Cold Brew Coffee

Servings: 8
Cooking Time: 120 Minutes

Ingredients:

- 12 Ounce coarse ground coffee
- heavy cream or milk
- sugar

Directions:

1. Place half the coffee grounds in a plastic container and slowly pour 3-1/2 cups water over the top of the grounds. Add remaining grounds and pour another 3-1/2 cups water over the top in a circular motion.
2. Press the grounds down into the water using the back of a spoon. Cover and transfer to the refrigerator and let sit for 18 to 24 hours.
3. Remove from refrigerator and strain into a clean container through a fine mesh strainer or double layer of cheese cloth.
4. Supply your smoker with wood pellets and follow the start-up procedure. Preheat the grill, with the lid closed, to 180° F.
5. Pour cold brew into a shallow baking dish and place directly on the grill grate. Smoke for 1 to 2 hours depending on desired level of smoke. Grill: 180 °F
6. Remove from grill and place over an ice bath to cool. Drink as is over ice, with cream or sugar or use in your favorite coffee recipes. Enjoy!

Smoked Grape Lime Rickey

Servings: 4
Cooking Time: 45 Minutes

Ingredients:

- 1/2 Pound red grapes
- 1/2 Cup plus 1 tablespoon sugar
- 1/2 Cup water
- 1 limes, sliced
- 2 limes, halved
- 1 Tablespoon sugar
- 1 L lemon lime soda

Directions:

1. Supply your smoker with wood pellets and follow the start-up procedure. Preheat the grill, with the lid closed, to 180° F.
2. Rinse grapes well and place in a shallow baking dish. Combine 1/2 cup sugar and water and stir until sugar dissolves. Pour over grapes.
3. Place the baking dish directly on the grill grate and smoke for 30 to 40 minutes until grapes are tender. Grill: 180 °F
4. Remove from the grill and pour entire contents of the baking dish in a blender. Puree on high until smooth then pass the mixture through a fine mesh strainer.
5. Increase Traeger temperature to 350°F. Grill: 350 °F
6. Toss the lime slices and lime halves with 1 tablespoon sugar and place directly on the grill grate. Cook for 15 to 20 minutes or until grill marks develop. Remove from grill and set slices aside. When cool enough to handle, juice grilled lime halves. Grill: 350 °F
7. To build the drink, fill a pint glass with ice. Pour in 1-1/2 ounce grilled lime juice, 1-1/2 ounce smoked grape syrup and top off with soda. Garnish with grilled lime slice. Enjoy!

In Delicious Fashion Cocktail

Servings: 2
Cooking Time: 20 Minutes

Ingredients:

- 2 Whole orange peel
- 2 Whole lemon peel
- 3 Ounce bourbon
- 1 Ounce Smoked Simple Syrup
- 6 Dash Bitters Lab Charred Cedar & Currant Bitters

Directions:

1. Supply your smoker with wood pellets and follow the start-up procedure. Preheat the grill, with the lid closed, to 350° F.
2. Place the lemon and orange peel directly on the grill grate and cook 20 to 25 minutes or until lightly browned. Grill: 350 °F
3. Add bourbon, Traeger Smoked Simple Syrup and bitters to a mixing glass and stir over ice. Stir until glass is chilled and contents are well diluted.
4. Strain into a new glass over fresh ice and garnish with grilled lemon and orange peel. Enjoy!

Bacon Old-fashioned Cocktail

Servings: 2
Cooking Time: 20 Minutes

Ingredients:

- 16 Slices bacon
- 1/2 Cup warm water (110°F to 115°F)
- 1500 mL bourbon
- 1/2 Fluid Ounce maple syrup
- 4 Dash Angostura bitters
- 2 fresh orange peel

Directions:

1. Smoke bacon prior to making Old Fashioned using this recipe for Applewood Smoked Bacon.
2. To Make Bacon: Supply your smoker with wood pellets and follow the start-up procedure. Preheat the grill, with the lid closed, to 325° F.
3. Place bacon in a single layer on a cooling rack that fits inside a baking sheet pan. Cook in Traeger for 15-20 minutes or until bacon is browned and crispy. Reserve bacon for later. Let the fat cool slightly; you'll use the fat to infuse the bourbon. Grill: 325 °F
4. Combine 1/4 cup of warm (not hot) liquid bacon fat with the entire contents of a 750ml bottle of bourbon in a glass or heavy plastic container.
5. Use a fork to stir well. Let it sit on the counter for a few hours, stirring every so often.
6. After about four hours, put bourbon fat mixture into the freezer. After about an hour, the fat will congeal and you can simply scoop it out with a spoon. You can fine-strain the mixture through a sieve to remove all fat if desired.
7. Combine ingredients with ice and stir until cold. Strain over fresh ice in an Old Fashioned glass and garnish with reserved bacon and orange peel. Enjoy!

Smoky Mountain Bramble Cocktail

Servings: 2
Cooking Time: 15 Minutes

Ingredients:

- 16 Ounce blackberries
- 2 Cup sugar
- 10 smoked blackberries
- 3 Ounce vodka
- 1 1/2 Ounce Alpine Distilling Preserve Liqueur
- 1 1/2 Ounce lemon juice
- 1 Ounce smoked blackberry syrup

Directions:

1. Supply your smoker with wood pellets and follow the start-up procedure. Preheat the grill, with the lid closed, to 180° F.
2. To make Smoked Blackberry Simple Syrup: Place blackberries on a grill mat and smoke for 15 to 20 minutes. Grill: 180 °F
3. Combine 1 cup water and sugar in a small sauce pan and warm over medium heat until sugar dissolves. Remove from heat and place 2/3 of blackberries in the simple syrup and macerate.
4. Strain through a fine mesh strainer and store for up to 14 days.

5. To make the cocktail: Muddle 4 to 5 smoked blackberries in a cocktail shaker. Add vodka, Preserve Liqueur, lemon and smoked blackberry syrup. Add ice and shake vigorously. Double strain into an old fashioned glass.
6. Garnish with a smoked blackberry and lemon twist. Enjoy!

Smoked Jacobsen Salt Margarita

Servings: 2
Cooking Time: 1 Day

Ingredients:

- kosher sea salt
- 3 Cup Jacobsen Co. Honey
- 6 Ounce tequila
- 4 Ounce fresh squeezed lime juice
- 1/2 Cup Jacobsen Salt Co. Cherrywood Smoked Salt or smoked kosher salt
- 2 Ounce simple syrup
- 2 Teaspoon orange liqueur

Directions:

1. If making your own smoked salt, take kosher sea salt (however much you want to smoke) and spread it out on a tray.
2. Supply your smoker with wood pellets and follow the start-up procedure. Preheat the grill, with the lid closed, to 165° F.
3. Place tray of salt directly on the grill grate and smoke for about 24 hours, stirring the salt every 8 hours. Once it has smoked for 24 hours, take off grill and use in all your favorite dishes. Note: If you want to skip the long smoke session, use Jacobsen Salt Co. Cherrywood Smoked Salt. Grill: 165 °F
4. Simple Syrup: Put the honey and 1 cup water in a small saucepan. Cook over low heat, stirring, for about 20 min.
5. Fill a cocktail shaker with ice. Add tequila, lime juice, simple syrup and orange liqueur. Cover and shake until mixed and chilled, about 30 seconds.
6. Place smoked salt on a plate. Press the rim of a chilled rocks glass into the salt to rim the edge. Strain margarita into the glass. Enjoy!

Smoked Pumpkin Spice Latte

Servings: 4
Cooking Time: 45 Minutes

Ingredients:

- 1 Small sugar pumpkin
- olive oil
- 1 Can sweetened condensed milk
- 1 Cup whole milk
- 2 Tablespoon Smoked Simple Syrup
- 1 Teaspoon pumpkin pie spice
- pinch of salt
- cinnamon
- whipped cream
- shaved nutmeg
- 8 Ounce smoked cold brew coffee

Directions:

1. Supply your smoker with wood pellets and follow the start-up procedure. Preheat the grill, with the lid closed, to 325° F.
2. Cut the sugar pumpkin in half, scoop out the seeds and discard. Place the pumpkin halves cut side up on a baking sheet and brush lightly with olive oil.
3. Place the sheet tray directly on the grill grate and cook 45 minutes or until the flesh is tender. Remove from heat and place on the counter to cool. Grill: 325 °F
4. When the pumpkin is cool enough to handle, scoop out the flesh and mash until smooth.
5. Place 3 Tbsp of the pumpkin puree in a separate bowl and reserve the remaining for another use.
6. Add the sweetened condensed milk, whole milk, Traeger Smoked Simple Syrup, pumpkin pie seasoning and salt to the pumpkin puree. Whisk to combine.
7. Pour the cold brew over ice, add desired amount of pumpkin spice creamer and top with whipped cream, cinnamon, and shaved nutmeg if desired. Enjoy!

Zombie Cocktail Recipe

Servings: 2
Cooking Time: 45 Minutes

Ingredients:

- fresh squeezed orange juice
- pineapple juice

- 2 Ounce light rum
- 2 Ounce dark rum
- 2 Ounce lime juice
- 1 Ounce Smoked Simple Syrup
- 6 Ounce smoked orange and pineapple juice
- 2 grilled orange peel, for garnish
- 2 grilled pineapple chunks, for garnish

Directions:

1. Supply your smoker with wood pellets and follow the start-up procedure. Preheat the grill, with the lid closed, to 180° F.
2. Smoked Orange and Pineapple Juice: Pour equal parts fresh squeezed orange juice and pineapple juice into a shallow sheet pan and smoke for 45 minutes. Remove and let cool. Measure out 3 ounces of juice and reserve any remaining juice in the refrigerator for future use. Grill: 180 ˚F
3. Add dark and light rums, 3 ounces smoked orange and pineapple juice, lime juice and Traeger Smoked Simple Syrup to a mixing glass.
4. Add ice, shake and strain over clean ice into a Tiki glass.
5. Garnish with a grilled orange peel and grilled pineapple. Enjoy!

Ryes And Shine Cocktail

Servings: 2

Cooking Time: 30 Minutes

Ingredients:

- 2 lemon, cut into wheels for garnish
- 6 Tablespoon granulated sugar
- 2 Ounce rye
- 1 Ounce bourbon
- 3 Ounce lemon juice
- 1 Ounce Smoked Simple Syrup
- 6 Dash Fernet-Branca

Directions:

1. Supply your smoker with wood pellets and follow the start-up procedure. Preheat the grill, with the lid closed, to 325° F.
2. Toss lemon wheels with granulated sugar to coat on both sides. Place wheels directly on the grill grate and cook for 15 minutes on each side or until grill marks form. Grill: 325 ˚F
3. Add rye, bourbon, lemon juice, Traeger Smoked Simple Syrup and Fernet-Branca to a shaker and shake until slightly diluted (about 10 to 15 seconds).
4. Pour into a fresh glass, serve neat and garnish with a grilled lemon wheel. Enjoy!

Honey Glazed Grapefruit Shandy Cocktail

Servings: 2

Cooking Time: 20 Minutes

Ingredients:

- 4 grapefruits
- 4 Tablespoon honey
- granulated sugar
- 2 Ounce bourbon
- 1 Ounce Smoked Simple Syrup
- 4 Ounce honey glazed grilled grapefruit, juiced
- 2 Bottle Ballast Point Grapefruit Sculpin

Directions:

1. Supply your smoker with wood pellets and follow the start-up procedure. Preheat the grill, with the lid closed, to 375° F.
2. For the honey glazed grapefruit: Slice one grapefruit in half and coat with 2 tablespoons honey.
3. Take the other grapefruit and slice into wheels. Toss the wheels in granulated sugar until well coated.
4. Place the grapefruit halves and wheels directly on the grill grate, cut side down, and cook for 20 to 30 minutes. Remove from grill and set the wheels aside. Grill: 375 ˚F
5. Squeeze the grapefruit halves into a measuring cup. It should yield about 2 oz juice.
6. Pour the grapefruit juice into a shaker and add bourbon and Traeger Smoked Simple Syrup then top with ice. Shake for 10-15 seconds.
7. Strain into glass, add ice and fill with beer. Garnish with the grilled grapefruit wheel. Enjoy!

Smoked Salted Caramel White Russian

Servings: 4
Cooking Time: 20 Minutes

Ingredients:

- 16 Ounce half-and-half
- salted caramel sauce
- 6 Ounce vodka
- 6 Ounce Kahlúa

Directions:

1. Supply your smoker with wood pellets and follow the start-up procedure. Preheat the grill, with the lid closed, to 180° F.
2. Pour the half-and-half in a shallow baking dish and place directly on the grill grate. In another shallow baking dish, pour 2 to 3 cups of water and place on the grill next to the half-and-half.
3. Smoke both the half-and-half and water for 20 minutes. Remove from the grill and let cool. Grill: 180 ˚F
4. Place the half-and-half in the fridge until ready to use. Pour the smoked water into ice cube trays and transfer to the freezer until completely frozen.
5. Separate the smoked ice cubes into four glasses. Drizzle the salted caramel sauce around the inside of the glass.
6. Pour 1-1/2 ounce vodka and 1-1/2 ounce Kahlúa into each of the glasses and top with the smoked half-and-half. Enjoy!

Smoking Gun Cocktail

Servings: 2
Cooking Time: 45 Minutes

Ingredients:

- 2 Jar vermouth soaked cocktail onions
- 3 Ounce vodka
- 1 Ounce dry vermouth

Directions:

1. Supply your smoker with wood pellets and follow the start-up procedure. Preheat the grill, with the lid closed, to 180° F.
2. To make the smoked onion vermouth: Pour jar of vermouth soaked cocktail onions onto a shallow sheet pan. Smoke for 45 minutes. Remove from grill and set aside to chill. Grill: 180 ˚F
3. To make the cocktail: Add vodka, 1 teaspoon liquid from the smoked onions and dry vermouth to a mixing glass. Shake and strain into a chilled martini glass.
4. Garnish with smoked cocktail onions on a skewer. Enjoy!

Smoked Ice Mojito Slurpee

Servings: 2
Cooking Time: 30 Minutes

Ingredients:

- water
- 1 Cup white rum
- 1/2 Cup lime juice
- 1/4 Cup Smoked Simple Syrup
- 12 Whole fresh mint leaves
- 4 Sprig mint
- 4 Whole lime wedge, for garnish

Directions:

1. Supply your smoker with wood pellets and follow the start-up procedure. Preheat the grill, with the lid closed, to 180° F.
2. For optimal flavor, use Super Smoke if available. Grill: 180 ˚F
3. Remove water from grill and pour smoked water into ice cube trays. Place in freezer until frozen.
4. Add rum, lime juice, Traeger Smoked Simple Syrup, mint and smoked ice to a blender.
5. Blend until a slushy consistency and pour into glasses.
6. Garnish with a mint sprig and lime wedge. Enjoy!

Delicious Old Fashioned

Servings: 2
Cooking Time: 60 Minutes

Ingredients:

- 2 orange
- 2 Cup cherries
- 3 Ounce bourbon

- 1 Ounce Smoked Simple Syrup
- 8 Dash Bitters Lab Apricot Vanilla Bitters

Directions:

1. Supply your smoker with wood pellets and follow the start-up procedure. Preheat the grill, with the lid closed, to 180° F.
2. While Traeger preheats, slice whole orange into wheels.
3. Place cherries on a small sheet pan and place in the Traeger. Place orange slices directly on the grill grate.
4. Smoke cherries for 1 hour and oranges for 25 minutes, depending on taste, before removing from the grill. Let oranges and cherries cool. Grill: 180 ˚F
5. Pour bourbon into glass, followed by Traeger Smoked Simple Syrup and bitters. Add ice and stir for 45 seconds or until drink is well-diluted.
6. Strain contents into new glass over fresh ice. Skewer orange wheel and add cherry for garnish. Enjoy!

Grilled Hawaiian Sour

Servings: 2

Cooking Time: 15 Minutes

Ingredients:

- 2 Whole pineapple, trimmed and sliced
- 1/2 Cup palm sugar
- 3 Ounce bourbon
- 2 Ounce grilled pineapple juice
- 2 Ounce Smoked Simple Syrup
- 10 Ounce lemon juice
- 2 grilled pineapple chunk, for garnish
- 2 pineapple leaf, for garnish

Directions:

1. Supply your smoker with wood pellets and follow the start-up procedure. Preheat the grill, with the lid closed, to 350° F.
2. For the Grilled Pineapple Juice: Dust pineapple slices with palm sugar. Place directly on the grill grate and cook for 8 minutes per side. Grill: 350 ˚F
3. Remove from grill and let cool. Reserve a few pieces for garnish. Run remaining pineapple pieces through centrifugal juicer to extract juice.
4. To Make the Drink: Add bourbon, grilled pineapple juice, simple syrup and lemon juice to a cocktail strainer with ice. Shake vigorously. Double strain into a chilled coupe glass. Garnish with grilled pineapple chunk and pineapple leaf. Enjoy!

Dublin Delight Cocktail

Servings: 2

Cooking Time: 20 Minutes

Ingredients:

- 2 orange, sliced
- 3 Fluid Ounce Teeling Whiskey
- 1 1/2 Fluid Ounce Smoked Simple Syrup
- 6 Dash aromatic bitters
- 6 Fluid Ounce Guinness beer
- 2 Amarena cherry, for garnish

Directions:

1. Supply your smoker with wood pellets and follow the start-up procedure. Preheat the grill, with the lid closed, to 450° F.
2. Place orange slices directly on the grill grate and cook 20 to 25 minutes. Remove from grill and let cool. Grill: 450 ˚F
3. In a mixing glass, add whiskey, Traeger Smoked Simple Syrup and bitters. Add ice and shake. Pour over a beer glass filled with ice and top off with cold Guinness.
4. Garnish with a grilled orange slice and Amarena cherry. Enjoy!

Smoky Scotch & Ginger Cocktail

Servings: 2

Cooking Time: 60 Minutes

Ingredients:

- 1 Ounce ginger syrup
- 1/2 Ounce brandied cherry juice
- 1/2 Ounce agave nectar
- 4 Ounce scotch
- 1 1/2 Ounce lemon juice
- 2 Slices grilled lemon, for garnish
- 2 cherry, for garnish

Directions:

1. Supply your smoker with wood pellets and follow the start-up procedure. Preheat the grill, with the lid closed, to 180° F.
2. For the smoked ginger cherry syrup: Place ginger syrup, cherry juice and agave nectar in a shallow dish and place the dish directly on the grill grate.
3. Smoke for 60 minutes, or until the mixture has picked up the smoke flavor. Remove from grill and allow to cool for 30 minutes. Grill: 180 °F
4. Place smoked ginger cherry syrup, scotch and lemon juice into a shaker tin and shake with ice. Strain into a glass over fresh ice and garnish with a grilled lemon wheel and cherry. Enjoy!

Delicious Boulevardier Cocktail

Servings: 2
Cooking Time: 60 Minutes

Ingredients:

- 4 oranges
- 1/2 Cup honey
- 1500 mL rye whiskey
- 1 1/2 Ounce Campari
- 1 1/2 Ounce sweet vermouth
- 2 Tablespoon granulated sugar
- 3 Ounce grilled orange infused rye

Directions:

1. Supply your smoker with wood pellets and follow the start-up procedure. Preheat the grill, with the lid closed, to 350° F.
2. Slice 2 oranges in half and coat cut side with honey. Peel remaining orange and place peels on the grill. Cook 20 to 25 minutes. Grill: 350 °F
3. Remove from grill and let cool. Place orange halves cut side down directly on the grill grate and cook 20 to 30 minutes or until dark grill marks appear. Remove orange halves and allow to cool. Grill: 350 °F
4. Place orange halves into a bottle of rye whiskey and let steep for 10 to 12 hours. The longer they steep, the sweeter and more pronounced the orange flavor will be.
5. Add all ingredients into a mixing glass and stir until diluted. Strain into a fresh coupe glass and serve neat.
6. Garnish with grilled orange peel. Enjoy!

Smoked Apple Cider

Servings: 2
Cooking Time: 30 Minutes

Ingredients:

- 32 Ounce apple cider
- 2 cinnamon sticks
- 4 whole cloves
- 3 star anise
- 2 Pieces orange peel
- 2 Pieces lemon peel

Directions:

1. Supply your smoker with wood pellets and follow the start-up procedure. Preheat the grill, with the lid closed, to 225° F.
2. Combine the cider, cinnamon stick, star anise, clove, lemon and orange peel in a shallow baking dish.
3. Place directly on the grill grate and smoke for 30 minutes. Remove from grill, strain and transfer to four mugs. Grill: 225 °F
4. Finish with a slice of apple and a cinnamon stick to serve. Enjoy!

Strawberry Mule Cocktail

Servings: 2
Cooking Time: 15 Minutes

Ingredients:

- 8 grilled strawberries, plus more for serving
- 3 Ounce vodka
- 1 Ounce Smoked Simple Syrup
- 1 Ounce lemon juice
- 6 Ounce ginger beer
- fresh mint leaves

Directions:

1. Supply your smoker with wood pellets and follow the start-up procedure. Preheat the grill, with the lid closed, to 400° F.
2. Place strawberries directly on the grill grate and cook 15 minutes or until grill marks appear. Grill: 400 °F
3. For the cocktail: Add vodka, grilled strawberries, Traeger Smoked Simple Syrup and lemon juice to a shaker. Shake vigorously.

4. Double strain into a fresh glass or copper mug with crushed ice.
5. Top with ginger beer and garnish with extra grilled strawberries and fresh mint. Enjoy!

Smoked Plum And Thyme Fizz Cocktail

Servings: 2
Cooking Time: 60 Minutes

Ingredients:

- 6 fresh plums
- 4 Fluid Ounce vodka
- 1 1/2 Fluid Ounce fresh lemon juice
- 2 Ounce smoked plum and thyme simple syrup
- 4 Fluid Ounce club soda
- 2 Slices smoked plum, for garnish
- 2 Sprig fresh thyme, for garnish
- 8 Sprig thyme
- 2 Cup Smoked Simple Syrup

Directions:

1. Supply your smoker with wood pellets and follow the start-up procedure. Preheat the grill, with the lid closed, to 180° F.
2. Cut plums in half and remove the pit. Place the plum halves directly on the grill grate and smoke for 25 minutes. Grill: 180 °F
3. For the Plum and Thyme Simple Syrup: After 25 minutes, remove plums from the grill and cut into quarters. Add plums and thyme sprigs to 1 cup of Traeger Smoked Simple Syrup. Smoke the mixture for 45 minutes. Remove from grill, strain and let cool. Grill: 180 °F
4. Add vodka, fresh lemon juice and smoked plum and thyme simple syrup to a mixing glass.
5. Add ice and shake. Strain over clean ice, top off with club soda and garnish with a piece of thyme and slice of smoked plum. Enjoy!

Smoke And Bubz Cocktail

Servings: 2
Cooking Time: 45 Minutes

Ingredients:

- 16 Ounce POM Juice
- 2 Cup pomegranate seeds
- 6 Ounce sparkling white wine
- 2 lemon twist, for garnish
- 2 Teaspoon pomegranate seeds

Directions:

1. Supply your smoker with wood pellets and follow the start-up procedure. Preheat the grill, with the lid closed, to 180° F.
2. For the Smoked Pomegranate Juice: Pour POM juice and a cup of pomegranate seeds into a shallow sheet pan. Smoke on the Traeger for 45 minutes. Pull off grill, strain, discard seeds and let sit until chilled. Grill: 180 °F
3. Add 1-1/2 ounces of the smoked pomegranate juice to the bottom of a champagne flute.
4. Add sparkling white wine, a few fresh pomegranate seeds and a lemon twist to garnish. Enjoy!

RECIPE INDEX

G

H

I

T

www.ingramcontent.com/pod-product-compliance
Ingram Content Group UK Ltd.
Pitfield, Milton Keynes, MK11 3LW, UK
UKHW051132260726
13967UKWH00010B/3000